THE
Cold
War
File

By
ANDY EAST

 The Scarecrow Press, Inc.
Metuchen, N.J., & London
1983

The novelization series enumerated below are copyrighted in the following interests:

1)   "The Avengers": ABC Television Ltd., a subsidiary of the Associated British Picture Corporation Ltd., London.

2)   Derek Flint series: 20th Century-Fox Film Corporation.

3)   "Get Smart": Talent Associates-Paramount Ltd.

4)   "The Girl from U.N.C.L.E.": Metro-Goldwyn-Mayer, Inc.

5)   "I Spy": Triple-F Productions.

6)   "It Takes a Thief": Universal Television, Inc.

7)   "The Man from U.N.C.L.E.": Metro-Goldwyn-Mayer, Inc.

8)   "Mission: Impossible": Desilu Productions, Inc. (1967-68) and Paramount Pictures Corporation (1969).

Library of Congress Cataloging in Publication Data

East, Andy.
  The Cold War file.

  Includes bibliographies and index.
  1. Spy stories, English--History and criticism.
2. Spy stories, English--Bio-bibliography. 3. Spy
stories, American--History and criticism. 4. Spy
stories, American--Bio-bibliography. 5. World
politics in literature. I. Title.
PR830.S65E3 1983   823'.0872'09   83-7584
ISBN 0-8108-1641-5

To David

In memory of his father, Michael

CONTENTS

"How many a man has dated a new era in

his life from the reading of a book?"

Thoreau

PREFACE

I have attempted to evoke the Cold War era by writing a reference volume in the brisk, no-nonsense style of an intelligence dossier. The book contains seventy-seven evaluations of spy series of varying popularity. Alphabetized by author, each segment identifies the series figure(s), analyzes significant books in each canon, and judges each series on the merits of its viability. Entries are also included on Ace Books, Fawcett, New American Library, and Universal-Award, in recognition of their invaluable contributions to the genre. I think the title of The Cold War File aptly describes the book's overall concept and purpose.

INDIVIDUAL ENTRY SYMBOLS

The following symbols are used in the evaluations throughout this book:

CWF	identifies each Cold War File entry, followed by the appropriate number and author. Example: CWF 50. Mason, F. Van Wyck
EOP	entry out of print
EsOP	entries out of print
HB	hardback edition
HB-HB	two consecutive hardback editions
HB-R	hardback edition, followed by a paperback reprint
MN	movie novelization (i.e., Our Man Flint)*

---

*In keeping with the format of this book, all film adaptations shall be referred to as visual projects, except in the entry symbols noted above.

MT	movie tie-in edition (i.e., Where the Spies Are)
PBO	paperback original
PBO.MN.	paperback original and movie novelization represented by the same edition
PBO.MT.	paperback original and movie tie-in represented by the same edition
PBO.TN	paperback original and television novelization represented by the same edition
R	reprint, generally a paperback edition
R.MT.	paperback reprint and movie tie-in represented by the same edition
R-R	two consecutive paperback reprints
SOP	series out of print
SSP	series still in print
TN	television novelization (i.e., "The Man from U.N.C.L.E.")
(...).	and so on

ABOUT THE BOOK

The evaluations in this book are intended only as a guide and, as such, are designed to provide the serious student with a basic framework from which a more comprehensive study of the Cold War series thriller may be pursued.

Every attempt has been made to identify the paperback source in all cases, whether an original or reprint edition. I have not made a random guess as to a given paperback origin where that information was not available.

Also included are two appendixes. The first relates to spy series which continued after 1969, while the second is a revised listing of the evaluated series which have changed paperback outlets since 1969 (i.e., James Bond and Nick Carter, among others). A secret agent index completes The Cold War File.

THE BIBLIOGRAPHIES

The bibliographies in this volume have been classified by

series and appear at the end of each CWF entry rather than at the book's conclusion. Reprints issued after 1969 are notated by symbol in the respective series bibliography, and referenced in the corresponding segment of the appropriate appendix.

Each bibliography also indicates variations between the U.S. and British titles (or other foreign source) and release dates, as well as visual project editions.

Concerning pen names, I have used the name by which a given author is best known. Honoring the manner established throughout The Cold War File, pseudonyms are generally termed cover identities.

The devotee might wish to contact the Passaic Book Center (594 Main Avenue, Passaic, New Jersey 07055) to further his or her interest in the spy fiction of the sixties. They have perhaps the world's largest stock of hard-to-find and out-of-stock paperback espionage novels, as well as other mysteries.

I sincerely hope that this book may prove of value and interest to the serious student of espionage literature.

Andy East
Louisville, Kentucky
November 1982

The author is fully aware that M.I.5. and M.I.6. are now referred to, respectively, as D.I.5. and D.I.6. In order to place these British intelligence bodies within the proper context of The Cold War File, they have been given the designations indicative of the era depicted in this book.

ACKNOWLEDGMENTS

No author can truthfully say that he alone has invested all of the diverse elements which enter into the completion of a book. Therefore, I would like to express my gratitude to the following for their contributions:

Authors: William B. Aarons; Norman Daniels; Donald Hamilton; Shawn McCarthy; and Jack Seward.

Publishers (all based in the U.S. except where noted): Ace-Charter Books; Ballantine Books; Bantam Books; Berkley-Jove Publishing Group; Doubleday and Co.; E. P. Dutton; Farrar, Straus and Giroux, Inc.; Fawcett Books Group; Harcourt Brace Jovanovich; Harper and Row Publishers, Inc.; Horwitz Grahame Books Pty. Ltd. (Cammeray, Australia); Alfred A. Knopf, Inc.; Macmillan Publishing Co.; William Morrow and Co.; New American Library; Stein and Day Publishers; Charles E. Tuttle Co., Inc. (Tokyo, Japan); and Walker and Co.

Agents (all based in the U.S. except where noted): Julian Bach Literary Agency; Brandt and Brandt Literary Agents, Inc.; Jonathan Clowes Ltd. (London); George Greenfield, of John Farquharson Ltd. (London); Donald MacCampbell, Inc.; McIntosh and Otis Literary Agency; Harold Matson Co., Inc.; Scott Meredith; Robert P. Mills Ltd.; Harold Ober Associates, Inc.; and Roslyn Targ Literary Agency.

Motion Picture Studios: M. G. M. /U. A. Entertainment Co., and 20th Century-Fox Film Corporation.

And Special Thanks To: The law firm of Fulop and Hardee, on behalf of Glidrose Productions Ltd. (London); Ms. Judith Wallace, of Horwitz Grahame Books Pty. Ltd. (Cammeray, Australia); Danny Biederman and Robert Short; Professor Richard Knudson, of The Dossier; Barbara, of the Passaic Book Center, Passaic, New Jersey; Carl Smith, owner of CBS Book Distributors, Louisville; and the many helpful staff members of the Louisville Free Public Library (main branch) and Copy Boy, Inc. (Louisville).

INTRODUCTION

The passing of the James Bond phenomenon of the sixties and the maturing of the spy novel to the present day have prompted a significant number of books examining this elusive genre as a whole, but no single volume covering exclusively the spy novel of the sixties. It is the objective of this book to provide the serious student of the espionage novel with an evaluative guide that reflects both the pioneering and contributing efforts of the period.

It was, of course, during the sixties that the respective effects of such masters as "Sapper" and Eric Ambler were realized to help bring the character conceptions of James Bond and George Smiley into proper focus.

The development of the sixties spy thriller can be divided into three categories: 1) the transformation of Ian Fleming's James Bond into the paperback sensation of the decade; 2) the appearance of the paperback spy original, as typified by those of Edward S. Aarons, Stephen Marlowe, and Donald Hamilton, and 3) the sobering consequences of the realistic spy novel, as exemplified by John le Carré and Len Deighton.

JAMES BOND

The effects of the 007 rage have been analyzed to death during the past fifteen years, and, for this reason, it is unnecessary to discuss them here. However, in order to place the Bond-Fleming cycle in the proper context with the espionage thriller of the sixties, it would be helpful to identify two fundamental points.

First, Bond didn't make a significant impression on the U.S. paperback market until 1961, eight years after Casino Royale (Macmillan, 1954), the first Fleming thriller,

had achieved considerable success in Britain. The year 1961,
then, marked the initiation of the 007 boom, triggered in
part, by President John F. Kennedy's revelation in Life magazine (March 17th, 1961) that he enjoyed the Fleming books.

    Second, the Bond phenomenon reached its zenith in
1965 with the publication of Ian Fleming's posthumous Bond
novel, The Man with the Golden Gun (New American Library),
and the heralded release of Sean Connery's fourth 007 film
caper, Thunderball (United Artists), but began to disintegrate
shortly thereafter.

    By 1968 the American public's waning interest in the
cloak-and-dagger yarn paralleled its disillusionment with Vietnam, as well as the "closed-door" operations of Western intelligence agencies as a whole. Beginning that year, Bond's
plummeting performance in the marketplace demonstrated his
lack of staying power with the bookbuying audience, thus show-
ing that he was subject to the treacherous whims of changing
global politics.

    Although the James Bond films have continued unabated
into the eighties, the books have never regained their initial
momentum. When Roger Moore's fourth Bondian opus, Moonraker (United Artists), was released in 1979, only four Ian
Fleming titles were available in the U.S.

    However, in the last few years Agent 007 has enjoyed
a respectable revival, including John Gardner's two extant
James Bond novels, License Renewed (Richard Marek, 1981)
and For Special Services (Coward, McCann, and Geoghegan,
1982), both of which attained bestseller status and the Flem-
ing-styled film version of For Your Eyes Only (United Artists,
1981), starring Roger Moore as James Bond.

    Since 1980 the Bond entries have been distributed in
paperback by Berkley-Jove as well as by Fleming's principal
publisher of the sixties, New American Library.

THE PAPERBACK SPY ORIGINAL

The advent in the sixties of original espionage novels in
paperback provided the genre with its most illustrious moments. Fawcett-Gold Medal Books tested this viable format
in 1955 with the introduction of Edward S. Aarons' Sam Durell and Stephen Marlowe's Chester Drum, followed in 1960

by Donald Hamilton's first two Matt Helm books, Death of a
Citizen and The Wrecking Crew.

Along with the highly successful Nick Carter series
(Universal-Award and Ace-Charter), which still is not penned
by a single author, the Durell and Helm canons are the sole
survivors of the paperback spy craze of the sixties.   Their
continued prosperity paved the way for the likes of "The Executioner" and "The Destroyer" (both published by Pinnacle
Books) in the seventies.

The majority of the sixties spy efforts fall into the
paperback original group, and, in the context of volatile
world politics, Don Smith's Phil Sherman--"Secret Mission"
series, which first appeared under the Universal-Award imprint in 1968, was one of the first to reflect the changing
complexion of the global Cold War.

Apart from the aforementioned spy staples, some of
the more durable series, notably James Dark's Mark Hood
novels (New American Library), and the television tie-ins
for "The Man from U.N.C.L.E." (Ace Books) and "I Spy"
(Popular Library), fall into this ample category.

Le CARRE AND DEIGHTON

The long-term effects of works by John le Carré and Len
Deighton eventually became so devastating to James Bond
that the realistic school of spy fiction surely must have influenced Ian Fleming's steady decline in popularity after 1967,
as others have suggested.

However, the credible ground of espionage was so
quickly covered by Len Deighton's The Ipcress File (Simon
and Schuster, 1963), John le Carré's The Spy Who Came In
from the Cold (Coward-McCann, 1964), and to a certain extent, Adam Hall's The Quiller Memorandum (Simon and Schuster, 1965), that most of the later efforts in this sector seemed
tame by comparison.   More importantly, this last group relied greatly on the enigmatic politics of the Cold War, and
it is this single historical sphere that unites all espionage
fiction of the sixties.

THE COLD WAR AND THE SPY NOVEL

The summer of 1965 may well be the first time in recorded

history in which fact actually courted fiction: President
Johnson committed 193,000 U.S. troops to Southeast Asia
in July 1965, the same month that the paperback spy novel
invaded America.*

Unquestionably, the spy novel of the sixties reflected
the shockwaves of the Cold War in its many guises, whether
the clearly defined cultural divisions manifested in the Bond
books or the more disturbing ideological conflicts professed
by le Carré and Deighton.   Given this precarious relationship, I chose to concentrate on series fare for two reasons:
1) the symbols of the Cold War seemed easier to define
through the actions of a continuing secret agent character,
and 2) the identification between author and protagonist, especially Ian Fleming and James Bond, suggested the unique format for this book on espionage fiction.

*By July 1965, New American Library had distributed the spy
fiction of Ian Fleming, John le Carré, William Haggard, Desmond Cory, James Dark, David St. John (E. Howard Hunt),
and Bill Ballinger.   This prolific activity was aggressively
manifested throughout the U.S. market.

THE CONSPIRATORS

†   of the   †

COLD WAR FILE

† CWF 1. AARONS, EDWARD S. †

BACKGROUND: Innovative, prolific suspense author, generally associated with the developing years of the paperback original.

Born in 1916 in Philadelphia. Won a collegiate short-story contest at the age of seventeen and published his first two mystery novels, Death in a Lighthouse and Murder Money, in 1938. After serving in the Coast Guard during World War II, Aarons penned numerous suspense works under the cover identitites of Edward Ronns and Paul Ayres. These early thrillers were later reprinted under his own name.

Shortly after the end of World War II Aarons married Ruth Ives; widowed, he later married Grace Dyer.

Terror in the Town (1947) and State Department Murders (1950) were among the early mysteries of this CWF author, then writing as Edward Ronns. Dead Heat (1950), based on the Casey, Crime Photographer radio feature, was the only novel Aarons wrote as Paul Ayres.

However, when Aarons instigated the "Assignment" dossier in 1955, involving C.I.A. agent Sam Durell, he achieved global recognition. Here, writing as Aarons, he offered more intriguing characters and settings.

After being embroiled in international espionage for six years, Aarons resurfaced on the domestic crime scene in 1961 with a novelization, based on the courtroom drama The Defenders, a highly controversial visual project restricted to the home sector.

Until his death in 1975, Aarons functioned as a primary constituent of the Fawcett Intelligence Group (see separate reference). Aarons' series operative, Sam Durell, continues to serve in the group's paperback original division, Gold Medal, which also includes Donald Hamilton's Matt Helm (see separate reference).

CWF AGENT: Durell, Sam.

7

CWF HISTORY: Sam Durell was born in Bayou Perche Rogue, Louisiana, in 1926. Cajun stock. Son of Jonathan Durell, Jr. and Mary-Ellen Lamont Durell.

Durell is described as a tall, muscular man with piercing blue eyes. A photograph dating back to 1955 shows a thin moustache on CWF agent Durell.

Graduated cum laude from Yale University. Served with the O.S.S. from 1943 to 1945, followed by two years with the G-2 in the Pentagon.

Durell joined the C.I.A. in March, 1951, as an operative in the agency's K Section. Durell's current superior is identified as General Dickinson McFee. From files dated 1955, the location of K Section as relevant to this file was recorded as 20 Annapolis Street, Washington, D.C. Cover identity: The Johnson-Kimball Company. Exact cover function unknown, except as a successful business establishment. (Note: In 1956, McFee ordered Durell to remove the aforementioned moustache).

Agent Durell is inclined to erratic expressions of anger and openly admits to gambling tendencies.

Speaks fluently a dozen languages and is competent at a number of foreign dialects. Highly proficient in marksmanship and unarmed combat. Standard field weapon: .38 Special. Adept in the use of larger, more lethal weaponry, notably the .50mm machine gun, as recorded in the file, Assignment: Sulu Sea (1964). Further, Durell has been trained in scuba techniques.

Durell's romantic involvement has been limited to one Deirdre Padgett, formerly of Price John, Maryland. However, it should be noted here that Ms. Padgett was a key figure in a crucial K-Section mission in 1955, identified from the Aarons dossier as Assignment to Disaster. Durell's relationship with Ms. Padgett, outside his activities with K Section, is not pertinent to this file. Further, agent Durell has encountered women from his past in the field, and is well-seasoned in the selective arts of seduction.

Properly termed, Sam Durell is a field operative for the C.I.A. The assignments requiring his special talents have sent him around the globe, to its most incendiary locales.

Unlike many CWF agents, Durell does not possess any known code names. In the field, however, he has on occasion been referred to as "Cajun."

Officially, Durell is designated as a subchief of field operations for K Section, although he continues to perform his duty in the fashion demanded of an active agent. Like all K-Section operatives, Durell has consistently displayed resourcefulness, objectivity, and an impassive attitude toward both professional and personal problems, when engaged in the field.

(Note: All missions evaluated below, as derived from the Durell dossier, are prefixed with the designation, "Assignment").

OPERATIVE DATA: In general, the Durell series is marked by an established plot structure: General McFee dispatches Durell on a hazardous mission to counter subversive intimidation abroad.

However, Mr. Aarons' acute perception of the relationship between the unwavering function of intelligence and volatile global politics separates the "Assignment" saga from the more predictable entries of the sixties.

In Assignment to Disaster (1955), K Section sanctioned Durell to find a man who had vanished from a missile base in the New Mexico desert--and to liquidate him if he had leaked any information concerning a top-secret atomic project. The man's identity: Calvin Padgett, Deirdre's brother.

Assignment to Disaster manifested an atmosphere of tension and suspicion which even today is a reflection of the C.I.A. This mood extended to the contrasting relationships between Durell and Deirdre, since the mission involved her brother, and that of his initial superior, Buritt Swayney.

Assignment to Disaster, along with Donald Hamilton's Death of a Citizen (1960), is one of the most significant contributions in the development of the paperback spy original of the sixties.

Preceding by several years the serious spy fiction of John le Carré and Len Deighton (see separate references), this novel was perhaps the first of the immediate postwar period to examine the dark side of "The Company." Its theme, perfected throughout the "Assignment" series, has been imitated often.

Further, Aarons balanced Durell's mission with the potential disaster of the desert missile project, recalling the explosion of the first atomic bomb near Alamogordo, New Mexico, in July, 1945.

Thus, in his first assignment for K Section, Aarons confronted his series agent with a double challenge: a dangerous secret and a devastating nuclear menace. In Assignment to Disaster Sam Durell proved his value as a C.I.A. agent.

In Assignment: Treason (1956) the treachery theme of Assignment to Disaster was more fully realized. Durell's mission was to unmask a traitor--within K Section.

After Assignment: Treason the Durell books of the fifties ominously foreshadowed the Cold War.

In Assignment: Suicide (1956) Durell posed as a Soviet
M. V. D. agent in order to slip behind the Iron Curtain.   K Section
had learned of a neo-Stalinist domination plot within the Soviet
Union, and General McFee ordered Durell to circumvent a plot to
provoke the U. S. into an atomic war--to be triggered by a Soviet
ICBM during a May Day parade in Moscow.   Durell's sole contact:
a beautiful yet highly unreliable Soviet agent known only as Valya.

Assignment: Madeline and Assignment: Angelina (both 1958)
advanced the lethal femme fatale theme introduced in Assignment:
Suicide.   Of the two, Assignment: Angelina transpired as the more
explosive.   A mysterious woman, identified from K-Section files as
Angelina, was believed to be the crucial link in four savage murders.

Aarons continued to refine his Mata Hari theme in Assignment: Helene (1959) and Assignment: Zoraya (1960).   Integrating
the accelerating political turmoil in the books' respective locales of
Southeast Asia and the Middle East, Aarons endowed Durell with a
callous quality that had been conspicuously absent from earlier missions.

Although Aarons had established a loyal audience well before
the spy craze of the sixties, he emphasized plots during this period
that mirrored the shattering climate of the Cold War.   Turkey, for
instance, was a hot-bed of contention in the early years of the Cold
War.   In Assignment: Ankara (1961), a plane on which Durell was
traveling was shot down by the Russians--in Turkish territory.
Durell's mission concerned investigation of the possible sabotage of
a secret N. A. T. O. radar base, situated twenty miles from the
Turkish-Soviet frontier.

Assignment: Sorrento Siren (1963) displayed an underlying
current of ferocity that characterized the C. I. A. during the Cold
War.   A K-Section agent stationed in Paris, identified as Jack Tal-
bott, was accused of stealing a set of valuable scrolls in Geneva.
Assigned to find him, Durell journeyed to Southern Italy where he
encountered a ruthless, jaded countess, later revealed as the link
to the mystery of the scrolls and a potentially dangerous international incident.

Many K-Section operatives believe Assignment: School for
Spies (1966) to be the best of the series.   Full details are given
below.

Accused of treason, Durell was hunted by the C. I. A. when
he refused to leave Europe.   This harsh theme was complemented
by several insidious elements:

1)   A blueprint outlining the complete infiltration of K Section.

2)   A mysterious girls' school in a remote section of Central
Europe.   Note: the operative might wish to compare this

segment with John Gardner's Amber Nine (1966) (see separate reference).

3)   Deirdre Padgett's purported defection to the East.

Assignment: School for Spies thus masterfully conveyed the desolate existence of a C. I. A. agent at the apex of the Cold War in Europe.

It should be noted here that Assignment: School for Spies was preceded by the account of Durell's hazardous mission to the Middle East, Assignment: The Cairo Dancers, acknowledged with K Section in 1965.   The Durell thrillers that followed Assignment: School for Spies illustrated with great authenticity the rising fever of the Cold War around the globe.

In Assignment: Cong Hai Kill (1966), Durell was embroiled in a scorching guerilla war in the jungles of Southeast Asia--in the thick of the Vietnam conflict--while the machinations of the Mafia in Southern Italy and the international nuclear market provided the focus of Durell's mission in Assignment: Palermo, recorded with K Section in 1966.

Manipulating the seemingly outlandish notion of global weather control, Aarons crafted a devastating spy novel with Assignment: Black Viking (1967).   K Section suspected that Peking was involved in fomenting destructive weather patterns throughout the world and Durell was ordered to ally with the K. G. B. to avert a worldwide cataclysm.

By 1968 a number of popular espionage novelists, ranging from Van Wyck Mason to James Dark (see separate references), were using a blending of the traditional secret-agent format and the growing fascination with outer space to bolster the waning cloak-and-dagger phenomenon.   Aarons' most inventive Durell entry, Assignment: Moon Girl (1967) enhanced this brief trend.   Durell was assigned to find a provocative Russian-Chinese girl, just returned from the moon, who was prepared to reveal to the world the mysteries of her foray.

The "hippie" movement and the search for a priceless portrait figured in Durell's most perplexing adventure, Assignment: Nuclear Nude (1968).   Traveling from the Florida Keys to Singapore with a group of "flower children," Durell unmasked the avaricious motives of an Oriental power broker, known only as Madame Hung, whose ruthless search for a crucial formula threatened the world with a nuclear war.

SUMMARY: The success of Edward Aarons' bestselling "Assignment" series can be substantiated by the following factors:

1)   Appearing as a series operative in the mid-fifties, Edward

Aarons' intrepid C. I. A. agent, Sam Durell, provided the basis for the archetypal secret agent who would dominate the popular spy fiction of the Cold War.

2) The canon was the first to examine the realistic backgrounds of the C. I. A. as well as the locales that figured in their global operations.

However, the Durell dossier manifested two major deficiencies:

1) The consistent "Assignment" stamp on each successive Durell docket helped induce a mood of formularization in espionage series fiction, as typified in Don Smith's Phil Sherman-- "Secret Mission" series (see separate reference).

2) Apart from the topicality evidenced throughout the series, both the general plot structure and the Durell character varied little from book to book. Compare this aspect with the development of Donald Hamilton's Matt Helm (see separate reference).

STATUS: Despite the death of spymaster Aarons in 1975, Sam Durell remains "on hazardous duty" with K Section, which is still directed by General McFee.

Since 1977 the "Assignment" files have been signed by one Will B. Aarons, as recorded in Assignment: Tyrant's Bride (1980), while the original Durell entries are in constant rotation by the Fawcett Intelligence Group (see separate reference). The series has now surpassed the forty-title mark. SSP.

FIELD BIBLIOGRAPHY

Aarons, Edward S. Assignment: Angelina. New York: Fawcett-Gold Medal, 1958. PBO.

_____. Assignment: Ankara. New York: Fawcett-Gold Medal, 1961. PBO.

_____. Assignment: Black Viking. New York: Fawcett-Gold Medal, 1967. PBO.

_____. Assignment: Budapest. New York: Fawcett-Gold Medal, 1957. PBO.

_____. Assignment: Burma Girl. New York: Fawcett-Gold Medal, 1961. PBO.

_____. Assignment: The Cairo Dancers. New York: Fawcett-Gold Medal, 1965. PBO.

_____. Assignment: Carlotta Cortez. New York: Fawcett-Gold Medal, 1959. PBO.

_____. Assignment: Cong-Hai Kill. New York: Fawcett-Gold Medal, 1966. PBO.

_____. Assignment: The Girl in the Gondola. New York: Fawcett-Gold Medal, 1964. PBO.

_____. Assignment: Helene. New York: Fawcett-Gold Medal, 1959. PBO.

_____. Assignment: Karachi. New York: Fawcett-Gold Medal, 1962. PBO.

_____. Assignment: Lili Lamaris. New York: Fawcett-Gold Medal, 1959. PBO.

_____. Assignment: Lowlands. New York: Fawcett-Gold Medal, 1961. PBO.

_____. Assignment: Madeline. New York: Fawcett-Gold Medal, 1958. PBO.

_____. Assignment: Manchurian Doll. New York: Fawcett-Gold Medal, 1963. PBO.

_____. Assignment: Mara Tirana. New York: Fawcett-Gold Medal, 1960. PBO.

_____. Assignment: Moon Girl. New York: Fawcett-Gold Medal, 1967. PBO.

_____. Assignment: Nuclear Nude. New York: Fawcett-Gold Medal, 1968. PBO.

_____. Assignment: Palermo. New York: Fawcett-Gold Medal, 1966. PBO.

_____. Assignment: Peking. New York: Fawcett-Gold Medal, 1969. PBO.

_____. Assignment: School for Spies. New York: Fawcett-Gold Medal, 1966. PBO.

_____. Assignment: Sorrento Siren. New York: Fawcett-Gold Medal, 1963. PBO.

_____. Assignment: Stella Marni. New York: Fawcett-Gold Medal, 1957. PBO.

_____. Assignment: Suicide. New York: Fawcett-Gold Medal, 1956. PBO.

_____. Assignment: Sulu Sea. New York: Fawcett-Gold Medal, 1964. PBO.

_____. Assignment to Disaster. New York: Fawcett-Gold Medal, 1955. PBO.

_____. Assignment: Treason. New York: Fawcett-Gold Medal, 1956. PBO.

_____. Assignment: Zoraya. New York: Fawcett-Gold Medal, 1960. PBO.

CONSULT APPENDIX I FOR SERIES CONTINUATION

END OF CWF 1

† CWF 2. THE ACE INTELLIGENCE GROUP †

CONTENTS: The objectives of the Ace Intelligence Group were directed for the most part toward the visual-project novelization, an area which received only polite attention from the allied units. A novelization is often referred to as a tie-in.

Before considering the contributing elements of the A. I. G., it is necessary, given its concentration in the visual-project field, to define the terms "novelization" and "tie-in":

1) Novelization: a published book adapted from an original script. A previously published book, as distinct from an original script, is rarely used in the preparation of a novelization.

2) Tie-in: a published book which suitably promotes any type of visual project. Generally, this refers to a previously published book (or books), from which a visual project has been adapted. However, a novelization could be loosely considered as a tie-in, as the representations of the A. I. G. will illustrate.

Through the ambitious efforts of the A. I. G., the novelization became an established publishing category by the mid-sixties. Although the A. I. G. recruited only two series during the sixties, namely "The Man from U. N. C. L. E." and "It Takes a Thief," the group's achievements launched the format into large-scale popularity.

It is believed in many intelligence sectors that "The Man from U. N. C. L. E." was the most distinguished visual project to be

presented in the home territory. Inspired by the style of the James
Bond visual projects, "The Man from U. N. C. L. E." served from
1964 to 1968 and quickly attracted an audience which rivaled that of
the 007 contingent.

Utilizing authorized visual-project files, the A. I. G. produced
no fewer than twenty-three U. N. C. L. E. books, thereby exceeding any
other espionage novelization series of the period.

The A. I. G. summoned several CWF authors for field duty
during the U. N. C. L. E. operation, namely Michael Avallone, Fredric Davies, J. Hunter Holly, Peter Leslie, David McDaniel, John
Oram, John T. Phillifent, Thomas Stratton, and Harry Whittington
(see separate references).

Beginning in 1965 with The Thousand Coffins Affair by Michael Avallone, the novelization series continued until 1970, two
years after the visual project expired.

The U. N. C. L. E. series was the first of its kind to enjoy
bestseller status, and its success intensified the use of the format
in such later secret-agent series as "I Spy," "Mission: Impossible,"
and "Get Smart."

In 1966 "The Girl from U. N. C. L. E.," a home visual project
derived from the original series, was initiated by M. G. M., the
same production source responsible for "The Man from U. N. C. L. E."
However, the three resulting novelizations, adapted from the former
effort, were sponsored by the N. A. L. /Signet Intelligence Group
(see separate reference); A. I. G. writers Avallone and Leslie were
drafted by the N. A. L. for this supplementary operation.

Unlike the U. N. C. L. E. series, Ace's novelizations for "It
Takes a Thief" were penned by a single CWF author, identified as
prolific conspirator Gil Brewer (see separate reference).

Although A. I. G. published only three novelizations based upon
that popular home visual project, during 1969 and 1970, the series
was well received in most intelligence areas. However, it failed to
generate the sensationalism or publicity of the U. N. C. L. E. novelizations. The operation ended in 1970.

Illustrated with striking color file photos, the Ace editions
of "The Man from U. N. C. L. E." and "It Takes a Thief" depicted
respectively the intriguing exploits of U. N. C. L. E. agents Napoleon
Solo and Illya Kuryakin, and master thief Alexander Mundy who was
manipulated into a choice of counterespionage service for the S. I. A.
or a prison term. Both series were published as paperback originals.

The A. I. G. is no longer in existence and Ace has since
intensified their marketing strategies in the areas of gothics and
science fiction. Officially, the New York-based publisher is now
known as Ace-Charter.

For additional information on the U. N. C. L. E. novelization project, consult the individual files relevant to the aforementioned CWF authors.

Pursuant to this last point, no field data was available on one Joel Bernard or his contribution to the U. N. C. L. E. series, The Thinking Machine Affair (1970), which was listed as the twenty-first entry in the A. I. G. /U. N. C. L. E. dossier.

END OF CWF 2

† CWF 3. ALDRIDGE, JAMES †

BACKGROUND: Australian author of espionage and suspense fiction. Official name: Harold Edward Aldridge. Born in 1918.

One of the many serious spy novelists who attempted during the sixties to follow in the path of John le Carré. Critical response: excellent. Commercial response: poor.

Aldridge showed promise with The Diplomat (1950), a carefully plotted suspense novel with dominant political overtones. However, not being a prolific author, it was thirteen years before Aldridge returned to the mystery scene, with A Captive in the Land. This effort was the first of his two novels about Rupert Royce, the subject of this file.

Although Aldridge continued to impress critics with his later books, notably A Sporting Proposition (1973) and The Untouchable Juli (1976), written around his second series character, Kit Quayle, his Royce thrillers especially are so disciplined in plotting and characterization that they nearly qualify as straight fiction as well as contributions to the suspense genre. Note: Unlike most espionage authors of the period, Aldridge minimized the use of chronological and geographical details.

CWF AGENT: Royce, Rupert.

CWF HISTORY: Born into a wealthy English family, Royce entered the family business, the Royce Shipping Line, and eventually inherited the concern.

Royce later forfeited his company stock to his mother; subsequently secured employment with the Naval Meteorological Office, situated in Greenland, where he was purportedly engaged in a number of clandestine spy missions for the Admiralty.

However, an incident involving Royce with a Soviet pilot, identified only as Vodopyanov, cast his loyalties under suspicion.

While employed by the Meteorological Office, Royce rescued Vodopyanov and literally hauled the Russian across miles of polar ice. Vodopyanov was retained by the Americans in Thule, Greenland --on the pretense of his being seriously ill after the paralyzing ordeal.

Royce was later sent to Moscow by Admiral Lille, a close family friend who transpired as the head of a special Admiralty department. Officially, it was recorded that Royce visited the Soviet capital to develop the skills required of him by the Meteorological Office. Secretly, Royce had been sent on yet another intelligence assignment.

From this vantage point, Royce's activities in Moscow precipitated the following developments:

1) Royce became involved with Vodopyanov's wife, Nina. This action infused in Royce an uncontrollable sense of betrayal, prompting him to develop his seditious attitudes toward his faithful wife, Jo, and his country.

2) Although the Soviets had previously wished to honor Royce as "The Hero of the Soviet Union," for rescuing Vodopyanov, his later movements in Moscow caused the Russians to arrest the Englishman on allegations of spying.

3) Subsequently brainwashed by the Soviets, Royce returned to England where he was branded a traitor in the highest intelligence circles.

Apart from his association with the Meteorological Office and Admiral Lille, Royce did not openly profess any further involvement with Whitehall. It should be noted here, however, that the accusations of Royce's treacherous sympathies figured into his later actions regarding the family shipping line.

OPERATIVE DATA: Aldridge's two Royce books, A Captive in the Land (1963) and The Statesman's Game (1966), are clearly in the le Carré class.

In A Captive in the Land Aldridge recounted the Vodopyanov affair, and Royce's ambiguous foray to Moscow. The Stateman's Game surpassed A Captive in the Land in its plotting, characterization, and penetrating perception of the Cold War.

Beyond these qualities, Aldridge demonstrated a rare acumen for simplifying complex financial details. In The Statesman's Game, Royce offered the family shipping line a staggering opportunity: a multimillion-dollar shipping deal with the Soviet Union. Aldridge deftly maneuvered the Royce Shipping Line against the studied motives of multinational oil concerns, N. A. T. O., Whitehall, and Soviet official-dom to delineate the nearly indiscernible boundary between international finance and global intelligence.

Integrating the Chinese and British paranoid fears of the U. S. S. R., Aldridge intensified The Statesman's Game to make a statement on the Cold War and its perilous relationship to big-power politics that few wanted to hear.

Unlike the cynical protagonists associated with le Carré, Deighton, and Hall (see separate references), Rupert Royce was depicted as an elusive master of espionage and high finance, totally oblivious to the fatalism of the Cold War.

Throughout The Statesman's Game, Aldridge's allusions to literary figures like Shelley and F. Scott Fitzgerald accented the intellectual facet of Royce's personality.

SUMMARY: James Aldridge's Rupert Royce thrillers were conceived in the general mold of John le Carré and Len Deighton (see separate references). Aldridge imparted an atmosphere of disciplined seriousness that pointed to the style le Carré would develop in his post-Cold War achievements.

Although the Royce series was a limited one, Aldridge successfully competed in the espionage market with authors like le Carré, Deighton, and Hall (see separate references). Aldridge's solemn narrative style quickly placed him on a par with these celebrated masters of the Cold-War spy novel, as well as with the action-oriented allies of Ian Fleming (see separate reference).

Royce transcended the weary operatives crafted by le Carré and Deighton (see separate references), and emerged as a worldly protagonist in the fashion of the late Van Wyck Mason and William Haggard (see separate references).

STATUS: The passage of the Cold War, coupled with the constantly changing face of world politics, make it highly unlikely that Rupert Royce would be summoned by the Meteorological Office for current field duty. SOP.

FIELD BIBLIOGRAPHY

Aldridge, James. A Captive in the Land. Garden City, N. Y.: Doubleday, 1963. HB.

_____. The Statesman's Game. Garden City, N. Y.: Doubleday, 1966; New York: Curtis paperback, 1969. HB-R.

END OF CWF 3

ar File

RY: See also Fleming, Ian--CWF 25.

 DATA: In the context of the Bond series, Colonel Sun
 changing climate of the Cold War in the midst of the
flict and, most significantly, Britain's relation to Red
8, a year which has been recognized by historians as
oint between the Cold War and détente.

el Sun is, in many ways, Amis's fictionalized com-
Fleming's deficiencies, despite his affection for Bond
 creator.

 007's superior, was kidnapped by Colonel Sun of the
eration Army of China, and this fusion provided the
s: "M," the symbol of a romanticized, pre-World War
as, for the first time, subjected to the fanaticism of
a world power which in 1968 was perceived as the great-
 world peace.

's treatment of "M" in Colonel Sun reverted back to his
ith the Fleming character in The James Bond Dossier:

What would have done 'M' good would have been to have
meone burst into his eighth floor office without waiting
 the green light ... and jab him heartily in the ribs
th the muzzle of a Walther PPK 7.65 mm, or even the
spised Beretta .25."*

the first time in the Bond series since Doctor No (1958),
ignified a formidable yet credible threat, as opposed to
 Fleming's Sir Hugo Drax in Moonraker (1955). With
 Amis centralized the action entirely on Bond, rather
sensationalism that typified Fleming's books after Doc-

 created a nemesis for 007 who was a genuine menace,
r No, from whom the character of Colonel Sun was ob-
ved. Further, Amis did not require the use of such
e organizations as S.M.E.R.S.H. and S.P.E.C.T.R.E.
his plot in Colonel Sun.

ould be pointed out that Amis honored certain obligatory
he alluring femme fatale in the person of Ariadne Alex-
tic locales (Greece), the meticulous appreciation of the
ry delights, and 007's excruciating torture at the hands
 sadist.

trospect, Colonel Sun is not a continuation of the Ian

mis, The James Bond Dossier. New York: New
ibrary, 1965, ch. 7, pp. 62-63.

† CWF 4. AM

BACKGROUND: Born in London i
began writing at the age of eleven
project at the suggestion of a prej

While attending St. John's
James Michie, edited Oxford Poet
English teacher until 1963.

Amis's abilities as a write
ably best-known as a subtle satiri

Amis's novel Lucky Jim (1
troversy in England because of its
postwar generation. He penned se
notably That Uncertain Feeling (19
Take A Girl Like You (1960).

Lucky Jim was released as
ing the same heated publicity that
Uncertain Feeling was similarly ac
(1962). In the area of visual proj
Esquire in the late fifties while he
ton University.

Amis has also authored a s
Enemy (1962), and published two p
(1956) and A Look Round the Estat
flections of his Oxford Poetry days

Amis's achievements in the
eclipsed, however, the furor creat

In 1965 Amis's provocative
published, which immediately assur
with Ian Fleming's legendary secre
biographies and commentaries that
Amis's analysis of the Bond series
written defense against Fleming's c

The following year, The Ant
resounding critical praise for Amis
of the Cold War.

Under the cover identity of
the first post-Fleming James Bond
subject of this file.

CWF AGENT: Bond, James.

OPERATIV
mirrored t
Vietnam co
China in 19
the turning

Cold
mentary on
and his late

"M,
People's Li
novel's foc
II Britain,
Red China,
est threat t

Ami
annoyance

"
s
f
w
d

For
the villain
the likes of
Colonel Sur
than on the
tor No.

Ami
unlike Doct
viously der
Fleming-st
to flesh ou

It s
elements:
androu, ex
finest culir
of a maste

In r

*Kingsley
American

Fleming dossier. Instead, it is a dedicated attempt to humanize James Bond with a believable challenge to his values, as exemplified by the kidnapping of "M" and by Colonel Sun's avaricious threat to both the West and the Soviet Union.

Beyond this realm, the premise of Colonel Sun has been more fully realized with John Gardner's recent Bond thrillers, notably License Renewed (1981) and For Special Services (1982).

Like Fleming's 007 novels, Colonel Sun is a dated document of espionage fiction. Colonel Sun's sympathies were clearly based on Maoist Communism, and, from that viewpoint Sun's plot, which manipulated Bond and "M" in a scheme to intimidate the Russians through nuclear force, was deeply rooted in the politics of the Cold War.

SUMMARY: Kingsley Amis's Colonel Sun reflected the author's opinions about Fleming's weaknesses as suggested in his earlier study, The James Bond Dossier.

Apart from the deployment of the expected Fleming elements, Colonel Sun is credited with bestowing 007 with a more believable quality.

STATUS: Given the current resurgence in Bond's popularity, Colonel Sun should be reissued in the American sector to complement this revival.

It should be noted that Colonel Sun has already been reprinted in British territory, under the Panther paperback imprint.

Despite all the Fleming books which have been adapted as visual projects, Colonel Sun has been ignored for this purpose. Further, recent field reports suggest that the Amis property is likely to remain unfilmed, given the political deviation from Maoist Communism since Mao's death in 1976. EOP, in American sector only.

FIELD BIBLIOGRAPHY

Amis, Kingsley. Colonel Sun. (Robert Markham, cover identity). New York: Harper and Row, 1968; New York: Bantam paperback, 1969. HB-R.

CONSULT FLEMING, IAN--CWF 25 FOR SERIES ADDITIONS

END OF CWF 4

† CWF 5.   ATLEE, PHILIP †

BACKGROUND: Cover identity of James Atlee Phillips, prominent American author of the Joe Gall counterespionage series and other suspense works.   Born in 1915.

Under the Atlee cover, Phillips penned The Naked Year (1954), which earned an enthusiastic response from Raymond Chandler: "I admire Philip Atlee's writing tremendously, the hard economy of style, the characterizations...."

This recommendation justified Atlee's admission into the Fawcett Intelligence Group (see separate reference) in 1963, joining Edward S. Aarons, Donald Hamilton, Dan J. Marlowe, and Stephen Marlowe (see separate references).

Atlee remained with the Fawcett group until 1977, executing twenty-two contracts involving Joseph Liam Gall: Code name--the Nullifier.

It should be noted that the designation, "contract," served as the code identification for the highly successful Gall series.

Prior to recruiting Gall, Atlee wrote four hard-boiled suspense novels under his real name.   These are: The Case of the Shivering Chorus Girls (1942), Suitable for Framing (1949), Pagoda (1951), and The Deadly Mermaid (1954).

These early mystery works were favorably received in the United States and in England, although The Deadly Mermaid was not directly purchased for British distribution.

James Atlee Phillips currently resides in Fayetteville, Arkansas.

No further information is available on this CWF author since his withdrawal from the Fawcett Intelligence Group.

CWF AGENT: Gall, Joseph Liam.

CWF HISTORY: Descended from Irish stock.   Approximate year of birth given as 1924.   Exact month and place of birth unknown.

At the age of eighteen, Gall flew the Himalayan route during the early years of World War II.   Employer: the China National Airline.

Later enlisted in the Marine Corps and eventually suffered a severe ankle injury on Iwo Jima.   Admitted to the Klamath Veterans' Hospital on the West Coast.   After a year of extensive physiotherapy, Gall regained partial use of the injured foot and, shortly thereafter, married a young woman whose identity has never been revealed.

The marriage did not last and Gall accepted an offer to operate an airline charter service in Burma, transporting troops and ammunition.

Once again Gall suffered an ankle injury, this time during a crash landing, and he returned to the Klamath Falls Hospital. During his recuperative period, Gall was approached by a man identified as Howard Shale, who recruited him as a counterespionage operative for "the agency," a clandestine intelligence unit sponsored by the State Department.

Upon completing the obligatory training courses, Gall was assigned to routine, purely administrative missions throughout the world. During a revolution in Bolivia, however, Gall experienced the savage side of his new profession when a contact was killed during a bomb explosion in Sucre.

Gall was ordered to ally with the Cubans in the late fifties. Operative locale: the Oriente hills. When the Bay of Pigs incident occurred in 1961, Gall submitted his resignation to Shale; it was instantly and adamantly rejected.

The agency's files also revealed that Gall admired Egypt's Gamal Abdul Nasser at a time when the United States was building a strong relationship with Israel.

"The agency" entered a new phase when Howard Shale was shot down in a helicopter near Saigon. He was replaced by Carl Wiley, a former member of the U.S. Foreign Service. It was an unenviable position for Wiley, considering that Shale had been the most decorated member of "the agency."

The circumstances of a mission involving a mysterious baroness caused Wiley to jump to his death from an upper floor of the Bethesda Medical Tower, and in 1966 Neal Pearsall was appointed to replace Wiley as the director of the agency's action division.

Through all these chaotic changes Gall remained with "the agency" as a contract killer.

Gall's early sanctions carried him around the globe to such locales as the Caribbean, the Canary Islands, Spain, Sweden, Texas, and Mexico. When not engaged on a contract, Gall resided in a fashionable house on a remote Ozark hill in Arkansas.

Although "the agency" is no longer in existence, it is well known in intelligence circles that the organization was situated in Washington, D.C., and that Gall, who retired from the Marine

Corps with the full rank of Major, was its best contract assassin.

Full details on CWF agent Gall are given below.

OPERATIVE DATA: Following Fawcett constituents Aarons and
Hamilton, Philip Atlee introduced a lean, grim style that probably
influenced Don Pendleton, Warren Murphy, and other advocates of
the avenger genre of the seventies.

Further, Atlee himself was apparently motivated by Donald
Hamilton (see separate reference), inasmuch as he used the first
person throughout the entire Gall series.

Atlee established the pattern for the series with The Green
Wound (1963), the first contract assigned to Gall. For a first entry
in a series, The Green Wound was a perplexing spy tale, drawing
an array of disturbing events and realistic characters into a destructive web.

A damaging letter that involved a millionaire's wife, the
brutal murder of an anti-Castro Cuban in Austin, Texas, a daring
hijack flight into Monterrey, Mexico, and a suitcase containing
nearly a quarter of a million dollars developed as crucial factors
in Gall's initial contract.

The Green Wound launched Gall against his most insidious
antagonist, Asmodeous. Purportedly Asmodeous was suspected of
fomenting a race riot in a small southern town, identified only as
Lafcadio, on the day that an all-black government had been elected
to power.

Considering the racial theme and the time in which it was
written, The Green Wound soberly reflected the civil conflicts prev-
alent in the U.S. in the early and mid-sixties.

Atlee's perceptive sense of topicality was his strongest asset
as a spy novelist of the sixties.

Gall's pursuit of the nebulous Asmodeous ranked as one of
the most suspenseful events in the field action of the sixties, and
Atlee was able to maintain the tension of The Green Wound in the
later Gall books as well.

As a matter of record, it should be noted here that Gall's
first assignment was reissued in 1967 as The Green Wound Contract, identifying it with the authorized seal of the bestselling series, as was done with Edward S. Aarons' "Assignment" dossier
(see separate reference).

Atlee heightened the complexity of Gall's profession in The
Silken Baroness (1964). Gall's cover was carefully established as

Harry Malloy, author of escapist fiction. His contract: meet an elusive baroness, and then avoid her--until advised of the treacherous motives of "the agency." In 1966, this Gall docket was submitted into the field as The Silken Baroness Contract.

As the series progressed, Atlee blended his crisp style with the authentic trappings of the Cold War.

The political implications of U.S. involvement in Southeast Asia punctuated The Death Bird Contract (1966), wherein the Nullifier was ordered to investigate the past of Lewis Wardlaw, a flamboyant Texas diplomat slated to become the Under Secretary of State to the Far East.

Atlee's suggestion of a Chi-Com spy ring operating in Mexico symbolized the callous philosophy of the Cold War. Without reservation, The Death Bird Contract transpired as the most realistic in the Gall canon.

Many field agents hailed The Paper Pistol Contract (1966) as the best of the Gall adventures of the sixties.

Identified only as Tumatus, a French atomic test was slated to occur in Tahiti. Gall's contract: in order to counteract President de Gaulle's arrogant recognition of Red China, he was to sabotage the test and make it appear to be a deliberate act of Chi-Com provocation.

Given the devastating theme conveyed in The Paper Pistol Contract, the subsequent Gall books reflected both the consistency in Atlee's style and the advanced state of the Cold War. The Star Ruby Contract (1967) and The Skeleton Coast Contract (1968) exemplified this subtle transformation.

In The Star Ruby Contract, Gall journeyed to Burma under the cover identity of Captain Joseph Mallory, the operator of a contract aviation service. This mission involved the deployment of a Gurkha regiment to the Sino-Burmese border--to drive Red Chinese troops out of Burma.

Atlee's perception of Asian politics, from an American viewpoint, was staggering in its unremitting characterization of the Cold War.

Africa was the setting for The Skeleton Coast Contract. Aided by two ruthless mercenaries, Gall's assignment was to smuggle a large cache of uncut gemstone alluvial diamonds from the Skeleton Coast of Southwest Africa to Rhodesia.

Acknowledged as Gall's most grueling sanction, The Skeleton Coast Contract demonstrated the physical demands of the agent's profession, as the Nullifier was embarked on a suicidal foray across the barren Kalahari Desert, embroiled in bizarre Pygmy

customs and apartheid power. This extensive action was preceded
by a calculated maneuver into a Kenyan jail and an explosive escape
attempt.

It was this dossier entry that confirmed Gall's reputation as
a brutal, amoral intelligence operative, second only to Donald Hamilton's Matt Helm (see separate reference).

SUMMARY: Philip Atlee's Joe Gall series penetrated the quagmire
of the Cold War with an uncompromising style that may have set the
precedent for the avenger genre of the seventies.

It should be mentioned that, like Fawcett ally Donald Hamilton, Atlee employed the first person throughout the Gall dossier.
However, the overall effect was not as dramatic in the latter series,
and Atlee clearly lacked Hamilton's expertise in the area of firearms.

Prompted by Gall's mass acceptance in the mid-sixties, The
Tombstone Epitaph offered this evaluation of the series: "Up-to-the-
minute newsworthiness. Every bit as good as the best in the field."

STATUS: For a time, it appeared that Gall had survived the spy
phenomenon, along with Fawcett confederates Aarons and Hamilton.
However, the sudden cancellation of his "contract" in 1977 made it
clear that Gall's services were no longer required.

Given the present climate of the espionage market, it is
highly unlikely that Joseph Liam Gall, a.k.a. the Nullifier, will be
recalled to active field duty. SOP.

FIELD BIBLIOGRAPHY

Atlee, Philip. The Death Bird Contract. New York: Fawcett-
Gold Medal, 1966. PBO.

_____. The Green Wound. New York: Fawcett-Gold Medal,
1963. Reissued in 1967 as The Green Wound Contract. PBO.

_____. The Ill Wind Contract. New York: Fawcett-Gold Medal,
1969. PBO.

_____. The Irish Beauty Contract. New York: Fawcett-Gold
Medal, 1966. PBO.

_____. The Paper Pistol Contract. New York: Fawcett-Gold
Medal, 1966. PBO.

_____. The Rockabye Contract. New York: Fawcett-Gold
Medal, 1968. PBO.

_____. The Silken Baroness. New York: Fawcett-Gold Medal, 1964. Reissued in 1966 as The Silken Baroness Contract. PBO.

_____. The Skeleton Coast Contract. New York: Fawcett-Gold Medal, 1968. PBO.

_____. The Star Ruby Contract. New York: Fawcett-Gold Medal, 1967. PBO.

_____. The Trembling Earth Contract. New York: Fawcett-Gold Medal, 1969. PBO.

CONSULT APPENDIX I FOR SERIES CONTINUATION

END OF CWF 5

† CWF 6.   AVALLONE, MICHAEL   †

BACKGROUND: Immensely prolific author of paperback originals. Avallone has operated under numerous cover identities, namely Nick Carter, Troy Conway, Priscilla Dalton, Mark Dane, Jean-Anne dePre, Dora Highland, Steve Michaels, Dorothea Nile, Edwina Noone, Vince Stanton, Sidney Stuart, and Max Walker.

Using these names and his own, Avallone has written mystery, spy, gothic, science fiction, and juvenile novels, as well as books adapted from various visual projects.

Born in Manhattan in 1924.   Spent childhood in the Bronx amidst sixteen brothers and sisters.

Entered U.S. Army after high school and served as a sergeant in Europe during World War II.   Returned to New York in 1945.

Eight years later Avallone created Ed Noon, a glib, New York-based private detective whose later activities in the highest levels of American intelligence are one of the subjects to be considered in this evaluation.

Avallone has written over thirty Noon books and approximately one hundred short stories featuring his popular character.

Although Avallone is best known for his Noon mysteries, he has earned a considerable reputation as an author of visual-project novelizations.   His contributions to the espionage genre by way of "The Man from U.N.C.L.E." and "The Girl from U.N.C.L.E." are also covered in this file.

Avallone's numerous visual-project assignments also have included these 1968 entries--Hawaii Five-O, Krakatoa--East of Java, Mannix, (...).

Under the aforementioned cover of Max Walker Avallone shadowed the activities of the I. M. F. intelligence unit in two 1968 "Mission: Impossible" reports, Code Name: Judas and Code Name: Rapier (see also Tiger, John--CWF 69).

More recently, Avallone wrote a visual-project novelization based on the Peter Ustinov mystery-comedy Charlie Chan and the Curse of the Dragon Queen (1981).

The author's prolific short-story output has continued unabated to the present, generally in mystery-suspense publications.

Avallone is a prominent member of the Mystery Writers of America and during the mid-sixties he represented both the Ace and N. A. L. /Signet Intelligence Groups (see separate references).

Note: before considering the CWF agents in this file, it should be pointed out that all novelization entries here, as elsewhere, will be given only brief treatment since in most cases the visual project author was not the original creator.

CWF AGENTS: 1) Noon, Ed.
                   2) Solo, Napoleon, and Illya Kuryakin.
                   3) Dancer, April, and Mark Slate.

CWF HISTORIES: 1) Ed Noon: began his practice in the early fifties in a modest Manhattan office. Noon's involvement in the Cold War was a guarded one, but in the mid-sixties he became personal intelligence agent to the President of the United States.

For security reasons, all other details are classified.

2) and 3) Napoleon Solo and Illya Kuryakin; April Dancer and Mark Slate: Top-flight operatives for U. N. C. L. E., otherwise known as United Network Command of Law Enforcement.

Born in Canada, Solo was Chief Enforcement Officer for U. N. C. L. E. during the Cold War era. Kuryakin, native Russian, was his lethal confederate.

April Dancer, American, was U. N. C. L. E. 's most resourceful female operative. Mark Slate, British subject, often assisted Ms. Dancer on her perilous missions.

During the Cold War era, the headquarters for U. N. C. L. E. were located a few blocks from the United Nations building in New York. Full details are given below.

In 1964 U. N. C. L. E. acquired a row of weathered brownstone buildings, with a more fashionable whitestone situated at the south end of the older structures.   A public garage was stationed at the north end of the block.   Deteriorating shops and businesses occupied the street level of the brownstones while the upper segments housed low-rent apartments.

Del Floria's Tailor Shop was established in a brownstone near the center of the block.   To all appearances, this concern was somewhat more prosperous than the adjoining tenants.   It was, in fact, the secret entrance to the U. N. C. L. E. command center.

The Masked Club, an exclusive key-club restaurant, commanded the first two floors of the whitestone; a respectable suite of offices occupied the third.   The acronym U. N. C. L. E. adorned the suite entrance.   According to U. N. C. L. E. files, the inner offices housed capable employees sorting mail and acknowledging visitors.

This line of buildings concealed the most efficient intelligence organization in the world, wherein a three-story building, hidden from the public, contained an elaborate technological system, a thoroughly skilled multinational staff, and an impenetrable surveillance network.

The overall impression of this "ghost" structure was that of a steel maze, lacking any stairways.   Four elevators accommodated all pedestrian traffic.   This was the command center for U. N. C. L. E. as it was known during the sixties.   For reasons unknown, U.N.C.L.E. ceased global operations in January 1968.

The function of U. N. C. L. E. was the enforcement of a high moral code among the peoples and nations of the world.   As a self-contained international agency, U. N. C. L. E. 's actions were not accountable to any nation, government, corporation, or global leader; an objective that would be reaffirmed if the nucleus of the U.N.C.L.E. organism were revived today.

U. N. C. L. E. 's chief adversary was T. H. R. U. S. H.   This entity was properly identified as the "Technological Hierarchy for the Removal of Undesirables and the Subjugation of Humanity."

Solo and Kuryakin's chief during the sixties was Mr. Alexander Waverly.

During the span of its Cold War service, U. N. C. L. E. was divided into eight sections:

1)   Policy and Operations
2)   Operations and Enforcement
3)   Enforcement and Intelligence
4)   Intelligence and Communications
5)   Communications and Security
6)   Security and Personnel

7)   Propaganda and Finance
8)   Camouflage and Deception

OPERATIVE DATA: 1) In transforming Noon from a private detective into a secret agent, Avallone intensified the character's
cynical nature to provide him with the attitude required for the
hazardous aspects of his new profession.   This also applied to the
espionage plots.

Of all the "spy-to-the-President" thrillers, The Doomsday
Bag (1969) was acknowledged as the most authentic and topical:
Noon was assigned to locate a top-secret agent, known only as "the
Bagman," who had vanished with a black satchel.   Its contents:
classified thermonuclear war codes.

Appearing during the height of America's nuclear awareness
in the Cold War era, The Doomsday Bag coldly depicted the potential menace presented by a shadowy man who was susceptible to
compromise by a friendly yet competitive world power.

2) and 3)   Avallone was the initial novelization author for
both U. N. C. L. E. projects.

Acknowledging that the tie-in novel previously had been dismissed by the more disciplined sectors of commercial publishing,
it is to Avallone's credit that his inventive style enhanced this format with both substance and mass acceptance.

The Thousand Coffins Affair (1965) involved the total obliteration of two remote areas in Scotland and Africa.   Suspecting
T. H. R. U. S. H. provocation, Mr. Waverly dispatched Solo to Germany
to investigate the death of U. N. C. L. E. agent Stewart Fromes, an
incident which Waverly believed to be linked to the cataclysmic
events in Africa and Scotland.   An Ellery Queen mystery aided Solo
in his mission to discover the scope of T. H. R. U. S. H. 's blueprint.

In The Birds of a Feather Affair (1966), April Dancer, the
girl from U. N. C. L. E., infiltrated T. H. R. U. S. H. to rescue confederate Mark Slate.

A resurgence of Nazism and a new global antagonist, identi-
fied from U. N. C. L. E. transcripts as T. O. R. C. H., prompted Mr.
Waverly to summon April and Mark in The Blazing Affair (1966).
Their mission: prevent the rise of a new "master race."

SUMMARY: Avallone's translation of his private-eye protagonist,
Ed Noon, into a secret agent displayed the gifted author's ability to
perform in any paperback genre.

Concerning the visual projects mentioned in this report,
"The Man from U. N. C. L. E." featured Robert Vaughn and David

McCallum in the respective roles of Napoleon Solo and Illya Kuryakin. M. G. M. 's immensely popular home series remained in the
field from 1964 to 1968.

Deploying authorized home files, M. G. M. launched eight
U. N. C. L. E. theatrical projects, released in global intelligence sectors between 1966 and 1968.

Stefanie Powers appeared as "The Girl from U. N. C. L. E."
in another home visual project from M. G. M. Initiated in 1966,
this sequel series lasted only a year, and featured Noel Harrison
as Mark Slate. However, it should be noted that Mary Ann Mob-
ley played April Dancer in the project pilot, aided by Norman Fell
as a veteran U. N. C. L. E. agent.

The late Leo G. Carroll commanded the U. N. C. L. E. network as Mr. Waverly in both home visual projects as well as the
theatrical initiatives.

It is widely known that Ian Fleming (see separate reference)
supplied the names April Dancer and Napoleon Solo, the latter derived from a gangster figure in his seventh James Bond novel,
Goldfinger (1959). In TV Detectives (1981), Richard Meyers revealed that Fleming also developed the project's pilot film, The Vulcan Affair (1964).

STATUS: 1) Because Avallone has remained active in the mystery
field, the Ed Noon series could be successfully reissued. SOP.

2) and 3) Recent field reports have indicated that the
U. N. C. L. E. organization is currently being reshaped for global
operations. Upon successful realization of this project, the original U. N. C. L. E. novelizations should be seriously evaluated for
reactivation; otherwise a distribution action of this magnitude would
serve no worthwhile purpose. SOP.

FIELD BIBLIOGRAPHY

Note: for the purpose of this bibliography, only the Noon entries
designated by the code phrase "spy to the President" have been
listed.

Avallone, Michael. Assassins Don't Die in Bed. New York: New
American Library, 1968. PBO. (Noon)

_____. The Birds of a Feather Affair. New York: New Amer-
ican Library, 1966. PBO. TN. ("The Girl from U. N. C. L. E.")

_____. The Blazing Affair. New York: New American Library,
1966. PBO. TN. ("The Girl from U. N. C. L. E.")

_____. The Doomsday Bag. New York: New American Library, 1969. PBO. (Noon)

_____. The February Doll Murders. New York: New American Library, 1967. PBO. (Noon)

_____. The Thousand Coffins Affair. New York: Ace Books, 1965. PBO. TN. ("The Man from U. N. C. L. E.")

CONSULT APPENDIX I FOR SERIES CONTINUATION

CONSULT ACE AND N. A. L. /SIGNET INTELLIGENCE GROUPS FOR ADDITIONAL AUTHOR REFERENCES

END OF CWF 6

† CWF 7. BALLINGER, BILL S. †

BACKGROUND: Seasoned American mystery writer, with impressive credits dating from the late forties: The Body in the Bed (1948), The Body Beautiful (1949), Portrait in Smoke (1950), The Tooth and the Nail (1957), (...).

Ballinger's suspense volumes have been printed in twenty-eight foreign countries and thirteen languages. Author also has penned mysteries under the cover identities of B. X. Sandborn and Frederic Freyer.

Principal constituent of the N. A. L. /Signet Intelligence Group (see separate reference) during the mid-sixties.

Responsible for more than 150 visual-project scripts before encountering valuable operative for immediate field duty in 1965. That year a special project was realized in which Ballinger had been involved as writer. Designated Operation C. I. A. (Allied Artists), the mission concerned the activities of American secret agent Mark Andrews (Burt Reynolds), assigned to Southeast Asia.

This last fact is particularly relevant to this file. Full details are given below.

CWF AGENT: Hawks, Joaquin.

CWF HISTORY: Son of a Nez Percé Indian chieftain and a Spanish gentlewoman. Hawks served briefly as an undercover operative for the C. I. A. in Southeast Asia. Term of duty: 1965 to 1966.

Proficient in several languages, including Nez Percé, Spanish, English, French, German, and numerous Arabic and Asian dialects.

Adept at karate and scuba diving, as derived from government training.

Hawks's superior was Horace Berke, Director of Operations, Los Angeles. Operated under the code name "Swinger."

Hawks's dark, lithe appearance enabled him to impersonate Europeans, Asians, Arabs, Malayans, or Indians with equal conviction.

OPERATIVE DATA: Hawks's resourcefulness in the field was proven in The Chinese Mask (1965) in which he posed as a Chinese circus performer to rescue three Western scientists imprisoned in Peking.

Further, his cover identities as an Arab seaman and a French salesman in The Spy in the Jungle (1965) insured the success of his mission into Laos to circumvent a Chi-Com plot to undermine U.S. nuclear-missile defense capabilities.

Hawks demonstrated his expertise as a scuba diver in The Spy in Bangkok (1965), a hazardous assignment which required "Swinger" to locate a sunken treasure off the Siamese coast.

SUMMARY: Bill S. Ballinger's Joaquin Hawks series was probably the first to survey the explosive political situation in Southeast Asia during the mid-sixties. Ballinger's perception of the Chi-Com and Soviet threat in Southeast Asia was highly accurate.

The series had much to recommend it at the time of its inception. Ballinger's measured balance of inventive plotting, credible characters, and well-paced action distinguished it from other paperback original espionage series of the period.

Also, Ballinger's meticulous attention to the finer points of Southeast Asian culture, as well as his topical locales, added to the canon's authenticity.

However, the American public's weariness over Vietnam quickly diminished the viability of the Hawks series.

STATUS: Given the constantly changing political climate in Southeast Asia, especially in the region's pro-Soviet sectors, it is highly unlikely that CWF agent Hawks would be recalled to active service. Present whereabouts unknown. SOP.

FIELD BIBLIOGRAPHY

Ballinger, Bill S.   The Chinese Mask.   New York: New American
    Library, 1965.   PBO.

_____.   The Spy at Angkor Wat.   New York: New American
    Library, 1966.   PBO.

_____.   The Spy in Bangkok.   New York: New American Li-
    brary, 1965.   PBO.

_____.   The Spy in the Java Sea.   New York: New American
    Library, 1966.   PBO.

_____.   The Spy in the Jungle.   New York: New American Li-
    brary, 1965.   PBO.

END OF CWF 7

† CWF 8.   BARKER, ALBERT †

BACKGROUND: American author of action-oriented espionage and
suspense novels.   Series characters include Hank McRae and Reefe
King, the latter being the subject of this file.

Dragon in the Spring (1973) and The Straw Virgin (1975) are
among his nonseries mystery efforts.   The Big Fix (1973), another
straight suspense thriller, should not be confused with Roger Simon's
hard-boiled genre novel of the same title.

Contributing member of the Universal-Award Intelligence
Group (see separate reference).

CWF AGENT: King, Reefe.

CWF HISTORY: Handsome American actor who was drafted as a
free-lance operative for the C.I.A. in the late sixties.   No other
details available.

The sole emphasis of the King series was action, and, as is
the fashion in entries of this nature, character delineation tends to
be limited at best.

In general, King's performance in the field lacked the pro-
fessionalism of a James Bond or Matt Helm.

OPERATIVE DATA: Barker's Reefe King series manifested little
originality. In Gift from Berlin (1969), the first of the series,
King transpired as no more than a satisfactory 007 imitation, and
Barker's use of the first person added nothing to the formularized
plot.

Utilizing his experience as an actor in Gift from Berlin,
King was assigned to investigate a mysterious drug which transformed film stars into sex fanatics. Despite his choice of Cold-
War-ravaged Berlin as locale, Barker failed to establish agent King
as a credible Cold-War protagonist. Gift from Berlin evolved as an
unlikely mixture of Ian Fleming and Harold Robbins with the slightest trace of Donald Hamilton.

The action values in this brief series were no more than ade-
quate. Granted, Barker's allusions to the film world blended with
King's background, but in the context of the Cold-War secret agent
motif, the concept was inappropriate.

SUMMARY: Albert Barker's Reefe King series, among the spate of
007 effigies to come out of the spy craze, lacked anything memorable to recommend it as escapist fare.

STATUS: Considering the more durable spy series of the period
that would be worthy of reissue, it's ironic that Charter Books
briefly reprinted Gift from Berlin in 1980. SOP.

FIELD BIBLIOGRAPHY

Barker, Albert. Gift from Berlin. New York: Universal-Award,
    1969. PBO.

CONSULT APPENDIX I FOR SERIES CONTINUATION

CONSULT APPENDIX II FOR SERIES TRANSITION

END OF CWF 8

† CWF 9. BLACK, GAVIN †

BACKGROUND: It is a matter of record in most intelligence sectors that Gavin Black is a cover identity for Oswald Wynd.

Born in 1913 in Tokyo, Japan, of Scottish parents. Attended
the American School in Tokyo; later went to Edinburgh University.

Upon graduation Wynd joined the Scots Guard and eventually served in the Intelligence Corps in Malaya. This experience was to prove useful later in the recruitment of CWF agent Paul Harris, the subject of this file.

Captured, as a POW Wynd was confined to prison camps in both Japan and Malaya.

In 1945 Wynd came to the U.S., returning to Scotland less than a year later.

An early Wynd novel earned the coveted Doubleday $20,000 Fiction Prize, an event which launched the author on a gratifying career as a suspense writer.

All of Wynd's mystery titles, including the acclaimed Paul Harris thrillers, were published in the U.S. by Harper & Row and were given the prestigious "Joan Kahn-Harper Novel of Suspense" imprint.

Wynd's short stories have been published in such magazines as the Saturday Evening Post, Woman's Day, and Good Housekeeping.

Mr. Wynd currently resides in Fife, Scotland.

For obvious reasons, Wynd will be designated as Black throughout this report.

CWF AGENT: Harris, Paul.

CWF HISTORY: Born in Singapore, Malaya. Served in the Intelligence Corps during World War II, undertaking numerous assignments in the Far East.

Entered the business sector after the war. By 1960 Harris had capitalized on his tested experience to form the multinational shipping line of Lindquist, Harris, and Hok-Lin.

Based in Kuala Lumpur, Malaya, the shipping group soon acquired a reputation of low esteem in the world market because of its arrogant initiative in dealing with Red China and her allies, excluding Albania.

These activities attracted the attention of the C.I.A., and in 1961 Harris was recruited as a "limited" operative for that agency. Harris's sponsor was identified as Clem Winburgh, one of the C.I.A.'s best agents in the Orient.

Purportedly Harris utilized his business acumen and influence with the Chi-Coms to satisfy his obligations with the C.I.A. However, on several occasions the C.I.A. has, not surprisingly, accused Harris of being a Red agent.

Proficient in numerous Asian dialects, including southern Chinese and Cantonese.

Highly adept at traditional martial arts and standard C. I. A. weaponry techniques.

OPERATIVE DATA: Initially, Gavin Black's Paul Harris invites a direct comparison with James Aldridge's Rupert Royce (see separate reference). Unquestionably, the similarity of both protagonists' financial expertise would appear to support such an analysis.

However, the Harris dossier differs from the Royce series in two significant ways:

1) Black conceived Harris as a finely developed balance between the archetypal action agent and the cynical Whitehall servant.

2) Black's depiction of the Chi-Coms, unlike that of many espionage novelists of the period, was wholly objective, avoiding any personal attitudes the author might have formulated during his intelligence and prison-camp years.

The focus of the Harris series was the economic relationships of the Cold War, in much the same fashion as Aldridge's thrillers. However, Black emphasized the Far East while Red China received only peripheral attention from Aldridge.

Among the six Harris books published in the sixties, A Wind of Death (1967) exemplified Black's fictional thesis: the characterization of the Chi-Coms as being equally avaricious in both the diplomatic and economic arenas.

Harris was ordered to stalk Lum Ping, a former Red leader during the Malaysia Civil War. Ping had gained control of a jungle fortress near Thailand, identified from agency maps as Khota Baru, in Kelantan, Malaya.

Harris joined forces with Betty Hill, a prominent British surgeon based in Kuala Lumpur, and penetrated a Chi-Com supply line to Ping's guerilla army in Thailand. Thus, Harris's mission stretched from Kuala Lumpur to the jungles of Thailand.

A distinguished Chinese family and two double agents figured into Harris's most perilous sanction.

As in the other Harris entries, A Wind of Death was narrated in the first person, and, coupled with the clarity of detail manifested throughout the series, the Harris books compare favorably with the works of Len Deighton (see separate reference).

SUMMARY: Gavin Black's Paul Harris canon represented yet a

finer line between James Aldridge's Rupert Royce thrillers and the realistic school fostered by John le Carré and Len Deighton (see separate references).

Generally, Black offered the expected values of tense plotting, credible characters, and authentic locales, and, like James Aldridge (see separate reference), he demonstrated a seasoned financial acumen and a feverish pace that distinguished him from le Carré.

The Harris series was more specific than Aldridge's in its sobering perception of Red China's global role in the Cold War.

Throughout the series, Black consistently conveyed Red China's eagerness to undermine Western stability through the calculated manipulation of the free enterprise system.

Since the Harris dossier concentrated on the economic aspects of the Cold War and its relationship to Red China and the West, the series survived well beyond the passing of the 007 craze.

STATUS: Several of the early Harris books have been reissued in recent years as classic espionage novels, despite the maturation of Communist China after the death of Mao-Tse Tung. SSP.

FIELD BIBLIOGRAPHY

Black, Gavin. The Cold Jungle. New York: Harper & Row, 1969. HB-R. See also The Cold Jungle in Appendix I.

_____. A Dragon for Christmas. New York: Harper & Row, 1963; Avon paperback, 1967. HB-R.

_____. The Eyes Around Me. New York: Harper & Row, 1964. HB-R. See also The Eyes Around Me in Appendix I.

_____. Suddenly at Singapore.... London: Collins, 1961. HB.

_____. A Wind of Death. New York: Harper & Row, 1967. HB-R. See also A Wind of Death in Appendix I.

_____. You Want to Die, Johnny? New York: Harper & Row, 1966. HB-R. See also You Want to Die, Johnny? in Appendix I.

CONSULT APPENDIX I FOR SERIES CONTINUATION

CONSULT APPENDIX II FOR SERIES TRANSITION

END OF CWF 9

† CWF 10.   BOLAND, JOHN †

BACKGROUND: John Bertram Boland is better known in England for his action and suspense fiction, but he gained a devoted audience in the U.S. when his "The Gentlemen" series was represented by the Universal-Award Intelligence Group (see separate reference) in the late sixties.

Boland's first novel, White August (1955), was critically lauded as a science-fiction-oriented thriller, and its success encouraged him to continue writing. By 1970, Boland had produced over twenty-five thrillers, including Counterpol (1963) and Counterpol in Paris (1964), both of which involved series agent Kim Smith.

Boland's other suspense volumes include Negative Value (1960) and Breakdown (1968).

Of British origin, Mr. Boland was born in 1913.

CWF AGENTS: "The Gentlemen."

CWF HISTORY: "The Gentlemen" was the code name assigned to a ruthless yet sophisticated unit of bank robbers. The leader of this elite group was identified as John George Norman Hyde, a former British Army commando, who had attained the full rank of Colonel during World War II.

This crack criminal squad consisted of seven men under Hyde's command, all of whom were former British Army officers.

In 1961 "The Gentlemen" escaped from a British maximum-security prison, known only as Bladely, and were never recaptured. However, it is known that this exclusive group had been secretly summoned for intelligence missions of a "seek-and-destroy" nature which M.I.6. refused to acknowledge or execute.

The supporting members of Hyde's squad were generally known under the following names: Race, Mycroft, Porthill, Rutland-Smith, Lexy, Weaver, and Stevens.

No additional information has been reported since 1962.

OPERATIVE DATA: Considering its brevity, the "Gentlemen" series remains one of the most inventive and entertaining espionage series of the sixties.

The first in the canon, The League of Gentlemen (1958) merely disclosed the personal histories of Hyde and his worldly allies.

The Gentlemen Reform (1961) recounted the group's dangerous escape from Bladely.

Whereas most spy novelists focused their efforts on a single
operative, Boland was able to maintain the reader's interest in eight
equally intriguing provocateurs.

In general, Boland crafted the series to reflect both the pursuits and abilities of his group creation. Further, Boland's careful
balance was so effective that the reader acquired a sense of intimate
relationship with "The Gentlemen."

In The Gentlemen at Large (1962) Boland perfected the premise of his preceding entry. Hyde and squad were still being hunted
after the Bladely escape when they were secretly assigned to foment
a war in the Middle Eastern oil sheikdom of Accaria and to restore
a pro-British prince to the throne.

Boland's third "Gentlemen" adventure is unquestionably the
best of the series, as he managed to occupy all eight commandos
in grueling desert combat during their assault on Accaria.

SUMMARY: In the wake of the phenomenally successful 1967 visual
project, The Dirty Dozen (M. G. M.), adapted from E. M. Nathan-
son's 1965 bestseller, Universal-Award distributed The Gentlemen
at Large and The Gentlemen Reform to the American paperback market in 1968, emphasizing the obvious similarities to the Lee Marvin
visual war project.

The year 1968 signaled the beginning of the spy novel's decline in popularity and yet this unconventional series garnered a
strong following well into the seventies.

The acceptance of "The Gentlemen" as the "Dirty Dozen" of
the Cold War, and the audacious originality of Boland's overall concept, offered the jaded reader escapist fare that was both satisfying
and timely.

STATUS: Since Universal-Award's withdrawal from the market in
1977, Charter Books has reissued several of the former agency's
files. "The Gentlemen" was not among these series, but given the
success of such commando-style objectives as Steve White's "S-COM"
adventures, it is recommended that Boland's "Gentlemen" dossier be
reactivated for immediate distribution. SOP.

FIELD BIBLIOGRAPHY

Boland, John. The Gentlemen at Large. London: Boardman,
    1962; New York: Universal-Award paperback, 1968. HB-R.

_____. The Gentlemen Reform. London: Boardman, 1961;
New York: Macmillan, 1964; New York: Universal-Award
paperback, 1968. HB-HB-R.

_____. The League of Gentlemen. London: Boardman, 1958;
Boston: Beacon, 1961. HB-HB.

END OF CWF 10

† CWF 11. BREWER, GIL †

BACKGROUND: Prolific American author of paperback originals,
specializing in mysteries and, relevant to this file, visual-project
novelizations.

Apart from his "It Takes a Thief" tie-ins, the subject of
this file, Brewer's novels have generally leaned toward the grim,
hard-boiled genre.

Appearing under such major paperback imprints as Ace,
Avon, Fawcett, and Lancer, Brewer's taut suspense efforts include
Flight to Darkness (1952), Nude on Thin Ice (1960), and Sin for Me
(1967). Since the early fifties, Brewer has produced over thirty
paperback originals, many of which have been well received in Eng
land

Contributing member of the Ace Intelligence Group (see
separate reference).

CWF AGENT: Mundy, Alexander.

CWF HISTORY: Former professional thief. In 1967 Mundy was
paroled from San Jobal Prison in the custody of the S. I. A., a
highly secret intelligence organization based in Washington, D. C. --
exact location unknown.

The S. I. A. obtained a suspension of Mundy's prison term,
provided that he assume the role of thief for the agency whenever
summoned by intelligence chief Noah Bain. The director of the
S. I. A. was August Henderson.

Mundy's tastes and capabilities were remarkably similar to
one James Bond, and his activities often brought him into the most
exotic surroundings, from the Swiss Alps to the Mediterranean.

Skilled in such required espionage arts as safecracking,

casino gambling, seduction, and the various classes of armed and unarmed combat.

Before being "recruited" into the S. I. A., Mundy focused his attention on jewelry capers, usually on the Continent.

Mundy's handsome, athletic figure attracted incomparably elegant women in his worldly travels--women who often became the objects of his polished expertise.

Alister Mundy, Alexander's father, was a master thief and occasionally aided his son on assignments for the S. I. A.

Mundy's "field duty" with the S. I. A. ended in August 1970.

OPERATIVE DATA: Like Ace's "The Man from U. N. C. L. E." visual-project novelizations, Gil Brewer's tie-ins for "It Takes a Thief" featured ravishing locales and explosive action.

Unlike the U. N. C. L. E. home files, the novelizations for "It Takes a Thief" didn't instantly follow the series, which was initiated by Universal in 1968; only three S. I. A. missions were authorized for distribution by the Ace Intelligence Group.

Brewer's tense narrative manner characterized the Mundy dossier, and, in this respect, it was this CWF author who dominated the novelizations for "It Takes a Thief," in contrast to the multiauthored U. N. C. L. E. project.

The first file, The Devil in Davos (1969), recounted Mundy's perilous secret assignment at an exclusive ski resort in the Swiss Alps.

The Mediterranean Caper (1969) launched Mundy on a search for a coded textbook which contained the coveted guide for a new ABM (Anti-Ballistic Missile) system.

Mundy's unique talents were challenged beyond expected limits in The Mediterranean Caper: the textbook in question was in the safe of a K. G. B. agent, and Mundy was ordered to rescue Marina, the daughter of a prominent Soviet missile scientist, Vasilei Kotov.

SUMMARY: Gil Brewer's novelizations for "It Takes a Thief" imparted both the author's taut style and the salient values of Universal's popular home visual project, which starred Robert Wagner as Alexander Mundy, Malachi Throne as Noah Bain, and Fred Astaire as Alister Mundy.

The project spanned the years 1968 to 1970.

STATUS: Mundy has not been reported in the field since 1970.

However, a wealthy Los Angeles businessman, identified as one Jonathan Hart, purportedly bears an incredible resemblance to Mr. Mundy. SOP.

FIELD BIBLIOGRAPHY

Brewer, Gil. The Devil in Davos. New York: Ace Books, 1969. PBO. TN.

_____. The Mediterranean Caper. New York: Ace Books, 1969. PBO. TN.

CONSULT APPENDIX I FOR SERIES CONTINUATION

END OF CWF 11

† CWF 12. BRIDGE, ANN †

BACKGROUND: Cover identity of Lady Mary Dolling Saunders O'Malley. Born in 1899. Married a distinguished diplomat and accompanied him on diplomatic missions around the world.

This experience served as the inspiration for Julia Probyn, whom Ms. Bridge recruited in The Lighthearted Quest (1956).

Bridge's adroit mixture of romance and espionage in her Julia Probyn novels garnered resounding praise from critics, and she created one of the first romantic spy series to achieve an international following.

Her early mysteries include Singing Waters (1946) and Dark Moment (1952). Peking Picnic (c. 1950), a Bridge non-suspense volume, earned the Atlantic $10,000 Novel Award.

Ann Bridge died in 1974.

CWF AGENT: Probyn, Julia.

CWF HISTORY: Nationality: British.

Extremely resourceful and charming, Julia Probyn traveled widely and was proficient in numerous languages and customs.

Although not directly associated with any global intelligence

network, the alluring adventuress possessed two connections with
M. I. 6:

1) Probyn's cousin, Colin Monro, was a principal operative for
   the department.

2) In 1965 Ms. Probyn married Colonel Philip Jamieson, a
   high-ranking official of the aforementioned segment of British
   Intelligence. He was killed during a mission in Africa in
   1969.

OPERATIVE DATA: The Dangerous Islands (1963) provided the
focal point of the Probyn dossier.

Here Ms. Bridge demonstrated a skillful combination of
romance and intrigue that has yet to be equaled. Even with its
many diverse elements, The Dangerous Islands evolved into an absorbing, authentic Cold-War yarn.

Julia encountered Colonel Jamieson for the first time in this
entry, after discovering a mysterious "gadget" in the Scottish Hebrides Islands. Their alliance developed into a richly satisfying romance that captivated Ms. Bridge's demanding audience.

Acting in an official capacity, Colonel Jamieson aided Julia
in locating a Soviet satellite tracking system in the Hebrides. A
hazardous foray through the Scilly Islands in Southwest England also
figured into Julia's most perplexing adventure.

In its evaluation of Ms. Bridge's fifth Probyn assignment,
the Columbus Dispatch commented: "Romance, suspense, and adventure combine to make this a novel to win new friends for Julia
Probyn and to delight her established fans."

SUMMARY: Ann Bridge conceived the best romantic spy series with
her Julia Probyn novels. Characterized by credibly drawn plot
lines, with a clearly defined sense of romance and espionage, the
Probyn canon stands alone in the Cold-War fiction of the sixties.

STATUS: Given the seemingly endless popularity of the modern romantic novel, the Probyn series would find a receptive audience in
today's market.

Since the plots were not dictated by the possibilities of the
Cold War, Ann Bridge's efforts in the genre are not dated. SOP.

FIELD BIBLIOGRAPHY

Bridge, Ann. The Dangerous Islands. New York: McGraw-Hill,

1963; New York: Berkley-Medallion paperback, 1964.
HB-R.

_____. Emergency in the Pyrenees. New York: McGraw-Hill,
1965; New York: Berkley-Medallion paperback, 1966. HB-R.

_____. The Episode at Toledo. New York: McGraw-Hill, 1966;
New York: Berkley-Medallion paperback, 1967. HB-R.

_____. The Lighthearted Quest. New York: Macmillan, 1956;
New York: Berkley-Medallion paperback, 1964. HB-R.

_____. The Malady in Madeira. New York: McGraw-Hill,
1969. HB.

_____. The Numbered Account. New York: McGraw-Hill,
1960; New York: Berkley-Medallion paperback, 1963. HB-R.

_____. The Portuguese Escape. New York: Macmillan, 1958;
Berkley-Medallion paperback, 1963. HB-R.

_____. The Tightening String. New York: McGraw-Hill, 1962;
New York: Berkley-Medallion paperback, 1963. HB-R.

END OF CWF 12

† CWF 13.   CAILLOU, ALAN †

BACKGROUND: Renowned author of suspense and fast-paced adventure fiction. Born in 1914.

Although the above surname suggests French nationality, the author is actually British.

"Alan Caillou" was established as the operative field cover for one Allan Lyle-Smythe who devised the identity in 1955 with Rogue's Gambit, a mystery published exclusively in the British sector. Alien Virus (1957) and The Mindanao Pearl (1959), two early Smythe thrillers, were also restricted to the United Kingdom territories.

The following year, Smythe penned The Plotters (1960), a tightly conceived espionage tale, published by the distinguished Harper and Row, which generated praise from major American suspense critics.

In 1964 "Caillou" entered the arena of the paperback-original series with Marseilles, the first of his Mike Benasque mysteries.

<u>Who'll Buy My Evil</u>?, the second and last of the Benasque suspense sequence, was published in 1966.

The Benasque thrillers, although modest in the sales and commentary areas, provided Caillou with enough of a following to foster his most significant project to date--the Cabot Cain series, the subject of this file.

The first three assignments of this six-volume action dossier, were distributed in 1969. The second entry, <u>Assault on Ming</u> (1969), was nominated for the Mystery Writers of America Special Award, although, curiously, there is no listing for either Allan Lyle-Smythe or Alan Caillou in the current M. W. A. directory.

While the Cain series was still in progress, Caillou instigated the <u>Private Army of Colonel Tobin</u> adventures for action-oriented Pinnacle Books. The latter canon remains in print today.

It was the Cain missions, however, that earned Caillou the enthusiastic acceptance of both readers and critics. By 1972 the Cain books had attained sales exceeding 500,000.

Hereafter in this file, Smythe shall be referred to as Caillou.

CWF AGENT: Cain, Cabot.

CWF HISTORY: Dangerous, professional provocateur for Department B-7 of Interpol. Based in Paris. Superior identified as one Colonel Matthias Fenrek.

Proficient in both traditional and advanced espionage disciplines.

Specialized in the most lethal applications of unarmed combat. On the basis of this factor alone, Cain quickly developed a reputation in the field that was respected by allied and hostile intelligence agencies alike.

No known code names or numbers. According to B-7 files, Cain's strongest asset was his flexibility in any foreign setting, especially the Far East.

Well versed in European and Oriental languages. Before entering B-7 Cain had taught a course in Advanced Oriental Studies at the Sorbonne. Exact date of tenure uncertain but it is known that Cain was on loan from Stanford University. Also conducted a course at the Institute for Oriental Military Studies. Again, exact date of term unknown.

Cain served with B-7 from 1969 to 1975.

No further record.

OPERATIVE DATA: Despite the fact that Caillou's dossier was consistently well-received in the espionage market, its initiation in 1969 coincided with Don Pendleton's Executioner series, which dramatically altered the course of escapist fare.

In the face of the changes precipitated by Pendleton and his action allies, it is to Caillou's credit that his efforts achieved bestseller rank in 1969, a year which was marked by the continued decline in popularity of the Cold-War spy novel.

Although all six of the Cain assignments were designated by the word, "Assault," Caillou eschewed the formula approach to spy fiction.

Assault on Ming (1969) typified the Cain series in general terms. As in most cloak-and-dagger offerings of the late sixties, the emphasis was strictly on action. In some rare instances the plots commented on the hardened state of the Cold War.

In Caillou's most celebrated Cain entry, a Chi-Com death merchant identified as Alexander Ming resurfaced in the Hong Kong-Macao area. Cain was ordered to terminate Ming--by any expedient means.

The M. W. A. nomination for Assault on Ming was well deserved, for Caillou's vivid delineation of the Hong Kong and Macao locales was as effective as his topical plot. In this respect, Caillou simultaneously evoked the timeless culture of these two Asian cities and their concealed peril.

Ming was involved in any enterprise that would intensify his criminal syndicate, and he possessed a highly trained army of lethal assassins to support him.

Further, Caillou won the reader's sympathy for the alluring Sally Hyde, who was enslaved by Ming. Cain's mission encompassed Ms. Hyde's release.

In Assault on Ming Caillou conveyed the hazardous climate of Hong Kong and Macao. Finally, Cain's showdown with Ming heightened the ferocious pace of the book, and, taking into account the balance of the other elements, Assault on Ming came through as one of the finest action spy thrillers of the late sixties.

SUMMARY: Alan Caillou's Cabot Cain saga utilized the demanding elements of the spy genre to achieve a superior series in the post-secret-agent craze era.

STATUS: Caillou's later Private Army of Colonel Tobin series was successfully reissued in 1980, although it failed to achieve either the sales or prestige of the Cabot Cain dossier. On this basis, the Cain series might, with an ambitious action-paperback publisher, enjoy a profitable distribution today. SOP.

FIELD BIBLIOGRAPHY

Caillou, Alan. <u>Assault on Kolchak</u>. New York: Avon, 1969. PBO.

_____. <u>Assault on Loveless</u>. New York: Avon, 1969. PBO.

_____. <u>Assault on Ming</u>. New York: Avon, 1969. PBO.

CONSULT APPENDIX I FOR SERIES CONTINUATION

END OF CWF 13

† CWF 14. CARTER, NICK †

BACKGROUND: House cover. Adapted for the espionage field from the detective character conceived by Ormond G. Smith.

John Russell Coryell actually wrote the first three Carter stories, the first of which appeared in the <u>New York Weekly</u> in 1886. The series was continued by a number of other authors, notably Frederic Van Rensselaer Dey, who produced over 1,000 episodes.

In 1964 book packager Lyle Kenyon Engel transformed Nick Carter into an intrepid secret agent, and, through Universal-Award, a New York-based paperback house, an army of writers have assumed Carter's mantle, the first assignment being <u>Run-Spy-Run</u> (1964).

By the time Universal-Award vacated the intelligence market in 1977, more than one hundred Carter books had appeared, accounting for a global distribution exceeding 20,000,000.

The following year, Charter Books (now known as Ace-Charter, and owned by Berkley-Jove Publishing) acquired several Universal-Award properties, including Nick Carter. They continued the series, initiating new missions while reactivating several of the original Universal-Award files. The series is distributed in association with Condé Nast Publications.

As the popularity of spy novels skyrocketed, Nick Carter evolved as the symbol of the Universal-Award Intelligence Group (see separate reference).

Although lacking the substance of the constituents of the Fawcett Intelligence Group (see separate reference), the Carter thrillers have survived into the eighties, allowing, of course, for the acquisition transfer period from Universal-Award to Charter.

Considered as either detective or espionage agent, Nick Carter has appeared in more stories and books than any other character in suspense fiction.

CWF AGENT: Carter, Nick.

CWF HISTORY: Top agent for AXE, a clandestine intelligence group based in Washington, D. C. The chief of AXE is known only as Mr. Hawk.

The letters in AXE do not signify any operative title. Since its start in the mid-fifties, the agency has been symbolized by an axe.

AXE is responsible to the National Security Council, the Secretary of Defense, and the President of the United States.

Since 1957 Nick Carter has operated under the code designation N-3. Also known in the field as Killmaster.

As required for all AXE agents, Carter's right forearm manifests the small blue tattoo of an axe.

Carter served in the U.S. Army during World War II and, before joining AXE, acted as field operative for the O.S.S.

Devoted student of physical fitness. Highly adept at yoga and other rigorous practices designed to maintain peak physical condition--the paramount requirement for all AXE agents.

Carter is a recognized master of the martial arts in its many forms. Skilled in standard espionage abilities, as demanded by Mr. Hawk.

As recorded in 1964, Agent N-3 possesses three weapons for operative duty:

1) "Wilhelmina"--. 9mm Luger. Carter appropriated this pistol from one Colonel Pabst, a trusted A. D. C. to Heinrich Himmler, in the S. S. Barracks at Munich--after he liquidated Pabst.

2) "Hugo"--Italian stiletto. Razor-thin ice-pick blade and a bone handle no thicker than a heavy pencil. Concealed blade until activated. Fast and quiet.

3) "Pierre"--round pellet containing sufficient quantities of lethal X-5 gas to eliminate instantly a roomful of people.

OPERATIVE DATA: The thrust of the Killmaster series is a sharply defined integration of action and sex. However, since no single author is responsible for the series, this file will simply list in alphabetical order N-3 missions of the sixties, emphasizing the inherent Cold War themes.

The Amazon (1969). N-3 searched for a crucial "electronic brain" in the Amazon Delta.

Amsterdam (1968). A double agent recruited for a global spy network.

Assignment: Israel (1967). A former Nazi henchman, identified as "The Butcher," conspired a holocaust in the Middle East.

Berlin (1969). Feared revival of Nazism.

A Bullet for Fidel (1965). Fictionalized account of the Cuban Missile Crisis.

Checkmate in Rio (1964). Suspected sabotage of the AXE apparat in Rio de Janeiro.

The China Doll (1964). N-3 was assigned to penetrate "the forbidden city of Peking" and the Chi-Com's nefarious spy network, C. L. A. W.

The Chinese Paymaster (1967). Another double agent in the service of Peking.

Danger Key (1966). C. L. A. W. dispatched top Chi-Com saboteurs, including one Mr. Judas, into Florida--under the cover of Cuban refugees.

The Defector (1969). N-3's assignment: prevent a top American scientist from defecting to Red China.

Double Identity (1967). N-3's double turned up in Tibet.

Dragon Flame (1966). A sinister Chinese society, the Tiger Tong, was involved in smuggling high-ranking Chi-Com leaders.

The Eyes of the Tiger (1965). A golden tiger idol belonging to Hitler, hidden in a Swiss vault, was desperately sought by AXE, the Germans, and the Japanese.

The Filthy Five (1967). A convoluted Chi-Com plot to assassinate the new President of the United States.

Fraulein Spy (1964). N-3 was assigned to locate a top Nazi leader--Martin Boorman.

The Golden Serpent (1967). AXE and the C. I. A. were

involved in a "war" for territorial supremacy that extended all the way from Texas to California.

Hanoi (1966). N-3 was ordered to locate a new launching site near Hanoi--guarded by Chi-Com soldiers and staffed by high-level German scientists.

The Human Time Bomb (1969). Chemical warfare perpetrated to undermine the entire defense network of the U.S.

Istanbul (1965). N-3 was sanctioned to liquidate four men who were an integral part of a global opium conspiracy.

The Judas Spy (1968). N-3 confronted his most insidious nemesis, Mr. Judas, in the jungles of Indonesia.

A Korean Tiger (1967). N-3 stalked a traitor who possessed valuable atomic secrets--and also was marked for termination by the Chi-Coms and the Soviets. One of N-3's most perilous missions.

Macao (1968). Killmaster was assigned to "persuade" the jaded Princess da Gama into "suicide"--before the Chi-Coms and the Portuguese succeeded in eliminating her.

The Mind Poisoners (1966). N-3 assumed the identity of a college professor to avert a nefarious plot aimed at the student peace movement.

Mission to Venice (1967). N-3 was delegated to locate a missing H-bomb--somewhere in the Adriatic.

Operation Moon Rocket (1968). America's leading astronauts were being ruthlessly eliminated. N-3's mission: find the Chi-Com's resident provocateur.

Operation Snake (1969). An ancient love ritual plunged AXE and the Chi-Coms into a secret war in the Himalayas.

Operation Starvation (1966). N-3 unmasked a brilliant Chi-Com blueprint to control the world's food supply.

Rhodesia (1968). N-3 in Africa--embroiled in racial hatred and a desperate search for Nazi gold.

Run-Spy-Run (1964). N-3's first recorded mission for AXE: Operation Jet. N-3 tracked a traitor on a grueling journey stretching from New York to London.

Safari for Spies (1964). Casablanca: N-3 was ordered to circumvent growing Chi-Com influence in Africa.

The Sea Trap (1969). Mr. Judas established an island

fortress in the Caribbean designed to annihilate America's nuclear-submarine defense capacity.

Seven Against Greece (1967). A calculated Chi-Com scheme structured to upset the balance of global power, manipulating the Balkans as a battleground.

Temple of Fear (1968). N-3 was dispatched on a mission of assassination in Tokyo--assuming the identity of a man believed long dead.

The Terrible Ones (1966). N-3 returned to the Caribbean to avert a Chi-Com destruction plot. Code name: Operation Blast.

The 13th Spy (1965). AXE and the K. G. B. entered into an uneasy alliance to discover the identity of the lone agent responsible for selling high-level embassy documents to Peking.

The Weapon of Night (1967). N-3's most perplexing mission: find the cause behind the power blackouts that devastated every sector of the U. S.

SUMMARY: The success of the Nick Carter series probably can be explained by its consistently up-to-date reflection of the Cold War.

During the Cold War era, the series focused more closely on the machinations of Red China and less on the global motives of the Soviet Union.

Although a score of authors contributed to the Killmaster dossier, the approach to the series was, unquestionably, formularized.

The blistering pace of the Killmaster books initiated the format for later action series, notably Don Smith's (see separate reference) "Secret Mission," another Universal-Award offering, and "The Destroyer." However, series of this type generally lacked the substance of Donald Hamilton's Matt Helm and Edward S. Aarons' Sam Durell adventures (see separate references).

However, with over 20, 000, 000 Killmaster books in print, the above critical observations are trivial. The best recommendation for the Nick Carter series came from Ladislas Farago, former news chief for Radio Free Europe during the Cold War: "What colleague of mine from the Corps diplomatique or Intelligence, I wonder, is the real author using the pen name Nick Carter?"

Variety proclaimed it "America's number one espionage agent" while Film Daily commented, "Carter has inherited the mantle of the late Ian Fleming's James Bond."

STATUS: N-3 is still on active duty with AXE, serving under Mr.

Hawk. Because of the large volume of Killmaster files, the series is subject to rotation by Ace-Charter (Berkley-Jove Publishing Group), who also distribute new missions on a monthly basis. The Universal-Award Intelligence Group (see separate reference) is no longer in existence. SSP.

FIELD BIBLIOGRAPHY

Carter, Nick. The Amazon. New York: Universal-Award, 1969. PBO.

————. Amsterdam. New York: Universal-Award, 1968. PBO.

————. Assignment: Israel. New York: Universal-Award, 1967. PBO.

————. Berlin. New York: Universal-Award, 1969. PBO.

————. The Bright Blue Death. New York: Universal-Award, 1968. PBO.

————. A Bullet for Fidel. New York: Universal-Award, 1965. PBO.

————. Carnival for Killing. New York: Universal-Award, 1969. PBO.

————. The Casbah Killers. New York: Universal-Award, 1969. PBO.

————. Checkmate in Rio. New York: Universal-Award, 1964. PBO.

————. The China Doll. New York: Universal-Award, 1964. PBO.

————. The Chinese Paymaster. New York: Universal-Award, 1967. PBO.

————. The Cobra Kill. New York: Universal-Award, 1969. PBO.

————. Danger Key. New York: Universal-Award, 1966. PBO.

————. The Defector. New York: Universal-Award, 1969. PBO.

————. The Devil's Cockpit. New York: Universal-Award, 1967. PBO.

————. The Doomsday Formula. New York: Universal-Award, 1969. PBO.

_____. Double Identity. New York: Universal-Award, 1967.
PBO.

_____. Dragon Flame. New York: Universal-Award, 1966.
PBO.

_____. The Eyes of the Tiger. New York: Universal-Award,
1965. PBO.

_____. The Filthy Five. New York: Universal-Award, 1967.
PBO.

_____. 14 Seconds to Hell. New York: Universal-Award, 1968.
PBO.

_____. Fraulein Spy. New York: Universal-Award, 1964.
PBO.

_____. The Golden Serpent. New York: Universal-Award,
1967. PBO.

_____. Hanoi. New York: Universal-Award, 1966. PBO.

_____. Hood of Death. New York: Universal-Award, 1968.
PBO.

_____. The Human Time Bomb. New York: Universal-Award,
1969. PBO.

_____. Istanbul. New York: Universal-Award, 1965. PBO.

_____. The Judas Spy. New York: Universal-Award, 1968.
PBO.

_____. A Korean Tiger. New York: Universal-Award, 1967.
PBO.

_____. The Living Death. New York: Universal-Award, 1969.
PBO.

_____. Macao. New York: Universal-Award, 1968. PBO.

_____. The Mind Poisoners. New York: Universal-Award,
1966. PBO.

_____. Mission to Venice. New York: Universal-Award, 1967.
PBO.

_____. Operation Che Guevara. New York: Universal-Award,
1969. PBO.

_____. Operation Moon Rocket. New York: Universal-Award,
1968. PBO.

_____. Operation Snake. New York: Universal-Award, 1969.
PBO.

_____. Operation Starvation. New York: Universal-Award,
1966. PBO.

_____. Peking/The Tulip Affair. New York: Universal-Award,
1969. PBO.

_____. The Red Guard. New York: Universal-Award, 1969.
PBO.

_____. The Red Rays. New York: Universal-Award, 1969.
PBO.

_____. Rhodesia. New York: Universal-Award, 1968. PBO.

_____. Run-Spy-Run. New York: Universal-Award, 1964.
PBO.

_____. Safari for Spies. New York: Universal-Award, 1964.
PBO.

_____. Saigon. New York: Universal-Award, 1964. PBO.

_____. The Sea Trap. New York: Universal-Award, 1969.
PBO.

_____. Seven Against Greece. New York: Universal-Award,
1967. PBO.

_____. Spy Castle. New York: Universal-Award, 1966. PBO.

_____. Temple of Fear. New York: Universal-Award, 1968.
PBO.

_____. The Terrible Ones. New York: Universal-Award, 1966.
PBO.

_____. The 13th Spy. New York: Universal-Award, 1965.
PBO.

_____. The Weapon of Night. New York: Universal-Award,
1967. PBO.

_____. Web of Spies. New York: Universal-Award, 1966.
PBO.

CONSULT APPENDIX I FOR SERIES CONTINUATION

CONSULT APPENDIX II FOR SERIES TRANSITION

END OF CWF 14

† CWF 15.   CLEEVE, BRIAN †

BACKGROUND: Born in 1921 in Ireland.   Brian Brendon Talbot
Cleeve is not generally regarded as a series author; however,
Cleeve's Sean Ryan espionage thrillers, the subject of this file,
have been compared to the works of Ian Fleming and John le Carré
(see separate references).

The first Ryan book, Vote X for Treason, was published in
the U.S. in 1965, having appeared a year earlier in Britain.

Like Fleming, Cleeve was affiliated with British Intelligence
during World War II.   The content of Cleeve's espionage novels
evidently did not violate the Official Secrets Act, for the author in
question apparently operated under his own name.

Several of Cleeve's suspense works, including his Sean Ryan
entries, have alternate titles for the respective American and British editions.   An early Cleeve mystery, Birth of a Dark Soul (1953),
was published the following year in the U.S. as The Night Winds.
The cover titles for the Ryan dossier will be disclosed in this file.

Cleeve has written over a dozen suspense novels, including
Assignment to Vengeance (1961) and You Must Never Go Back (1968),
and in 1971 he edited three volumes of The Dictionary of Irish Writers.

More recently, Cleeve has concentrated on the romantic
thriller genre with a series of single-name books, notably Kate
(1978), Judith (1978), and Hester (1980).

CWF AGENT: Ryan, Sean.

CWF HISTORY: Irish convict.   Place and date of birth unknown.

Paroled from prison in 1964 on condition that he work for
British Intelligence.

Reputedly trained as an international terrorist.   No known
association with the I.R.A.

Upon entering the field, Ryan employed the methods indigenous to the terrorist trade, which contributed to his fearsome reputation.

Ryan was categorized as a counterspy in British Intelligence
reports and files.   Eyes Only.

Recruited into the Secret Service by one Major Courtenay,
he initially worked under "local" British agent known only as Mr.
Dryburgh.   Full details to follow.

OPERATIVE DATA: Cleeve's series is unique in that it often focused on the Cold War through a single geopolitical sphere, namely
Ireland.

Throughout the brief series, Cleeve explored the turmoil experienced in Ireland during the mid-sixties and often predicted developments that would characterize the country after 1969. Cleeve
also covered the Cold-War-at-large.

Vote X for Treason (1965) involved a fanatical political party
which threatened to plunge Great Britain into anarchy.

Ryan's assignment: posing as a messenger for the cryptic
Dryburgh, discover the motives of the New Party.

A scandalous political secret concerning a top-level British
cabinet minister figured into Vice Isn't Private (1966), in which
Cleeve gravely depicted the indiscretions of Whitehall as the mask
of hidden treachery that extended across Europe and into the structured fiber of the Common Market.

Ryan's mission of breaking into a British maximum-security
prison was integrated, with savagery, into the principal plot.

Cleeve provided the cabinet minister, Home Secretary Gar-
rett Cameron-Harvey, with a respectable background which, on the
surface, transcended suspicion. His reflections on Ireland were
restricted to the prison segment of the book, but led to an almost
Satanic quality in Ryan's confrontation with his antagonists.

As Anthony Boucher noted: "A fine plot of violence related
with force and a sense of tragedy."

SUMMARY: More than any other espionage series of the sixties,
Brian Cleeve's Sean Ryan thrillers read as a bitter mixture of Ian
Fleming and John le Carré. This disturbing effect makes the ser-
ies all the more memorable.

STATUS: The viability of this type of spy series has been stated
in earlier evaluations, notably of James Aldridge and Bill S. Ballinger (see separate references). SOP.

FIELD BIBLIOGRAPHY

Cleeve, Brian. Counterspy. New York: Lancer paperback, 1966.
    R. U.S. paperback title for Vote X for Treason.

_____. Dark Blood, Dark Terror. New York: Random House,
    1965; New York: Lancer paperback, 1967. HB-R.

_____. Vice Isn't Private. New York: Random House, 1966; New York: Lancer paperback, 1967. HB-R.

_____. Violent Death of a Bitter Englishman. New York: Random House, 1967; New York: Lancer paperback, 1968. HB-R.

_____. Vote X for Treason. New York: Random House, 1965; New York: Lancer paperback, 1966. HB-R. See also Counter-spy.

END OF CWF 15

† CWF 16. CORY, DESMOND †

BACKGROUND: Cover identity of Shaun McCarthy, British author of suspense and espionage fiction. Born in Sussex in 1928.

Although McCarthy wrote City of Kites (1955) as Theo Callas, his Cory alias is accepted as a separate personality.

In 1951 Cory published two books in Britain and quickly established his auspicious career as a mystery writer.

Begin, Murderer! was lauded as a tightly plotted murder mystery that rivaled the works of such celebrated genre masters as Agatha Christie and Ellery Queen.

Cory's second novel promised an even more enduring contribution to modern suspense fiction. Secret Ministry was the first of Cory's Johnny Fedora espionage series, the subject of this file.

The Fedora canon lasted twenty years, with fifteen representative titles, concluding with Sunburst in 1971.

Cory served as a major constituent in both the N. A. L. / Signet and Universal-Award Intelligence Groups (see separate references) during the mid- and late sixties.

Most of the Fedora titles were reprinted in paperback during the James Bond era, often under alternate titles. Johnny Goes East (1958), for instance, was published in 1968 as Mountainhead by Universal-Award. This practice was more common in the Fedora books distributed by Universal-Award than in the ones reprinted by New American Library.

Cory excelled in other areas of the suspense field. In 1957 he created his flamboyant aristocratic figure, Mr. Pilgrim, in two memorable mysteries, Pilgrim at the Gate (1957) and Pilgrim on the Island (1959).

Such non-Fedora thrillers as The Head (1960) and The Stranglehold (1961) reverted back to the more traditional suspense format evidenced in Begin, Murderer!

For all the critical praise lavished on the Fedora thrillers, Cory is probably best known for Deadfall (1965), a gripping suspense work which was adapted as an engaging visual project starring Michael Caine, released in 1968 by 20th Century-Fox.

In recent years, Cory has written highly readable thrillers marked by an overwhelming sense of contemporaneity. These include A Bit of a Shunt Up the River (1974), The Circe Complex (1975), and Bennett (1977). These volumes were published as Doubleday Crime Club editions.

One of the most controversial developments of the spy phenomenon was the contentious attitude toward Ian Fleming (see separate reference) by the publishers of such competing espionage authors as James Leasor, Philip McCutchan, and George Brown Mair (see separate references).

The Fedora series was also involved in this ambitious effort to surpass Fleming in terms of both sales and critical reaction.

CWF AGENT: Fedora, Sean (a.k.a. Johnny) O'Neill.

CWF HISTORY: Sean O'Neill Fedora was born of a Spanish father and Irish mother. Parents were liquidated by the Falangists (a.k.a. Spanish Fascists) during a holiday journey on the Spanish coast in the late thirties.

Fedora later migrated to Chicago, where he became a pianist in a local cabaret. Earned a criminal reputation from a notorious involvement in one of the last Chicago gang wars.

Disappeared from Chicago in 1939, and turned up in Paris in early 1940. Later that year, Fedora was recruited into a British spy unit commanded by a man known only as Squires.

Fedora was then submitted to an extensive three-year term of counterespionage service with the F.B.I. and the French Maquis. During this period, however, Fedora executed several missions for Squires.

During World War II Squires allied Fedora with two agents of equal ability, namely James Emerald and Jean de Meyrignac, as assassins for the French Underground.

By May 1945 Squires' liquidation squad had eliminated eighty-three Nazis, consisting of Gestapo, Army officers, quislings, and traitors. Fedora, Emerald, and de Meyrignac themselves eliminated forty-two Nazis--and were the only survivors in Squires' group.

In 1951 Squires recommended Fedora for a confidential mission with an intelligence unit known only as "The Secret Ministry." The group's "Minister" was identified as a man named Holliday.

Until 1971 Fedora was engaged as a free-lance assassin for British Intelligence, contending with Nazi war criminals and other inimical elements of the Cold War. Concerning the latter, Fedora encountered a Soviet master spy, known only as Feramontov, on several missions in Europe during the mid-sixties.

Fedora frequently operated with the aforementioned Mr. Emerald and one Sebastian Trout, an inquiry agent. Jean de Meyrignac vanished shortly after the end of World War II.

Fedora manifested a cultured knowledge of Spain, which was part of his origin, and was often dispatched into that territory.

No known code names or designations. No record in the field since 1971.

OPERATIVE DATA: Preceding the introduction of Ian Fleming's James Bond by two years, the Johnny Fedora thrillers achieved a concise level of topicality without falling into the le Carré-Deighton mold.

The early Fedora books were concerned with the bitter motives of Nazis and war criminals in the immediate postwar world. The later entries delved into the diversity of the Cold War.

In Secret Ministry (1951), Fedora was drafted back into the free-lance market, assigned to seek out and destroy a crack squad of Hitler's henchmen, based in London, who were assassinating former R.A.F. pilots.

In his initial Fedora mission, Cory delineated his operative's savage nature and predatory attitude toward women, notably the alluring Davida Kane.

Cory's Czech villain, Malinsky, emanated the disciplined callousness that also characterized his later nemesis, Feramontov.

Further, Cory objectively defined the postwar philosophies of both British Intelligence and the Nazis.

Cory endowed Fedora with an equal mixture of amorality and urbanity in his first postwar assignment by testing his gambling acumen at an exclusive London club.

Fedora was noted for his antagonism toward the Nazis, and in This Traitor, Death (1952), he was ordered to liquidate "The

Nightingale, " Hitler's most lethal "femme fatale, " while the scattered fragments of the Gestapo and a cache of coveted Nazi gold figured into his mission.

His cover: a worldly Frenchman, Pierre Darreaux, a former member of the infamous Diamond Resistance group.

In Intrigue (1954) Cory created a sadistic twist in Fedora's mission involving his search for Panagos, a savage Bulgarian agent who was ordered to "deliver" Trieste to the Russians.

Posing as a Nazi in Height of Day (1955), Fedora embarked on a grueling archaeological foray into the deadly Kob'ei region of the African Congo. His mission: bring a "dead" man back alive-- from a remote sector of the Congo from which no man had ever returned.

This Fedora entry demonstrated the operative's endurance as he journeyed through the treacherous African Congo, while Madrid Schneider, the expedition's interpreter, developed as Fedora's most formidable female challenge, even in comparison to his later conquests.

In addition, Height of Day manifested an erudite knowledge of the African culture and locale.

The feverish pace of Height of Day was intensified in High Requiem (1956), in which Fedora returned to Africa to penetrate a secret desert atomic base primed for a cataclysmic assault.

Johnny Goes North (1956) reiterated Cory's Nazi theme. Fedora's assignment: recover a fortune in Reich gold belonging to a double agent who had long since been murdered for his treachery.

Johnny Goes East (1958) launched Fedora on a bizarre mission concerning a global spy network extending from London to Nepal, and a mysterious plane crash in the frigid Himalayas.

Johnny Goes South and Johnny Goes West (both 1959) marked a turning point in Cory's classic series. In both entries Cory initiated Cold War themes that would dominate his later books.

The explosive politics of Latin America underlined Johnny Goes South. Fedora infiltrated the armed fortress of a South American dictator, and a civil conflict threatened to spread to U.S. borders in this assignment.

In Johnny Goes West Fedora and Sebastian Trout were dispatched into the steaming Venezuelan jungle to investigate the death of one Robert West, an unscrupulous adventurer who had tapped the secret of Carnotite. According to Intelligence files, Carnotite was a valuable mineral oil with a high uranium content--and devastating nuclear potential.

This book employed the services of the E. I. E., otherwise known as Emerald Investigations and Explorations Company, Ltd., a London-based investigative firm which Emerald, Fedora, and Trout had established several years earlier.

Undertow (1962) represented the peak of the series. In this entry Cory fused the finer points of his Nazi themes with his sobering perception of the Cold War.

Fedora confronted Soviet master spy Feramontov in a lethal hunt for coveted documents crucial to the Cold War. The settings: Franco's Spain and a sunken Nazi U-Boat on the floor of the Gibraltar Straits.

In Undertow Cory perfectly balanced the spectacular and suspenseful elements in a manner that distinguished Johnny Fedora from James Bond. Compare, for instance, with Ian Fleming's Thunderball (1961).

In Undertow Cory's underwater passages of the narrative were dominated by the antagonistic relationship between Fedora and Feramontov. With Thunderball, however, Fleming achieved exactly the opposite--intensifying the aquatic machinations of S.P.E.C.T.R.E. in the Bahamas rather than the development of James Bond's climactic battle with Emilio Largo.

Cory, then, endowed Feramontov with a seething animalistic charisma that identified him as a formidable challenge to Fedora. Further, Fedora's final confrontation with Feramontov's savage henchman, Moreno, on a submerged submarine capped Cory's tightly conceived plotting, evident throughout the book.

In the books following Undertow, Cory advanced Fedora into the obscurity of the Cold War.

Franco's Spain was more prominently displayed in Shockwave (1963) in which Fedora stalked Feramontov through the euphoric night life of Madrid to prevent the execution of "Operation Hammerhead," an intricate Soviet plan directed against U.S. military power in Spain. (Shockwave was published as Hammerhead in British territory.)

Fedora faced his Soviet nemesis for the third time in Feramontov (1966). With the setting once again in Spain, Cory employed the glittering Spanish paradise of Barcelona to flesh out the bitter confrontation between Fedora and Feramontov.

In Feramontov, Cory launched his intrepid secret agent on a more complex plane, involving the Soviet master spy in the international drug market and the heartless manipulation of desperate human pawns.

Having explored the intricacies of the Cold War, Cory

challenged Fedora with a paralyzing dilemma in Timelock (1967):
On a suicidal mission which he had only five hours to complete,
Fedora was besieged with amnesia--while in the merciless grip of
a master sadist.

SUMMARY: Anthony Boucher's review of Undertow in the New York
Times illustrates the differences between Johnny Fedora and James
Bond, as well as the motivation for the heated competition between
Ian Fleming and other comparable authors in the espionage market:

> "Desmond Cory seems to me to accomplish in Undertow
> precisely what Fleming is aiming at. This is a sexy,
> colorful, glamorous story of intrigue and violence, com-
> plete with spectacular setpieces ... and even a torture
> scene. And it is written with finesse, economy, humor,
> and full inventive plotting. For my money, Johnny Fe-
> dora, professional killer for British Intelligence, more
> than deserves to take over James Bond's avid audience."

On the Fedora series as a whole, the Buffalo Evening News
commented, "Johnny Fedora, assassin, brings a steely touch to
cloak-and-daggering."

STATUS: Given the current revival in the James Bond saga, the
Fedora series should be reissued in preference to the works of
such authors as James Leasor, Philip McCutchan, and George
Brown Mair (see separate references). SOP.

FIELD BIBLIOGRAPHY

Cory, Desmond. Dead Man Falling. London: Frederick Muller
Ltd., 1953. HB-R. See also The Hitler Diamonds.

_____. Dead Men Alive. New York: Universal-Award paper-
back, 1969. R. U.S. paperback title for Height of Day.

_____. Feramontov. New York: Walker, 1966; New York:
Universal-Award paperback, 1968. HB-R.

_____. The Gestapo File. See This Traitor, Death.

_____. Hammerhead. London: Frederick Muller Ltd., 1963.
HB-R. See also Shockwave.

_____. Height of Day. London: Frederick Muller Ltd., 1955.
HB-R. See also Dead Men Alive.

_____. High Requiem. London: Frederick Muller Ltd., 1956;
New York: Universal-Award paperback, 1969. HB-R.

_____. The Hitler Diamonds. New York: Universal-Award paperback, 1969. R. U.S. paperback title for Dead Man Falling.

_____. Intrigue. London: Frederick Muller Ltd., 1954. HB-R. See also Trieste.

_____. Johnny Goes East. London: Frederick Muller Ltd., 1958. HB-R. See also Mountainhead.

_____. Johnny Goes North. London: Frederick Muller Ltd., 1956. HB-R. See also The Swastika Hunt.

_____. Johnny Goes South. London: Frederick Muller Ltd., 1959; New York: Walker, 1964; New York: New American Library paperback, 1966. HB-HB-R.

_____. Johnny Goes West. London: Frederick Muller Ltd., 1959; New York: Walker, 1967; New York: Universal-Award paperback, 1968. HB-HB-R.

_____. Mountainhead. New York: Universal-Award paperback, 1968. R. U.S. paperback title for Johnny Goes East.

_____. The Nazi Assassins. See The Secret Ministry.

_____. The Secret Ministry. London: Frederick Muller Ltd., 1951. HB-R. See also The Nazi Assassins in Appendix I.

_____. Shockwave. New York: Walker, 1964; New American Library paperback, 1965. HB-R. U.S. hardback and paperback title for Hammerhead.

_____. The Swastika Hunt. New York: Universal-Award paperback, 1969. R. U.S. paperback title for Johnny Goes North.

_____. This Traitor, Death. London: Frederick Muller Ltd., 1952. HB-R. See also The Gestapo File in Appendix I.

_____. Timelock. New York: Walker, 1967; New York: Universal-Award paperback, 1968. HB-R.

_____. Trieste. New York: Universal-Award paperback, 1968. R. U.S. paperback title for Intrigue.

_____. Undertow. London: Frederick Muller Ltd., 1962; New York: Walker, 1963; New York: New American Library paperback, 1965. HB-HB-R.

CONSULT APPENDIX I FOR SERIES CONTINUATION

END OF CWF 16

† CWF 17. CREASEY, JOHN †

BACKGROUND: Born in Southfields, Surrey, England, in 1908.

Published first novel at the age of 24, collecting a total of 743 rejection slips in the process.

Unquestionably, Creasey is the most prolific author in the suspense genre, with over 600 titles to his credit, under no fewer than twenty-eight cover identities. This accomplishment should not be compared with the achievements of paperback original authors Michael Avallone and Norman Daniels (see separate references), because most of Creasey's works were initially distributed in hard-bound editions, followed by periodic paperback reprints of his numerous series titles.

Since his death in 1973, Creasey's books have continued to appear in both hardback and paperback, with several unpublished volumes available for future release.

Like prolific paperback author Michael Avallone (see separate reference), Creasey came from a large family (nine children). Perhaps, then, a relationship exists between highly productive mystery authors and their family backgrounds.

As a point of reference, Creasey's major series are enumerated below, with appropriate cover identities.

1) George Gideon series, written as J. J. Marric.

2) Roger West series, written as Creasey.

3) The Toff series, written as Creasey.

4) Dr. Palfrey series (the subject of this file), written as Creasey.

5) Department Z series, written as Creasey.

6) Patrick Dawlish series, written as Gordon Ashe.

7) Dr. Cellini series, written as Kyle Hunt in the U.S.; Michael Halliday in Britain.

8) Superintendent Folly series, written as Jeremy York.

9) Mark Kilby series, written as Robert Caine Frazer.

10) The Liberator and Bruce Murdoch series, written as Norman Deane.

11) The Baron series, written as Anthony Morton.

Creasey also turned out mysteries under the following identities: M. E. Cooke, Patrick Gill, Charles Hogarth, Brian Hope, Colin Hughes, Abel Mann, Peter Manton, Richard Martin, and Rodney Mattheson, and he employed the Halliday cover for other works published exclusively in the United Kingdom, in addition to the aforementioned Dr. Cellini series distributed in that territory.

CWF AGENT: Palfrey, Dr. Stanislaus Alexander.

CWF HISTORY: Leader of a clandestine intelligence organization known only as Z-5.

During World War II Z-5 allied with Department Z, an equally secret counterespionage division of British Intelligence, to oppose the Axis intelligence services. Department Z was commanded by one Gordon Craigie, Scottish subject. All other information remains classified under the Official Secrets Act.

Department Z ceased operations in 1957 but Z-5 continued into the Cold War period.

Dr. Palfrey had one requirement of his select group: secrecy--even in the most hazardous situations.

Given the constantly perilous status in which the Z-5 operatives found themselves, as well as the focus on Dr. Palfrey throughout the series, it would be inappropriate to reveal the identities of the subordinate Z-5 agents.

Further, the Official Secrets Act and Dr. Palfrey's insistence on secrecy takes precedent over any motive for public disclosure.

However, it is known that in 1948 Dr. Palfrey controlled a global network of 500 Z-5 agents, of varied nationalities and creeds. Naturally an individual with even a trace of Communist indoctrination was immediately rejected as a candidate for Z-5.

Until the organization was formally disbanded in 1973, its function was the preservation of democracy in all sectors of the globe. In this respect, Z-5, based in London, was not responsible to any national intelligence agency or military power.

OPERATIVE DATA: The Palfrey series remains in its own sphere, removed from such contrasting series as those concerning operatives like Quiller and Nick Carter.

While the early Palfrey entries were clear in their unwavering Allied and post-war attitudes, the later books established new themes that adroitly blended espionage and science fiction. Undeniably, this seemingly unlikely integration provided the basis for most of the Z-5 missions which appeared during the mid-sixties.

An early Palfrey thriller, The Plague of Silence (1948), fostered this innovative trend, as it concerned a cluster of bizarre deaths caused by mosquito bites that brought on loss of voice and eventually total paralysis.

Creasey balanced the crisp, efficient movement of the global Z-5 organization in crisis against the calculated motives of the impenetrable, obscure enemy with precision and economy. Further, Creasey accomplished this without displaying preference for either element.

Creasey advanced this concept with The Touch of Death (1954) in which Z-5 was propelled on a terrifying search for a lethal ore, but it wasn't until the mid-sixties that Creasey perfected his tested formula.

The tendency toward science fiction in the Palfrey series were heightened in The Terror (1966) and The Famine (1967).

The Terror rivaled the premise of Ian Fleming's third James Bond thriller, Moonraker (1955). In this entry Palfrey nearly exhausted the resources of Z-5 in a desperate race to deflect the planned course of a cataclysmic missile armed with a deadly warhead that was targeted for England.

Nuclear destruction themes involving spacecraft were common in the espionage fiction of such period authors as James Dark, Philip McCutchan, and Van Wyck Mason (see separate references).

With The Terror Creasey surpassed the efforts of these and other genre practitioners, conceiving a highly probable plot that progressed at a non-stop pace. Beyond the recognized boundaries of the espionage fiction of the sixties, The Terror portended the state of nuclear vulnerability in which the world now finds itself.

Creasey offered his most horrifying Palfrey plot in The Famine as Z-5 confronted the parasitical, subhuman Lozi colonies, which were fortified beneath the earth's surface.

SUMMARY: John Creasey manifested a skillful integration of espionage and science-fiction elements in his Dr. Palfrey thrillers.

The long-term effects of this series can be observed in both the secret-agent fiction and visual projects of the sixties as well as in the development of the contemporary science-fiction genre.

This is not to suggest, of course, that the Palfrey books were solely responsible for the current science-fiction trends in both the general-fiction and visual-project areas. Rather, that the value of the Palfrey missions is inestimable in the evolution of the traditional espionage genre into the modern realms of science fiction, as the book and visual-project audiences accept them today.

STATUS: Although Z-5 is no longer in operation, the original Palfrey files are in periodic rotation by several paperback publishers, which is not surprising given the number of Creasey titles in existence. SSP, subject to rotation.

FIELD BIBLIOGRAPHY

Creasey, John. The Blight. New York: Walker, 1968. HB-R. See also The Blight in Appendix I.

_____. The Children of Despair. London: Jay, 1958. HB-HB-R-R. British hardback reprint title for The Children of Hate. See also The Children of Hate below and The Killers of Innocence in Appendixes I and II.

_____. The Children of Hate. London: Evans, 1952. HB-HB-R-R. See also The Children of Despair and The Killers of Innocence in Appendixes I and II.

_____. Dark Harvest. London: Long, 1947. HB-HB. See also Dark Harvest in Appendix I.

_____. The Dawn of Darkness. London: Long, 1949. HB.

_____. Death in the Rising Sun. London: Long, 1945. HB-HB. See also Death in the Rising Sun in Appendix I.

_____. The Depths. London: Hodder, 1963; New York: Walker, 1967. HB-HB-R. See also The Depths in Appendix I.

_____. The Drought. London: Hodder, 1959; New York: Walker, 1967. HB-HB-R. See also Dry Spell.

_____. Dry Spell. London: Four Square paperback, 1967. R. British paperback title for The Drought.

_____. The Famine. London: Hodder, 1967; New York: Walker, 1968. HB-HB-R. See also The Famine in Appendix I.

_____. The Flood. London: Hodder, 1956; New York: Walker, 1969. HB-HB-R. See also The Flood in Appendix I.

_____. The Hounds of Vengeance. London: Long, 1945. HB.

_____. The House of the Bears. London: Long, 1947. HB-HB. See also The House of the Bears in Appendix I.

_____. The Inferno. London: Hodder, 1965; New York: Walker, 1966. HB-HB-R. See also The Inferno in Appendix I.

_____. The Legion of the Lost. London: Long, 1943; New York: Day, 1944. HB-HB.

_____. The Man Who Shook the World. London: Evans, 1950. HB.

_____. The Mists of Fear. London: Hodder, 1955. HB-HB.
See also The Mists of Fear in Appendix I.

_____. The Oasis. London: Hodder, 1969. HB-HB. See also
The Oasis in Appendix I.

_____. The Perilous Country. U.S. title for The Valley of
Fear. HB. See also The Valley of Fear and The Perilous
Country in Appendix I.

_____. The Plague of Silence. London: Hodder, 1948; New
York: Walker, 1968. HB-HB-R. See also The Plague of Silence in Appendix I.

_____. The Prophet of Fire. London: Evans, 1951. HB.

_____. The Shadow of Doom. London: Long, 1946. HB.

_____. The Sleep. London: Hodder, 1964; New York: Walker,
1968. HB-HB-R. See also The Sleep in Appendix I.

_____. The Sons of Satan. London: Long, 1948. HB.

_____. The Terror. New York: Walker, 1966; New York:
Berkley-Medallion paperback, 1968. HB-R.

_____. The Touch of Death. London: Hodder, 1954; New York:
Walker, 1969. HB-HB-R. See also The Touch of Death in Appendix I.

_____. Traitor's Doom. London: Long, 1942. HB-HB-R.
See also Traitor's Doom in Appendixes I and II.

_____. The Valley of Fear. London: Long, 1943. HB-HB.
See also The Perilous Country in this listing and in Appendix I.

_____. The Wings of Peace. London: Long, 1948. HB-HB.
See also The Wings of Peace in Appendix I.

CONSULT APPENDIX I FOR SERIES CONTINUATION

CONSULT APPENDIX II FOR SERIES TRANSITION

END OF CWF 17

† CWF 18.   DANIELS, NORMAN †

BACKGROUND: Phenomenally prolific author of paperback originals. Of all the authors covered in this file, Daniels has probably produced more paperback volumes than any other.   He and his wife, gothic novelist Dorothy Daniels, have penned more than 200 paperback originals in a wide range of categories, from mysteries to family sagas.

Before entering the paperback field, Daniels wrote several monthly series for Doc Savage and other pulp magazines.   Under the cover identity of G. Wayman Jones, Daniels created The Black Bat, which preceded Batman.   He also wrote a series of books based on the popular comic strip, Don Winslow of the Navy.

Daniels conceived scripts for the "Nick Carter" radio program.   He wrote for live television in its early days, and later adapted episodes for a number of filmed shows in Hollywood, including "Alfred Hitchcock Presents," "Ford Theatre," and "General Electric Theatre," among many others.

Daniels scored impressively with numerous visual-project novelizations, notably The Detectives (1962) and Arrest and Trial (1963), and, relevant to this file, two adaptations of "The Avengers."

In the mystery arena, Daniels' achievements are exceptional, especially in the espionage series genre.

Daniels' Bruce Baron and John Keith dossiers, both of which will be examined here, enjoyed considerable popularity during the mid- and late sixties.

After Don Pendleton's Mack Bolan propelled the adventure market into new dimensions in 1969, Daniels successfully ventured into the field with three books featuring man-of-action Kelly Carvel. This brief series consisted of: The Rape of a Town (1970), One Angry Man (1971), and License to Kill (1972).

Before recruiting these series operatives, Daniels penned several suspense novels in the mold of the grim, hard-boiled thriller, notably The Captive (1959), Deadly Game (1959), and Lady for Sale (1960).

Daniels has excelled in other mass market categories, apart from the mystery genre: In 1965 he published Strike Force, a savage war novel in the tradition of The Guns of Navarone.   That was reissued in 1969 as Killer Tank.

More recently, Daniels has been crafting a Civil War series featuring the Turner family: Wyndward Passion (1978), Wyndward Fury (1979), Wyndward Peril (1980), and Wyndward Glory (1981).

Wyndward Passion consists of two previously published volumes, Law of the Lash (1968) and Master of Wyndward (1969). A fifth novel in the series is scheduled for future publication.

Daniels' works have been published by such paperback houses as Avon, Berkley, Lancer, Pyramid, and Warner Books.

CWF AGENTS: 1) Baron, Bruce.
             2) Keith, John.
             3) Steed, John.

CWF HISTORIES: 1) Bruce Baron: President of Baron's Bank of Hong Kong. Characterized from intelligence files as urbane, shrewd, and well-versed in the culture of the Orient.

In addition to his banking interests, Baron was involved in other successful enterprises in Hong Kong during the mid-sixties, chiefly: A jewelry store, a travel agency, a restaurant-cabaret, a bar and grill, a tailor shop, a sports palace, and a brothel. Each of these concerns served a useful purpose for Baron, other than the obvious one of profit--each outlet provided a crucial link for Baron as an agent for the C. I. A.

Baron's assigned territory: Hong Kong. However, on occasion, he was summoned outside the British Crown Colony.

2) John Keith: Intrepid operative for A. P. E., otherwise known as the American Policy Executive, a highly secret intelligence organization that was unique in its structure--each A. P. E. agent operated alone in the field, generally unknown to other agency members.

It is not known if a director or command center existed for A. P. E. However, thorough agent covers were developed for the unwavering preservation of American foreign policy throughout the world, as the situation demanded--this being the official function of A. P. E. (which was disbanded in 1971).

John Keith's cover established him as a member of a prominent public relations firm, Skinner, Maywell, and Finch, with global representation that included New York and London. This respectable concern received contracts from foreign governments for various public relations projects during the Cold War period.

The clients of this firm included, among other countries, Cuba and the Soviet Union. It was through these "contacts" that Keith and other A. P. E. constituents "encountered" potential missions. Details on Keith to follow.

Adept at foreign languages, firearms, and unarmed combat. No record on location of training or extensive war record.

Operated under the code name of Darius. Considered as an "agent-in-place" by allied and inimical intelligence agencies.

3) John Steed: British subject. Worldly free-lance agent for British Intelligence. No recorded code names or designations; known in the field under his own name.

Identifying marks: derby hat and cane.

Superior: "Mother" (1968-69 only).

Allies: Peel, Emma, and Tara King. Mrs. Peel met Steed as the result of a motor car accident in 1965. Worked with Steed from 1965 to 1968. No known sexual associations. Mrs. Peel was allied with Steed until her missing husband, one Peter Peel, returned from the Amazon. Extremely athletic and dangerous.

Tara King succeeded Mrs. Peel as Steed's partner from 1968 to 1969. No further record.

OPERATIVE DATA: 1) Norman Daniels' Bruce Baron thrillers represented a creative concept for an espionage series of its period.

Unlike many agents of the Cold War era, Baron was a man of wealth and influence who utilized these advantages to serve the global objectives of the C.I.A.

Further, Baron's seasoned knowledge of Hong Kong afforded him an advantageous view of the Chi-Coms and their operations. No known connections in Macao, situated on the other side of Hong Kong Harbor.

In The Baron of Hong Kong (1967) Baron employed his network to protect a high-ranking member of the Chi-Com party, to avoid risk of a nuclear confrontation between the U.S. and Red China. The mission also involved a heroin ring based in Hong Kong, with agents linking the infamous Red Guard and a mysterious South American contact.

2) John Keith entered the field with Overkill (1964), within months of Nick Carter's recruitment in Run-Spy-Run (1964).

Daniels launched the paperback spy original into a new sphere with his Keith series. He deftly fused consistently satisfying plots with a taut, first-person narrative style, and, to complement this level of development, Daniels intensified the plot movement in each entry with a pulsating pace that blended in with the series' contributing values.

Overkill concerned the intricate nuclear machinations of the U.S., the Soviet Union, and Red China in a treacherous death-chase that extended from Moscow to Albania.

While the missions for many series of that period explored themes relating to the instigation of World War III, Daniels presented a stunning twist on the Soviet-Chinese hegemony that was curiously ignored by competing authors, making Overkill one of the more daring spy thrillers of the Cold War era.

In Spy Ghost (1965) Daniels journeyed into even more provocative espionage territory as Keith investigated reports of Soviet manipulation of the occult sciences for the purpose of gaining global domination in outer space.

Despite the seemingly implausible material in Spy Ghost, Daniels executed the plot, especially the segments involving seances and space lore, with precision and conviction.

Spy Ghost was, unquestionably, one of the most imaginative cloak-and-dagger entries to emerge from the spy phenomenon.

Operation K (1965), considered more streamlined than Overkill and Spy Ghost, nonetheless displayed Daniels' narrative magnetism. Keith's mission was to check the audacious abduction of Nikita Khrushchev by an insidious international criminal consortium, before he could be delivered to the Chi-Coms.

Of all the Keith yarns, Operation K manifested a meticulous attention to detail, particularly in respect to A. P. E.'s calculated counterploy to rescue the former Soviet leader.

Daniels maintained the originality of the early Keith books in the later entries, concluding with Operation S-L (1971).

3) In The Magnetic Man (1968), in which Norman Daniels captured the sensationalism of "The Avengers," John Steed embarked on a perilous foray to Hong Kong to intercept some crucial documents. After being assaulted, Steed discovered that the papers had been replaced by a large sum of money.

Steed and his new ally, Tara King, devised a chilling intrigue worthy of "The Avengers" to probe the mystery behind the treacherous interplay in Hong Kong.

SUMMARY: While the specific concepts of the Bruce Baron and John Keith series were different, both series reflected Norman Daniels' special gift for blending action and suspense.

Further, the above evaluation of The Magnetic Man speaks for itself, to which could be added Daniels' versatility in the paperback field.

STATUS: 1) and 2) Apart from a few dated allusions to the Chi-Coms in the Baron and Keith dossiers, both series would perform well in the current espionage market. SOP.

3) It is unfortunate that visual-project novelizations are not reissued, for Norman Daniels' "The Avengers" ranks as one of the finest examples of this misunderstood genre, surpassing the efforts of predecessor John Garforth (see separate reference).

Daniels deftly conveyed the futuristic atmosphere of the popular ABC home visual project which starred Patrick Macnee as John Steed, Diana Rigg as Emma Peel, and Linda Thorson as Tara King. SOP.

FIELD BIBLIOGRAPHY

Daniels, Norman. The Baron of Hong Kong. New York: Lancer
    Books, 1967. PBO. (Baron)

_____. Baron's Mission to Peking. New York: Lancer Books,
    1967. PBO. (Baron)

_____. The Hunt Club. New York: Pyramid Publications,
    1964. PBO. (Keith)

_____. The Magnetic Man. New York: Berkley-Medallion,
    1968. PBO. TN. ("The Avengers")

_____. Moon Express. New York: Berkley-Medallion, 1969.
    PBO. TN. ("The Avengers")

_____. Operation K. New York: Pyramid Publications, 1965.
    PBO. (Keith)

_____. Operation N. New York: Pyramid Publications, 1966.
    PBO. (Keith)

_____. Operation T. New York: Pyramid Publications, 1967.
    PBO. (Keith)

_____. Operation VC. New York: Pyramid Publications, 1967.
    PBO. (Keith)

_____. Overkill. New York: Pyramid Publications, 1964.
    PBO. (Keith)

_____. Spy Ghost. New York: Pyramid Publications, 1965.
    PBO. (Keith)

CONSULT APPENDIX I FOR SERIES CONTINUATION

END OF CWF 18

† CWF 19. DARK, JAMES †

BACKGROUND: Former naval officer who turned to suspense writing in the early fifties.

Acknowledging the author's possible obligations to the Official Secrets Act, "James Dark" may have been devised as a cover identity. However, since the author's early non-espionage works, notably Dame on the Lam (1952), A Guy Must Live (1954), and The Squealer (1954), were attributed to James Dark, it is highly probable that such is his real name.

It wasn't until 1965 that Dark appeared in U.S. territory, beginning with Come Die with Me, the first in his Mark Hood-Intertrust series, the subject of this file.

A number of Dark's books were initially distributed by Horwitz Publications, the Australian publishing firm that launched prolific mystery writer Carter Brown (Alan G. Yates) outside the United States. In addition to the Hood entries, Dark's non-series espionage thriller, Spy from the Grave (1964), was also published by Horwitz. (Horwitz was based in Sydney during the Cold War field term of the Hood dossier [1965-1971]. Currently established as Horwitz Grahame Books Pty. Ltd., the publisher is now situated in Cammeray, Australia. An allied branch, identified under the original name of Horwitz Publications, is located in Hong Kong, B.C.C.)

Dark acted as a prominent constituent of the N. A. L. /Signet Intelligence Group (see separate reference).

N. A. L. published the Hood series in the U.S. sector throughout its six-year run, concluding with Sea Scrape in 1971. It is to Dark's credit that he remained on the publisher's paperback docket after the secret-agent phenomenon began to disintegrate in 1968.

No further record since 1971.

CWF AGENT: Hood, Mark.

CWF HISTORY: Born in New York in 1932. Mark Kingsley Hood was educated in England, where he played championship cricket; qualified as a doctor at Oxford.

Developed a solid reputation as a diver and competition race-car driver.

Became established as a free-lance writer in the early sixties. Published several articles on racing in the best international sports magazines. Hood served as the executive officer on a destroyer in the U.S. Navy during the Korean War. Later entered Naval Intelligence.

In the early sixties Hood was recruited into a clandestine intelligence organization known only as Intertrust. Full details are given below:

1) Structure: formed by the United States, France, Great Britain, and the Soviet Union.

2) Global Objective: the aversion of nuclear proliferation.

3) Focus: non-political.

4) Location: Geneva, Switzerland--an undistinguished building situated on Lake Geneva near the old Palace of Nations.

5) Cover: technical publishing house.

6) Hood's Superiors: Mr. Fortescue and Mr. Blair, respectively of British and American origins. Both names cover identities, devised by Intertrust for obvious security reasons.

7) Official Term of Field Existence: 1965 to 1971.

During his training period Hood achieved a high level of proficiency in the martial arts. When not actively engaged on an assignment for Intertrust, Hood advanced his self-defense pursuits at the fashionable International Club in Geneva. His Japanese instructor was one Mr. Murimoto.

Murimoto accompanied Hood on a mission in the Far East, but otherwise Hood's only ally was the top British operative for Intertrust, Thomas Tremayne.

Tremayne executed covers in the field as a nuclear scientist and an auto mechanic, among other guises, and Hood's mastery as a sportsman provided him with an effective cover on several occasions. Cover identity also recorded as Arthur Conant, a worldly tourist.

Adept with firearms. Standard field weapons: .32 Colt automatic and .38 caliber pistol.

Hood traveled extensively as a field agent for Intertrust, with assignments ranging from the Bahamas to Hong Kong.

No relationship existed between Intertrust's top American operative and one Charles Hood, the continental provocateur recruited in 1964 by James Mayo (see separate reference).

No trace of Hood since the dissolution of Intertrust in 1971.

OPERATIVE DATA: The major virtue of the Hood series was its crisp action. However, Dark augmented the progression in each entry with knowledgeable attention to exotic locales and with Hood's fascination for action sports in general and martial arts in particular. In this respect, Dark's contributions to the evolution of the man-of-action genre place him close to Edward S. Aarons, Donald Hamilton, and Philip Atlee (see separate references).

The focus of the entire series was Intertrust's global circumvention of nuclear subversion, with Mark Hood initially conceived as a slick mixture of James Bond and Matt Helm.

The avaricious designs of a Nazi war criminal identified as one Heinrich Gauss, as well as the seizure of three U.S. torpedo boats in Bahamian waters, prompted Intertrust to summon Hood in Come Die with Me (1965).

Dark's utilization of the colorful Bahamian settings challenged Ian Fleming's Thunderball (1961) (see separate reference) as Hood savagely confronted Gauss in Nassau, uncovering a plot for biological warfare that would have insured the revitalization of Nazism.

Gauss's command center: a remote and impenetrable fortress in the Brazilian mountains.

This Dark mission should not be confused with the British edition of Diamonds Are Deadly (1969) by James Eastwood (see separate reference). The book was published as Come Die with Me in that territory.

In the three books which followed Come Die with Me, Dark sharpened his definition of the Intertrust apparat in the thick of the Cold War. Not surprisingly, these files were plotted in several Asian trouble spots.

The Bamboo Bomb (1965) transpired as Hood's most baffling assignment for Intertrust. The Chi-Coms were suspected of designing a ruinous atomic test in the Malay Archipelago, and, to execute Intertrust's directives of nullifying the test and revealing it as political blackmail, Hood was to gain access across the Strait of Malacca and convince the Chi-Coms of his treacherous inclinations.

Dark's nefarious Chi-Com puppet, Ramsuddin, was characterized as the archetypal political nemesis in his position as the Minister of Reconstruction and Development for the Island of Sumatra.

As he had with the Bahamian locales in Come Die with Me, Dark masterfully employed the Malayan background in The Bamboo Bomb, especially the perilous environs of Singapore.

Hong Kong Incident (1966) concerned the feared annihilation of the U.S. Seventh Fleet in the Pacific. In this Hood entry the enigmatic locales of Hong Kong and Macao exemplified the treachery of a Chi-Com defector and an ominous border incident.

Hood's cover: a world-class driver in competition at the Macao Grand Prix, with Tremayne as his mechanic.

The action and suspense values of the Hood series were pushed to the limit in Assignment Tokyo (1966). The diplomatic quagmire of Tokyo complicated Hood's mission of investigating three mysterious deaths on Oba Island, the site of a global missile-defense system, otherwise known as Miss-Sat.

Dark infiltrated a new subject area for a paperback spy original with his incisive evaluation of the political complexities existing between the U.S. and Japan and their mutual relationship to the Cold War throughout the Far East during the Vietnam era.

Inspired to use the character of American Ambassador Hubert P. Tomlinson, Dark focused on the precarious diplomatic interplay which often influenced U.S. policy in Japan in its role as a deterrent against the threat of the Chi-Coms and the Soviet Union.

The tempestuous "femme fatale" figure of Toi came across as Hood's most challenging sexual encounter.

On the escapist side, Dark allied Hood with Tremayne as he added a considerable amount of martial arts lore to the narrative. Dark adroitly fused to the main plot Hood's barbarous karate contest with the formidable Hiroshi Sato at the Meinjin Martial Arts Exhibit in Tokyo.

Comparable to Jack Seward's (see separate reference) Curt Stone thrillers, Dark's Assignment Tokyo, with its worldly knowledge of Japanese culture developed as one of the finest examples of paperback espionage fiction.

Intertrust dispatched Hood to the Caribbean in Operation Scuba and Throne of Satan (both 1967).

Tremayne posed as a renowned nuclear scientist in Operation Scuba, accompanied by Hood as his capable bodyguard. Vacationing in Jamaica, the audacious operative team was assigned to investigate a series of bizarre ship collisions in Caribbean waters.

With an authenticity equal to that of Assignment Tokyo, Dark included an impressive yet intimidating atomic vessel display near Cuban territory, lending strength to the gravity of the overall plot. Inclusion of Hood's tested aquatic abilities and several chilling underwater setpieces raised Operation Scuba to the rank of one of the best in the Hood dossier, second only to Assignment Tokyo.

A seething desire for revenge and a maddened scheme directed towards the world's combat forces added to the mystery of the Throne of Satan. Intertrust dispatched Hood and Tremayne to the island of Dominica to foil a plot, designated "Operation Sugarstrike" by a malevolent conspirator known as Dominat, that would have surpassed the ravaging potential of the Cuban Missile Crisis.

In The Sword of Genghis Khan (1967) Hood and Murimoto journeyed to the Asian sector to confront one General Khan, who possessed the megalomaniacal traits of a long-deceased ancestor. His stronghold: a formidable mountain fortress in Inner Mongolia.

The disappearance of several rocket scientists and an incendiary siege across Asian waters highlighted this apocalyptic Hood mission, which also proffered a Chi-Com cultural exhibition in Peking. The discovery of a rare narcotic in Paris and certain Asian and Arabic areas, namely the Gobi and Libyan Deserts, also figured in this critical Intertrust initiative.

The later Hood books introduced futuristic elements bordering on science fiction in the fashion of John Creasey's (see separate refference) Dr. Palfrey thrillers.

In Operation Octopus (1968) search for a missing Polaris submarine led Hood to an aquatic city "on the tongue of the ocean"-- triggered for a cataclysmic assault against the U.S. in a scheme dating back to the bloodstained fantasies of Nazi Germany.

Intertrust devised an ingenious cover for Hood: a traitor specializing in selling valuable Naval weaponry secrets to competing global powers. The setting: New Orleans.

Hood was on vacation in Spying Blind (1968), his itinerary including the glittering paradise of Monte Carlo, when he encountered one Norman Edgell, an avaricious aerospace magnate, on his yacht, the Argosy.

Edgell proposed a staggering project to Hood: aid him in the calculated hijacking of a Soviet moon probe as it landed on earth. His ally was to be Edgell's ravishing daughter, Lynne, who was also a desperate drug addict.

Dark succeeded admirably with this entry, refining the burgeoning espionage trend toward space themes, one which developed more fully in 1968. Dark's action and suspense values in Spying Blind matched his efforts in Assignment Tokyo and Operation Scuba.

The last two Hood books of the sixties, Operation Ice Cap and The Invisibles (both 1969), were merely satisfactory reprisals of earlier missions.

In Operation Ice Cap, two nuclear-powered submarines were reported by Holy Loch in Scotland to have literally melted above the Arctic Circle, while The Invisibles concerned a nebulous plot to dominate through voodoo the global nuclear weapons market on a remote Caribbean island.

In both instances Dark exceeded the boundaries of credibility established in Operation Octopus and Spying Blind, but the general excellence of the Hood canon negate the structural deficiencies of these 1969 entries.

SUMMARY: James Dark's Intertrust series emerged as one of the most important developments in the evolution of the paperback spy novel of the sixties. Dark was perhaps the first espionage author to confront the complex issue of global nuclear proliferation, translating it into popular genre fiction.

Further, Dark's achievements with the series strongly emphasized the escapist values of action and suspense, as well as the specialized interests of his protagonist, Mark Hood. In this last respect, Dark made an indelible contribution to the espionage fiction of the Cold War era with his seasoned knowledge of the martial arts, weaponry, commercialized sports, and the Far East.

Unquestionably, Dark's series ranks on a par with the operative dossiers of Edward S. Aarons, Norman Daniels, and Donald Hamilton (see separate references).

STATUS: Considering the present state of intensified nuclear awareness in most intelligence sectors, every effort should be directed toward the reactivation of the Hood series. High priority for all territories. SOP.

FIELD BIBLIOGRAPHY

Dark, James. Assignment Hong Kong. Sydney, Australia: Horwitz Publications, 1966. PBO. See also Hong Kong Incident.

_____. Assignment Tokyo. New York: New American Library, 1966. PBO. U.S. paperback title for Operation Miss-Sat.

_____. The Bamboo Bomb. New York: New American Library, 1965. PBO.

_____. Come Die with Me. New York: New American Library, 1965. PBO.

_____. Hong Kong Incident. New York: New American Library, 1966. PBO. U.S. paperback title for Assignment Hong Kong.

_____. The Invisibles. New York: New American Library, 1969. PBO.

_____. Operation Ice Cap. New York: New American Library, 1969. PBO.

_____. Operation Miss-Sat. Sydney, Australia: Horwitz Publications, 1966. PBO. See also Assignment Tokyo.

_____. Operation Octopus. New York: New American Library, 1968. PBO.

_____. Operation Scuba. New York: New American Library,
1967. PBO.

_____. Spying Blind. New York: New American Library, 1968.
PBO.

_____. The Sword of Genghis Khan. New York: New American
Library, 1967. PBO.

_____. Throne of Satan. New York: New American Library,
1967. PBO.

CONSULT APPENDIX I FOR SERIES CONTINUATION

END OF CWF 19

† CWF 20. DAVIES, FREDRIC †

BACKGROUND: Combined cover identity of Ron Ellik and Fredric
Langley.

Known as a science-fiction advocate and computer program-
mer, Ellik was recruited by David McDaniel (see separate reference)
for the U. N. C. L. E. field project in 1967. (McDaniel dedicated his
1968 "Man from U. N. C. L. E." novelization, The Utopia Affair, to
Ellik: "a squirrel with a cross of gold.")

From 1958 to 1961 Ellik served as co-editor of the science-
fiction magazine Fanac and co-authored with Bill Evans the science-
fiction novel The Universes of E. E. Smith (1968).

Langley's collaboration with Ellik consisted of one U.N.C.L.E.
novelization, as part of the Ace Intelligence Group (see separate reference).

CWF AGENTS: Solo, Napoleon, and Illya Kuryakin.

CWF HISTORIES: See also Avallone, Michael--CWF 6.

OPERATIVE DATA: The Cross of Gold Affair (1968) adequately reflected the salient values of the "The Man from U. N. C. L. E."
visual-project novelization series. However, Davies' contribution
lacked the narrative energy apparent in the efforts of Michael
Avallone, J. Hunter Holly, Peter Leslie, and David McDaniel (see
separate references).

The interrogation of a minor T. H. R. U. S. H. agent, identified only as Alain, revealed a blueprint to monopolize the global gold market by an emerging African nation.

Ordered by Mr. Waverly to interview several commodity brokers in New York, Solo uncovered a connection between Gambol and Associates, a leading brokerage house, and a consortium of investors controlled by T. H. R. U. S. H.

Solo's suspicions were aroused by the actions of Jason Gambol, president of the Gambol organization, but, according to U. N. C. L. E. files, T. H. R. U. S. H. 's key architect of this scheme was one Avery D. Porpoise.

Predictably, U. N. C. L. E. successfully averted T.H.R.U.S.H.'s avaricious objectives.

SUMMARY: The Cross of Gold Affair added nothing of new interest to "The Man from U. N. C. L. E." visual-project tie-in series.

In some sectors, Langley's name has been listed as Steve Tolliver.   No further information.

STATUS: See Avallone, Michael--CWF 6.

FIELD BIBLIOGRAPHY

Davies, Fredric. The Cross of Gold Affair. New York: Ace Books, 1968. PBO. TN.

CONSULT ACE INTELLIGENCE GROUP FOR ADDITIONAL AUTHOR REFERENCES

END OF CWF 20

† CWF 21. DEIGHTON, LEN †

BACKGROUND: Well-known British author of realistic spy and war novels.

Leonard Cyril Deighton was born in London in 1929. His father was chauffeur to Campbell Dogsdon, Keeper of Prints and Drawings for the British Museum.

During World War II, the Deighton family lived within the fashionable Dogsdon household, and it was the intricate hierarchical rivalries within the domestic staff that fostered Deighton's acute perception of human behavior. It is possible that the accumulation of these early experiences were instrumental in the formation of Deighton's conception of the contemporary Cold War operative.

As an English schoolboy, Deighton was evacuated from London during World War II. He was later employed as a railway clerk, before entering the R.A.F., serving as a photographer during his term of duty.

Deighton procured an art education grant from St. Martin's School of Art and later attended the Royal College of Art. Concurrently working as a waiter in a Piccadilly restaurant, it was during this period that he cultivated an interest in the culinary arts. This pursuit eventually led to his illustrated cookery feature for The Observer, which in turn provided the inspiration for Len Deighton's Cookstrip Cook Book (1965), based partly on his columns.

After graduating from art school, Deighton presided over the art department of a leading London advertising agency and in the late fifties he moved to New York where he secured work as an illustrator.

In the meantime Deighton had expanded his talents to include writing.

The Ipcress File (1962), Deighton's first novel, was credited, along with John le Carré's The Spy Who Came In from the Cold (1963) and Adam Hall's The Quiller Memorandum (1965) (see separate references), with the development of the realistic school of spy fiction.

The book was an immediate success in both the critical and sales arenas, and it quickly transpired that both the more serious devotees of espionage fiction and James Bond's growing audience responded enthusiastically to Deighton's cynical, anonymous British agent.

It must be emphasized here that reviewers and readers alike instantly regarded Deighton's protagonist as an anti-hero. It is still debatable whether Len Deighton or John le Carré (see separate reference) actually developed the largest countercult to Ian Fleming (see separate reference) during the mid-sixties.

Departing briefly from the alleys of international intrigue, Deighton authored the visual-project script for Oh, What a Lovely War! (1969), a lavish musical production with noticeable anti-war overtones. Deighton also has produced contemporary spy novels, removed from the ideologies of the Cold War, such as Catch a Falling Spy (1976). This entry was published in Britain as Twinkle, Twinkle, Little Spy.

The renowned British author was distinguished as well for his graphic, compelling espionage novels derived from authentic World War II history. Punctuated with the gripping realism that characterized Deighton's earlier efforts in the suspense field, these works include Yesterday's Spy (1975), SS-GB (1978), and XPD (1981). Fighter (1978) and Blitzkrieg: From the Rise of Hitler to the Fall of Dunkirk (1980) reflected Deighton's extensive knowledge of military and world history.

Deighton's straight war novels, generally isolated from the demands of the modern espionage genre, included Bomber (1970) and Goodbye, Mickey Mouse (1982), as well as a collection of war-oriented short stories, Eleven Declarations of War (1971).

Like many British authors, Deighton has long since left his native land to escape its severe tax laws. He currently lives in Ireland.

Deighton is a distinguished representative of the Fawcett Intelligence Group (see separate reference).

CWF AGENT: No recorded name (other than "Harry Palmer" in three visual projects of the mid-sixties). For the purpose of this file, Deighton's operative shall be referred to as Deighton's spy.

CWF HISTORY: Deighton's spy was born in Burnley, England. Exact date unknown. Working class background.

Served without distinction in the British Army, followed by three years in Military Intelligence. Superior was a man known as Ross.

Later joined the W.O.O.C. (P), a small yet significant spy unit associated with the War Office. The paramount chief of the W.O.O.C. (P) was identified as Dawlish (recorded in 1963). However during a 1962 assignment Deighton's spy acted under the orders of a top W.O.O.C. (P) officer, Dalby. It should be noted here that Deighton's spy worked for the W.O.O.C. (P) in a purely civilian capacity.

During the Cold War era the W.O.O.C. (P) functioned in much the same manner as M.I.5. or the C.I.A. Deighton's spy was dispatched to missions in Lebanon, Paris, Lisbon, Leningrad, as well as both sectors of Berlin in the thick of the Cold War.

The W.O.O.C. (P) was last encountered in the field in 1974.

Deighton's spy came into contact with certain individuals in the field during the Cold War era who otherwise would have been avoided by agents of the C.I.A. and M.I.5., notably Colonel Alexeyevitch Oleg Stok, K.G.B., and one General Midwinter, a megalomaniacal oil millionaire from Texas.

Adept at scuba diving, as substantiated in a 1963 assignment in Portugal that involved the location of a sunken submarine. Full details under OPERATIVE DATA.

Proficient in the culinary arts, an aid to his standing as a bachelor. Other interests included classical music.

Although characterized as a solitary field operative, Deighton's spy occasionally allied with a female agent, known only as Jean. Also associated with one Samantha Steel, purportedly of Israeli Intelligence, during a 1964 mission in Berlin, and an audacious female provocateur, identified only as Charly. During an assignment in Helsinki, worked briefly with a Finnish contact, Dr. Olaf Kaarna.

OPERATIVE DATA: The importance of the Deighton dossier in relation to the Cold-War espionage novel of the sixties cannot be overstressed.

Deighton's unconventional approach to the spy novel of the period, observed by both critics and readers upon the initial release of The Ipcress File in 1962, partly explains the complexity of the series, from The Ipcress File to An Expensive Place to Die (1967).

However, several other elements are integral to Deighton's series. 1) A painstaking evaluation of the global intelligence services, in every intricate functional detail, both in terms of the central plot and the strategic machinery of the Cold War. (In several books, notably The Ipcress File (1962), Funeral in Berlin (1964), and Billion Dollar Brain (1966), the format of a top-secret intelligence file, often utilizing footnotes and appendixes, was adopted.)

2) A serious consideration of the technological aspects of Cold War intelligence techniques and operations. While this feature figured, in a general way, into the archetypal Deighton plot, it was perhaps more prominent in Horse Under Water (1963), which contained an appendix on telephone tapping, and in Billion Dollar Brain (1966) in which the global manipulation of computers for military use contributed to the development of the plot.

3) Deighton complemented these technical and structural fragments with allegorical references, varying in nature, which created the effect of a puzzle in terms of the plot's progression. In The Ipcress File, for instance, an astrological forecast for an Aquarian preceded most of the chapter passages, while the fundamental rules of chess punctuated most chapters of Funeral in Berlin. (Elsewhere this faction of the Deighton framework was far more ambiguous, as in Horse Under Water, wherein the integral plot instruments of a secret code translation, a high-level cabinet letter (dated 1941), and a top-priority file register were introduced before the first chapter.)

4) It has been repeatedly stated that Deighton's plots were

superseded by his technological and allegorical segments. Simply expressed, Deighton conceived themes which reflected Britain's deterioration as a world power and, in part, as a global intelligence entity. Within the realm of the realistic spy thriller of the period, Deighton was distinguished from John le Carré (see separate reference) by his contention that, ironically, Britain possessed more technological competence than the U.S. or the Soviet Union. Further, Deighton also stressed that Britain was highly suspicious of Red China's global motives, in a manner transcending the actions of the U.S. and the Soviet Union.

5) Deighton employed the first person throughout the series, an element which undeniably enhanced the obscurity of his operative.

Details on the plots relevant to the Deighton dossier are given below.

The disappearance of several prominent British biochemists in The Ipcress File was the result of a maliciously calculated plot directed at the very core of British Intelligence.

Deighton's spy allied with W.O.O.C. (P) staffers Jean and Carswell to penetrate the designs of an elusive agent with wartime associations with Polish Intelligence, identified from W.O.O.C. (P) files as "Jay."

The emphasis throughout The Ipcress File was on the British Intelligence apparat, and while Deighton clearly defined the aims of the belligerent operative bodies, their strategists generally remained veiled from field observers.

The dimensions of The Ipcress File extended into Ba'albek, Lebanon, where Deighton's spy and Dalby attempted to rescue one of the missing biochemists, identified as Raven.

Deighton ended with a twist at the climax of the mission, which embodied the devious interplay between Deighton's spy, Ross, Dalby, and Jay; the significance of "Ipcress"; a file on Soviet military aid throughout the Near East; and the manipulative use of brainwashing.

Unquestionably, The Ipcress File was a major achievement in the evolution of the Cold War spy novel.

In Horse Under Water Deighton's spy was assigned to Portugal and required to locate a sunken German vessel situated off the Portuguese Coast, which contained a coveted cache of international currency intended for renegade Nazis.

In addition to the earlier referenced appendix on telephone tapping, Deighton infused Horse Under Water with a considerable amount of operative detail relative to the intelligence trade, notably on the finer points of underwater strategy and the utilization of counterfeit currency in foreign territories.

Given the prominent role of warships in Horse Under Water, Deighton included extensive information on an Italian tanker, the Olterra, and on Kurier, a signal device used by the Germans in their naval operations during World War II.

Throughout Horse Under Water Deighton probed the unstable political climate in Europe during the early sixties, examining the remaining Fascist factions in Western Europe. He also deftly threaded the political implications of the global drug market and the treacherous motives of a British naval officer (who maintained two other cover identities) into the W. O. O. C. (P) underwater initiative.

The sexual encounter of Deighton's spy with Charly, a fiery British "femme fatale," ranked as the best of the series, blending in smoothly with the central plot.

Deighton was constantly being measured against Ian Fleming (see separate reference) during the sixties, and in Horse Under Water, of all his missions, Deighton's spy's proficiency as a frogman contested James Bond's aquatic skill in Thunderball (1961).

For some inexplicable reason Horse Under Water was not distributed in the U. S. until 1968.

Funeral in Berlin, an instant bestseller after its publication in 1964, has remained the most frequently analyzed of Deighton's series entries. Allied with the opportunistic Johnnie Vulkan, Deighton's spy was assigned to execute the "transport" of a top Soviet scientist, Semitsa, and this account emerged as one of the fictional symbols of the Cold War, along with John le Carré's The Spy Who Came In from the Cold (1963) (see separate reference) and, to a lesser extent, Adam Hall's The Quiller Memorandum (1965) (see separate reference).

Involved with Deighton's spy was Colonel Alexeyevitch Oleg Stok, a former Red Army officer who later reached the highest ranks of the Soviet K. G. B. The tense interplay between them throughout Funeral in Berlin typified the mounting rivalries in the aftermath of the Berlin Wall crisis.

Deighton established a broader geopolitical base with this entry, intensifying the conflict between Deighton's spy and Stok with the enigmatic presence of James J. Hallam (F. R. S. A.) and the calculating Samantha Steel, as well as the Nazi elements in the plot, to be expected given the German locale.

Further, the mystique which Deighton created for the elusive character of Paul Louis Broom, identified by the W. O. O. C. (P) as an agricultural biologist, bestowed Funeral in Berlin with a haunting quality that was absent from the other books, except perhaps An Expensive Place to Die.

Deighton's master stroke in Funeral in Berlin, however, was

executed with his devious manipulation of the novel's East and West
Berlin settings, the divided city becoming a Cold War mosaic in
which all of the complex elements were blended by the inspired
chess-game allegory.

Funeral in Berlin was unquestionably one of the few espionage classics to come out of the sixties.

Billion Dollar Brain and An Expensive Place to Die represented, in many respects, Deighton's cynical reaction to Ian Fleming (see separate reference). In Billion Dollar Brain Deighton, with
the fanatical Texas nemesis, General Midwinter, scornfully mocked
such Fleming adversaries as Goldfinger and Sir Hugo Drax (Moonraker).

Midwinter's San Antonio-based organization, identified from
W. O. O. C. (P) files as Facts for Freedom, controlled by a formidable computer and politically defined as right-wing, was totally committed to obliterating global Communism, programmed to begin with
an invasion of the Soviet Republic of Latvia. Midwinter's blueprint
also called for the deployment of a deadly virus in the critical target sector.

In Billion Dollar Brain Deighton's spy was both challenged
and intimidated by the resourceful Harvey Newbegin, who had entered into the intrigues of Funeral in Berlin by way of his penetration of Midwinter's espionage network. Further, Colonel Stok manifested a passionate interest in the activities of Deighton's spy with
Facts for Freedom.

Deighton's electrifying use of locales like New York, San
Antonio, Helsinki, Leningrad, and Riga endowed Billion Dollar Brain
with a worldly quality that transcended the somewhat disdainful tone
of his earlier thrillers.

The style and content of Deighton's imaginative format was
refined to near perfection in An Expensive Place to Die. The narrative in this entry was more contemptuous even than in Funeral in
Berlin, for he portrayed the futility of Deighton's spy in a fatalistic
mission concerning a Chi-Com-backed H-bomb scheme involving the
highest levels of the C. I. A., British Intelligence, and the French
Sureté.

With An Expensive Place to Die Deighton analyzed the most
vulnerable weaknesses of the Western spy organizations as well as
their paranoid, often childish fears of Red China and the Soviet
Union.

In this precarious arena An Expensive Place to Die excelled
le Carré's The Spy Who Came In from the Cold (1963) (see separate reference) and, next to Funeral in Berlin, measured as Deighton's best series entry, on a par with The Ipcress File.

Considering the principal scope of the book--Deighton's spy's

Parisian interplay between a U.S. nuclear expert and a Chi-Com scientist--Deighton delineated Cold War Paris with much the same impassivity which Ian Fleming (see separate reference) conveyed Tokyo in You Only Live Twice (1964).

However, Deighton's somewhat moral judgment of Paris in An Expensive Place to Die surpassed Fleming's Oriental foray, evoking the general feeling that it was both the postwar degradation and the Cold War climate that infected the city with such a bleak mood for Deighton's spy and his colleagues.

The calculating figures of psychiatrist M. Datt, Sureté Chief Inspector Loiseau, and the ravishing Maria Chauvet reflected the reality that the genuine menace of the Cold War was not the threat of the East but the corrosive ring of suspicion and deception which dominated the intelligence apparat of the West. This is probably the only link Deighton shared in common with le Carré (see separate reference).

Deighton's conception of M. Datt's mysterious clinic in the Avenue Foch emerged as one of his most chilling presentations, and An Expensive Place to Die offers Deighton's commentary on the future of the Cold War, as of 1968. He imbued it with a forboding sense of futility and bitterness.

An Expensive Place to Die eventually developed as an understated masterpiece of contemporary espionage fiction, as signified by Deighton's taut plotting and enigmatic characters and his progression beyond the ambiguities of the Cold War.

SUMMARY: Len Deighton, with his unique approach to the realistic spy novel, taking into account the author's fascination with the technological aspects of global espionage, contributed more to its evolution than most of the practitioners of the period. This would exclude John le Carré (see separate reference) whose narrative method, as revealed in CWF 41, was directed toward the psychological features of the Cold War servant.

Richard Condon, bestselling author of The Manchurian Candidate (1959), commented on Deighton: "No novelist, past or present, has done so much for international intrigue."

Assigned the cover identity of Harry Palmer, Michael Caine appeared as Deighton's anti-hero in three visual projects of the Cold War era: The Ipcress File (Universal, 1965), Funeral in Berlin (Paramount, 1966), and Billion Dollar Brain (United Artists, 1967).

Shelving both the Dawlish post and the W.O.O.C.(P), producer Harry Saltzman delegated to Australian actor Guy Doleman the role of Ross, Palmer's superior in M.I.5.

STATUS: Although Deighton's spy's most recent mission was Spy

Story (1974), Deighton's W.O.O.C. (P) dossier remains in active paperback distribution today. It should be noted, however, that the field publishing sources have changed since the sixties. SSP.

FIELD BIBLIOGRAPHY

Deighton, Len. The Billion Dollar Brain. New York: Putnam, 1966; New York: Dell paperback, 1967. HB-R.

_____. An Expensive Place to Die. New York: Putnam, 1967; New York: Dell paperback, 1968. HB-R.

_____. Funeral in Berlin. London: Jonathan Cape, 1964; New York: Putnam, 1965; New York: Dell paperback, 1965. HB-HB-R.

_____. Horse Under Water. London: Jonathan Cape, 1963; New York: Putnam, 1968; New York: Dell paperback, 1969. HB-HB-R.

_____. The Ipcress File. London: Hodder, 1962; New York: Simon & Schuster, 1963; New York: Fawcett-Crest paperback, 1964. HB-HB-R.

CONSULT APPENDIX I FOR SERIES CONTINUATION

CONSULT APPENDIX II FOR SERIES TRANSITION

END OF CWF 21

† CWF 22. DIMENT, ADAM †

BACKGROUND: Born in 1945, on a Dorsetshire farm, among the grass roots of England.

Attended several private schools; began writing at the age of seventeen. Early job as advertising copywriter afforded both the experience and spare time to pursue his chosen craft.

His first novel, The Dolly, Dolly Spy (1967), introduced Philip McAlpine, a British secret agent cast slightly in the anti-hero mold of Len Deighton's spy (see separate reference) but invested also with the "mod" attributes of the late sixties.

Achieving bestselling-author status after The Dolly, Dolly Spy was published in 1967, Diment produced two more McAlpine thrillers,

The Great Spy Race and The Bang, Bang Birds, both released in 1968. The New York Times crowned Diment as "Ian Fleming's successor" and it appeared that his bizarre mixture of Cold War espionage and the psychedelic explosion would be the salvation of the waning spy genre.

The initial public reaction seemed to support this contention, for the young British author was given unprecedented media attention, including international television and magazine interviews as well as promotional posters on London buses. However, despite an ambitious campaign by Bantam Books, which emphasized the erudite tastes and sleek attire of the avant-garde spy novelist, the fervor over Diment and McAlpine proved to be short-lived. Still, Bantam managed to convey Diment's frenzied conception of espionage with hypnotic, sex-oriented covers.

By 1971 the mass interest in Diment had so diminished that Think Inc. (1971), the fourth and final McAlpine entry, was not published in the U.S. and received only a modest distribution in Britain and other European territories; Diment soon vanished from the suspense field.

CWF AGENT: McAlpine, Philip.

CWF HISTORY: British subject.   Formerly an industrial security agent for British Electric Household Tools, or B.E.H.T.   Superior identified as Stafford, an ex-Army intelligence officer.

Attended middle-grade public school.   Later expelled from a distinguished university for alleged sexual involvement with the daughter of a local millionaire.   Names of both the academic institution and the millionaire's family remain unknown.

After securing employment with B.E.H.T., McAlpine leased a three-room flat in Hampstead, which he shared with Veronica Lom, a woman of desirable dimensions.

Trained in the basic Oriental martial arts, with expertise in the areas of driving and flying.   (In 1966 McAlpine acquired an MGB sports car, and was registered as a licensed pilot.)

In December 1966 Stafford offered McAlpine's services to a clandestine intelligence unit veiled within the Ministry of Labour, recorded only as Department 6 (Location: Suffolk House in the British city of the same name).   McAlpine made contact with one Mr. Quine for a special assignment.

Pursuant to his term of duty with Department 6, McAlpine manifested language fluency in French and Greek.

Traveled extensively throughout the Mediterranean, notably Corfu, Greece.

McAlpine was known to have indulged in addictive drugs, including hashish, a potent form of marijuana (cannabis), which has been known to produce the following effects: 1) laziness, 2) psychic instability, 3) amorality, 4) loss of drive and ambition, 5) grayish-yellow skin color, 6) abnormal body and speech patterns, and 7) general conditions of poor health. Nonetheless, McAlpine functioned as an agent of the highest caliber for Department 6.

No further record since 1971.

OPERATIVE DATA: Format varied little throughout the McAlpine series. Diment conceived a fairly taut narrative style which displayed his protagonist's unconventional qualities, underscoring his more professional talents such as flying and the martial arts.

The Dolly, Dolly Spy (1967) briefly generated a positive response, assisted by the impact of the psychedelic cult of the late sixties; but by this time the secret-agent genre had been virtually exhausted on all levels.

Diment competently handled the segments involving McAlpine's interest in hashish, and, although he maintained a rapid story pace, the plots were drawn from the basic standards of the genre.

In The Dolly, Dolly Spy Quine assigned McAlpine to fly a Nazi war criminal out of Egypt and return him to the United States.

In The Great Spy Race (1968) McAlpine competed against eight capable and lethal agents for a coveted dossier of the Chi-Com agents-in-place in the Far East.

Diment parodied Len Deighton (see separate reference) in The Great Spy Race by addressing each chapter with either a serious or satirical quotation, from Heinrich Himmler to popular myths about sex, and even a few specimens of his own special brand of wry humor.

SUMMARY: Adam Diment developed a unique concept for the weathered spy genre of the late sixties, implementing a number of elements indigenous to the youth culture movement of the period. However, the ingenuity of the series could not withstand the general decline in popularity of the Cold-War spy novel.

STATUS: The confinement of the series within the chaotic ideologies of the late sixties makes it highly unlikely as a candidate for reissue. SOP.

FIELD BIBLIOGRAPHY

Diment, Adam. The Bang, Bang Birds. New York: E. P. Dutton, 1968; New York: Bantam paperback, 1969. HB-R.

_____. The Dolly, Dolly Spy. New York: E. P. Dutton, 1967; New York: Bantam paperback, 1968. HB-R.

_____. The Great Spy Race. New York: E. P. Dutton, 1968; New York: Bantam paperback, 1969. HB-R.

CONSULT APPENDIX I FOR SERIES CONTINUATION

END OF CWF 22

† CWF 23. EASTWOOD, JAMES †

BACKGROUND: British native. Born in 1918. Former foreign correspondent with extensive experience in Central Europe.

As a journalist, Eastwood developed interests in criminology and Hungarian culture, both reflected in the subject of this file, Anna Zordan.

Before recruiting Ms. Zordan in 1965, Eastwood capably displayed his talents in the suspense field with his celebrated mystery, Murder Inc. (1952). That same year Eastwood novelized the Humphrey Bogart visual project Deadline U. S. A.

Like many espionage authors of the Cold War era, Eastwood has ventured since in new directions, as evidenced by his straight suspense novel, Henry in a Silver Frame (1972).

CWF AGENT: Zordan, Anna.

CWF HISTORY: Born in 1938 in Budapest, Hungary to a Hungarian father and American mother. Educated at the finest schools in the U. S. and Europe.

Andreas Zordan, Anna's father, was a distinguished diplomat during World War II and served in a number of important posts throughout the world.

After the war, Anna Zordan entered the business sector and

eventually became an international free-lance agent for the British automation and machine-tool markets.

Anna Zordan's parents were found murdered in their Vienna apartment in 1965, but Viennese authorities uncovered no apparent motive for their deaths. Shortly after her parents were cremated, Anna confronted a mysterious German in her London flat, who alleged that her father had used his global contacts to channel refugees from Eastern Europe for the purpose of establishing a spy network that purportedly involved Red China.

Enraged at this accusation, Anna liquidated the German antagonist, who possessed an armed advantage. The German was later identified as one Otto Hagmann.

As a result of the incident, Anna encountered a man known only as Mr. Sarratt, the head of a clandestine British intelligence unit; Sarratt later recruited Ms. Zordan for a field term of four years. She was trained at "The Studio," command center for Sarratt's group, based in Kent.

Zordan was characterized as tempestuously amoral, dangerously proficient in both the conventional and cultured schools of self-defense, yet highly sensitive.

No known code names or designations. No field record after 1969.

OPERATIVE DATA: Eastwood incorporated all of the basic ingredients into his three-volume Zordan dossier. However, it was far from being formularized, for Eastwood conceived a spy series that was both topical and intriguing.

Anna Zordan was initially perceived as an oversimplified imitation of Peter O'Donnell's Modesty Blaise (see separate reference). However, it has been fully documented in retrospect that Eastwood's operative ambitiously rivaled agent Blaise in the field, especially in terms of plot and narrative pace. In contrast to O'Donnell's comic-oriented themes, Eastwood established a tense line of realism.

Ms. Zordan faced the Chi-Coms in her first two assignments, The Chinese Visitor (1965) and Little Dragon from Peking (1967).

In The Chinese Visitor a list containing the names of prominent international military, political, scientific, and media figures marked for assassination turned up in London. Sarratt assigned Anna Zordan to investigate the multiple threat under the cover identities of actress and senator's daughter.

Anna eventually allied with a man identified as Edwin Steiner, leader of a fanatically anti-Communist organization. It was here that the full significance of the Hagmann incident was revealed.

Sarratt's key agent then unmasked a scheme calculated to create an atmosphere of global suspicion at the highest levels of governments from the capitals of Europe to Peking. The termination of H'an Yang, a pro-Western Chinese diplomat, provided the crucial link between the assassination list and a devastating plot that harbored the threat of a nuclear war.

While Ms. Zordan admirably displayed her sexual and athletic abilities in The Chinese Visitor, Sarratt extended her training to include the following:

1) The detection and use of hidden microphones, transmitters, explosives, and booby-traps.

2) Languages.

3) Advanced self-defense techniques.

4) Methods of jail escape.

Eastwood magnified the theme of Chi-Com domination in Little Dragon from Peking in which Anna penetrated an exclusive Aegean resort to investigate the grisly death of a German chemist. The resort was managed by the Zimmerman family, whom Sarratt categorized as arrogantly Neo-Nazi in both the military and political spheres.

Anna's perilous foray into the restricted sexual and material pleasures of the privileged led to the discovery of a Chi-Com plot to hijack a transcontinental plane and arm it with a nuclear bomb—a "little dragon from Peking."

In Little Dragon from Peking Eastwood brought into the plot several contentious political elements besides the Nazis and the Chi-Coms, notably the Soviets, East Germans, and Syrians. This operative action intensified Eastwood's scope of the Cold War.

Eastwood dramatically altered that focus in Diamonds Are Deadly (1969) in which he probed the chaotic political climate in England during the late sixties: A sequence of violent events throughout England prompted Sarratt to launch Anna Zordan into this explosive sector.

The chilling effect of live-television coverage of the incidents and the theft of twelve scripts for a new spy program figured in Zordan's disturbingly realistic mission.

SUMMARY: Anna Zordan challenged Modesty Blaise with topical plots and a suspenseful progression that compared favorably to Ian Fleming (see separate reference) and his imitators.

It was 1967, however, before the Zordan thrillers appeared in paperback, a year which portended the inevitable decline of the

spy genre. Consequently Eastwood forfeited a well-deserved following to the more flamboyant dossier of Peter O'Donnell (see separate reference).

STATUS: The presence of the Chi-Coms in The Chinese Visitor and
Little Dragon from Peking reduces the possibility of a reissue mis-
sion for Anna Zordan. However, in the event that one Modesty
Blaise resurfaces in the field, it would be highly recommended that
Ms. Zordan also be recalled for competitive duty. SOP.

FIELD BIBLIOGRAPHY

Eastwood, James. The Chinese Visitor. New York: Coward-
    McCann, 1965; New York: Dell paperback, 1967. HB-R.

_____. Come Die with Me. British hardback title for Diamonds
    Are Deadly. HB. See also Come Die with Me in Appendix I.

_____. Diamonds Are Deadly. New York: McKay, 1969. HB-
    R. See also Diamonds Are Deadly in Appendix I.

_____. Little Dragon from Peking. New York: Coward-
    McCann, 1967. HB-R. See also Seduce and Destroy.

_____. Seduce and Destroy. New York: Dell paperback, 1968.
    R. General paperback title for Little Dragon from Peking.

CONSULT APPENDIX I FOR SERIES CONTINUATION

END OF CWF 23

† CWF 24. THE FAWCETT INTELLIGENCE GROUP †

CONTENTS: Fawcett Books contributed more to the sixties spy
novel than any other paperback publisher. Still in existence today,
the F. I. G. consists of two major imprints, Gold Medal and Crest.

GOLD MEDAL (PBO): The constituents adhering to this faction
symbolized the development of the paperback secret agent.

    Edward Aarons initiated the archetypal Cold-War paperback
operative with his Sam Durell dossier, beginning with Assignment
to Disaster (1955). Although the Sam Durell "Assignment" series
displayed enough plot diversion to reflect the ambiguities of the

Cold War, the continuous designation of "Assignment" on each
Aarons docket created the impression of formularization in some
intelligence sectors.

The appearance in 1955 of Stephen Marlowe's Chester Drum
in The Second Longest Night tested the novelty of a spy series related in the first person. However, it wasn't until Matt Helm entered the field in 1960 with Death of a Citizen and The Wrecking
Crew that the use of the first person narrative in the secret-agent
genre began to realize its full potential.

The inventiveness of Donald Hamilton's Matt Helm series
generally shaped the structure of subsequent Gold Medal entries in
the F. I. G. and the paperback-spy-original genre as a whole. The
lean style of the Helm missions is reflected in that of the later
members, notably Philip Atlee's Joe Gall series and Dan J. Marlowe's Earl Drake thrillers.

The distribution of Death of a Citizen and The Wrecking Crew
in 1960 signified a major development in the evolution of the paperback spy original, for Matt Helm personified the Cold War operative, and yet Donald Hamilton conceived his protagonist with the
cynicism of the Hammett-style private detective.

The introduction in The Green Wound (1963) of Philip Atlee's
Joe Gall, known in the field as the "Nullifier," advanced the paperback spy original even further. Atlee's grim characterizations and
taut style provided the foundation for the avenger category of paperback hero that would dominate the action market during the seventies,
as typified by Don Pendleton's Mac Bolan and his imitators.

However, it should be noted that Donald Hamilton actually
generated the cell for Atlee's conception in Death of a Citizen in
which Matt Helm was transformed from a peaceful man into an instrument of violence.

Dan Marlowe's Earl Drake started in the paperback field
more as a crime figure than a secret agent. Introduced as Chet
Arnold in The Name of the Game Is Death (1962), he was transformed into series character Drake in 1969 with One Endless Hour
and Operation Fireball.

Thereafter the Drake missions generally honored the "Operation" prefix and contained many elements of the generic espionage
format. However, the plots often challenged those of the avenger
genre, appearing at regular intervals throughout the seventies.

Further, Neil MacNeil's The Spy Catchers (1966), a relevant
Cold War thriller concerning the menacing penetration of a top-
security intelligence complex, was also a Gold Medal title.

Although MacNeil's series involved a crack team of adven-
turers, Tony Costaine and Bert McCall, The Spy Catchers was the
only spy insert in the paperback-original feature.

The F. I. G. also sponsored Peter Rabe's Manny deWitt intrigue series, consisting of three Gold Medal entries.

CREST(R): Crest is strictly a reprint line. The two chief constituents of this segment, John Gardner and Peter O'Donnell, penned novels that were generally regarded as secret agent parodies: respectively, the Boysie Oakes and Modesty Blaise books. During the sixties each series was represented by three titles under the Crest banner.

Several more serious spy works also displayed the Crest stamp, notably Len Deighton's The Ipcress File (1962) and the following non-series thrillers by James Hall Roberts: The Q Document (1964) and The February Plan (1966).

While The Ipcress File has appeared under the Ballantine imprint in recent years, the Roberts entries have long since vanished from the field.

Most of the aforementioned Gold Medal and Crest principals can be cross-referenced under their matching files. This excludes the efforts of Neil MacNeil and James Hall Roberts, neither subject to examination here. (It might be mentioned that Neil MacNeil and James Hall Roberts served as the cover identities for W. Todhunter Ballard and Robert L. Duncan, respectively.)

Today only the missions of Matt Helm and Sam Durell remain in active F. I. G. distribution, comprising both Cold War era and post-1969 entries.

The Helm thrillers have survived into the eighties, with nineteen extant titles. Although Edward S. Aarons died in 1975, his Durell books have been subject to constant rotation while additions to the popular series have been authored by Will B. Aarons.

In the broader realm of Cold War spy and action fiction, the works of Helen MacInnes and Alistair MacLean were reprinted by Fawcett during the period and have continued under the Crest line to the present day.

The F. I. G. also sponsored several visual-project tie-ins, enumerated in a selective bibliography at the conclusion of this CWF evaluation.

FIELD VISUAL PROJECT BIBLIOGRAPHY

The dates listed here refer to project release and not to original publication.

Deighton, Len. The Ipcress File. New York: Fawcett-Crest paperback, 1965. R. MT.

Gardner, John. The Liquidator. New York: Fawcett-Crest paperback, 1966. R. MT.

Hamilton, Donald. The Ambushers. New York: Fawcett-Gold
Medal, 1967. PBO. MT.

_____. Murderers' Row. New York: Fawcett-Gold Medal, 1966.
PBO. MT.

_____. The Silencers. New York: Fawcett-Gold Medal, 1966.
PBO. MT.

_____. The Wrecking Crew. New York: Fawcett-Gold Medal,
1969. PBO. MT.

O'Donnell, Peter. Modesty Blaise. New York: Fawcett-Crest paperback, 1966. R. MT.

END OF CWF 24

† CWF 25. FLEMING, IAN †

BACKGROUND: Ian Lancaster Fleming was born in 1908 in London;
son of Major Valentine Fleming, conservative member of Parlia-
ment, and Evelyn Beatrice (St. Croix Rose) Fleming.

Educated at Eton, the Royal Military Academy at Sandhurst,
and the universities of Munich and Geneva.

After failing to qualify for the diplomatic service, Fleming
became a foreign correspondent with Reuters News Agency. In
1933 he was dispatched to Moscow to cover the shocking trial involving six British engineers who had been arrested on espionage
charges by the Soviet O. G. P. U.

Although the engineering firm of Metropolitan-Vickers was
one of the most prestigious of its kind in England, Fleming's account of the trial focused on the Soviet system of justice and its
relationship to a major Western power. On the basis of this assignment, Fleming earned a reputation in the global news world as
a tough, uncompromising journalist who possessed an almost mad-
dening penchant for detail.

Fleming elected to leave Reuters in 1933 and entered the
merchant banking field in the City, securing a position with the
firm of Cull & Company in Bishopgate. Two years later Fleming
joined the elite stockbroking concern of Rowe & Pitman, where he
eventually became a junior partner.

During his six years in the business sector, Fleming cultivated a book collection which focused on the achievements of human
progress.

In the spring of 1939 Fleming was ostensibly assigned to
Moscow as a foreign correspondent for the London Times. He was,
however, secretly acting as an "agent-in-place" for the Foreign Office. Fleming was selected as the personal assistant to Admiral
John Godfrey, the newly appointed Director of Naval Intelligence,
and was given the full rank of Lieutenant, R. N. V. R.

Assigned to the now-infamous Room 39 in the Admiralty,
Fleming was responsible for a number of crucial intelligence duties,
including 1) The indoctrination of field agents; 2) the interrogation
of enemy operatives; 3) the deciphering of codes; and 4) the topo-
graphical interpretation of enemy territories.

During this period Fleming organized and controlled the Number 30 Assault Unit, a crack outfit of 300 Royal Commandos whose
missions were often carried out in perilous sectors of Nazi territory.
It often has been postulated that James Bond was based in part on
the archetypal British commando.

The year 1941 proved to be auspicious in the well-ordered
evolution of James Bond, for two events occurred which eventually
would influence Fleming's conception of Secret Agent 007.

First, Fleming confronted several German agents at the daring game of chemin de fer. The place: the fashionable Estoril
Casino in Portugal. Fleming's defeat--even after acquiring additional funds--has been irrefutably documented as the basis for
Bond's "official" contest with one LeChiffre, a paymaster for the
Soviet espionage network called S. M. E. R. S. H. , at Royale-Les-Eaux
in 1951. That game, however, was baccarat.

Second, Fleming studied the career of a malicious Nazi officer named Otto Skorzeny, who had been involved on the command
level with the German assault on Crete in 1941. In addition to
utilizing this notion for his Number 30 unit, Fleming stored Skorzeny's flamboyant appearance in his memory, retrieving it when he
conceived Sir Hugo Drax, 007's megalomaniacal nemesis in Moonraker (1955).

Fleming was not decorated for his wartime service and he
subsequently became foreign manager of the Kemsley Newspaper
Syndicate.

In 1952 Fleming married Lady Anne Rothemere in Port
Maria, Jamaica. Casino Royale, the first James Bond thriller,
was published a year later. The Flemings had one son, Caspar,
who died in 1974.

The 007 books achieved instant success in Britain, but the

American acceptance of James Bond was slow in coming. It wasn't until President John F. Kennedy revealed his interest in the Bond novels in a 1961 Life magazine article that the 007 phenomenon took hold in the United States.

Two years later the release of the first 007 visual project, Dr. No, starring Sean Connery as James Bond, served to intensify the Fleming movement in the United States.

As well as producing one Bond book a year at his Jamaican retreat, Goldeneye, until his death in 1964, Fleming authored two non-fiction books, The Diamond Smugglers (1957) and Thrilling Cities (1963), and one children's story, Chitty Chitty Bang Bang (1964).

The critical reaction to 007 was sharply divided on both sides of the Atlantic. Fleming's most passionate advocate was Kingsley Amis (see separate reference) whose The James Bond Dossier (1965) is still regarded as the definitive defense of the Bond series. Further, mystery writer Raymond Chandler and New York Post commentator Max Lerner consistently lauded Fleming's books.

The opposition to Bond was no less fervent, however. The late Anthony Boucher, who reigned as the authoritative suspense critic for the New York Times until his death in 1968, and spy novelist John le Carré (see separate reference) made no secret of their contempt for Bond and Fleming.

However, the biggest controversy of Fleming's career coincided in time with the Kennedy comment in 1961. Irish producer Kevin McClory filed a lawsuit against Fleming on the grounds of copyright infringement regarding the use of certain material in the eighth James Bond novel, Thunderball (1961).

McClory alleged that Fleming openly derived specific plot and character elements for Thunderball from the screenplay of a proposed visual project, James Bond: Secret Agent, on which McClory collaborated with Fleming and veteran writer Jack Whittingham during 1958-59.

It was 1963 before a final decision was made in the case, the visual-project rights being awarded to McClory. McClory allied with regular Bond producers Albert R. Broccoli and Harry Saltzman for the visual-project adaptation of Thunderball (1965), starring Sean Connery as 007. The visual effort accumulated the largest box-office volume of the early Bond projects and retained this distinction into the seventies.

Tragically, Ian Fleming died too soon to enjoy the fruit of his efforts--the 007 boom of the mid-sixties, which profoundly influenced the espionage fiction of the period, especially in the paperback sector.

The Bond surge began to wane in 1968, but its popularity, though considerably diminished, has continued to the present day in the form of the perennial visual-project series and the continuation of the 007 dossier--by Kingsley Amis, using the cover identity of Robert Markham for <u>Colonel Sun</u> (1968), and, more recently, by John Gardner in <u>License Renewed</u> (1981) and <u>For Special Services</u> (1982). (See separate references Amis and Gardner.)

It is well known that several of the Fleming-Bond books achieved global bestseller status, and, pursuant to 007's unprecedented paperback bonanza during the mid-sixties, the late Ian Fleming symbolized the efforts of the N.A.L./Signet Intelligence Group (see separate reference), although he was not an official member.

Many of his devoted followers feel that Fleming will never be equaled in the spy genre, believing, as Kingsley Amis concluded in <u>The James Bond Dossier</u>, "He leaves no heirs."

CWF AGENT: Bond, James.

CWF HISTORY: Born in Wattenschied, Germany, on November 11, 1920, to a Scottish father, Andrew Bond, and a Swiss mother, Monique Delacroix.

Andrew Bond was a foreign representative for the Metropolitan-Vickers Electrical Company and simultaneously associated with the Allied Military government. Therefore the Bond family traveled extensively during the twenties and early thirties.

Bond's parents were killed in a climbing accident in the Aiguilles Rogues near Chamonix in 1931. Shortly thereafter Bond was given into the custody of his aunt, Charmian Bond, who lived in Kent, England. Bond had an elder brother, Henry.

In the fall of 1933 Bond gained admission into Eton but was dismissed two years later for an alleged sexual encounter. He then entered his father's old school, Fettes, for a brief stay, but by the age of 16, he had migrated to the University of Geneva where two incidents occurred which affected his future profession, at least in terms of the legendary reputation which would eventually be his.

On the Aiguilli de Midi ski run near Chamonix, Bond discovered the passion of competitive skiing, a sport which was to figure in his postwar occupation.

More importantly, Bond's association with the notorious Marthe de Brandt, the daughter of a judge and distinguished courtesan, attracted the "official" attention of the British Secret Service.

Acquiring a fortune by the age of 25, de Brandt opened an exclusive establishment in Paris which catered to the desires of

jaded males among the privileged and the powerful. It was later
revealed that Marthe de Brandt utilized this pleasure spot as a
cover for her true profession an an ambitious yet ruthless spy in
the pay of the British Secret Service.

Ms. de Brandt was immediately attracted to young James
Bond when he first visited Paris in 1937, and she educated him in
the arts of sophistication and seduction. They traveled everywhere
together, from the races at Le Mans to the elegant passions of Le
Boeuf sur le Toit.

Bond was approached that summer by a man named Maddox
who officially represented himself as a military attaché with the
British Embassy in Paris. Unofficially, Maddox informed Bond that
he was aware of his relationship with Marthe de Brandt--and that
she had become a Nazi agent.

Maddox, representing the British Secret Service, gave Bond
his first mission: liquidate Marthe de Brandt.

While on an otherwise pleasant motor holiday in the French
countryside, Bond jammed the accelerator, causing the car to plunge
into the river. The incident accomplished Bond's assignment, and
the impact of the accident produced the now-familiar three-inch scar,
which figured in his recorded description:

"Height: 183 centimetres; weight: 76 kilograms; slim build;
eyes: blue; hair: black; scar down right cheek and on left shoulder;
signs of plastic surgery on back of right hand; all-round athlete; expert pistol shot, boxer, knife-thrower; does not use disguises. Languages: French and German. Smokes heavily (N. B.: special
Turkish-Balkan cigarettes, with three gold bands, specially made by
Morlands of Grosvenor Street); vices; drink, specifically, a dry vodka martini, shaken and not stirred, and women. Not thought to accept bribes." (From Russia, With Love, Ch. 6.)*

Maddox initiated Bond into the basic training regimen of the
British Secret Service, including a rigorous course on casino techniques instructed by one Steffi Esposito, an American gambling expert. Bond was then assigned to join a party of Roumanians at the
casino in Monte Carlo for a game of baccarat. Bond was, of
course, expected to defeat the group, headed by a man known only
as Vlacek. To this end, Esposito taught Bond an exercise called
"The Luminous Reader." This event seasoned Bond as a professional gambler, and it was also during this time that Bond met
René Mathis, with whom he would ally on two postwar assignments.

Throughout World War II, Bond served with the Ministry of
Defense, achieving the full rank of Commander, R. N. V. R.

*From Russia, With Love by Ian Fleming. (© 1957 Glidrose Pro-
ductions Ltd.) Reprinted by permission of Macmillan and Co.,
Jonathan Cape, Ltd.

In 1946 Bond was encouraged to submit an application for postwar service in the Ministry of Defense. It was here that Bond met "M," otherwise known as Admiral (later Sir) Miles Messervy, who would become his chief. By the early fifties Bond had secured the designation of 007, the "00" signifying his license to kill in the line of duty.

Bond was married briefly to Comtesse Teresa di Vicenzo, the half-English, half-Corsican daughter of Marc-Ange Draco, the ruthless czar of the Union Corse, a powerful Corsican crime syndicate. Bond encountered the Comtesse, whom he affectionally called Tracy, at Royale-Les-Eaux in 1961, and in 1962 they were married by the British Consul. On the day of her wedding Tracy was brutally murdered by an assassin in a passing Maserati on the Autobahn. Bond recognized the assailant and avenged Tracy's death while on a mission in Japan in 1963.

Agent 007 worked efficiently with allied intelligence units, principally the C.I.A. and the French Deuxième Bureau, in which the aforementioned René Mathis was employed. When engaged in American territory, Bond often operated with C.I.A. agent Felix Leiter, who subsequently became a member of Pinkerton's. Full details under OPERATIVE DATA.

Despite the publicity which followed James Bond during the sixties--Ian Fleming's bestselling-author status, multi-million-dollar merchandising campaigns, and extensive literary and pictorial coverage in Playboy that resulted from the early visual projects--Agent 007 has maintained his effectiveness in the field and is currently on active duty with the British Secret Service.

Officially, the "00" section was abolished in the late seventies. Secretly, Bond's status was renewed in 1980 by "M," who is still head of the British Secret Service. Headquarters for the British Secret Service remain situated in an obscure grey building near Regent's Park in London. (Until 1965 the cover for the intelligence apparat was Universal Export; for security reasons it was changed to Transworld Consortium; in 1980 it became Transworld Export.)

Bond's use of field weapons will be examined more fully under OPERATIVE DATA, but he has been known to carry a knife strapped to his left forearm and to employ steel-capped shoes.

OPERATIVE DATA: Ian Fleming developed a formula for his James Bond novels, meticulously conceived over the years. In most of the early Bond books, 007 was assigned to penetrate S.M.E.R.S.H., the Soviet espionage network. For instance, in Casino Royale (1953) he was ordered to defeat LeChiffre, identified as paymaster for S.M.E.R.S.H., in a baccarat game at the elite Royale-Les-Eaux casino.

In this first Bond novel, Fleming introduced three key elements which would eventually define the 007 format:

1) The menacing villain (such as LeChiffre).

2) The beautiful "femme fatale" (such as field agent Vesper Lynd).

3) The careful attention to the fine art of gambling. This fascination with detail would be applied to other areas of expertise in future entries.

Casino Royale can be credited with establishing Bond's assured, sophisticated character, especially his knowledge of gambling and culinary arts.

Felix Leiter and René Mathis were also introduced in this book, as were office personnel Bill Tanner, M's Chief-of-Staff, and Miss Moneypenny, M's dutiful secretary.

Further, it was disclosed in Casino Royale that Bond kept a .38 Colt Police Positive under his pillow at night while his earliest field weapon was recorded as a .25 Beretta.

Live and Let Die (1954) depicted 007 at his most ruthless as he dispatched into a shark pit an enemy agent known only as "The Robber."

Bond's motive--vengeance: "The Robber" had performed the same action against C.I.A. operative Leiter, inflicting permanent loss of the American agent's right hand.

In Live and Let Die Fleming more fully delineated the avaricious quality of Bond's nemesis. Buonaparte Ignace Gallia, a.k.a. Mr. Big, was building a Soviet spy network in the U.S., manipulating his own crime syndicate, from Harlem to the Florida Keys to the Caribbean.

Mr. Big's Haitian background generated some adverse racial reaction when the book was initially published because the S.M.E.R.S.H. master spy utilized the inner core of the "Negro world" to achieve the objectives of the Kremlin on U.S. soil. It was also revealed that Mr. Big was head of the Black Widow Voodoo Cult; he was believed to be the zombie of Baron Samedi, the Prince of Darkness.

A captivating Haitian woman, using the names of Solitaire and Simone Latrelle, betrayed Mr. Big to come to Bond's aid on a treacherous trail that stretched from New York to the paradisiacal waters of Jamaica where they faced torturous death by keel-hauling on Mr. Big's yacht, the Secatur.

Bond was assisted in Jamaican territory by the head of Station C, Strangways, and a Cayman Islander identified only as Quarrel.

Agent 007 successfully completed this perilous mission, which added two important elements (both of which figured in later entries) to the structure of the series:

1) The exotic locale of Jamaica.

2) Agent 007's proficiency at underwater techniques, employed to infiltrate Mr. Big's island, the Isle of Surprise.

In Moonraker (1955) Fleming intensified the malevolent character and ambitions of Bond's adversary to such an extent that Sir Hugo Drax's scheme to destroy London with an atomic rocket was indicative of the scope of later blueprints for destruction, notably Doctor No (1958), Goldfinger (1959), and Thunderball (1961).

In this respect, Moonraker evolved as the archetypal 007 novel, influencing most of the later books and the popular visual-project series.

Bond's gambling acumen was displayed as he unmasked the cheating activities of Sir Hugo Drax, a renowned British industrialist, at London's exclusive men's club, called Blades. The game: bridge.

It is well known that Drax used his global resources to build "Moonraker," the super-atomic rocket that would protect England from annihilation.

Diamonds Are Forever (1956), characterized by a conspicuous lack of the spectacular elements which marked Live and Let Die and Moonraker, ranked as one of 007's least intriguing missions.

Posing as a minor-league diamond smuggler, Bond was assigned to ally with the provocative Tiffany Case to eliminate a smuggling pipeline that extended from French Guinea to Las Vegas.

Upon encountering Felix Leiter near the House of Diamonds in New York, 007 learned that he was now employed by Pinkerton's. Both agents were interested in the illicit activities of the ruthless Spangled Mob, which included global diamond smuggling.

Despite Fleming's effective use of graphic locales in Diamonds Are Forever, especially the passages involving casino life in Las Vegas and the tension of the Saratoga race track, many field operatives felt that the absence of a megalomaniacal menace sacrificed the promise of the plot. However, Bond challenged two of his most sadistic opponents in Diamonds Are Forever, notably two "torpedos" known as "Wint" and "Kidd."

From Russia, With Love (1957) is still acknowledged as 007's most realistic mission, as Fleming departed from what appeared to be his formula.

The lure of the coveted Spektor decoding machine persuaded "M" to send 007 to Istanbul to work with the enticing Tatiana Romanova, a clerk attached to the Turkish capital's Soviet embassy, in order to obtain the deciphering device and transport it to England. Ms. Romanova claimed that she was in love with Bond, and desired exile in England.

It is well known that 007's "mission" was an integral part of a S. M. E. R. S. H. conspiracy to liquidate Bond in a fashion that would have humiliated the British Secret Service.

The key participants were 1) Kronsteen: Soviet master chess player, known as "The Wizard of Ice." Head of the Planning Department of S. M. E. R. S. H.; 2) Rosa Klebb: the barbarous head of Otydel II, Operations and Executions branch of S. M. E. R. S. H.; and 3) Donovan "Red" Grant: Renegade Irish assassin, Chief Executioner for S. M. E. R. S. H.

Fleming slowly unveiled the dimensions of his plot as 007 and Tatiana faced Grant on a treacherous train journey from Istanbul to London. Like the novel itself, Bond's savage battle with Grant on the "Orient Express" transpired as a major development in the 007 dossier.

The achievements of "Q" Branch were heightened in From Russia, With Love, for Bond was supplied with an "overnight bag," which was equipped with: 1) fifty rounds of .25 ammunition; 2) two flat throwing knives; 3) a cyanide death pill; 4) fifty gold sovereigns; and 5) a silencer for his Beretta.

M's agent in Istanbul, the enigmatic Darko Kerim, who had controlled Station T since before World War II, emerged as 007's most potent ally.

Even with John Gardner's satisfying additions to the Bond series, many operatives remain adamant in their opinion that From Russia, With Love is the best of the 007 canon.

The beginning of Doctor No (1958) concerned 007's recovery from his grueling encounter with Rosa Klebb during the climax of From Russia, With Love, in which the Soviet spy chief injected him with a toxic "fugu" poison.

In this instance, 007's defensive inadequacy warranted the following changes in his field weaponry: 1) A 7. 65 Walther PPK, to be deployed as 007's main field weapon, and 2) A Smith & Wesson Centennial Airweight .38 revolver, to be used for long-range work.

The deaths of Strangways and his secretary, Mary Trueblood, prompted "M" to dispatch 007 to Jamaica to investigate. Aided by Quarrel and the sensuous Honeychile Rider, Bond trekked into Crab

Key, the desolate island of Dr. Julius No, where he unmasked a
Soviet-backed plan directed against the communication capabilities
of U.S. rockets.

Doctor No is credited with the inception of the Bond phenomenon, derived principally from the following elements:

1) The devastating dimensions of Dr. No's blueprint, and its
   implications, considering the proximity of Crab Key to U.S.
   territory.

2) Bond's calculated manipulation of Honeychile Rider throughout
   the mission.

3) The sadistic nature of Dr. No, who submitted 007 to a horrifying survival test. Also, Quarrel was killed during the
   course of 007's mission. The Cayman Islander was literally
   scorched to death by a mobile flame thrower.

4) Dr. No's Eurasian background, specifically a mixed Chinese-
   German origin, suggested an arrogant betrayal of the Chi-Com
   cause to serve Russia.

Goldfinger (1959) requires little examination; its notoriety has
gradually fashioned it as the culmination of the series.

Auric Goldfinger's plot to plunder Fort Knox was perceived
as a magnification of Sir Hugo Drax's atomic machinations in Moonraker. In a similar vein, Goldfinger's cheating patterns in the game
of Canasta were derivative of Drax's activities at Blades.

Fleming's resourceful use of locales in Miami, Geneva, London, and Fort Knox, as well as detailed focus on Bond's golf contest with Goldfinger, displayed his narrative talent in its purest form.

The presence of Pussy Galore, a lesbian gangster whose
Harlem gang joined Goldfinger's crime consortium for the Fort Knox
operation, sharpened 007's manipulative talents.

To shadow Goldfinger across Europe, 007 was provided with
an Aston-Martin D. B. III motor car which included, among other
defensive refinements, a Colt .45 hidden in a trick compartment
under the driver's seat.

Despite all its strengths, however, Goldfinger has never been
regarded in the same light as From Russia, With Love and Doctor
No, and certainly not on a par with Moonraker.

For Your Eyes Only (1960), which consists of five short
stories, offered some of Fleming's finest writing.

In "From a View to a Kill" a S. H. A. P. E. dispatch rider
was eliminated, and 007 was sent to S. H. A. P. E. headquarters in

Versailles to circumvent the assassination plot. Well-known in most intelligence sectors, the acronym S. H. A. P. E. signifies Supreme Headquarters Allied Powers Europe.

The death of the Havelocks, a prominent British couple residing in Jamaica, motivated "M" to avenge their savage murders in "For Your Eyes Only." Bond was allied with the couple's vindictive daughter, Judy, as he tracked the killers--an ex-Gestapo agent, identified as one Von Hammerstein, and his Cuban hit-man, Major Gonzales.

Agent 007 was equipped with a Savage 99F rifle, complete with a Weatherby 6 x 62 scope, while Ms. Havelock was armed with bow and arrow.

In "Risico" 007's mission involving the global drug trade in Rome emerged as one of his most challenging assignments. Briefly, Agent 007 found it difficult to discern the identity of the Redland conspirator: perhaps Kristatos, a notorious double agent with strong ties to the C. I. A., or perhaps a ruthless yet charming international smuggler named Enrico Colombo.

These three short entries were adapted by Fleming from outlines he had prepared for a proposed James Bond television series for CBS in the late fifties. Excluding "From a View to a Kill," these stories were in fact used as the basis for the 1981 James Bond visual project, For Your Eyes Only, starring Roger Moore as 007.

The two remaining entries, "Quantum of Solace" and "The Hildebrand Rarity," initially appeared in Cosmopolitan and Playboy, respectively.

Thunderball (1961) was the first Bond book to feature S. P. E. C. T. R. E. and its maniacal master, Ernst Stavro Blofeld. Representing the Special Executive for Counterintelligence, Terrorism, Revenge, and Extortion, Blofeld initially controlled his espionage syndicate from 136 bis Boulevard Haussmann, Paris.

Blofeld deployed S. P. E. C. T. R. E. strategist Emilio Largo, a native Sicilian with an international reputation in café society, to execute Plan Omega: the theft of two atomic bombs from a N. A. T. O. bomber identified as the Vindicator, and a blackmail scheme aimed at the Western nuclear global powers.

Designated "Operation Thunderball" by The Ministry of Defense, 007 was sent to Nassau to pursue M's theory concerning the hijacking. Assisted by Felix Leiter, who had been drafted back into the C. I. A., Bond commanded a full-scale underwater counteroffensive against Largo to recover the bombs, before they could be activated to destroy an American city.

Initially, however, it was imperative for 007 and Leiter to

discover the significance of Largo's hydrofoil yacht, the Disco Volante, and his ambitious treasure-hunt endeavor.

Fleming intensified Bond's prowess as a gambler with an intriguing chemin de fer contest against Largo at the exclusive Nassau Casino. Further, 007's feverish battle with the treacherous S. P. E. C. T. R. E. agent, Count Lippe, at a British health spa in the opening chapters of Thunderball ranked among the best of the series.

Punctuated by a plethora of brand names and factual attention to the details of scuba lore, Thunderball has remained an excellent 007 entry, despite Fleming's two-year contention with Kevin McClory over the visual-project rights.

With the exception of On Her Majesty's Secret Service (1963), the later Bond novels paled in comparison to the earlier thrillers.

Narrated by a young French-Canadian woman, Vivienne Michel, The Spy Who Loved Me (1962) recounted 007's rescue of Ms. Michel from two hoodlums at a resort motel in the Adirondacks. This was the only Bond book in which the usual trappings of Fleming's format were absent, and, for this reason, many field operatives dismissed The Spy Who Loved Me as the weakest entry in the series.

In On Her Majesty's Secret Service, 007 unmasked an insidious S. P. E. C. T. R. E. blueprint involving biological warfare.

Posing as one Sir Hilary Bray, a distinguished genealogist from London's College of Arms, Bond penetrated Blofeld's alpine stronghold in the Swiss Alps, Piz Gloria, to verify the S. P. E. C. T. R. E. master's claim to the title of a French nobleman, Comte de Bleuville.

The best chapters depicted 007's daring ski escape from Piz Gloria and his later helicopter assault on the S. P. E. C. T. R. E. command center, aided by Tracy's father, Marc-Ange Draco.

Bond's relationship with Tracy was recollected in On Her Majesty's Secret Service. While Blofeld's murderous aide, Irma Bunt, initially appeared as a villain in the mold of Rosa Klebb, her actions depicted her as a slick imitation of Goldfinger's fanatical Korean manservant, Oddjob.

By the time You Only Live Twice (1964) appeared, readers and critics alike believed that Fleming's sensationalism had reached unacceptable limits. Assigned to an important mission in Japan, which involved a crucial defense document recorded as Magic 44, 007 eventually encountered Blofeld and Irma Bunt, and avenged Tracy's death.

You Only Live Twice was hindered by a travelogue approach to the plot and Blofeld's demented vision of himself as a samurai warrior. The former S. P. E. C. T. R. E. chief was obsessed with luring any vulnerable Japanese citizen to an honorable death in an exotic garden.

Elements from Diamonds Are Forever and Goldfinger were reprised in the posthumous The Man with the Golden Gun (1965). In this entry, 007 challenged Scaramanga, a free-lance Cuban assassin armed with a gold-plated Colt .45, who was embroiled in a K.G.B. plot to sabotage Western business interests in the Caribbean.

Apart from Scaramanga's fetish with guns, The Man with the Golden Gun had little to recommend it as a genuine 007 thriller.

Octopussy and the Living Daylights (1966), another Fleming collection, maintained the pace and style of For Your Eyes Only.

The original volume offered "Octopussy" and "The Living Daylights," which were initially published in Playboy and Argosy, respectively. Another Playboy entry, "The Property of a Lady" was added to the 1967 Signet paperback edition.

In "Octopussy" Bond was sent to Jamaica on a "nostalgic" mission: to contact Major Dexter Smythe (O.B.E.), a former Royal Marine intelligence officer, and "recollect" certain treacherous acts committed during World War II, chiefly the illicit acquisition of a valuable cache of Nazi gold.

Fleming conveyed a haunting quality in this entry, contrasting Major Smythe's fond reminiscences with a chilling incident about climbing a perilous Austrian peak. The activities of the Foo brothers, a pair of shrewd export-import merchants who were literally masters of the Chinese colony in Jamaica, were adroitly fused into the principal plot.

Within the context of the Nazi-gold segment, Fleming's commentary on the currency movements in Macao and Tangier and on the Bretton Woods Convention masterfully displayed what Kingsley Amis (see separate reference) once termed "the Fleming effect." Further, Fleming's hypnotic portrayal of Major Smythe's savage and bizarre death developed into one of his most electrifying presentations.

"The Living Daylights," punctuated by a strong line of tension and topicality, concerned 007's assignment of liquidation in Cold-War-ravaged Berlin. For this mission Bond was equipped with 1) the .308 International Experimental Target Rifle, 2) a pair of binoculars, 3) a microphone, and 4) a black velvet hood. (This entry originally appeared in Argosy as "Berlin Escape.")

SUMMARY: Ian Fleming's James Bond series inspired the super-agent genre of the sixties, and its unique elements continue to influence both fictional and visual projects involving espionage themes.

Although estimates vary, the Bond books have reportedly generated global sales exceeding 42,000,000.

The contents of the James Bond visual projects, recognized as the most successful series in contemporary history, have become legendary. This file will simply note the completed 007 projects, indicating the agent who played Bond in each entry:

Dr. No (1962--Britain; 1963--U.S., United Artists), Sean Connery.

From Russia, With Love (1963--Britain; 1964--U.S., United Artists), Sean Connery.

Goldfinger (1964--United Artists), Sean Connery.

Thunderball (1965--United Artists), Sean Connery.

Casino Royale (1967--Columbia), David Niven.

You Only Live Twice (1967--United Artists), Sean Connery.

On Her Majesty's Secret Service (1969--United Artists), George Lazenby.

Diamonds Are Forever (1971--United Artists), Sean Connery.

Live and Let Die (1973--United Artists), Roger Moore.

The Man with the Golden Gun (1974--United Artists), Roger Moore.

The Spy Who Loved Me (1977--United Artists), Roger Moore.

Moonraker (1979--United Artists), Roger Moore.

For Your Eyes Only (1981--United Artists), Roger Moore.

Octopussy (1983--United Artists), Roger Moore.

STATUS: Although the paperback distribution of the James Bond dossier has been erratic, Agent 007 remains a viable force in the present espionage market.

It is expected that by the summer of 1983 all of the Ian Fleming entries will be available in paperback editions, distributed by New American Library and Berkley Books.

For additional information on the various Fleming biographies and commentaries, the field operative is advised to consult Jon Breen's Edgar-winning reference guide, What About Murder? (Scarecrow Press, 1981). SSP.

FIELD BIBLIOGRAPHY

Fleming, Ian Bonded Fleming. New York: Viking Press, 1965.
HB. Omnibus Edition: For Your Eyes Only, The Spy Who
Loved Me, and Thunderball.

_____. Casino Royale. London: Jonathan Cape, 1953; New
York: Macmillan, 1954; New York: New American Library
paperback, 1960. See also You Asked For It. HB-HB-R-R.

_____. Diamonds Are Forever. New York: Macmillan, 1956;
New York: Perma Books paperback, 1957; New York: New
American Library paperback, 1961. HB-R-R.

_____. Doctor No. New York: Macmillan, 1958; New York:
New American Library paperback, 1959. HB-R.

_____. For Your Eyes Only. New York: Viking Press, 1960;
New York: New American Library paperback, 1961. HB-R.

_____. From Russia, With Love. New York: Macmillan, 1957;
New York: New American Library paperback, 1958. HB-R.

_____. Gilt-Edged Bonds. New York: Macmillan, 1961. HB.
Omnibus Edition: Casino Royale, Doctor No, and From Russia,
With Love.

_____. Goldfinger. New York: Macmillan, 1959; New York:
New American Library paperback, 1960. HB-R.

_____. Live and Let Die. London: Jonathan Cape, 1954; New
York: Macmillan, 1955; New York: Perma Books paperback,
1956; New York: New American Library paperback, 1959. HB-
HB-R-R.

_____. The Man with the Golden Gun. New York: New Ameri-
can Library, 1965; New York: New American Library paperback,
1966. HB-R.

_____. Moonraker. New York: Macmillan, 1955; New York:
New American Library paperback, 1960. HB-R. See also
Too Hot to Handle.

_____. More Gilt-Edged Bonds. New York: Macmillan, 1965.
HB. Omnibus Edition: Diamonds Are Forever, Live and Let
Die, and Moonraker.

_____. Octopussy. New York: New American Library paper-
back, 1967. R. Paperback title for Octopussy and the Living
Daylights. Contains one additional short story, "The Property of
a Lady."

_____. Octopussy and the Living Daylights. New York: New
American Library, 1966. HB. Original hardback title.

_____. On Her Majesty's Secret Service. New York: New American Library, 1963; New York: New American Library paperback, 1964. HB-R.

_____. The Spy Who Loved Me. New York: Viking Press, 1962; New York: New American Library paperback, 1963. HB-R.

_____. Thunderball. New York: Viking Press, 1961; New York: New American Library paperback, 1962. HB-R.

_____. Too Hot to Handle. New York: Perma Books paperback, 1957. R. Original U.S. paperback title for Moonraker.

_____. You Asked For It. New York: Popular Library, 1955. R. Original U.S. paperback title for Casino Royale.

_____. You Only Live Twice. New York: New American Library, 1964; New York: New American Library paperback, 1965. HB-R.

CONSULT APPENDIX I FOR SERIES CONTINUATION

CONSULT APPENDIX II FOR SERIES TRANSITION

END OF CWF 25

† CWF 26. GALWAY, ROBERT C. †

BACKGROUND: This file is meant to be informative rather than evaluative.   Specifically, the subject is Robert Connington Galway, cover identity of British spy novelist Philip McCutchan (see separate reference).

As Galway, McCutchan penned a number of books bearing the designation "Assignment," which have been identified in many intelligence sectors as a continuation of Edward S. Aarons' (see separate reference) Sam Durell espionage series--it is well-known that each Durell entry is recognized by the "Assignment" stamp.

Recent field inquiries have confirmed that Galway's "Assignment" entries are not series efforts and therefore bear no relation to the contents of the Durell dossier.

The objective of this file, then, is to distinguish the Galway "Assignment" books from those of the late Mr. Aarons (see separate reference).   The field bibliography which follows this report will adequately advise all operatives of the titular differences.

To the point, McCutchan's Galway titles have appeared exclusively in British territory. In addition to his "Assignment" volumes, McCutchan-Galway has written The Timeless Man (1963) and The Negative Man (1971).

Given the unusual nature of CWF 26, the remaining standard evaluative categories have been deleted.

FIELD BIBLIOGRAPHY

Galway, Robert C. Assignment: Andalusia. London: Hale, 1965. HB.

_____. Assignment: Argentina. London: Hale, 1969. HB.

_____. Assignment: Finland. London: Hale, 1969. HB.

_____. Assignment: Gaolbreak. London: Hale, 1968. HB.

_____. Assignment: London. London: Hale, 1963. HB.

_____. Assignment: Malta. London: Hale, 1966. HB.

_____. Assignment: New York. London: Hale, 1963. HB.

_____. Assignment: Sea Bed. London: Hale, 1969. HB.

_____. Assignment: Tahiti. London: Hale, release date unavailable. HB.

CONSULT APPENDIX I FOR FICTION CONTINUATION

END OF CWF 26

† CWF 27. GARDNER, JOHN †

BACKGROUND: Born in Newcastle, England, in 1926; his father was a clergyman. Educated at Wangate Grammar School.

During World War II Gardner served in the Fleet Air Arm as well as the Royal Marines.

Following military service Gardner entered St. John's College in Cambridge, with an interest in theology. Influenced by his father's vocation, Gardner attended a theological college at Oxford; was subsequently ordained. After five years in holy orders, he left the church an agnostic.

In the late fifties Gardner turned to journalism and earned a remarkable following as a theatre critic for a small newspaper at Stratford-on-Avon, becoming such a recognized authority on Shakespeare that he soon found himself in great demand as a lecturer in both Britain and the United States.

However, it was Gardner's revelation of his desperate battle with alcoholism in Spin the Bottle (1963) that brought him to the attention of the publishing and reading sectors. This therapeutic work launched a distinguished career for Gardner as one of England's finest suspense novelists.

Although Gardner is currently enjoying critical and public praise for his continuation entries of Ian Fleming's James Bond series (see separate reference), notably License Renewed (1981) and For Special Services (1982), he has demonstrated his capable talents in other areas of the mystery genre.

Gardner authored a number of espionage novels belonging to the realistic school, including The Werewolf Trace (1977), and The Dancing Dodo (1978). The Nostradamus Traitor (1979), The Garden of Weapons (1981), and The Quiet Dogs (1982) formed the "Kruger trilogy," featuring hero Herbie Kruger.

A Complete State of Death (1969) was lauded as a provocative crime novel and was adapted as a visual project in 1973, with Charles Bronson, under the operative title of The Stone Killer.

Gardner successfully ventured into the short-story arena with Hideaway (1968) and The Assassination File (1974), two collections of espionage tales which were published exclusively in England. But, next to his maturation of Agent 007, Gardner is probably best known for his intriguing excursions into the Sherlockian mystery with The Return of Moriarty (1974) and The Revenge of Moriarty (1975).

With all these accomplishments, Gardner's Cold War operative Boysie Oakes, subject of this file, provided the British author with a heated cycle of controversy that is not likely to characterize his term as the successor to Ian Fleming and Kingsley Amis (see separate reference) as author of James Bond novels.

Mr. Gardner was also a major constituent of the Fawcett Intelligence Group (see separate reference) from 1965 to 1968.

CWF AGENT: Oakes, Brian Ian "Boysie."

CWF HISTORY: In August 1944 in Paris, British Army Sergeant Brian Ian Oakes saved the life of Major James George Mostyn of British Intelligence, who was attacked by two German assassins in a dark alley off Boulevard Magenta.

In 1956, Mostyn, second-in-command to the Department of
Special Security, spotted a story in the London Gazette concerning
the death of Philip William Redfern, with whom Oakes had owned
and operated a café since 1947. An accompanying photograph of
Oakes reminded Mostyn of the 1944 Paris incident.

Mostyn drafted Oakes into the Department in the spring of
1956 and assigned him the code name of "The Liquidator," also
known as "L."

By 1965 Oakes, as "L," had officially eliminated approximately twenty-five Redland agents. However, it was later disclosed
that "L" was involved in a clandestine relationship with an ex-
undertaker identified as Charles Griffin, which figured into his activities with the Department. To wit: "L" subcontracted his liquidation missions to Griffin, whose reputation as a callous mercenary
is well known in intelligence circles.

Given Oakes' reputation within the Department, his agree-
ment with Griffin masked the most ingenious deception ever practiced within the sealed bastions of British Intelligence. The truth
behind the Oakes myth was not restricted, however, to the agent's
contempt for the art of assassination--for "L" was literally para-
lyzed with fear when confronted with the demands of human existence, especially airplane travel. Still, it should be noted that there
was one area in which "L" did not require Griffin's services. The
late Ian Fleming (see separate reference) often referred to it as
"womanizing."

Immediately after his induction Oakes entered "The Espionage School" (exact location unknown) and regained his peak physical
condition. As to be expected, "L" was trained in marksmanship
and clandestine security techniques.

Mostyn supervised Oakes' personal reading, assigning such
authors as Cervantes, Luther, Murdoch, and (make special note)
Ian Fleming and Kingsley Amis (see separate references). However, Oakes failed to respond satisfactorily to Mostyn's cultural
indoctrination and likewise did not benefit from the required language courses.

The Department has only seven recorded missions involving
"The Liquidator," from 1964 to 1975. "L" has been inactive since
that time and his present whereabouts is unknown.

Mostyn was eliminated by an enemy agent during Oakes'
final mission in 1975. The tragic incident was purportedly related
to a revenge motive for a secret-service assassination in Mexico
which, according to intelligence files, occurred in 1964.

The Department of Special Security is no longer in existence.

OPERATIVE DATA: "L" was assigned to assassinate an English

duke in The Liquidator (1964), ostensibly as part of a training exercise. Code name: "Coronet." Location: an R. A. F. airfield identified from Department records as Gayborough. Weapon employed: a modified Lee Enfield Mark III .303 rifle, with a Tasco variable scope and camera attachment.

However, several double agents within the Department turned "Coronet" into a more explosive incident involving the theft of a top-secret aircraft, the Vulture.

"L" subsequently confronted one of the doubles aboard the Vulture. Although the identities of the Redland operatives concerned in this case remain classified under the Official Secrets Act, it is known that a free-lance master spy, identified as Shereik, was an integral part of the "Coronet" initiative, purportedly in the pay of Redland.

As a result of "Coronet," "L" was designated a menace by Redland. The following year Moscow filtered an exact double of "The Liquidator" into the field in Understrike (1965)--one Vladimir Solev, a top agent for the K. G. B.

The mission focused on the sabotage of nuclear submarine trials in San Diego Bay where the U. S. S. Playboy, the principal project submarine, housed six new deadly trepholite warheads. "L" successfully prevented Redland from subverting the tests.

Oakes' proficiency as a womanizer proved valuable to the Department in Amber Nine (1966) in which he was assigned to Klara Thirel's girls' school in Switzerland. The Thirel establishment reportedly specialized in training for the killing, torturing, and maiming of formidable male intelligence agents. Amber Nine provided Oakes' most pleasurable assignment for the Department, given his smooth manipulation of Petronella.

As for sexual prowess, it was a matter of record within the Department that at the time of "Coronet," "L" was, in fact, intimately involved with Iris MacIntosh, Mostyn's desirable, auburn-haired secretary.

In his fourth Oakes entry, Madrigal (1967), Gardner introduced a daring change which radically altered the complexion of the series: under orders to terminate a treacherous spy in East Berlin --a former Department operative--"L" was unable to locate Griffin.

With Madrigal, Gardner probed the complexities of both the realistic espionage novel and the Cold War.

Basically, Madrigal involved an official British-Soviet "swap" at the notorious Checkpoint Charlie that was to have resulted in the liquidation of a double agent, identified as "Rabbit" Warren. From this vantage point, Gardner conceived an unconventional spy thriller that venomously mocked le Carré and Deighton (see separate references) with his satirical examination of the U.S.-Soviet hegemony in Berlin and the Chi-Com's isolated perception of the Cold War in Europe.

Within his main plot Gardner fused a Chi-Com scheme directed toward Britain that both parodied and challenged the Len Deighton (see separate reference) style of spy thriller.

Gardner's vision of the Chi-Coms in Madrigal authentically reflected their global objectives in the late sixties, especially in the segments dealing with the People's Liberation Army and its interest in the British-Soviet exchange. In this respect, Gardner commented on the feverish rivalry between the Soviet Union and Red China.

In addition to these elements, Gardner inserted an unexpected twist into the British-Soviet switch theme which assailed the ideologies expressed in the works of le Carré and Deighton (see separate references).

Specifically, Mostyn encountered Griffin for the first time in Madrigal; and, given his initial predicament, Oakes' confrontation with an elusive, nefarious master spy known only as Madrigal ironically justified his reputation for ruthlessness as "The Liquidator," which he had been struggling to expel from his mind.

Gardner heightened his antagonistic response to the realistic spy novel with Shakespearean allusions throughout Madrigal. Further, "L" displayed a more dispassionate attitude toward women in Madrigal, as evidenced by his dispassionate treatment of the fiery Rosy Puberty, a Chi-Com agent who figured in the British-Soviet intrigues at Checkpoint Charlie.

Madrigal, then, emerged as the best of the Oakes thrillers because it corrected the misconception that Gardner belonged to the anti-Fleming group. If anything, Madrigal prepared Gardner for his future assignment as author of the new James Bond novels.

SUMMARY: The Boysie Oakes series adroitly blended tongue-in-cheek humor with the highest level of suspense conceived in the spy fiction of the sixties, and John Gardner's slick economy of characterization and plotting made the series even more unique.

The author's conception of Boysie Oakes, alias "L" or "The Liquidator," as the reluctant yet deadly secret agent ranked as the most offbeat cloak-and-dagger creation to come out of the sixties, with the possible exception of Adam Diment's Philip McAlpine series (see separate reference). However, Madrigal drastically altered the face of the series to such an extent that it failed to attain the bestseller status of its three predecessors.

Unlike such noted spy novelists as Desmond Cory, James Leasor, Philip McCutchan, and George Brown Mair (see separate references), Gardner was not a participant in the competitive ploy to exceed Fleming's commercial and critical achievements. Still, the skill and imagination with which Mr. Gardner executed the Oakes thrillers amply qualified him to assume the throne of the late Ian Fleming (see separate reference).

The Book-Of-The-Month-Club offered the following observation in its evaluation of The Liquidator: "The Liquidator manages the tricky feat of being simultaneously a gripping spy story and a preposterous joke."

M. G. M. distributed a visual project concerning "L," adapted from The Liquidator. Released in 1966 the project featured Rod Taylor as "L," Trevor Howard as Mostyn, Jill St. John as Iris, Akim Tamiroff as Shereik, and Eric Sykes as Griffin.

STATUS: It is recommended that full details of the "L" dossier be renewed for public distribution. The incomparable narrative style of the series and John Gardner's newly tapped popularity with his James Bond thrillers should provide sufficient motive for this action. SOP.

FIELD BIBLIOGRAPHY

Gardner, John. Amber Nine. New York: Viking Press, 1966; New York: Fawcett-Crest paperback, 1968. HB-R.

_____. Founder Member. London: Joseph, 1969. HB.

_____. The Liquidator. New York: Viking Press, 1964; New York: Fawcett-Crest paperback, 1965. HB-R.

_____. Madrigal. London: Frederick Muller Ltd., 1967; New York: Viking Press, 1968; New York: Berkley-Medallion paperback, 1969. HB-HB-R.

_____. Understrike. New York: Viking Press, 1965; New York: Fawcett-Crest paperback, 1968. HB-R.

CONSULT APPENDIX I FOR SERIES CONTINUATION

END OF CWF 27

† CWF 28.   GARFORTH, JOHN †

BACKGROUND: British paperback author, generally associated with home visual-project novelizations.

Relevant to this file, Garforth wrote the early tie-ins for "The Avengers" home visual series, preceding Norman Daniels (see separate reference).

Garforth also wrote Sleep, and the City Trembles (1969), a suspense novel in the inimitable English tradition of James Hadley Chase.

CWF AGENT: Steed, John.

CWF HISTORY: See also Daniels, Norman--CWF 18.

OPERATIVE DATA: Garforth's contributions to this successful novelization series lacked the energy and pace of the later novels by Norman Daniels (see separate reference).

In the initial entries adapted from "The Avengers" visual project, Garforth employed a restrained style that failed to reflect the audacity of the British series. Further, Garforth minimized the striking characters of Steed and Emma Peel so that they were depicted as mere shadows of their visual counterparts.

On the positive side, Garforth's understated narrative style enhanced the British values of the visual project.

In The Passing of Gloria Munday (1967), Mrs. Peel established herself as a pop singer to investigate the bizarre death of a singing idol. Her cover, however, was seriously jeopardized when Steed was jailed on charges of murdering Gloria Munday, the afore-mentioned singing star.

The Communist sympathies in Franco's Spain and a fanatical organization identified only as REEL, U.S.A. figured as integral parts of the plot.

Heil Harris! (1967) underscored the revival of Nazism. Steed and Mrs. Peel were summoned to anatomize the identity of a mysterious German, believed to be Adolf Hitler residing in exile in the English countryside.

SUMMARY: As noted elsewhere, novelizations are not generally reissued, unless the project in question is scheduled for reactivation. Nonetheless, John Garforth's tie-ins for "The Avengers" adequately reflected the electrifying quality of the series.

STATUS: For reference purposes, the visual project was briefly revived in 1979 as "The New Avengers." See also Daniels, Norman--CWF 18. SOP.

FIELD BIBLIOGRAPHY

Garforth, John. The Floating Game. New York: Berkley-Medallion, 1967. PBO. TN.

_____. Heil Harris! New York: Berkley-Medallion, 1967. PBO. TN.

_____. The Laugh Was On Lazarus. New York: Berkley-Medallion, 1967. PBO. TN.

_____. The Passing of Gloria Munday. New York: Berkley-Medallion, 1967. PBO. TN.

CONSULT APPENDIX I FOR SERIES CONTINUATION

END OF CWF 28

† CWF 29. GARNER, WILLIAM †

BACKGROUND: British-born suspense novelist.

Born in 1920. Served in U.S. Air Force during World War II, achieving rank of flight lieutenant.

After the war Garner entered the corporate sector and eventually attained the position of product director for the multinational sales group, Monsanto Chemicals, Ltd.

However, Garner counteracted the competitive business world by cultivating diverse interests in the cultures of France and the Mediterranean, easily blending his knowledge of these pursuits into his books. Widely recognized as a passionate Francophile.

Overkill (1966), Garner's first mystery effort, introduced British secret agent Mike Jagger, the subject of this file. This title should not be confused with Norman Daniels' (see separate reference) initial John Keith mission of the same name, published two years earlier.

Finding a devoted following in the U.S. as well as Britain, Garner continued in the suspense field, after the Jagger series expired in 1969, with such works as The Manipulators (1970), Strip Jack Naked! (1971), A Big Enough Wreath (1975), (...).

Associated with the N.A.L./Signet Intelligence Group (see separate reference) from 1966 to 1968.

CWF AGENT: Jagger, Michael.

CWF HISTORY: Recruited into British Intelligence in 1966 for an important mission when the world's food supply was threatened by botulism.

Jagger's term of service lasted for three years; his superior was identified as the Master.

Because of his predilection for violence, Jagger was branded as a dangerous security risk--his actions in the aforementioned 1966 assignment resulted in the brutal deaths of two allied agents. Jagger was characterized, however, as a "self-contained man" by a West German operative, known only as Niemeyer, who was terminated during a mission in 1968.

Proficient at basic martial arts techniques, as required for all British Intelligence agents. Expert sports-car driver, as evidenced by the Lotus Cortina which he owned in 1968.

Sexual abilities evaluated as assertive. In 1968 Jagger reportedly occupied a three-story house in South London, which he shared with only the occasional female companion.

Jagger professed to being an avid reader, favoring the works of Christopher Marlowe.

No known code names or designations. No record after 1969.

OPERATIVE DATA: The three entries in the Jagger series do not fall exclusively into either the super-agent or realistic molds. Instead, Garner displayed qualities of both schools throughout the Jagger dossier.

Following Jagger's induction into British Intelligence in Overkill (1966), he was dispatched on an improbable mission which concerned a vague threat to the global food supply.

While Overkill obviously identified with the James Bond style of spy thriller, Garner avoided political overtones in his first Jagger novel.

His approach to the Cold War tale altered with The Deep

Deep Freeze (1968). Totally removed from the field of espionage after his first mission, Jagger was manipulated by the Master for a dangerous assignment dealing with the defection of an East German spy.

Although Jagger retained some of the Bondian trappings of Overkill, The Deep Deep Freeze was on more comfortable ground with the intricacies of Len Deighton and John le Carré (see separate references).

Set in Berlin, as well as other European locales, The Deep Deep Freeze unveiled a convincing and authentic Cold War plot, after the highly lauded efforts of Len Deighton, John le Carré, and Adam Hall (see separate references) had saturated the intelligence market.

Specifically, Jagger's second mission focused upon several key figures involved with the East German Abteilung:

1) Strawitz: Abteilung agent of East German descent.

2) Dr. Hieronymus Drieter: Captured by the Soviets during World War II; an Austrian physician convicted of conducting brain experiments on Allied P.O.W.'s.

3) Achim Von Treysa: Former leader of the Nazi's savage "Die Anonymen" assassination cell.

4) William Norrysse: Suspected by British Intelligence of being treacherous Redland agent, Red Leader.

Within this complex plot structure, Garner uitilized the Chinese-Japanese game of Go in the same fashion that Len Deighton (see separate reference) employed chess in Funeral in Berlin (1964). Throughout The Deep Deep Freeze, Garner addressed several chapter headings with Go quotations as well as revealing the Master's unequaled skill in playing the game.

Further, Garner offered Deighton-style appendixes on 1) electronically stimulated brain responses, 2) voice prints, and 3) the game of Go.

In an era when it was thought that Deighton, le Carré, and Hall had exhausted the possibilities of the realistic sector, William Garner conceived a Cold War thriller with The Deep Deep Freeze that simultaneously satisfied the demanding precepts of the genre and provided new groundwork for the waning format.

On The Deep Deep Freeze, the New York Times commented: "The Deep Deep Freeze is an impressive and absorbing tale of possible infiltration into British Intelligence, a couple of leftover Nazis in strange places, a Russian assassin, and a Japanese game called Go. William Garner's sure-handed control of these diverse elements is a pleasure to behold."

The final Jagger entry, The Us or Them War (1969), was a conventional tale concerning an unsuspecting scientist who designs the ultimate weapon. Jagger was sanctioned to preserve England's global interests.

Unlike The Deep Deep Freeze, The Us or Them War developed as a standard cloak-and-dagger spy novel and contributed little to the series.

SUMMARY: William Garner's Mike Jagger series is unique among the secret-agent fiction of the sixties in that the plots didn't fall into just one category.

Garner probed in The Deep Deep Freeze territory not previously penetrated by Len Deighton, John le Carré, Adam Hall, James Aldridge (see separate references) or other contemporaries.

In this respect, The Deep Deep Freeze might be termed an experimental espionage novel of Cold-War fiction.

STATUS: Given the alarming changes in the U.S.-Soviet contention for influence in Berlin since the Cold War era, The Deep Deep Freeze is not a promising choice for reissue, and the formularized elements apparent in The Us or Them War excludes Garner's third Jagger mission as a renewal candidate.

However, the cataclysmic theme delineated in Overkill would justify Jagger's initial assignment for reactivation, especially in view of the current resurgence of interest in the 007 type of spy thriller. SOP.

FIELD BIBLIOGRAPHY

Garner, William. The Deep Deep Freeze. New York: Putnam, 1968; New York: Berkley-Medallion paperback, 1969. HB-R.

_____. Overkill. New York: New American Library, 1966; New York: New American Library paperback, 1967. HB-R.

_____. The Us or Them War. New York: Putnam, 1969. HB-R. See also The Us or Them War in Appendix I.

CONSULT APPENDIX I FOR SERIES CONTINUATION

END OF CWF 29

† CWF 30.   GILMAN, DOROTHY   †

BACKGROUND: Cover identity for Dorothy Gilman Butters.   Born in 1923.

Although Ms. Gilman is primarily noted for her mysteries featuring Mrs. Pollifax, the C. I. A.'s most unlikely operative, she has penned several non-series thrillers, namely Uncertain Voyage (1967), The Clairvoyant Countess (1975), and A Nun in the Closet (1975).

Ms. Gilman's first Pollifax book, The Unexpected Mrs. Pollifax (1966), the only entry of the series to appear during the sixties, was critically acclaimed in both the U. S. and Britain.   Curiously, The Unexpected Mrs. Pollifax wasn't published in paperback (by Fawcett-Crest) until 1971 when it was adapted into a visual project, Mrs. Pollifax, Spy, starring the late Rosalind Russell in the title role.

The entire Pollifax dossier, which currently numbers five titles, was originally published by Doubleday, renowned for its distinctive suspense fiction.   Recognized as one of the most successful mystery series ever marketed by Doubleday, many of the books were later condensed in Reader's Digest.

A highly respected member of the Mystery Writers of America, Dorothy Gilman Butters presently resides in Nova Scotia.

Since Fawcett's paperback distribution of the series is associated with the seventies, Dorothy Gilman was not represented in the Fawcett Intelligence Group (see separate reference).

CWF AGENT: Pollifax, Emily (Mrs. Virgil)

CWF HISTORY: Mrs. Pollifax came to the attention of the C. I. A. when she applied for the "position" of spy at the agency's headquarters in Langley, Virginia.

At the time, Mrs. Pollifax, a respectable citizen of New Brunswick, New Jersey, was duly registered as a widow with two married children, identified as Jane and Roger.   The inevitable C. I. A. security check revealed no subversive affiliations.

Mrs. Pollifax's reason for seeking employment with the agency was a sincere desire to serve her country.   However, she made no secret of her growing dissatisfaction with a comfortable yet uneventful suburban existence.

Upon meeting Mrs. Pollifax, section director Carstairs, who had received his training in the O. S. S., was impressed by her uncomplicated manner. Mrs. Pollifax suited the requirements for a seemingly simple mission in Mexico City, which demanded the services of a courier, and Carstairs gave her the assignment.

Although Mrs. Pollifax was not subjected to the usual training procedures of the C. I. A., she has proven herself a capable operative and remains on active duty with the agency.

OPERATIVE DATA: In The Unexpected Mrs. Pollifax (1966), Mrs. Pollifax was instructed to contact an obscure bookseller in Mexico City, intercept a cache of crucial documents and transport them back into U.S. territory. However, her C. I. A. confrere turned out to be an enemy agent, and the machinations of a Chi-Com spy unit in South America complicated Mrs. Pollifax's mission.

Mrs. Pollifax eventually found herself in a Chi-Com mountain bastion in Albania where she unearthed a connection between that Chi-Com ally and their espionage network in South America: Red China was attempting to draw Cuba into its orbit, away from the Soviet Union. This calculated design intensified the Chi-Com threat to the United States.

Mrs. Pollifax joined forces with C. I. A. operative John Sebastian Farrell and together they averted the Chi-Com-Albanian plot.

Dorothy Gilman meticulously devised a durable framework in The Unexpected Mrs. Pollifax that would shape the overall direction of the later entries.

Defining Mrs. Pollifax as the most improbable of global agents, Gilman established the characterization and plotting elements in much the same manner as would be anticipated in a straightforward action-suspense series, such as Peter O'Donnell's Modesty Blaise (see separate reference).

This type of development is especially apparent in The Unexpected Mrs. Pollifax with the depiction of Farrell, Mrs. Pollifax's intrepid C. I. A. confederate. Gilman masterfully balanced Farrell's delineation with villainous figures. In Mrs. Pollifax's first mission, the politically nefarious menaces, as typified by General Perdido (the Chi-Com's resident strategist in South America) and Peking's chief Albanian conspirators, Colonel Nexdhet and Major Vassovic, reflected Red China's global objectives during the Cold War era.

However, Gilman's logical, efficient plotting throughout The Unexpected Mrs. Pollifax imparted a chilling contrast to the deceptively placid Mrs. Pollifax and the graphic characters she encountered on her mission.

This discernible line of tension clearly separated Mrs. Pollifax from the other narrative elements in The Unexpected Mrs. Pollifax.

The critical and public reaction to The Unexpected Mrs. Pollifax has earned Dorothy Gilman and her inventive operative an exceptional place among the secret-agent fiction of the sixties.

The New York Times Book Review observed: "The Unexpected Mrs. Pollifax should delight you whether you're looking for smiles or thrills."

SUMMARY: The smooth, intelligent fusion of credibly vivid characterization and suspenseful plotting in The Unexpected Mrs. Pollifax contributed to the measured development of a durable protagonist who has transcended the boundaries of Cold War espionage fiction.

As noted earlier, Rosalind Russell appeared as Dorothy Gilman's irresistible provocateur in Mrs. Pollifax, Spy (1971), a visual project based on The Unexpected Mrs. Pollifax. Employing the cover identity of C. A. McKnight, Ms. Russell scripted the United Artists release, which also featured Dana Elcar as Carstairs and Darren McGavin as C. I. A. agent Farrell.

STATUS: The indomitable success of the Pollifax series throughout the seventies has insured its continued distribution in the current suspense market. SSP.

FIELD BIBLIOGRAPHY

Gilman, Dorothy. The Unexpected Mrs. Pollifax. Garden City, N. Y.: Doubleday, 1966. HB-R. See also Mrs. Pollifax, Spy and The Unexpected Mrs. Pollifax in Appendix I.

CONSULT APPENDIX I FOR SERIES CONTINUATION

END OF CWF 30

† CWF 31. GRAY, ROD †

BACKGROUND: Author of the Eve Drum--"The Lady from L.U.S.T." books, one of the more readable sex-oriented espionage series.

Beginning with the first entry, The Lady from L. U. S. T. (1967), the Drum dossier generated a large following, expanding well into the seventies with over fifteen representative titles.

"The Lady from L. U. S. T." developed as a minor cult in Hispanic territories during the late sixties and early seventies.

No further information available.

CWF AGENT: Drum, Eve.

CWF HISTORY: American female athlete. Adept at firearms, knife-throwing, and the martial arts. Recipient of the Sixth Dan Belt in karate. Initially employed as a government secretary for unknown branch. Later resided in New York.

From 1967 to 1976 Ms. Drum served as a top-flight operative for L.U.S.T., an intelligence unit formally known as the League of Undercover Spies and Terrorists, based in Miami.

Founded in the early sixties, L.U.S.T. engaged in espionage activities of a criminal nature, summoned only when other allied outlets had been exhausted. For this reason L.U.S.T. possessed no official status. The head of L.U.S.T. was a man identified only as "The General." L.U.S.T. was disbanded in 1976.

In 1967 while vacationing in Port-au-Prince, Haiti, Ms. Drum encountered one George Norman, a fellow American tourist with whom Ms. Drum allegedly experienced a brief yet euphoric sexual relationship. On the strength of this physical attraction, Norman recommended Ms. Drum as a potential candidate for L.U.S.T.

Upon completing the required training courses at a remote farm near Washington, D.C., Eve Drum became a fully registered L.U.S.T. operative.

Although her indoctrination consisted of various defense and combat regimens, as well as more specialized techniques involving "the drop," "the cut," and "the safe house," L.U.S.T. superior David Anderjanian judged Ms. Drum's principal talent to be in the physical-sexual area.

Also known in the field as Agent Oh-Oh-Sex, Ms. Drum's measurements were officially recorded as 38-22-35.

OPERATIVE DATA: The general structure of this type of series remained fairly constant with each entry.

However, unlike the equally popular series "The Man from O.R.G.Y." by Ted Mark and "The Man from T.O.M.C.A.T." by Mallory T. Knight (see separate references), this series intensified the protagonist's physical prowess and sexual acumen.

Further, Gray's use of first-person narrative created an atmosphere of mystery that has otherwise eluded this category of spy fiction.

In The Lady from L.U.S.T. (1967) Eve was to seduce the

enigmatic Count Guido della Faxiola on his resplendent yacht as the only means of recovering a set of crucial N. A. T. O. documents.

On her initial L. U. S. T. mission, Oh-Oh-Sex confronted H. A. T. E., an international criminal body. In future entries such inimical intelligence networks as A. L. L. A. H. and D. R. A. G. O. N. would be appropriately recorded in L. U. S. T. files.

The Lady from L. U. S. T. was also distributed as Lust, Be a Lady Tonight.

SUMMARY: Throughout his Eve Drum series, Rod Gray integrated sexual magnetism with a lean narrative style to produce one of the more imaginative sex-dominated secret agent series of the sixties.

STATUS: Given the phenomenal commercial success garnered by this class of spy novel during the Bond mania, the reissue of "The Lady from L. U. S. T." series should not be ruled out, provided the current interest in espionage fiction continues to flourish. SOP.

FIELD BIBLIOGRAPHY

Gray, Rod. Five Beds to Mecca. New York: Tower Books, 1968. PBO.

_____. The Hot Mahatma. New York: Tower Books, 1968. PBO.

_____. Kiss My Assassin. New York: Tower Books, 1969. PBO.

_____. The Lady from L. U. S. T. New York: Tower Books, 1967. PBO. See also Lust, Be a Lady Tonight.

_____. Lay Me Odds. New York: Tower Books, 1967. PBO.

_____. Lust, Be a Lady Tonight. Alternate title for The Lady from L. U. S. T.

_____. The Poisoned Pussy. New York: Tower Books, 1969. PBO.

_____. The 69 Pleasures. New York: Tower Books, 1967. PBO.

_____. South of the Bordello. New York: Tower Books, 1969. PBO.

_____. To Russia with L. U. S. T. New York: Tower Books, 1968. PBO.

CONSULT APPENDIX I FOR SERIES CONTINUATION

END OF CWF 31

† CWF 32. HAGGARD, WILLIAM †

BACKGROUND: Cover identity of Richard Henry Michael Clayton, former British civil servant.

Born in Croydon, England in 1907. Educated at Lancing College and Christ College, Oxford. Entered the Indian Civil Service in 1931; subsequently appointed magistrate and sessions judge.

Served in the Indian Army during World War II. After additional education at the Staff College at Quetta, Clayton was advanced to the General Staff as an intelligence officer.

In 1945 Clayton was designated for ministry duty in Whitehall, an experience which doubtless contributed to the conception and background of Colonel Charles Russell, the subject of this file.

Clayton became an official of the Board of Trade and controller of enemy property in 1957. Twelve years later, he retired from government service.

In the realm of Cold War espionage fiction, Haggard's spy novels have been likened more to the works of John Buchan than to such contemporaries as Ian Fleming and John le Carré (see separate references).

Beginning with his first suspense effort, Slow Burner (1958), which introduced Colonel Russell, Haggard essayed a unique mixture of the engaging romanticism of Buchan with a chilling perception of the political and diplomatic interplay which controlled the mechanism of global intelligence throughout the Cold War era.

In the Russell series, Haggard expressed this perspective from the collective viewpoint of Whitehall, and, in the process, he frequently mirrored Britain's declining world status during the Cold War era.

Unlike many authors of international intrigue, Haggard was not evaluated as a strict adherent of either the action or realistic schools.

Haggard integrated a worldly quality into the Russell books that surpassed the branded expertise of Ian Fleming (see separate reference) and at the same time transcended such anti-Bond practitioners as Deighton and le Carré (see separate references). In fact, he managed to convey the finer points of both approaches.

Despite an ambitious paperback promotional campaign launched by New American Library in the mid-sixties, Russell failed to attain a strong commercial response in the U.S. market, although American critics consistently lauded each new Haggard thriller. This might be explained by Haggard's distinctive manner of erudition, which veiled the inherent right-wing philosophies in his books.

The success of Haggard's espionage thrillers is generally associated with his native England where his unique narrative style has been more fully appreciated. In contrast to New American Library, Britain's prestigious Penguin Books did exceedingly well with the Russell mysteries during the sixties, reprinting several of the titles at regular intervals.

Although Haggard has penned more than twenty Russell novels, his other works inevitably reflected the knowledgeable tone of his series entries. These include The Telemann Touch (1958) and Closed Circuit (1960). More recently, Haggard initiated a limited series involving another civil servant, Paul Martiny, in The Protectors (1972) and The Kinsman (1974).

The disappointing lack of response to Colonel Russell in the American paperback market discouraged other domestic houses from continuing New American Library's efforts. As a result the Russell entries following The Powder Barrell and The Hard Sell (both 1965) have been published only in hardback in the U.S.

However, the distribution of the Russell series has continued in the American sector, two of the more current being The Median Line (1981) and The Mischief Makers (1982).

Haggard was a major constituent of the N.A.L./Signet Intelligence Group (see separate reference), as well as a representative author of the Detective Book Club.

CWF AGENT: Russell, Colonel Charles.

CWF HISTORY: Head of the Security Executive, an elite military organization situated within Whitehall. The delegated function of the Security Executive is the preservation of British interests through diplomatic means, and it remains in existence today.

British subject. Described as being not particularly tall, with a measured gait and a meticulously cultivated moustache, Colonel Russell has honored the urbane fashion required of a career intelligence officer.

Served with distinction in an exclusive Army regiment. Later

assigned to India. Subsequently, Russell was appointed to the Whitehall General Staff before being designated as Chief of the Security
Executive.

Although forced into obligatory retirement at the age of 65,
Colonel Russell is occasionally summoned by Whitehall.

The Official Secrets Act prohibits further information on
Colonel Charles Russell being disclosed in this file, given that he
has been actively engaged as an intelligence head rather than an
operative. For this reason, specific dates relating to Colonel
Russell's background have been deleted.

OPERATIVE DATA: The common theme of the Russell books of the
Cold War period was a politically devastating crisis, typically masked
by the aristocratic façade of postwar Britain.

Further, Haggard provided a new focus for the espionage
series of the sixties with the directorial role of Colonel Russell.

However, it would be an oversimplified assertion to conclude
that Haggard glamorized his native England in the tales of the Security Executive. Quite the contrary, Russell often experienced a
smoother working relationship with his Soviet counterpart than with
the self-seeking advocates of his own government.

Another facet of the Russell dossier developed with Haggard's
masterful depiction of polished, successful British diplomats and
businessmen who were extremely vulnerable to some lure of corrup-
tion despite or because of their privileged status. To a lesser extent, this delineation also applied to the scientists in Haggard's
thrillers.

In Slow Burner (1958) the Security Executive was confronted
with the possibility that Britain's most destructive atomic secret--
"Slow Burner"--was in danger of falling into hostile sectors.

Slow Burner implanted the foundation for future Security Executive projects in two respects. For one thing, the influential
characters of William Nichol and Sir Jeremy Bates defined the precarious relationship between the possession of power in the British
government and the irresistible temptation of treachery, as presented within the general framework of Haggard's novels. And,
more relevant to the series, Colonel Russell's diplomatic finesse
was superbly displayed in Slow Burner.

Haggard intensified his basic fictional thesis in Venetian
Blind (1959). Here, he focused on one Gervas Leat, an immensely
resourceful and powerful British industrialist, and on a dangerous
and secret military project identified as "Negative Gravity," concerning the development of the ultimate weapon through the con-
quest of space.

Knowing of Leat's involvement in the "Negative Gravity" project, the Security Executive suspected that the industrialist's defense plant would be susceptible to sabotage.

With Venetian Blind Haggard expanded the operations of the Security Executive across Europe: Russell was challenged by an elusive spy ring based in Venice, known only as Kinder Three, and a bitter scientist of German-Jewish extraction, Professor Wasserman, who was situated in Düsseldorf, Germany.

Without exception, Venetian Blind qualified as the best of the series, as Russell was tested by the enigma of Gervas Leat, the disturbing actions of Professor Wasserman, the motives of two supposedly dedicated civil servants, Richard Wakely and Lionel Lowe-Anderson, and their common interest in "Negative Gravity."

Russell's studied diplomatic expertise was manifested at its finest in Venetian Blind. In its review of Venetian Blind, the New York Times commented, "International malefactions and private motives for murder ... [make] a colorful, intelligent thriller."

Haggard did not explore the staggering possibilities suggested by the Cold War in his Russell books of the early sixties.

In The Arena (1961) the Security Executive investigated the political ramifications of a proposed merger between a failing merchant banking firm and a mysterious corporation.

The Unquiet Sleep (1962) revolved around the damaging effects of a new drug that had gained strong popularity within the highest spheres of the British government.

The feared subversion of a crucial British defense secret, "Project-A," punctuated the tension of The High Wire (1963)--Haggard's formal initiation into the series fiction of the Cold War.

Russell penetrated the intentions of an insidious blackmailer and a devoted civil servant Rex Hadley, amidst the cataclysmic consequences of "Project-A."

In The High Wire Haggard effectively employed the "secret war" notion so natural to the espionage novel of the early sixties.

Whether from a desolate government installation on the very edge of London or in a lethal confrontation on a stranded cable car in the Italian Alps, rival agents competed for "Project-A."

The cable car incident, enacted between Hadley and a savage assassin identified only as Victor, marked a significant departure for Haggard, an author who is not exactly renowned for feverish action in his spy thrillers.

Although the cable car battle more closely resembled the

blistering fashion of Ian Fleming (see separate reference), Haggard's logical sense of plotting permitted him to retain his basic structure throughout The High Wire. In this respect, The High Wire offers a provocative comparison to Ian Fleming's On Her Majesty's Secret Service (1963), especially since there are alpine settings in both entries.

Although Colonel Russell unfortunately was restricted to a monitoring role in The High Wire, which regrettably must figure as his least effective mission with the Security Executive, Anthony Boucher praised the entry in his evaluation for the New York Times Book Review: "Especially commended to those who are weary of the standard villains of most tales of intrigue ... This is precisely-managed thriller-mongering, sardonic and acute."

While acknowledging Colonel Russell's understated function in The High Wire, this Security Executive initiative nonetheless compared favorably with Venetian Blind.

Haggard magnified his vision of the Cold War in the Russell books that followed The High Wire, often encompassing the most sensitive areas of global politics and science.

The Antagonists (1964) concerned an eccentric Balkan scientist, identified as Dr. Alexander Gorjan, who controlled an apocalyptic military secret. During a lecture tour in London, Gorjan attracted the attention of two competing foreign powers. This development prompted Colonel Russell to involve the Security Executive in Dr. Gorjan's activities.

In The Antagonists Haggard adroitly fused the machinations of the U.S., Britain, and the Soviet Union with Gorjan's avaricious motives.

Haggard was perhaps the first espionage novelist to fictionalize the growing influence of the Arab world. In The Powder Barrel (1965) Haggard explored the explosive political climate of an oil-rich sheikdom, which was also a British protectorate, and the repercussions to the global powers of a potential revolution.

Russell was engaged in discerning the objectives of an ambitious Arab sheik and a calculating French-Arab princess, to forestall civil conflict in the British protectorate. Further, the Security Executive discovered a startling conspiracy to cover up the liquidation of a British Foreign Minister in the chaotic oil sheikdom.

Uniting all of these contemporary elements into a cohesive whole, Haggard conceived an electrifying spy novel which portended the bitter, antagonistic diplomatic atmosphere that would enflame the Arab world in the seventies.

With The Powder Barrel Haggard advanced beyond the limits of the Cold War, offering a plausible view of the global politics that would ultimately lead to détente.

Given the new ground probed by William Haggard in The Powder Barrel, this Russell entry should be regarded in the same vein as John le Carré's The Spy Who Came In from the Cold (1963), Len Deighton's Funeral in Berlin (1964), and Adam Hall's The Quiller Memorandum (1965) (see separate references)--that is, as a significant contribution to the espionage fiction of the Cold War.

The Hard Sell (1965) developed as one of Haggard's least satisfying Russell thrillers. Reprising the subversion themes of Venetian Blind and The High Wire, it focused on the possible industrial sabotage of the Princess Rose, a new, medium-load aircraft, which was designed at the SAGA plant in Northern Italy. Russell allied with Mario Donnini, an Italian Communist police commissioner, to avert the plot.

Although The Hard Sell lacked the menace of his earlier books, Haggard maintained his wry commentary on the diplomatic and business worlds of the mid-sixties.

SUMMARY: Embodying the romanticism of John Buchan and his own unique conception of global diplomacy and intelligence, William Haggard crafted an espionage series that seriously analyzed Britain's relationship to the world-at-large during the Cold War era.

Depicting Colonel Charles Russell as the imperturbable chief of the Security Executive, Haggard altered the emphasis of his series in which he generally dominated action with credible, authentic plots.

Haggard's erudite narrative style, however, alienated many American readers, although British suspense devotees reacted enthusiastically to Colonel Russell's polished brand of Whitehall diplomacy.

The London Sunday Express described William Haggard as "The adults' Ian Fleming," and the New York Herald Tribune observed, "It is to William Haggard more than any other suspense writer today that credit must be given for the renaissance of the spy-adventure tale...."

STATUS: The inability of the Haggard thrillers to perform in the U.S. paperback market during the mid-sixties virtually eliminates the likelihood of a renewed distribution effort, although given Haggard's huge following in Britain during the period, the demand for the Russell dossier could conceivably be reshaped.

Although new Russell books have appeared in recent years, all of the Cold War era entries are out of circulation.

For all practical purposes, SOP.

FIELD BIBLIOGRAPHY

Haggard, William. The Antagonists. New York: Ives-Washburn, 1964; New York: New American Library paperback, 1965. HB-R.

_____. The Arena. New York: Ives-Washburn, 1961; London: Penguin paperback, 1963. HB-R.

_____. The Conspirators. London: Cassell, 1967; New York: Walker, 1968. HB-HB.

_____. A Cool Day for Killing. New York: Walker, 1968. HB.

_____. The Doubtful Disciple. London: Cassell, 1969. HB.

_____. The Hard Sell. London: Cassell, 1965; New York: Ives-Washburn, 1966; New York: New American Library paperback, 1967. HB-HB-R.

_____. The High Wire. New York: Ives-Washburn, 1963; New York: New American Library paperback, 1964. HB-R.

_____. The Powder Barrel. New York: Ives-Washburn, 1965; New York: New American Library paperback, 1966. HB-R.

_____. The Power House. London: Cassell, 1966; New York: Ives-Washburn, 1967. HB-HB.

_____. Slow Burner. New York: Little, 1958; New York: New American Library paperback, 1965. HB-R.

_____. The Unquiet Sleep. New York: Ives-Washburn, 1962; London: Penguin paperback, 1964. HB-R.

_____. Venetian Blind. New York: Ives-Washburn, 1959; New York: New American Library paperback, 1963. HB-R.

CONSULT APPENDIX I FOR SERIES CONTINUATION

END OF CWF 32

† CWF 33.   HALL, ADAM   †

BACKGROUND: Born in 1920 in Bromley, Kent. Cover identity of Elleston Trevor, award-winning British author of mysteries and espionage novels.

Trevor Dudley-Smith, who eventually changed his name legally to Elleston Trevor, was formally educated at Sevenoaks, and served in the R.A.F. during World War II.

Married Jonquil Burgess in 1946; one son, Jean-Pierre.

Trevor has produced a plethora of popular novels under no fewer than eight cover designations. Several of his books have been translated into visual projects, notably The Big Pick-Up (1955), adapted as Dunkirk (1958), and Flight of the Phoenix (1964) (the visual project appeared two years later).

Trevor has written a number of works under his own name, such as The V.I.P. (1960), The Shoot (1966), and more recently, his war-oriented thriller, The Damocles Sword (1981).

The identities under which Trevor has operated include Mansell Black, Roger Fitzalan, Adam Hall, Howard North, Simon Rattray, Warwick Scott, and Caesar Smith.

The Hugo Bishop mystery series, which Trevor initiated as Simon Rattray, established a suspenseful style with plots, involving the mechanics of chess, that were both exacting and absorbing. These include Bishop in Check (1953) and Dead Circuit (1955).

However, it was The Quiller Memorandum (1965), written under the Hall cover, that earned Trevor a global audience. This bestselling espionage thriller has been ranked with Len Deighton's The Ipcress File (U.S., 1963) (see separate reference) and John le Carré's The Spy Who Came In from the Cold (U.S., 1964) (see separate reference) as a model of the realistic spy novel.

The Quiller Memorandum garnered the Mystery Writers of America Edgar award for Trevor in 1965, as well as the French Grand Prix Littérature Policière. Published as The Berlin Memorandum in England, it was a book club selection in both the U.S. and Britain.

It is well known that The Quiller Memorandum spawned a highly successful suspense series that has endured into the eighties, as represented by The Scorpion Signal (1980) and The Peking Target (1982).

After achieving an international following in the mid-sixties, several of Trevor's books were reissued under the Adam Hall identity or his own name, chiefly those originally authored as Mansell Black, Warwick Scott, and Caesar Smith.

Relevant to the subject of this file on Quiller, Trevor is referred to as Hall.

CWF AGENT: Quiller.

CWF HISTORY: British subject. Quiller refused military service
in World War II. Without proper authorization, Quiller posed as a
German soldier in an attempt to sabotage the Nazis' mass extermi-
nation of European Jews.

Although Quiller was cited for bravery by the governments of
Holland, Poland, and Sweden, he adamantly refused any decorations.

Purportedly, Quiller is recognized in intelligence circles for
his expertise in the areas of memory, sleep-mechanism, suicidal
behavior patterns, critical-path analysis, driving under hazardous
situations, and ballistics.

Real identity unknown, Quiller is the code name of a field
operative employed by a clandestine British organization known only
as the Bureau. The Bureau is situated in Whitehall and is not officially recorded as a global body.

In 1965 Quiller's superior was identified only as "Control."
However, during a later mission, dated 1968, he was revealed as a
man named Parkis.

Although the specific date of Quiller's entrance into the Bureau has not been accurately documented, a 1965 assignment in Berlin certified his proficiency as an agent of the highest caliber.

The Berlin case is considered below.

OPERATIVE DATA: Adam Hall's The Quiller Memorandum has received considerable critical attention as one of the definitive examples of the realistic Cold War spy novel.

The Quiller Memorandum signified an irrefutable achievement
for Hall, given the primacy previously achieved in the field by John
le Carré and Len Deighton (see separate references). Hall was
obliged to seek dimensions that hadn't been pursued by his peers.

Apart from the authoritative detail which Hall summoned to
describe the complex operations of the Bureau, The Quiller Memorandum has secured classic status for its incisive depiction of Neo-
Nazism, related from the standpoint of the Cold War.

After Bureau operative Kenneth Lindsay Jones was murdered
in Berlin, Quiller was recruited by his local contact agent, identified only as Pol, to replace him. Ironically, Jones' assignment
had been to track down an elusive ex-Nazi officer, Heinrich Zossen,
whom Quiller had testified against at the 1945 Nazi Tribunal.

Having defined Quiller's function early in the book, Hall conceived a plot in The Quiller Memorandum that emerged as more of
a political issue than contemporary espionage fiction--the obscure
yet formidable threat of a reinvigorated Neo-Nazi cell in Berlin.

Hall derived the title from a Bureau memorandum passed on to Quiller which enumerated the names of more than forty Nazis who were suspected as Zossen's allies.

Many reviews of The Quiller Memorandum emphasized Hall's adroit mixture of authenticity and tension, and in this respect the author balanced each segment with chilling precision.

Quiller's search for Zossen eventually brought him into contact with Inga Lindt, purportedly a civil servant, and a mysterious German identified only as Oktober.

With an almost sadistic passion, Hall deftly fused Quiller's Berlin memorandum with the significance of both Inga and Oktober to flesh out the harsh, bitter consequences of the Neo-Nazi movement.

Hall's Berlin locales, the divided sectors as well as the Berlin Wall itself, emanated a well-defined topicality that easily rivaled that of le Carré and Deighton (see separate references).

Further, Quiller's tortured endurance of the effects of a narcotic injection imparted a dimension of the unbearable to The Quiller Memorandum that wasn't apparent in the works of le Carré and Deighton (see separate references).

Anthony Boucher's widely quoted evaluation of The Quiller Memorandum in the New York Times Book Review serves to exemplify the underlying philosophy of the series as a whole:

"A grand exercise in ambivalence and intricacy, tense and suspenseful at every moment, with fascinatingly complex characters, unusual plausibility in detailing the professional mechanics of espionage and a genuine, uncompromising tough-mindedness comparable to Le Carré's."

SUMMARY: Adam Hall's The Quiller Memorandum earned him a lasting position as one of the precursors of the realistic spy novel of the Cold War era. Hall's measured integration of perplexing characters and masterful attention to detail equated him with le Carré and Deighton (see separate references), at the same time that his trenchant perception of Neo-Nazism in Germany, expressed from the viewpoint of the Cold War, distinguished him from his contemporaries.

George Segal starred as Quiller in a 1966 visual project, The Quiller Memorandum (20th Century-Fox), which also featured Senta Berger and Max von Sydow. Nine years later, several of the characters in the 1965 bestseller inspired a British visual miniseries.

STATUS: The Quiller series has survived to the extent that the entries of the sixties and seventies are subject to rotation, and the newer Quiller missions have been favorably received in both the critical and commercial sectors. SSP.

FIELD BIBLIOGRAPHY

Hall, Adam. The Berlin Memorandum. London: Collins, 1965. HB. British title for The Quiller Memorandum.

_____. The 9th Directive. New York: Simon & Schuster, 1966; New York: Pyramid paperback, 1968. HB-R.

_____. The Quiller Memorandum. New York: Simon & Schuster, 1965; New York: Pyramid paperback, 1966. HB-R. See also The Berlin Memorandum.

_____. The Striker Portfolio. New York: Simon & Schuster, 1968. HB-R. See also The Striker Portfolio in Appendix I.

CONSULT APPENDIX I FOR SERIES CONTINUATION

CONSULT APPENDIX II FOR SERIES TRANSITION

END OF CWF 33

† CWF 34. HAMILTON, DONALD †

BACKGROUND: Versatile American mystery and western novelist, with strong following among critics and readers alike. Anthony Boucher, influential suspense critic for the New York Times until his death in 1968, was probably Hamilton's strongest advocate.

Born in Uppsala, Sweden, in 1916. His family moved to the U.S. eight years later, after which his father, a Swedish count, became an American citizen, renouncing his title in the process.

After serving four years in the Naval Reserve as a chemist, Hamilton became a free-lance writer in 1946. He married Kathleen Stick in 1941; they have four children. He currently resides in Santa Fe, New Mexico.

Highly respected member of the following writers organizations: Mystery Writers of America, Western Writers of America, and Outdoor Writers Association of America. Also noted as a hunter, outdoor photographer, and boating enthusiast. Hamilton integrated these interests into his books, including the Matt Helm series, the subject of this file.

Further, Hamilton's fascination for the Southwest, evidenced in his westerns, notably The Big Country (1957) and Texas Fever (1960), is also reflected in his works of suspense. Pursuant to his reputation as a master sportsman, Donald Hamilton on Guns and Hunting, a collection of previously published articles on both subjects, appeared in volume form for the first time in 1970.

More recently, Hamilton displayed his fondness for boating in Cruises with Kathleen (1980).

Most of Hamilton's books were issued as paperback originals and he is regarded in many sectors as a forerunner in the field. The author has remained a distinguished constituent of the Fawcett Intelligence Group (see separate reference).

Along with Mickey Spillane (see separate reference), Hamilton may be one of the first bestselling spy novelists of the sixties having an established audience before recruiting a series operative. His following remains strong, and in 1980 Hamilton infiltrated the international terrorist market with The Mona Intercept.

Predating the initiation of the Matt Helm series by thirteen years, Hamilton's Date with Darkness (1947) was praised as a notable example of the counterspy novel. In another realm, Hamilton's mastery of firearms was soundly demonstrated in Line of Fire (1955). This last characteristic is of great importance in this file's consideration of the Matt Helm series.

With Stephen Marlowe (see separate reference), Hamilton was probably one of the first espionage novelists of the sixties to utilize the first person in his books, preceding Len Deighton (see separate reference) by two years.

Other non-series suspense titles by Hamilton include The Steel Mirror (1948), Night Walker (1954), and Assignment: Murder (1956), which was later reprinted as Assassins Have Starry Eyes.

CWF AGENT: Helm, Matthew L.

CWF HISTORY: Agent Helm has been described as a "transplanted Scandinavian," but he was born in Minnesota and moved to New Mexico as a young boy.

Before the war Helm was employed as a photographer for a small newspaper in Albuquerque, New Mexico. During World War II, officially, Helm served in the U.S. Army, achieving the rank of captain by 1945. Secretly, he was a member of an elite assassination squad known as the wrecking crew, or "Mordgruppe," as the Nazis called it. The unit was also referred to as M-group in field intelligence reports. The commander of the wrecking crew was a man identified as Mac.

The wrecking crew assigned Helm to a hazardous mission concerning the liquidation of a high-ranking Nazi officer, General von Lausche, near the French town of Kronhcim. Helm's partner in the exercise was a lone female operative known as Tina. The assignment was properly executed, though Captain Helm's involvement with Tina extended beyond the required limits.

After being discharged from the Army in 1945, Helm became a successful free-lance photographer and author of western novels. Captain Helm married a New England girl, Beth, and moved to Santa Fe, New Mexico, where he pursued his chosen postwar profession.

In 1960 Helm was recalled to active duty under mysterious circumstances which eventually led to a divorce after fifteen years of marriage. Beth gained custody of their three children: Warren, Matthew Jr., and Betsy.

Helm's wartime ally, Tina, and a young Spanish woman identified as Barbara Herrera figured in Helm's return to the wrecking crew. Ms. Herrera was found brutally murdered in the bathroom adjoining Helm's photography studio. Purportedly Tina had been sent to "terminate" Ms. Herrera, who was suspected of being an enemy agent.

The wrecking crew, still directed by the man known as Mac, has its headquarters in Washington, D.C., although the location of the building remains a secret to the public. The agency requires the use of code names for all operatives. Although "Tina" was the designation accorded to Helm's wartime confederate, she represented herself as one Madeline Loris, a New Yorker visiting Santa Fe with her husband, Frank, when she encountered Helm at a cocktail party.

Captain Helm is still an active agent with the wrecking crew, operating under the code name of Eric, the same cover identity assigned to him during the war.

Helm's mastery of firearms is well documented in the M-group files. However, he has, on numerous occasions, defied the agency's regulation concerning the use of the .38 caliber as standard field weapon. In two instances, notably The Ambushers (1963) and The Shadowers (1964), Helm preferred the .22 caliber.

Regarding his assassination mission in The Ambushers, Helm employed a hand-loaded version of the .300 Holland and Holland Magnum Cartridge with a twenty-power Herrlitz scope to liquidate General Jorge Santos, a Cuban-backed dictator based in the Costa Verde jungle.

Agent Helm is proficient in the art of kendo, as recorded in Murderers' Row (1962), as well as the more conventional methods of unarmed combat. Also, Helm effectively adapted a heavily-buckled belt to rout an enemy agent in The Silencers (1962).

The only available information on Helm's residence suggests it was Santa Rosa, California, in 1962, two years after the Herrera incident in Santa Fe. However, a payoff scandal involving Helm in 1976 disclosed that he had bank accounts in both Santa Fe and Washington. Therefore, it is highly probable that Eric moved to Washington shortly after his divorce from Beth.

It is known that Helm relinquished his writing-photography career in 1960, prior to his reentry into the wrecking crew. However, two years later, in The Silencers, Eric posed as a free-lance photographer on assignment in New Mexico. Here he encountered a man identified as Frank "Buddy" McKenna, a pre-war newspaper associate, at a top-secret government party near Alamogordo, N.M., who was to play a crucial role in his mission.

Eric is described as one of the most dangerous operatives in the field. His lean, six-foot-four inch frame has provided him with a deceptively innocent appearance that has served him well.

OPERATIVE DATA: The development of the Matt Helm novels is noticeably different from other paperback original series of the period, as regards Donald Hamilton's detailed depiction of Matt Helm and the organization for which he works.

Death of a Citizen (1960), the first series entry, recounted Helm's postwar meeting with Tina and the events leading up to his return to the wrecking crew. It should be noted, however, that after Barbara Herrera's body was discovered, Helm allied with Tina on a perilous journey across New Mexico and Texas in his 1951 Chevy pickup, a staple in several of the later books.

It was, however, Helm's bitter confrontation with a mysterious woman in San Antonio, later identified as an M-group agent operating under the code name of Sarah, and the revelation of Tina's true postwar allegiances that prompted agency director Mac to reinstate Helm's status as Eric.

Hamilton's allusion to Helm's secured gun rack in his studio alerted the reader to the major role that gun lore would play in the evolution of the series--in Death of a Citizen, one of Helm's antagonists was armed with a .357 Magnum.

Anthony Boucher's admiration for both Hamilton and Helm was reflected in his review of Death of a Citizen, "A harsh and sometimes shocking story, told with restraint, power, and conviction."

In The Wrecking Crew (1960) Helm utilized his photographic and literary background to track down an elusive master spy, known only as Caselius. Bearing the same name as Mac's organization, the second Helm mission more clearly illustrated its savage function.

Eric's explosive showdown with Caselius in the Swedish ore country established the feverish pace for future assignments. This entry also initiated the constants of the weary male and female operatives in Eric's camp, both of whom eventually suffer horrifying deaths; the treacherous Tina-style "femme fatale" who suffers an equally brutal death at Helm's hands; and his tantalizing companion.

Helm's assignment in The Removers (1961) involved the liquidation of a vicious assassin named Martell, who was known to have "terminated" several of Mac's agents. Martell was employed at the time by the Fredericks mob in Reno, Nevada, where ironically, Helm's ex-wife, Beth, had married a local rancher, Lawrence Logan.

This pattern of circumstances provoked a violent battle between Eric and Martell that set the precedent for later missions, notably The Silencers (1962), The Ambushers (1963), and The Shadowers (1964). Mac's clandestine Recognition Room was also introduced in this entry.

The Silencers (1962) transpired as the most crucial development in the Helm dossier, being Hamilton's first large-scale book in the series. Full details are outlined below.

This effort featured Hamilton's most ingenious plot device--a deadly enemy spy, known only as Cowboy, who looked and acted the part.

The savage death of agent Sarah in Juarez, Mexico, and the discovery of a top-secret microfilm launched Helm and Sarah's sister, a provocative Texas woman identified as Gail Hendricks, on a grueling mission from El Paso, Texas, into the mountains of New Mexico to hunt down the man Mac believed to be Cowboy.

The book's ferocious climax, set in a desolate mountain church, ranked among the best in the series, and Hamilton's use of the first person was at its most effective in The Silencers. As Anthony Boucher observed in his review, "The resolute hardness of story, prose, and Helm should earn Hamilton the title of the Hammett of espionage."

Acknowledging the precedent established in The Silencers, the later entries consistently recognized the acceleration of the Cold War.

Although Murderers' Row (1962) lacked the scope of The Silencers, Hamilton's fifth Helm entry may well be the first postwar spy novel dealing with the vulnerability of the Polaris submarine. Helm was ordered to locate a missing nuclear scientist, Dr. Norman Michaelis, who had perfected a lethal Polaris warhead device known as A. U. D. A. P. (Airborne Underwater Detection Apparatus).

In The Ambushers (1963) a fanatical Nazi war criminal,
identified as Heinrich von Sachs (alias Kurt Quintana), based in
northern Mexico, and a Soviet missile smuggled out of Cuba figured in what many operatives regard as the best in the series,
due to its emphasis on adventure and gun lore. Eric's beautifully
enigmatic Russian counterpart, Vadya, and Mac's secret ranch in
Arizona were introduced in this mission.

The Ambushers is credited with augmenting Helm's following, partly by its treatment of the plausible threat of a rising Neo-
Nazi movement throughout Mexico and certain sectors of the Southwest.

The Shadowers (1964) remains the most suspenseful in the
dossier, although it lacked the magnitude of The Silencers or The
Ambushers.

Eric's assignment of assassinating a ruthless spy master,
recorded as one Emil Taussig, was intentionally related to his
cover marriage to an alluring space scientist, Dr. Olivia Mariassy.
An obsessive desire for revenge and the untimely death of Gail
Hendricks, with whom Helm had maintained a relationship, were
effectively integrated into the principal plot.

Hamilton's formidable villain, Karl Kroch, helped make The
Shadowers one of the finest espionage novels to come out of the
Cold War, especially as a paperback original.

The Ravagers (1964) is significant for its lack of a central
villain.   Assigned to transport secret plans for a new laser across
Canada, accompanied by the wife and young daughter of a renowned
scientist, Eric confronted a chain of murderous spies and avaricious
government agents.

The book featured a seemingly innocent termination device
that haunted most field operatives--excluding Eric--long after the
mission was completed.

Helm and Vadya matched wits with the nefarious Madame
Ling in The Devastators (1965), Hamilton's first Helm mission involving the Chi-Coms. The menace of bubonic plague was set
against a background of the complexities of big-power politics and
the cities of London and Glasgow.

In the thick of both the Cold War and the paperback spy
mania, sales of the Matt Helm books soared to the 5,000,000 mark.

Eric's elusive Chi-Com adversary, Mr. Soo, was introduced
in The Betrayers (1966).   The growing Asian antagonism over U.S.
involvement in Vietnam dominated this Helm entry.

Mac's senior man in the Hawaiian Islands, an explosives expert known as the Monk, was suspected of subversive involvement

with Peking. Eric's assignment was to avert a plot to destroy an American troopship, the General Herman Hughes.

The Menacers (1968) revolved around an incredible U. F. O. sighting on the Mexican coast. Helm was summoned to accompany to safety in Los Alamos, New Mexico, the woman who had witnessed the U. F. O. incident, one Annette O'Leary.

Reflecting the waning spy phenomenon, Hamilton emphasized the competitive motives of various government agencies, including M-group, in their bid to capitalize on the U. F. O. event.

It should be noted here that Vadya, Hamilton's most prominent Cold War symbol, was liquidated in The Menacers, perhaps another indication of the spy movement's decline.

The Interlopers (1969), Hamilton's last Helm entry of the sixties, found Eric posing as a dead communist assassin who had been designated to kill the President-elect.

SUMMARY: The continued success of this exceptional paperback series can be explained perhaps by three factors,

1) Donald Hamilton's careful delineation of Matt Helm and the apparat which employed his special talents.

2) The conspicuous absence of a formula approach to the series.

3) The consistent integration of the author's fascination with firearms and the Southwest throughout the series. Unquestionably, these two elements provided a strong attraction for the male reading audience.

More fundamentally, Hamilton's use of the first person suggests a historical link to the hard-boiled, private-eye genre of the forties. Simply stated, Donald Hamilton gave the paperback spy novel a new form when he created Matt Helm.

Finally, the critical praise accorded to the Helm series signaled a major precedent in itself for a paperback original. Anthony Boucher, for instance, did not approve of Ian Fleming's James Bond (see separate reference), but was one of Hamilton's strongest proponents. In his evaluation of The Shadowers he called Helm "One of the few credible secret agents in today's fiction. Helm is a genuinely tough and tough-minded protagonist; your reading diet lacks essential vitamins if you overlook him."

To date, over 20,000,000 Matt Helm books have been distributed to pro-Western operatives.

Between 1966 and 1969 veteran spy master Irving Allen and Columbia Pictures adapted four highly successful visual projects from the Donald Hamilton dossier. Conveying much of Matt Helm's glib manner, Dean Martin played him in The Silencers (1966), Murderers' Row (1966), The Ambushers (1967), and The Wrecking Crew (1969).

The first of these projects, The Silencers, believed by many field agents to be the best of the series, was based on Death of a Citizen as well as its namesake. This Allen-Columbia entry featured Stella Stevens as Gail Hendricks, Daliah Lavi as Tina, Nancy Kovacks as Barbara, and Cyd Charisse as Sarita (Sarah).

In 1975 Tony Franciosa played Donald Hamilton's lethal protagonist in Matt Helm, an ABC home visual project which generated a brief series, terminating in January 1976.

Franciosa portrayed Helm as an L. A. -based private detective. Apart from the use of the Helm character, the ABC visual project bore little resemblance to the Hamilton canon.

STATUS: Matt Helm, also known in the field as Eric, is still on active duty with the wrecking crew. Helm was engaged in six recorded assignments during the seventies, and the details of his latest mission, The Revengers (1982), were revealed in the fall of 1982. SSP.

FIELD BIBLIOGRAPHY

Hamilton, Donald. The Ambushers. New York: Fawcett-Gold Medal, 1963. PBO.

_____. The Betrayers. New York: Fawcett-Gold Medal, 1966. PBO.

_____. Death of a Citizen. New York: Fawcett-Gold Medal, 1960. PBO.

_____. The Devastators. New York: Fawcett-Gold Medal, 1965. PBO.

_____. The Interlopers. New York: Fawcett-Gold Medal, 1969. PBO.

_____. The Menacers. New York: Fawcett-Gold Medal, 1968. PBO.

_____. Murderers' Row. New York: Fawcett-Gold Medal, 1962. PBO.

_____. The Ravagers. New York: Fawcett-Gold Medal, 1964. PBO.

_____. *The Removers*. New York: Fawcett-Gold Medal, 1961.
PBO.

_____. *The Shadowers*. New York: Fawcett-Gold Medal, 1964.
PBO.

_____. *The Silencers*. New York: Fawcett-Gold Medal, 1962.
PBO.

_____. *The Wrecking Crew*. New York: Fawcett-Gold Medal,
1960. PBO.

CONSULT APPENDIX I FOR SERIES CONTINUATION

END OF CWF 34

† CWF 35. HARVESTER, SIMON †

BACKGROUND: Cover identity of Henry St. John Clair Rumbold-Gibbs. Born in 1909. Best known for his Dorian Silk secret service thrillers, although he penned over thirty additional books under this identity as well as his own name. Before his death in 1975, Gibbs had produced thirteen Silk novels.

Gibbs-Harvester traveled extensively throughout Africa and Asia, and his works reflected an incisive knowledge of the turbulent postwar politics indigenous to these sectors.

Prior to recruiting Silk, Harvester created five Asian missions for operative Malcolm Kenton: *Bamboo Screen* (1955), *Dragon Road* (1956), *The Paradise Men* (1956), *The Copper Butterfly* (1957), and *The Golden Fear* (1957).

Similarly, Harvester's Heron Murmur mystery series also saw a brief term of duty, consisting of two titles: *The Chinese Hammer* (1960), and *Troika* (1962), the latter published two years later in the U.S. as *The Flying Horse*.

The first Silk mission, *Unsung Road*, initially appeared in 1960, and subsequent entries bore the designation, "Road," notably *Assassins' Road* (1965) and *Zion Road* (1968).

Harvester's second Kenton effort, *Dragon Road*, has been incorrectly listed as a Silk thriller, although it is possible that the author may have devised the Silk title format from the aforementioned Kenton novel. Less understandably, *Bamboo Screen*, the first in the Kenton series, also has been referred to as a Silk entry.

Harvester's straight thrillers include Epitaph for Lemmings (1944) and Spider's Web (1953). While most of these books were not published in the U.S., such series inserts as Bamboo Screen did not materialize in the domestic market until Harvester achieved popularity with Dorian Silk. Bamboo Screen appeared in the U.S. in 1968.

All of the novels issued under Harvester's real name were likewise restricted to British territory, and were non-series contributions, among them The Six Mile Face (1952) and The Mortal Fire (1963).

Shadow of a Hidden Land (1966), by contrast, was one novel outside the Silk mold that received a generous distribution in both the U.S. and Britain.

CWF AGENT: Silk, Dorian.

CWF HISTORY: Little background data exists on this agent who dealt primarily with Afro-Asian politics.

British subject. Well-traveled in the Orient and Africa, Silk was accustomed to Eastern folkways.

Especially adept at driving foreign motor cars; also proficient in the rigorous disciplines of combat. Master in the art of seduction, particularly with women of Afro-Asian origins.

As a result of his global assignments in Asia and Africa, Silk cultivated the polished manner of a shuttle-diplomat--which made him doubly effective as a field operative for the British Secret Service.

Silk's last mission was in 1976. No further record.

OPERATIVE DATA: Despite the topicality manifested by Harvester throughout the Dorian Silk dossier, the basic format of the series, regarding pace and characterization, varied little during its progression.

This should not be viewed as criticism of the series, for the Arabic settings of Unsung Road (1960) lent an unusually high degree of authenticity. In the later entries, Harvester merely adapted his Afro-Asian expertise to the more sensitive aspects of the Cold War.

In Unsung Road the divided sympathies of Iran, Iraq, and Nasser's Egypt imperiled Silk's assignment involving Woolf, an avaricious intelligence chief based in North Africa, and a mysterious Arabic counterrevolutionary squad, known only as SAVAK.

Focusing on the chaotic Middle-Eastern political climate of the early sixties, Harvester adroitly portrayed the growing Arab contempt toward Western scientific power in the context of the region's volatile political atmosphere.

In its review of Unsung Road, Bestsellers observed, "Simon Harvester has a wonderful way with words and a unique style, staccato and poetic."

Posing as a globe-trotting businessman in Silk Road (1962), Silk was ordered to obtain crucial intelligence from a defector in Afghanistan.

Harvester portended the complex Middle-Eastern geopolitics of the seventies in Assassins' Road (1965). Silk's mission was to unveil the explosive activities of an elusive conspirator, "The Prophet," as a prelude to averting a new "Holy War." The principal locale of this Silk entry was Jerusalem.

SUMMARY: Simon Harvester's Dorian Silk uniquely conveyed the aftermath of Afro-Asian colonial independence in the immediate postwar environment, doing so with conviction and menace.

With its unstable Arab settings, Unsung Road typified the Silk dossier, particularly the author's erudite knowledge of tangled Afro-Asian politics.

Harvester successfully advanced his narrative structure into the seventies, and the series now represents a Western mosaic embodying the conflicting realms of the Cold War and détente.

STATUS: For the most part, the Silk entries written in the sixties failed to survive in the espionage market of the seventies. However, the later Silk assignments were well received in both the critical and sales sectors during the seventies, although the paperback distribution of the post-Cold War titles tended to be less than those of the previous decade. SOP.

FIELD BIBLIOGRAPHY

Harvester, Simon. Assassins' Road. New York: Walker, 1965; New York: MacFadden-Bartell paperback, 1967. HB-R.

_____. Battle Road. New York: Walker, 1967; New York: MacFadden-Bartell paperback, 1968. HB-R.

_____. Nameless Road. London: Jarrolds, 1969. HB. See also Nameless Road in Appendix I.

_____. Red Road. London: Jarrolds, 1963; New York: Walker,

1964; New York: MacFadden-Bartell paperback, 1967. HB-HB-R.

_____. Silk Road. London: Jarrolds, 1962; New York: Walker, 1963; New York: MacFadden-Bartell paperback, 1968. HB-HB-R.

_____. Treacherous Road. London: Jarrolds, 1966; New York: Walker, 1967; New York: MacFadden-Bartell paperback, 1968. HB-HB-R.

_____. Unsung Road. London: Jarrolds, 1960; New York: Walker, 1961; New York: MacFadden-Bartell paperback, 1968. HB-HB-R.

_____. Zion Road. New York: Walker, 1968. HB-R. See also Zion Road in Appendix I.

CONSULT APPENDIX I FOR SERIES CONTINUATION

END OF CWF 35

† CWF 36. HOLLY, J. HUNTER †

BACKGROUND: Cover identity of Joan Carol Holly, psychologist, teacher, and author of science-fiction short stories and novels. Born in 1932.

Ms. Holly's genre books include Encounter (1959), The Flying Eyes (1962), Dark Planet (1962), and The Dark Enemy (1965). Roger Elwood's science-fiction collection, Graduated Robots and Other Stories (1974), contained one of Ms. Holly's short stories, "Mind Traders."

Recruited to write The Assassination Affair (1967) for the U.N.C.L.E. visual-project novelization series.

CWF AGENTS: Solo, Napoleon, and Illya Kuryakin.

CWF HISTORY: See also Avallone, Michael--CWF 6.

OPERATIVE DATA: The Assassination Affair, appearing midway in the Ace project, emerged as one of the more satisfying entries. Holly's careful balance of suspense and action was acknowledged as exceptional, placing her on a level with U.N.C.L.E. masters Michael Avallone and David McDaniel (see separate references).

Further, the menace of world starvation in The Assassination Affair was decidedly more realistic than the archetypal U. N. C. L. E. novel.

The bizarre death in Chicago of U. N. C. L. E. operative Randolph prompted Mr. Waverly to assign Solo and Kuryakin to follow a lead involving a mysterious provocateur known only as Dundee, suspected of being associated with T. H. R. U. S. H.

The threat of a T. H. R. U. S. H. global famine blueprint, "Operation Breadbasket," figured into The Assassination Affair, and Ms. Holly tightly fused these diverse elements to produce an entertaining novelization.

SUMMARY: Despite the fact that J. Hunter Holly wrote only one U. N. C. L. E. entry, The Assassination Affair, she conceived a plot with suspense and action that surpassed the average series contribution. Indeed, Ms. Holly rivaled the more highly lauded novelization efforts of Michael Avallone and David McDaniel (see separate references).

STATUS: See also Avallone, Michael--CWF 6.

FIELD BIBLIOGRAPHY

Holly, J. Hunter. The Assassination Affair. New York: Ace Books, 1967. PBO. TN.

CONSULT ACE INTELLIGENCE GROUP FOR ADDITIONAL AUTHOR REFERENCES

END OF CWF 36

† CWF 37. HUNT, E. HOWARD †

BACKGROUND: Born in 1918. Former C. I. A. agent; popular author of suspense and espionage fiction.

Hunt graduated from Brown University in 1940, and later enjoyed success as a screenwriter, an editor for the March of Time, and a correspondent for Life magazine.

Hunt's twenty-year field experience with the C. I. A. in Europe, Latin America, and the Far East led to his appointment as a White House staff assistant to President Nixon in 1971.

The author's involvement in the 1972 Watergate scandal and his subsequent conviction on six counts of conspiracy are a matter of public record and therefore will not be expounded in this file. However, it might be noted that his wife of twenty-three years, Dorothy, died in a plane crash in December 1972, traveling to raise money for her husband's defense.

Hunt assumed a number of cover identities in the suspense field, notably Gordon Davis, John Baxter, Robert Dietrich, and David St. John. Many of the novels written under these pseudonyms were later reissued under the author's real name.

The subject of this file, the Peter Ward series, was initially penned as by St. John. Further, Hunt conceived a brief adventure dossier, concerning one Peter Trees, under the cover names of John Q. and John Quirk. These include: The Bunnies (1965), The Survivor (1965), and The Tournament (1966).

Hunt served as a distinguished member of the N.A.L./Signet Intelligence Group (see separate reference) during the mid-sixties.

CWF AGENT: Ward, Peter.

CWF HISTORY: The background of this CWF agent is somewhat obscure, but it is known that Ward functioned as a C.I.A. operative who had successfully utilized the cover of a Georgetown lawyer and socialite.

Ward was assigned to a branch of "The Company" known only as the Clandestine Services, based at C.I.A. headquarters in Langley, Virginia.

The Deputy Director of the Clandestine Services was identified as one Avery Thorne. Insiders described Thorne as a controlled man with white hair and an ageless face that held a touch of asceticism.

Unlike most C.I.A. officers, Ward was not restricted to a specific global sector for his missions. From 1965 to 1971 Ward was assigned to the politically inflamed spheres of Europe, Southeast Asia, South America, and the Orient, operating under the code name, Seraph.

Ward's training included the usual indoctrination in methods of combat, liquidation, camouflage, espionage, and deception. While his performance qualified Ward for active duty abroad, there was nothing exceptional about his progress.

The Clandestine Services group no longer exists and it appears that Ward and Thorne are no longer associated with the C.I.A. However, Ward's term of duty did produce some significant effects on the espionage novel of the sixties.

OPERATIVE DATA: The Peter Ward series did for the paperback original spy thriller what the realistic spy stories of John le Carré and Len Deighton (see separate references) did for the hardback genre.

Throughout the series, Hunt employed terminology indicative of the C. I. A. in actual practice, a keen reflection of the author's own experience as a former agent. One term in the Ward dossier was Chi-Com, which signified Chinese Communist during the Cold War era. This designation, like others of the period, is not in common use in current espionage fiction.

Beyond this facet of the series structure, Hunt described the operations of global intelligence and political agencies, covering both pro-Western and Communist sympathies with authoritative accuracy. This aspect of the series' development closely identified Hunt with the style practiced by Len Deighton (see separate reference).

Using Peter Ward as a focal point, Hunt conceived one of the most realistic of paperback spy originals to come out of the sixties.

Posing as a Canadian journalist in On Hazardous Duty (1965), Ward's assignment was to protect a Soviet scientist whose knowledge threatened the balance of power. Hunt added authenticity to his tightly knit plot with the detailed backgrounds of K. G. B. agent Belkov and the enticing Nicole Minette.

The precedent established in On Hazardous Duty was adroitly perfected in later missions. Deploying Ward as an instrument of global intelligence, related from the Western viewpoint, Hunt succinctly defined the intricacies of the Cold War.

The intensification of the Vietnam War underscored Festival for Spies (1966). In Cambodia, Ward's mission was to investigate the mysterious exile of pro-Western Prince Sonram.

Hunt's sober characterization of Chi-Com behavior in Southeast Asia during the period emerged with frightening clarity. Further, the cultural integration into the plot of the Cambodian virgin celebration accentuated the author's knowledge of Southeast Asia.

The Venus Probe (1966) developed as Hunt's most complex series entry, concerned with U.S. -Soviet contention for superiority in space, dealing with the disappearance of seven key Western scientists.

Hunt's conception of Ward in The Venus Probe was noticeably more detached, contrasting with the abundance of aeronautical expertise expressed throughout the book.

Ward was portrayed at his most violent in One of Our Agents Is Missing (1967) as he confronted Chinese antagonists in Tokyo. Hunt's uncompromising depiction of Ward at his most ruthless, challenging the operative with the malicious Chi-Com threat and internal treachery, signaled <u>One of Our Agents Is Missing</u> as the best in the series. The ambiguities of the Cold War was especially apparent in this effort, with the premise of a C. I. A. operative vanishing from the field with a large sum of U.S. government funds.

SUMMARY: E. Howard Hunt's Peter Ward series consistently conveyed a bitter tone that was not as apparent in other paperback original features of the period, with the possible exceptions of Donald Hamilton's Matt Helm and Edward S. Aarons' Sam Durell (see separate references).

The author's concern with authenticity, coupled with his own background as a C. I. A. agent, illustrated the complexities of the Cold War as fact and fiction. In this respect alone, the Ward dossier evolved as a major development in the paperback spy fiction of the sixties.

Although some of the later Ward entries were published in hardback, the appearance of the earlier efforts as paperback originals places the Hunt series in the latter category.

STATUS: Ward has been inactive since 1971. It should be noted, however, that the first six Ward assignments were reissued under Hunt's own name from 1972 to 1974. This action exploited the author's role in Watergate and revealed his former cover identity, David St. John.

It is highly probable that the Ward series, given Hunt's extensive knowledge of the C. I. A., would be well-received in the current market. SOP.

FIELD BIBLIOGRAPHY

Hunt, E. Howard (as David St. John). <u>Festival for Spies</u>. New York: New American Library, 1966. PBO.

_____. <u>Hazardous Duty</u>. London: Frederick Muller Ltd., 1966. HB. British title for <u>On Hazardous Duty</u>.

_____. <u>The Mongol Mask</u>. New York: Weybright, 1968. HB.

_____. <u>On Hazardous Duty</u>. New York: New American Library, 1965. PBO. <u>See also</u> <u>Hazardous Duty</u>.

_____. <u>One of Our Agents Is Missing</u>. New York: New American Library, 1967. PBO.

_____. <u>Return from Vorkuta</u>. New York: New American Library, 1965; London: Frederick Muller Ltd., 1967. PBO-HB.

_____. The Sorcerers. New York: Weybright, 1969. HB.
See also The Sorcerers in Appendix I.

_____. The Towers of Silence. New York: New American Library, 1966. PBO.

_____. The Venus Probe. New York: New American Library, 1966. PBO.

CONSULT APPENDIX I FOR SERIES CONTINUATION

END OF CWF 37

† CWF 38. JOHNSTON, WILLIAM †

BACKGROUND: American author long associated with visual-project novelizations. Born in 1924.

In addition to his service with the "Get Smart" home series, the subject of this file, Johnston has shadowed other projects in this arena, notably Captain Nice (1967), Then Came Bronson (1970), and, from the "Mod Squad" series, Home Is Where the Quick Is (1971).

Johnston has also ventured into the theatrical sector, with such efforts as Klute (1971) and Asylum (1972).

Under the cover identity of Susan Claudia, Johnston penned a series of gothics: Madness at the Castle (1966), The Searching Spectre (1967), The Silent Voice (1967), and Clock and Bell (1974).

Under his own name, Johnston has been less prolific in the straight fiction sector, producing The Marriage Cage (1960) and Barney (1970).

In 1970 Johnston adapted a segment of the Dick Tracy comic strip in a paperback format.

CWF AGENT: Smart, Maxwell.

CWF HISTORY: Known in the field as Agent 86, an American operative for C.O.N.T.R.O.L., a U.S. intelligence organization.

Although in the visual project C.O.N.T.R.O.L. was situated in Washington, D.C., the novelization series placed it underground in a New York gray-stone building, replete with the expected security mechanisms.

Smart was generally allied with a capable female, Agent 99, whom he eventually married in 1969. The head of C. O. N. T. R. O. L. was recorded as Chief, although he was occasionally referred to as Thaddeus.

Agent 86 challenged a number of K. A. O. S. constituents in the field, chiefly the Claw (a. k. a. the Craw), Dr. Yes (a. k. a. Dr. Yeh), Wayne Ways, Melvin Means, Whitestone, and V. T. Brattleboro, among countless others. F. L. A. G., otherwise known as Free Lance Agents Amalgamated, was involved in a 1965 mission. Full details under OPERATIVE DATA.

Described by both confederates and enemies as slight, tight-lipped, and neatly dressed, Smart was perceived as a respectable threat by K. A. O. S., an inimical espionage body, and its German master, Conrad Siegfried McTavish.

However, 86's internal performance has been characterized as ridiculously incompetent, and he was known to have driven Chief nearly to the breaking point. This applied, to a lesser degree, to several of Smart's colleagues--namely the aforementioned Agent 99; Agent 13, who was highly adept in the art of personal camouflage; Hymie, a former K. A. O. S. robot recruited into C. O. N. T. R. O. L. in 1965; and Admiral Harold Harman Hargrade, the agency's former chief. Fang, the spy dog, known in C. O. N. T. R. O. L. circles as K-13, was oblivious to Smart's treatment.

Agent 86 scored impressively in the intelligence community, despite his farcical image.

Smart's secret gear generated an enormous amount of interest, especially his shoe-phone, which served him well in the most perilous situations, and an invisible wall in his apartment that disposed of hostile agents.

However, 86's most potent weapon was a set of key phrases, as follows:

1) "Would you believe?"

2) "Sorry about that, Chief."

3) "Missed it by that much."

Although C. O. N. T. R. O. L. was disbanded in 1970, Smart turned up ten years later as an operative for P. I. T. S., or more formally, Provisional Intelligence Technical Services. He retained his original status as Agent 86.

OPERATIVE DATA: The "Get Smart" project, unlike most other

series of this nature, had a sole author--Johnston. Throughout its term, he displayed a sharply defined sense of satire that honored the complexion of the NBC visual dossier.

In Get Smart (1965), the initial entry, Smart was assigned to locate a crucial computer, F.R.E.D., which signified the Fechner-ized Radiological Electronic Decoder.

Johnston's brisk narrative style set the pace for future novel-izations. Penetrating the complex maze of the U.N. building in New York, Smart encountered a southern tourist with a deceptively Rus-sian accent, and a F.L.A.G. agent, Captain 49, who intended to de-stroy the U.N. from a submarine.

On this assignment Agent 86 was assisted by Fang and Blos-som Rose, F.R.E.D.'s desirable inventor.

The self-parodying quality of the home series permeated every facet of this first novelization, from Smart's outrageous briefing with Chief to F.L.A.G.'s Madison Avenue-style advertising of its services. Johnston manifested a seasoned knowledge of New York locales in Get Smart, and he wisely avoided the obvious progression into slap-stick humor.

In Missed It by That Much (1967), Johnston spoofed the gruel-ing spy epic in which Smart and Agent 99 trekked into the Congo to rescue a top scientist, Dr. Livingstrom, from the clutches of K.A.O.S.

The comic mood was heightened in this entry, and Whitestone, a magician-illusionist in the pay of K.A.O.S., emerged as one of the series' more engaging adversaries.

Johnston achieved the highest possible level of self-mockery in Max Smart: The Spy Who Went Out to the Cold (1968).

Ordered to accompany Professor Wormser von BOOM to a clandestine laboratory at the North Pole, 86 and 99 engaged on an incredible foray, extending from a camel caravan in the Sahara to a jet bound for the U.S.S.R., to deliver von BOOM to his destination.

SUMMARY: In his nine-volume novelization series, William John-ston superbly captured the satirical flair of the NBC visual project that featured Don Adams as Maxwell Smart, Barbara Feldon as Agent 99, and the late Edward Platt as Chief. The home series also offered such recurring operatives as Bernie Kopell, a.k.a. Conrad Siegfried McTavish, and Dick Gautier as Hymie.

NBC presented the series from 1965 to 1969; CBS sponsored the project for one season until its cancellation in 1970.

Adams returned as Agent 86 in Universal's The Nude Bomb

(1980), a theatrical visual project in which Smart, now engaged by P. I. T. S. , challenged K. A. O. S. 's plot to render the world naked.

No longer allied with Barbara Feldon as Agent 99, Smart was effectively assisted by Pamela Hensley, Andrea Howard, and Sylvia Kristel as Agents 36-22-34, respectively. Dana Elcar assumed the role of Chief.

The Universal release was distributed into the home sector as The Return of Maxwell Smart.

STATUS: The reissue of William Johnston's novelization series would not be justified unless the project were to be revived outside the theatrical arena. SOP.

FIELD BIBLIOGRAPHY

Johnston, William. And Loving It! New York: Tempo Books, 1967. PBO. TN.

_____. Get Smart! New York: Tempo Books, 1965. PBO. TN.

_____. Get Smart Once Again! New York: Tempo Books, 1966. PBO. TN.

_____. Max Smart and the Ghastly Ghost Affair. New York: Tempo Books, 1969. PBO. TN.

_____. Max Smart and the Perilous Pellets. New York: Tempo Books, 1966. PBO. TN.

_____. Max Smart Loses Control. New York: Tempo Books, 1968. PBO. TN.

_____. Max Smart: The Spy Who Went Out to the Cold. New York: Tempo Books, 1968. PBO. TN.

_____. Missed It by That Much. New York: Tempo Books, 1967. PBO. TN.

_____. Sorry, Chief. New York: Tempo Books, 1966. PBO. TN.

WOULD YOU BELIEVE THAT THIS IS THE END OF

CWF 38?

† CWF 39. KNIGHT, MALLORY T. †

BACKGROUND: Cover identity of Bernhardt J. Hurwood, prolific American writer with experience in films and television. Born in New York in 1926.

Hurwood has written a variety of works, ranging from a book on the occult, Vampires, Werewolves, and Ghouls (1968), to noveli- zations like Born Innocent (1975), to timely non-fiction like Confes- sions of a Sex Researcher (1976). Hurwood also penned Casebook: Exorcism and Possession (1974) under the name of Fr. Xavier and several books as D. Gunther Wilde.

Utilizing the cover name of Mallory T. Knight, Hurwood en- tered the espionage field in 1967 with the Tim O'Shane-"The Man from T. O. M. C. A. T." series.

A prominent member of the Mystery Writers of America, Hurwood served in the Universal-Award Intelligence Group (see separate reference).

CWF AGENT: O'Shane, Timothy.

CWF HISTORY: Former Marine Corps officer. During a term of special duty with the American Embassy in Paris in 1961, O'Shane mysteriously acquired a N. A. T. O. microfilm after a sexual liaison with one Marianne de Montreuil.

The contents of the microfilm: the minutes of an "Eyes On- ly" meeting concerning nuclear warhead depots and missile emplace- ments.

O'Shane reported to the embassy for an interrogation session with the Secretary of State, the French Foreign Minister, and the local NCO, at which time O'Shane learned that Marianne's diplomat- husband, Marquis Gervaise de Montreuil, had been found in the Siene, savagely murdered during O'Shane's rendezvous with his wife.

Upon satisfying his interrogators, O'Shane was transported to an obscure building in the United Kingdom where he was received by one Colonel Duncan MacSwiver, Scotsman.

This perplexing incident was designed as Captain O'Shane's "recruitment" into T. O. M. C. A. T., a global espionage network of- ficially known as Tactical Operations Master Counterintelligence Assault Team. Its chief was Colonel MacSwiver.

After becoming acquainted with MacSwiver, who emerged from both world wars as one of the Allies' most arrogant officers,

O'Shane was dispatched to T. O. M. C. A. T. I, a thousand-acre estate on Long Island which cloaked the intelligence organization's introductory training center.

The remainder of O'Shane's indoctrination was completed at such advanced T. O. M. C. A. T. bases as Barbados, Kuala Lumpur, Kobe, Rome, London, Reykjavik, and Little America.

During this latter period, O'Shane achieved proficiency in the following areas: 1) Language fluency, 2) marksmanship, 3) knife-throwing, 4) strategic flying, 5) demolition, 6) safecracking, 7) lock-picking, 8) cryptography, 9) hypnosis, 10) skiing, and 11) silent assassination.

After a final examination, in which O'Shane penetrated a Chi-Com culture center in Cairo, he was awarded the MS, or Master Spy degree. He was subsequently assigned to T. O. M. C. A. T. II, the operative segment of the intelligence apparat, situated on the top two floors of the affluent Park Towers apartment building in New York. The roof of that building was often altered for the purpose of concealing internal operations, ranging from top-priority briefings to field weaponry preparations.

The cover for T. O. M. C. A. T. was established in the mid-sixties as Global Air Services House, Limited. Ostensibly, this "firm" was involved in handling special charter flights and freight consignments into hazardous territories.

O'Shane operated under the code designation of Agent Petronius, and, in addition to his acquired talents, he was ranked as a master of sexual persuasion.

Pursuant to this last ability, the following women represented his most striking alliances:

1) Chastity Beld--willing secretary of Colonel MacSwiver.

2) Wanda Nafkiwicz--highly sensual cryptographer; Polish.

3) Penelope Box--provocative C. I. A. agent.

4) Fanny and Hilly Willick--delectable handmaidens to Priadua Paranassus, prominent Greek industrialist.

5) Dr. Tanya Bolshoygrud--mesmerizing dentist; Soviet extraction.

T. O. M. C. A. T. was dissolved in 1971, after which time there has been no further record of O'Shane.

OPERATIVE DATA: The distinguishing mark of the O'Shane series was the comic exaggeration of Agent Petronius' seemingly unlimited sexual power.

Knight deviated little from this premise throughout the series, and it is regrettable that O'Shane failed to summon his impressive arsenal of non-sexual talents in the field.

As with the sex-oriented thrillers of Rod Gray and Ted Mark (see separate references), the initial episode exemplified the chief virtues of the series.

In The Dozen Deadly Dragons of Joy (1967) O'Shane was ordered to infiltrate Mom-Za, a Chi-Com spy network controlled by one Alexander Graham Wang. O'Shane eventually discovered Wang's design for global domination: the deployment of twelve mysterious beauties to enslave sexually all American males in their path.

Suffice it to say, O'Shane's acumen in this area of unarmed combat was tested to the limit.

SUMMARY: Mallory T. Knight's "The Man from T. O. M. C. A. T." series cleverly parodied the indomitable sexual image of the tongue-in-cheek secret agent.

Like other advocates of the species, the format of the O'Shane dossier remained constant throughout its run. Unfortunately, Knight failed to utilize O'Shane's highly developed operative abilities, as described in the first entry, The Dozen Deadly Dragons of Joy (1967).

To promote its new series, Universal-Award encouraged readers to contact their "hero" in care of the publisher.

STATUS: The withdrawal of Universal-Award from the espionage market in 1977 probably insured the inactive status of Agent Petronius, although the T. O. M. C. A. T. operative has not been reported in the field since 1971.

The nature of the series would likely attract a receptive audience, as indicated by the periodic reissue of Ted Mark's "The Man from O. R. G. Y. " (see separate reference). SOP.

FIELD BIBLIOGRAPHY

Knight, Mallory T. The Dirty Rotten Depriving Ray. New York: Universal-Award, 1967. PBO.

_____. The Dozen Deadly Dragons of Joy. New York: Universal-Award, 1967. PBO.

_____. The Malignant Metaphysical Menace. New York: Universal-Award, 1968. PBO.

_____. *The Million Missing Maidens.* New York: Universal-Award, 1967. PBO.

_____. *The Ominous Orgy.* New York: Universal-Award, 1969. PBO.

_____. *The Peking Pornographer.* New York: Universal-Award, 1969. PBO.

_____. *The Terrible Ten.* New York: Universal-Award, 1967. PBO.

_____. *Tsimmis in Tangier.* New York: Universal-Award, 1968. PBO.

CONSULT APPENDIX I FOR SERIES CONTINUATION

END OF CWF 39

† CWF 40. LEASOR, JAMES †

BACKGROUND: Thomas James Leasor was born in 1923 in Erith, Kent, England. Educated at the City of London School and Oriel College, Oxford, where he edited *The Isis.*

Served with distinction in the British Army in Burma, India, and Malaya during World War II. Later achieved the rank of captain in the Royal Berkshire Regiment.

In 1948 Leasor joined the staff of the *Daily Express* where he worked as a columnist, foreign correspondent, and feature writer.

Leasor entered the fiction field with his critically acclaimed novel, *Not Such a Bad Day* (1946) and eventually garnered a sizeable following with his Dr. Jason Love series, the subject of this file.

Leasor also ventured into other literary sectors that accented his wartime experiences, including several volumes on military history, chiefly *The Clock with Four Hands: Based on the Experiences of General Sir Leslie Hollis* (1959), *Rudolf Hess: The Uninvited Envoy* (1961), *Singapore: The Battle That Changed the World* (1968), *The Green Beach* (1975), *The Boarding Party* (1979), *Code Name: Nimrod* (1981), and *The Red Fort: The Story of the Indian Mutiny of 1857* (1982).

The Sea Wolves was adapted from *The Boarding Party* into a 1980 visual project featuring Roger Moore, Gregory Peck, and David Niven.

The latter was summoned into the field as Dr. Jason Love in a 1966 intelligence operation in the Middle East. Full details under SUMMARY. (Leasor's involvement in the visual world dates back to 1959 when he became director of Pagoda Films.)

Leasor demonstrated a thorough knowledge of vintage motor cars in the Love dossier, and in 1969 he initiated a two-tome fiction series focusing on the worldly owner of Aristo Autos: They Don't Make Them Like That Anymore (1969) and Never Had a Spanner on Her (1970).

Like many espionage series of the Cold War era, the Dr. Love missions were inevitably forced into feverish competition with Ian Fleming's James Bond (see separate reference). The later entries were distributed exclusively in British territory, due to declining American interest in the series after 1969.

In addition to the six Love novels, which appeared between 1964 and 1973, Leasor also prepared a Love short-story collection, A Week of Love (1969). Leasor's more recent fictional efforts include Mandarin Gold (1974) and The Chinese Widow (1975).

Leasor functioned as a principal constituent of the N. A. L. / Signet Intelligence Group (see separate reference) from 1966 to 1967.

CWF AGENT: Love, Dr. Jason.

CWF HISTORY: British subject. Born in Old Bexley, Kent. Exact date of birth unverified.

Served in the British Army during World War II, in India and Burma. Becoming a private soldier in June 1942, Love entered the Royal East Kent Regiment, a. k. a. the Buffs. Later commissioned with the Royal Berkshire Regiment, attached to the 1st Lincoln in Arakan (Southwest Burma).

Love obtained a medical commission in March 1944 in Buthiadaung, India, and studied medicine, from 1946 to 1951, at Oriel College, Oxford, and St. Bartholomew's, London. Received M. B. B. S. medical degree in 1951; by 1964 Love was engaged in an active general practice, situated in Bishop's Combe near Taunton, Somerset.

Recipient of the brown belt in karate. Possessed a special passion for Cord automobiles. Relevant to this latter pursuit, Dr. Love subscribed to the U. S. -based Auburn-Cord-Dusenberg Car Club. Also a distinguished member of the East India and Sports Club, of Oxford and Cambridge.

In 1964 British Intelligence chief Douglas MacGillivray, a native Scotsman, was confronted with the task of selecting an agent to locate a missing operative in Teheran. The assignment demanded someone who could blend naturally into the Iranian landscape.

The simultaneous occurrence of the Annual International Malaria Conference in Teheran prompted MacGillivray to designate a doctor for the mission, and he decided on a British doctor who had briefly assisted him in India during the war--Dr. Jason Love.

OPERATIVE DATA: Not discounting the staggering effects generated by Ian Fleming (see separate reference) on the espionage genre during the mid-sixties, James Leasor fashioned a series, using the code designation "Passport," that was superior in one major respect: He devised frighteningly realistic Cold War plots that resurrected the darkest mysteries of the world's most exciting locales.

Throughout the series, Leasor surpassed many of his contemporaries by avoiding any hint of Bondian emulation or formularization.

Measured against these elements, the reluctant character of Dr. Love endowed Leasor's narratives with a disturbing quality that wasn't associated with other initiatives of the period, including John Gardner's equally recalcitrant operative, Boysie Oakes (see separate reference).

Enticed by the promise of a classic Cord, Love agreed to search for an anonymous British agent, known as K, who had vanished in Teheran. The liquidation of several intelligence contacts in the Arab sector convinced MacGillivray that it was crucial that the aforementioned Malaria Conference should be used to protect Love's cover in Teheran.

The threat behind K's disappearance was explained to Dr. Love as the feared sabotage of politically critical oil treaties and potential danger to the Sheik of Kuwait, monarch of one of the richest oil skeikdoms in the Middle East. Also, before dispatching Love on his mission, MacGillivray was alerted to a Soviet scientific expedition to Persepolis, scheduled to arrive shortly on an Ilyushin Aeroflot airliner.

Unknown to MacGillivray, a French doctor based outside Teheran, identified as one Dr. Simmias, was the Soviet control for Persia.

Having defined these integral segments, Leasor booked Dr. Love on a <u>Passport to Oblivion</u> (1964), the first of the respectable doctor's perilous forays for MacGillivray. As noted earlier, the "Passport" signal emphasized the role of locales in the Love dossier.

Leasor's decisive fusion of all these elements resulted in a materialization of the settings in <u>Passport to Oblivion</u> in relation to the plot:

1) Love's encounter with a resident female agent in Rome, identified as Simone.

2) Dr. Simmias' calculated designs in Teheran and his connection to both the K incident and the imperiled oil treaties.

3) The use of The Oil Exploration Centre in Teheran as a cover for MacGillivray's group.

4) The integration of two Soviet agents, Axel Lukacs and Irina, in the Canadian Arctic, specifically Churchill, Manitoba.

5) The significance of the Soviet Illyushin Aeroflot aircraft in Teheran amidst the suspicion surrounding the oil treaties and the Sheik of Kuwait.

This last constituent provided the greatest level of tension in Passport to Oblivion as Simmias abducted Love on the Russian Aeroflot--eventually destined for the Soviet Union. This precipitated, in the Canadian Arctic, a deadly confrontation between Love and Simmias that developed as one of the best in spy fiction history.

Leasor's meticulous execution of his complex plot unveiled the mystery behind K's disappearance, revealing a cataclysmic scheme that was more politically volatile than the oil treaties.

Preceding William Haggard's The Powder Barrel (1965) (see separate reference) by a year, James Leasor's Passport to Oblivion was one of the first Cold War espionage novels to explore the specific dangers existing in the Arab world.

Leasor also introduced a chilling note of irony in Passport to Oblivion by giving similar professional backgrounds to Love and Simmias despite their mutual antagonism in the field. Further, Leasor probed an area generally ignored by his peers--showing the avaricious ploys of Whitehall with which MacGillivray was forced to contend.

In its review of the Leasor thriller, the Columbus Dispatch declared, "Passport to Oblivion is the reader's passport to unforgettable excitement in a world where danger wears many disguises. It is a Secret Service thriller in the most expert manner." Unquestionably, Passport to Oblivion emerged as one of the most provocative thrillers associated with the Cold War.

Leasor transposed the danger from Teheran to the Himalayas in Passport to Peril (1966) in which Dr. Love agreed to save the life of the son of the Nawab of Shahnagar. Ibrahim Khan, Love's Pakistani contact on holiday in Switzerland, was later found murdered.

Love's second mission involved an insidious big game consortium, a Himalayan-based Chi-Com espionage network that spanned Asia, and two crack assassins in the service of Red China.

In Passport to Peril Leasor conveyed Peking's global avarice with the same sobering objectivity which characterized his Soviet perceptions in Passport to Oblivion.

Leasor created a malevolent weapon in Passport to Peril which utilized the lethal precision of the Sniperscope and the principles of the laser. This liquidation device transpired as one of the most terrifying in Cold War fiction.

SUMMARY: Employing the code designation "Passport" in the early assignments of one Dr. Jason Love, James Leasor fashioned a series that unveiled the secrets of the most enigmatic global locales, originating espionage plots that were both authentic and haunting.

In one of its early Leasor evaluations, the London Evening Standard accented the massive field action to launch Dr. Love into James Bond's sphere, not without justification:

> "The reader will quickly realize that he is about to meet an heir-apparent to the golden throne of James Bond. The name is Dr. Jason Love, who from his Cord roadster (with Schwitzer-Cummins supercharger) to his judo, is a convincing contender mixed up in some suitably supercharged mayhem from Teheran to the frozen North."

David Niven was the reluctant Dr. Jason Love in Where the Spies Are (1966), an M. G. M. visual project adapted from Passport to Oblivion. Also summoned to the frenzied Leasor battleground were the late Françoise Dorleac, John Le Mesurier as MacGillivray, Cyril Cusack, Paul Stassino as Dr. Simmias, and Nigel Davenport as Parkington, Love's contact in the altered visual setting of Beirut. Leasor contributed field dialogue to the project.

In its promotion for the tie-in for Where the Spies Are, New American Library offered this intriguing definition of Leasor's inventive series concept:

> "Book yourself to a strange and danger-charged country. Where the unpredictable always happens. Where there's a knife in every handclasp and death in every smile. Where the woman you take to bed may be the enemy's secret weapon."

Although Where the Spies Are was dismissed in the public sector, it was favorably received in the critical arena and has slowly evolved as a classic of the spy genre.

STATUS: If revived today, James Leasor's espionage series would perform well in the present secret agent market. However, given the present state of instability in the Middle East, the reissue of Passport to Oblivion seems more likely than later entries, especially Passport to Peril, with its slightly dated Chi-Com themes. SOP.

FIELD BIBLIOGRAPHY

Leasor, James. Passport for a Pilgrim. London: Heinemann, 1968; Garden City, N. Y.: Doubleday, 1969. HB-HB.

_____. Passport in Suspense. London: Heinemann, 1967. HB. See also The Yang Meridian.

_____. Passport to Oblivion. London: Heinemann, 1964; New York: J. B. Lippincott, 1965. HB-HB. See also Where the Spies Are.

_____. Passport to Peril. London: Heinemann, 1966. HB. See also Spylight.

_____. Spylight. New York: J. B. Lippincott, 1966; New York: New American Library paperback, 1967. HB-R.

_____. A Week of Love. London: Heinemann, 1969. HB. Short-story collection.

_____. Where the Spies Are. New York: New American Library paperback, 1966. R. MT. Visual project title for Passport to Oblivion.

_____. The Yang Meridian. New York: Putnam, 1968; New York: Berkley-Medallion paperback, 1969. HB-R. U.S. title for Passport in Suspense.

CONSULT APPENDIX I FOR SERIES CONTINUATION

END OF CWF 40

† CWF 41. Le CARRE, JOHN †

BACKGROUND: Cover identity of David John Moore Cornwell, former British civil servant. Born in Poole, Dorsetshire, England, in 1931.

Educated at the Sherborne School, Berne University, and Lincoln College, Oxford. In 1956 Cornwell became a tutor at Eton.

Joined the Foreign Office, receiving the appointment of Second Secretary at the British Embassy in Bonn from 1960 to 1963. In 1964 Cornwell functioned as Consul in Hamburg.

It is well known that Cornwell's exposure to the closeted environment of the Foreign Office provided the inspiration for his espionage novels of the Cold War era, chiefly Call for the Dead (1961), The Spy Who Came In from the Cold (1963), The Looking Glass War (1965), and A Small Town in Germany (1968).

These works established the author's conception of an intelligence agent's existence as one of desperation and futility.

Although Cornwell-le Carré began with the disadvantage of competing with the Bond cult, he has emerged as the Graham Greene of the contemporary spy thriller.

Because of Cornwell's term with the Foreign Office, he was obligated under the Official Secrets Act to adopt a cover identity for security purposes, as was CWF author William Haggard (see separate reference). As a result, all of Cornwell's field projects have been executed as John le Carré.

While most practitioners of intrigue gained a respectable critical and/or public following acquired over an extended period, le Carré's grim perception of the Cold War earned him instant recognition in both sectors:

1) Call for the Dead was judged runner-up for first prize in the British Crime Writers Association awards in 1961.

2) Le Carré's third novel, The Spy Who Came In from the Cold, received the British Crime Writers Association's Gold Dagger award in 1963, followed one year later by the prestigious Edgar from the Mystery Writers of America.

3) Generating sales exceeding 250,000 in its U.S. hardback edition alone, The Spy Who Came In from the Cold seriously challenged the phenomenal bestselling achievements of Ian Fleming (see separate reference).

Le Carré's own controversial commentary on James Bond was published, somewhat ironically, in Henry Zieger's mockingly entitled biography, Ian Fleming: The Spy Who Came In with the Gold (1965):

> "Now this James Bond business, the really interesting thing, you know, is that Bond himself would be what I would describe as the ideal defector. Because if the money was better, the booze freer, the women easier over there in Moscow, he'd be off like a shot and defect to the Russians."
> "Bond, you see, is the ultimate prostitute. He replaces love with technique. For Bond it isn't a question of why you kill people but how; it isn't a question of whether you seduce people but when. None of this would matter and Fleming himself is least of all to blame, but when they have made an institution of Bond they must

either make him respectable or destroy
him...."*

Le Carré's reaction to Bond has often been characterized as
paranoid, but this seems too severe a judgment. It seems more
prudent to assert that le Carré's Secret Service protagonist, George
Smiley, signified a contemptuous revolt against Bond, an attitude
which doubtless influenced the anti-hero mold of such realistic allies as Len Deighton and Adam Hall (see separate references),
among others.

Curiously, the first two le Carré thrillers, Call for the Dead
(1961) and A Murder of Quality (1962), were initially represented by
the N.A.L./Signet Intelligence Group (see separate reference),
Fleming's U.S. paperback center during the Cold War era. Otherwise, le Carré's Cold War thrillers have been reprinted in the U.S.
by such prominent paperback houses as Bantam, Dell, Pocket Books,
and Popular Library.

Although le Carré doesn't fall into the prolific category, his
deliberated portrait of Smiley, the subject of this file, virtually
symbolized the realistic school of spy fiction during the sixties, and
in the opinion of many chiefs and operatives, to the present day.

A Small Town in Germany (1968), le Carré's only Cold War
novel in which Smiley was not featured, mirrored the author's experiences with the British Embassy in Bonn. Le Carré also authored
the non-suspense effort, The Naive and Sentimental Lover (1971).

Tinker, Tailor, Soldier, Spy (1974), The Honourable Schoolboy (1977), and Smiley's People (1980) comprise le Carré's post-
Cold War Smiley thrillers, all of which became international bestsellers.

CWF AGENT: Smiley, George.

CWF HISTORY: British subject. Described as short, fat, and
introspective, Smiley was initiated into the Secret Service in 1928
when he was interviewed by the Overseas Committee for Academic
Research at Oxford.

Following the mandatory term of training, Smiley was assigned as a lecturer at a small German university. During this
posting, Smiley also accompanied groups of suitably righteous students on vacations to Bavarian hunting camps.

At a clandestine location in Bonn, wholly removed from the

---

*Henry Zieger, Ian Fleming: The Spy Who Came In with the Gold
(New York: Duell, Sloane, and Pearce, 1965), ch. 5, p. 123.

German academy, there were those who were fully aware of Smiley's activities, especially his trips back to England with students who had been selected as potential agents. Smiley devised psychological tests for these candidates and yet he was never certain of how his recommendations were evaluated in Bonn or with his own department in London.

The fury of Nazism came home to Smiley in 1937 when he witnessed a university bonfire in which the works of such German authors as Mann, Heine, and Lessing were destroyed.

Two years later, Smiley was in Sweden under the cover of a respected agent for an established Swiss small-arms manufacturer, supported, naturally, by an authentic service record with the firm.

Until 1943 Smiley traveled extensively throughout Europe, acquiring the disposition of a shadowy man of tension. This four-year cover permitted Smiley to quietly intensify the British intelligence network across the Continent to counteract the Nazi siege.

Recalled to London in 1943, Smiley was advised by his superior, Steed-Asprey, to shelve the grueling pressures of foreign duty in favor of home service. Reluctantly, Smiley honored Steed-Asprey's wishes.

Near the end of the war, Smiley married Steed-Asprey's personal secretary, the Lady Ann Sercomb, a young English socialite-- a marriage tragically marked by Lady Ann's infidelity to Smiley.

The disclosure of a Soviet cipher clerk in Ottowa renewed a demand for a strategist of Smiley's caliber and he was again entangled in the Secret Service maze.

However, the complexion of the Service had been altered radically by the N. A. T. O. alliance, the rising fever of the U.S. - Soviet hegemony, and the appearance of new agents. Maston, the only prewar member who had remained with Smiley in the Service, was later appointed as the Ministers' Adviser on Intelligence in the "new" British Secret Service.

The Service was known privately as the Circus, a name suitably derived from its location in the frenzied environs of London's Cambridge Circus.

Smiley was initially relegated to an internal position, acquiring the nickname of "Mole," not to be confused with the in-house term signifying a double agent. In 1951 he transferred to Counterintelligence but returned to Maston's section ten years later. During the Cold War period, Smiley shifted in and out of the Service, functioning for the Circus at scattered intervals.

In 1977 Smiley became the chief of the British Secret Service, engaged in battle with his Soviet counterpart in the K. G. B., Karla.

OPERATIVE DATA: In a very real sense, le Carré's entries
featuring George Smiley contradicted the traditional notion of an
espionage series. Unlike such genre authors as Ian Fleming and
Donald Hamilton (see separate references), le Carré aimed for a
prolonged emotional response to Smiley's world of solitude within
the Secret Service.

While other spy novelists of the period were committed to
defining their operatives around the missions in which they figured,
le Carré slowly fused Smiley's maturation process with the crises
he faced in the Service.

It might be stated, then, that the Smiley books more closely
resembled a psychological cycle than an archetypal fictional series
focused on a central character.

In Call for the Dead (1961), le Carré's consummate portrayal
of George Smiley, Smiley interviewed Samuel Fennan, a government
official who had received an anonymous letter accusing him of Communist affiliations during the thirties. In a session characterized
as routine, Smiley's purpose was to verify Fennan's full security
clearance, given the latter's access to classified documents.

Fennan's subsequent suicide prompted the Circus to conduct
a formal inquiry to avert a politically damaging scandal.

From this plot inception, le Carré delineated Smiley as an
unobtrusive man who relied on his acumen for discerning the darkest human weaknesses in those he encountered.

Smiley's meeting with Fennan's widow, Elsa, depicted the
depth of his deceptively sympathetic attitude toward her. In this
case Smiley subtly arrived at the suspicion that the accusations in
the letter might have been well-founded.

Le Carré's portrayal of Elsa as a tortured woman intensified
that of George Smiley as a dedicated civil servant. Smiley's motive
in his interview with Mrs. Fennan was simply to discover the truth
behind the letter and her husband's suicide. In this respect, Call
for the Dead represented a departure in the English Cold War thriller, for le Carré emphasized Smiley's inflexible loyalty, in the
midst of a potential crisis within Whitehall, toward Britain and her
postwar ideologies.

Within the context of the plot, le Carré presented, through
Elsa's unwavering defense of her husband's accusations, a provocative contrast between Smiley and Fennan. Given Lady Ann's un-
faithfulness to Smiley, she might have abandoned him had he been
in Fennan's position.

The complexity of the Smiley character was compounded by
the introduction of Dieter Frey, a German Jew whom Smiley had
taught in Germany before the war.

The recollection of Frey's hatred of the Nazis in the academic realm permitted le Carré to probe Smiley's desolate nature. His bitterness changed Frey from one of Smiley's best prewar agents to a calculated Soviet operative obsessed with the intrigues of the Cold War.

Setting this conflict against Britain's pessimistic postwar atmosphere, le Carré completed his unique definition of espionage fiction with a portrayal of the British Secret Service of the Cold War as an entity savagely and irrevocably separated from the idealism that once had motivated its existence. Smiley's final, deadly confrontation with Frey literally symbolized le Carré's intention.

To fully complement Smiley's complex personality, le Carré climaxed the plot in Call for the Dead with a moral puzzle that served to resurrect all of the earlier elements--the letter, the suicide, Elsa, Frey, and the murder of a seemingly innocent man-- before unraveling the mystery of Fennan's death.

From this level le Carré delivered a compelling judgment of betrayal that simultaneously shaped Smiley's future progression and logically substantiated the circumstances surrounding Fennan's death.

A theatrical presentation of Edward II and an elusive agent known as Freitag played integral roles in the Fennan scandal, but solely in terms of fleshing out the London domain of the Circus. This also applied to the significance of the East German Steel Mission in London's Belsize Park, which figured into the intricate maze surrounding Fennan's death. This locale provided the shadowy introduction of Hans-Dieter Mundt, who emerged as a key operative in The Spy Who Came In from the Cold.

As was Maston, Peter Guillam, as the Circus's expert in Satellite espionage, was initiated into le Carré's intrigues in Call for the Dead.

In many respects Call for the Dead emerges as le Carré's best spy novel, in that it exists as an allegory of Britain's tragic loss of prestige and power in the postwar world.

The Washington Sunday Star observed of Smiley's first foray into espionage: "Watch George Smiley, he's really going places." Anthony Boucher, in his review for the New York Times, accented the suspenseful overtones of the book: "Subtle and acute ... marked by restraint, indirection, and intelligence."

As the title of le Carré's second Smiley entry suggests, A Murder of Quality (1962) is a traditional mystery story. Smiley, having left the Service, was asked to investigate a perplexing murder at Carne, a distinguished English public school. Le Carré displayed an awesome knowledge of the inflexible world of the English public school in A Murder of Quality, as typified by Smiley's interaction with the ordered characterizations of Terence Fielding, Felix D'Arcy, and Charles Hecht.

With A Murder of Quality le Carré smoothly preserved the resourcefulness of his protagonist, although Smiley's talents were employed in a setting far removed from the Secret Service.

The last two le Carré books of the sixties in which Smiley surfaced might be best described as his passage from the Cold War. In both The Spy Who Came In from the Cold (1963) and The Looking Glass War (1965) the emphasis was shifted elsewhere.

It would be repetitious to expound at great length on the significance of the fatalistic Alec Leamas in The Spy Who Came In from the Cold, for his mission involving Hans-Dieter Mundt, the head of operations for the East German Abteilung in ravaged Berlin, has qualified as the undisputed symbol of the realistic Cold War espionage novel.

Mundt was suspected by the Circus of liquidating one Karl Riemeck, a member of the German SED Praesidium. And Control ordered Leamas to eliminate Mundt.

In The Spy Who Came In from the Cold, le Carré established Alec Leamas as a man of conflict: respected as the Circus's key agent in West Berlin, he secretly despised his profession. Pursuant to this recognition, le Carré defined Leamas' relationship to Control, Smiley, Guillam, and the nucleus of the Circus. (It should be pointed out here that in The Spy Who Came In from the Cold, the British Secret Service was formally identified as the Circus.)

The Fennan case was recalled in this entry, with a fuller explanation of Mundt's role in that incident in which he utilized a cover at the East German Steel Mission.

George Smiley figured in the disclosure of Leamas' background when the West Berlin agent revealed his switch to Counterintelligence in 1951. Further, Smiley's name was invoked at the classic tribunal concerning Mundt's allegiances to the British Secret Service. Leamas was asked to outline his knowledge of Smiley at the tribunal and to verify a purported visit to Smiley's house in London.

Le Carré sketched an ominous portent for Smiley in The Spy Who Came In from the Cold with his tragic delineation of Leamas as an agent whose contempt for the Circus had reached a point of destructive desperation.

Although it is not known whether le Carré had planned as far back as 1963 to write Tinker, Tailor, Soldier, Spy (1974) and its two sequels, his well-conceived development of Leamas as a fatalistic figure foreshadowed Smiley's later crisis in that trilogy.

As in Call for the Dead, le Carré's depth of characterization was reflected in The Spy Who Came In from the Cold with the Jewish character of Fiedler, head of Counterintelligence for the Abteilung. Le Carré deployed Fiedler as an interrogator at the tribunal and, in this respect, used him as a balance between the tensions generated by Leamas and Mundt.

Further, Leamas' alliance with Liz Gold, identified as a librarian with Communist leanings, and their escape over the Berlin Wall into the Eastern sector typified the futility of Leamas' existence.

Unquestionably, le Carré achieved a feverish crescendo with the Leamas-Gold escape episode that crowned it as the most haunting in Cold War espionage fiction.

The Spy Who Came In from the Cold became an immediate global bestseller upon its publication, with critical praise emanating from all quadrants of the media. Ironically, le Carré's Cold War fiction nemesis, Ian Fleming, pronounced the book "A very fine spy story." The New York Herald Tribune commented: "It will haunt you ... for a long time.... Only rarely does a book of this quality appear--an inspired work."

Focusing on le Carré's radical contrast with Fleming, Show lauded: "In a world all too surfeited with glamorous James Bonds and Mata Haris, John le Carré has at last written a novel about espionage that is not only thrilling, but believable."

Graham Greene's recommendation alone, however, would have sealed the book's global reputation: "The best spy story I have ever read."

The Looking Glass War (1965) developed as le Carré's most isolated spy novel of the sixties--misunderstood in many ways, despite its bestseller status.

Reflecting the geopolitical schism in Europe caused by the acceleration of the Cold War, The Looking Glass War depicted the British Secret Service in a state of chaotic change, advanced far beyond the divided-Berlin climate of The Spy Who Came In from the Cold.

The death of a British agent, known variably as Taylor and Malherbe, and the simultaneous disappearance of a crucial microfilm prompted LeClerc, the head of an obscure intelligence group based in London, to confer with the Circus.

Smiley was assigned to the "North European Desk" in 1965, and, given Malherbe's contact point in Finland, he consulted with LeClerc on the matter. LeClerc summoned a seasoned agent, Leiser, to penetrate the Northern European sector.

Far more than The Spy Who Came In from the Cold, The Looking Glass War depicted the heightened climate of critical transition in the British Secret Service, especially in the constant suspicion manifested between LeClerc and Leiser, and a younger, more ambitious man, Avery.

Smiley surfaced infrequently throughout The Looking Glass War, more or less in the capacity of a Circus liaison, notably in Smiley's club where with LeClerc he jointly evaluated the progress of Leiser's mission. This meeting was inhabited, from Smiley's view, by some vaguely familiar Circus faces. Here, it seemed that le Carré intended to show how the Circus was being slowly affected by the changing power politics in Europe.

Of all le Carré's novels, The Looking Glass War emerged as his least memorable work, particularly in comparison to The Spy Who Came In from the Cold, because of the uncertainty in the futures of both Smiley and the Circus.

SUMMARY: John le Carré's conception of George Smiley in Call for the Dead represented the initiation of the realistic school of espionage fiction, with its depiction of the futility and inevitable betrayal of an agent's existence.

The entries featuring Smiley evolved more as a maturation cycle than a typical spy series. Excluding the Smiley mystery, A Murder of Quality, le Carré's early books portrayed Britain's tragic loss of power in the postwar world, measured against the global divisiveness created by the Cold War.

Smiley's treatment in the visual project arena has been an interesting one. Unlike James Bond, Smiley's appearance in this sector has improved with the passage of time.

British actor Rupert Davies briefly essayed the Smiley character in The Spy Who Came In from the Cold (Paramount, 1965) which featured Richard Burton as Alec Leamas, Claire Bloom, the late Peter Van Eyck as Hans-Dieter Mundt, and Oskar Werner as Fiedler.

Call for the Dead was tautly adapted as The Deadly Affair (Columbia, 1967) in which James Mason donned the Smiley mantle, although le Carré's improbable spy here was named Charles Dobbs. The visual project also offered Simone Signoret as Elsa Fennan, and Maximilian Schell as a more mature Dieter Frey.

Smiley was not portrayed at all in The Looking Glass War (Columbia, 1970), a visual project featuring Christopher Jones as Leiser, Sir Ralph Richardson as LeClerc, and Anthony Hopkins as Avery.

More recently, Sir Alec Guinness has garnered the image of le Carré's classic protagonist in two mini-series home visual projects, namely Tinker, Tailor, Soldier, Spy (PBS, 1980) and Smiley's People (Operation Prime Time, 1982). Guinness has become so closely identified with Smiley that Bantam Books currently depicts his likeness on several of their paperbound editions.

STATUS: Although le Carré's future direction is unknown at present, his espionage novels, especially the Cold War entries, continue to sell at an astounding rate. Bantam Books, whose first le Carré reprint was Tinker, Tailor, Soldier, Spy in 1975, has since acquired all of the author's celebrated spy thrillers, excluding A Small Town in Germany (1968), for mass market distribution. SSP.

FIELD BIBLIOGRAPHY

le Carré, John. Call for the Dead. London: Victor Gollancz Ltd., 1961; New York: Walker, 1962; New York: New American Library paperback, 1964. HB-HB-R. See also The Deadly Affair.

_____. The Deadly Affair. New York: New American Library paperback, 1967. R.MT. Visual project title for Call for the Dead.

_____. The Incongruous Spy: Two Novels of Suspense. New York: Walker, 1964. HB. Omnibus Edition: Call for the Dead and A Murder of Quality.

_____. The Looking Glass War. New York: Coward-McCann, 1965; Dell paperback, 1966. HB-R.

_____. A Murder of Quality. London: Victor Gollancz Ltd., 1962; New York: Walker, 1963; New York: New American Library paperback, 1964. HB-HB-R.

_____. The Spy Who Came In from the Cold. London: Victor Gollancz Ltd., 1963; New York: Coward-McCann, 1964; New York: Dell paperback, 1965. HB-HB-R-MT.

CONSULT APPENDIX I FOR SERIES CONTINUATION

CONSULT APPENDIX II FOR SERIES TRANSITION

END OF CWF 41

† CWF 42. LESLIE, PETER †

BACKGROUND: Prolific English author of paperback originals, especially mysteries, general fiction, and visual-project novelizations (although The Gay Deceiver (1967) and Liberation of the Riviera (1981) were issued originally in hardback). Born in 1923.

For the most part, Leslie's paperback fiction entries,

including The Plastic Magicians (1969) and The Extremists (1971),
have appeared exclusively in British territory. Leslie developed a
solid reputation during the mid-sixties for one of Britain's finest
novelization series, and his contributions in this area were not restricted to a single category.

Several of Leslie's visual-project adaptations, like his general fiction efforts, were distributed solely in Britain. These included The Frighteners (1968) from the "Daktari" home series; The
Night of the Tribolites (1968) and The Autumn Accelerator (1969),
both derived from "The Invaders" science-fiction home visual project; and a theatrical novelization, The Bitter Enders (1972).

Relevant to this file, Leslie contributed five novelizations to
the "The Man from U. N. C. L. E." home project and one entry to its
allied series, "The Girl from U. N. C. L. E." Leslie also penned an
episode from the "Secret Agent" visual series, Hell for Tomorrow
(1965).

Noted as an actor and journalist, Leslie represented both the
Ace and N. A. L. /Signet Intelligence Groups (see separate references).

CWF AGENTS: 1) Solo, Napoleon, and Illya Kuryakin.
              2) Dancer, April, and Mark Slate.

CWF HISTORIES: 1) See also Avallone, Michael--CWF 6.
                 2) See also Avallone, Michael--CWF 6.

OPERATIVE DATA: In his novelizations for "The Man from
U. N. C. L. E." Leslie reflected a smoother style than his confederates, although he occasionally lacked the pace of Michael Avallone
and David McDaniel (see separate references). Otherwise, he maintained the values of the visual series.

Leslie's first U. N. C. L. E. assignment, The Radioactive Camel Affair (1966), alarmingly conveyed the imminent threat of nuclear
proliferation amidst the global politics of the Cold War. A succes-
sion of thefts involving Uranium-235 prompted Mr. Waverly to send
Solo and Kuryakin to North Africa where it was feared T.H.R.U.S.H.
was building a belligerent nuclear power.

The Radioactive Camel Affair transpired as one of the more
credible U. N. C. L. E. entries, aided by Leslie's integration of detailed nuclear fission formulae into the plot.

A mysterious caravan crossing the North African desert and
the Nya Nyerere, an ambitious liberation army commanded by one
Colonel Ononu, were elements of Solo and Kuryakin's mission, which
spanned from Casablanca to Nasser's Egypt.

Solo and Kuryakin registered more extensive utilization of their U. N. C. L. E. field equipment throughout this operation, as with the resourceful use of the cigarette-case communicator to penetrate the movements of the caravan and the rapid deployment of the official U. N. C. L. E. combat gun against T. H. R. U. S. H. and hostile Arab factions.

Leslie's intriguing plot premise as well as his African erudition fashioned The Radioactive Camel Affair as one of the best assignments in the U.N.C.L.E. dossier, while depiction of T.H.R.U.S.H.'s lethal underground desert command center strengthened the escapist dimensions of this spy novelization.

The Diving Dames Affair (1967) was a chillingly offbeat U. N. C. L. E. thriller in which the deaths, near Rio de Janeiro, of two enticing members of D. A. M. E. S. (Daughters of America's Emergency Services) justified a perilous mission for Solo and Kuryakin in exotic South America.

Leslie inserted a plot twist that ingeniously masked a T. H. R. U. S. H. construction project in a remote section of Brazil.

As in The Radioactive Camel Affair, Leslie displayed an appreciation of the locale, which in The Diving Dames Affair was the torturous regions of the Brazilian jungle.

The originality of this entry was contained in the awesome scuba abilities of an elite corps of female agents employed by T. H. R. U. S. H. Eclipsing several of the earlier U. N. C. L. E. initiatives, The Diving Dames Affair represented a formidable challenge to Solo and Kuryakin in the action sector, although it lacked the credibility of The Radioactive Camel Affair.

The mystery behind the T. H. R. U. S. H. project veiled a blueprint that equaled their machinations in The Radioactive Camel Affair --the obliteration of six major cities in Argentina and Chile.

In a memorable interrogation scene Solo's resistance saved his life, as he utilized the technique of subliminal suggestion to confuse his captors.

Leslie neatly fitted the D. A. M. E. S. double death into the design of the principal plot.

Leslie offered an intriguing diversion in The Splintered Sunglasses Affair (1968)--the abduction of Solo from Del Floria's Tailor Shop, U. N. C. L. E. 's cover entrance. This incident placed Kuryakin in the perilous position of key agent, summoned by Mr. Waverly to the U. N. C. L. E. center.

Waverly ordered Kuryakin to locate a coveted list of primary T. H. R. U. S. H. operatives based in Europe, but the mission was gravely jeopardized when an Italian U. N. C. L. E. agent, identified as

Leonardo, was liquidated outside Turin after procuring the
T. H. R. U. S. H. document.

Meanwhile Solo's abductors were targeted as a man named
Carlsen, a top T. H. R. U. S. H. strategist, and his A. D. C., Lala
Eriksson.

Kuryakin's crucial task: find the connection between Carlsen
and the list, apart from the common denominator of T. H. R. U. S. H.

Leslie carefully balanced these plotting and characterization
fragments with the suspicion surrounding a major N. A. T. O. base
near the Italian Val d'Aosta, and in the manner of his preceding
U. N. C. L. E. assignments, Leslie demonstrated a slick familiarity
with this entry's majestic Italian settings.

Rivaling the fission formula aspect of The Radioactive Camel
Affair, Leslie adroitly blended the specialized mechanics of holography into the plot of The Splintered Sunglasses Affair. (From the
U. N. C. L. E. files, holography is defined as a method of photography employing the techniques of the laser, rather than the standard
lens.)

The brief kidnapping of Mr. Waverly in Holland at the outset
of The Unfare Fair Affair (1968) initially suggested a reprise of The
Splintered Sunglasses Affair. However, Leslie clearly distinguished
this entry from his previous U. N. C. L. E. missions.

Analyzing a multilingual lead relating to his capture, Mr.
Waverly was convinced that a network had been established to channel renegade criminals throughout Europe. Therefore, Waverly
sanctioned Solo and Kuryakin to infiltrate this pipeline, fearing that
T. H. R. U. S. H. could conceivably manipulate it for their global operations on the Continent.

The principal asset of this U. N. C. L. E. mission was Leslie's meticulous development of the criminal network along the dark
frontiers and borders of Eastern and Western Europe as Solo and
Kuryakin unmasked the motives of T. H. R. U. S. H. and an elusive
Corsican, identified as Bartoluzzi.

Posing as a Czech assassin, Kurim Cernic, Kuryakin joined
Solo on a pulsating, treacherous chase into East Germany that qual-
ifies as one of the finest action set pieces in the series.

Leslie also shadowed The Finger in the Sky Affair, originally distributed in British territory in 1966. However, since this entry wasn't issued in the U. S. until 1970, it will not be evaluated in
this file.

Leslie also wrote the final U. S. -distributed "The Girl from
U. N. C. L. E. " novelization, The Cornish Pixie Affair (1967), in
which April and Mark tracked a ring of political assassins.

Although the visual series was nearing the end of its run in 1967, this entry was especially well-written.

SUMMARY: 1) Peter Leslie's crisp narrative style in his "The Man from U. N. C. L. E." novelization contributions compared favorably with the allied activities of Michael Avallone, J. Hunter Holly, and David McDaniel (see separate references).

However, he surpassed his colleagues with his incisive perception of global locales and careful attention to technical detail.

2) Acknowledging the brevity of "The Girl from U. N. C. L. E." novelization project in the U. S., Leslie's The Cornish Pixie Affair ranked with the previous operations of Michael Avallone (see separate reference). The paperback series continued in British territory through 1968.

STATUS: See also Avallone, Michael--CWF 6.

FIELD BIBLIOGRAPHY

Leslie, Peter. The Cornish Pixie Affair. New York: New American Library, 1967. PBO. TN. ("The Girl from U.N.C.L.E.")

_____. The Diving Dames Affair. New York: Ace Books, 1967. PBO. TN. ("The Man from U. N. C. L. E. ")

_____. The Finger in the Sky Affair. London: Four Square, 1966. PBO. TN. ("The Man from U. N. C. L. E. ")

_____. The Radioactive Camel Affair. New York: Ace Books, 1966. PBO. TN. ("The Man from U. N. C. L. E. ")

_____. The Splintered Sunglasses Affair. New York: Ace Books, 1968. PBO. TN. ("The Man from U. N. C. L. E. ")

_____. The Unfare Fair Affair. New York: Ace Books, 1968. PBO. TN. ("The Man from U. N. C. L. E. ")

CONSULT ACE AND N. A. L. /SIGNET INTELLIGENCE GROUPS FOR ADDITIONAL AUTHOR REFERENCES

END OF CWF 42

† CWF 43.   LLEWELLYN, RICHARD †

BACKGROUND: Cover identity of Richard David Vivian Llewellyn Lloyd.   Born in 1906 in St. David's, the cathedral city of Pembrokeshire in South Wales.

Until the age of six, Lloyd spoke only his native Welsh.   In 1912 attended a private school in London; became well versed in English and subsequently attained an art scholarship.

Continued his education in Venice, Florence, and Rome, also learning the hotel business.   Studied Roman history and European art.

In 1924 Lloyd joined the British Regular Army, later assigned to India.

Seven years later Lloyd returned to London, securing employment as a journalist and an assistant visual project director. By the mid-thirties, Lloyd was producing his own visual projects in various European locations.

In 1937 Lloyd's first published work, Poison Pen, a play which he wrote under the Llewellyn cover, played in the British sector for two years.

Lloyd-Llewellyn achieved a worldwide following in 1939 with the publication of his now-classic novel, How Green Was My Valley, which was adapted into a memorable visual project in 1941 starring Walter Pidgeon and Maureen O'Hara.   This excellent work remains in print today.

Lloyd reentered the army in 1939, serving in North Africa and Europe until 1946.   His prewar novel, None But the Lonely Heart (ca. 1940), appeared as a 1944 visual project featuring Cary Grant and Ethel Barrymore.

After the war, Lloyd worked successfully in both the publishing and visual project arenas in New York and Hollywood.   In 1949 he journeyed to Argentina, spending the next ten years completing Up, Into the Singing Mountain (1960), the sequel to How Green Was My Valley.

Lloyd later resided on the Masai Reserve in Kenya, an experience that provided him with background for another bestseller, A Man in a Mirror (1961).

During the early sixties Lloyd alternated between Europe and Argentina, producing six major novels in the process.

Lloyd-Llewellyn is unique among CWF authors in that he

entered the espionage market thirty years after he began his writing career. Edmund Trothe, his contribution to the field, is the subject of this file.

CWF AGENT: Trothe, Edmund.

CWF HISTORY: Regarding the Trothe dossier, it should be emphasized that his initially recorded mission, The End of the Rug (1968), centered around his personal history in relation to a Neo-Nazi ring.

For general purposes, Trothe served as a British Secret Service operative for a Whitehall Ministry. Although acknowledged as a veteran agent, the exact term of his duty is not known.

In 1968 Trothe's department was appropriated by the Ministry of Administration. Pursuant to this action, Trothe was referred to Ms. Lesley Shafford, the newly appointed Junior Minister, for a staff interview. Trothe subsequently reported, however, to his regular superior, identified only as the Blur, for a new briefing.

Until Trothe's section was disbanded in 1973 it was controlled by the Ministry of Administration, subject to the expected staff changes.

Trothe's wife of more than twenty years, the former Melissa Ebbleton, was tragically murdered in 1968. The Trothes had two children, Frederick and Patti. Trothe's family figured into the aforementioned intelligence initiative, considered below.

OPERATIVE DATA: Returning from an unsuccessful mission in Central Europe, Trothe was ordered to penetrate a Neo-Nazi ring which had been gaining momentum in Germany.

The End of the Rug was originally evaluated as a realistic espionage novel of the le Carré (see separate reference) design, although its general plot more closely resembles Adam Hall's The Quiller Memorandum (1965) (see separate reference).

While it is difficult to conceive that a serious spy thriller published as late as 1968 could have explored new ground, Llewellyn at least managed to intensify the psychological elements of le Carré's efforts. This is not to suggest that Llewellyn surpassed le Carré's works.

The major contribution offered to the genre by The End of the Rug was the intricate manner in which Llewellyn fused Trothe's hazardous assignment with his personal crises, to wit: 1) his wife's fatal affair with another man, 2) his daughter's dangerously unsuitable choice of a husband, 3) his son's destructive addiction to drugs,

4) the deceptive forfeiture of the Trothe ancestral home, and 5) his own involvement with a sensuous girl named Tanis.

Llewellyn created the same tone of betrayal that character-ized le Carré's early Cold War thrillers, in terms of Trothe's per-sonal dilemmas and the staggering political implications of the ne-farious Neo-Nazi sphere which threatened the power structure of Europe. This complex integration of elements strengthened the theme of Trothe's futility as a Secret Service agent, and in this respect, The End of the Rug compares favorably with le Carré's Call for the Dead (1961) (see separate reference).

However, as against the dynamic progress achieved earlier in the field by John le Carré, Len Deighton, Adam Hall, and James Aldridge (see separate references), Llewellyn's first series entry appeared too late in the espionage phenomenon to make any lasting impact on the genre.

The New York Times Book Review, however, jubilantly praised Llewellyn's excursion into the grim battleground of the Cold War: "Trothe is by no means the average fictional spy, for we learn a great deal about what he is and thinks.... One of the more original spy plots in some time."

The Trothe series was brief, The End of the Rug followed by But We Didn't Get the Fox (1969), White Horse to Banbury Cross (1970), and The Night Is a Child (1972). This perhaps suggests that even a novelist of Llewellyn's proven ability found it difficult to ad-vance the realistic format beyond four books.

SUMMARY: Richard Llewellyn's The End of the Rug amplified le Carré's theme of betrayal in both the areas of plot and the con-ception of his protagonist, Edmund Trothe. Unquestionably, this can be attributed to Llewellyn's gifted narrative talent, as evidenced by his classic novel, How Green Was My Valley (1939).

However, Trothe's first recorded mission was hampered by appearing in 1968, a year marking the gradual dissipation of the Cold War espionage genre.

STATUS: Given the astounding resurgence in popularity of John le Carré (see separate reference) since 1977, the Trothe series could be successfully reactivated today, probably exceeding its ini-tial performance in the intrigue market. SOP.

FIELD BIBLIOGRAPHY

Llewellyn, Richard. But We Didn't Get the Fox. Garden City, N.Y.: Doubleday, 1969. HB-HB-R. See also But We Didn't Get the Fox in Appendix I.

_____. The End of the Rug. Garden City, N.Y.: Doubleday, 1968; London: Joseph, 1969; New York: Popular Library paperback, 1969. HB-HB-R.

CONSULT APPENDIX I FOR SERIES CONTINUATION

END OF CWF 43

† CWF 44. McCUTCHAN, PHILIP †

BACKGROUND: Born in Cambridge, England, in 1920. Received a thorough education at St. Helen's College in Southsea-Hants, Hampshire and the Royal Military Academy at Sandhurst, Berkshire.

Like a number of Cold War-era espionage novelists, Philip Donald McCutchan scored impressively in both the academic and military sectors. Served in the Royal Navy in World War II, achieving the full rank of Lieutenant, R.N.V.R.

After the war McCutchan sailed on various Far Eastern liners, venturing to Australia. Later became an assistant master at a preparatory school.

McCutchan decided to become a writer in 1956; four years later Gibraltar Road, the first of his popular Commander Shaw counterspy thrillers, subject of this file, was published.

While the Shaw books were gaining a substantial following in both the U.S. and British markets, McCutchan completed several non-series suspense works, notably Sladd's Evil (1965) and A Time for Survival (1966).

Initially, however, McCutchan produced straight fiction, not confined to a specific genre. An early McCutchan effort was Whistle and I'll Come (1957). As his reputation grew, McCutchan encored this viable format in later novels, chiefly Marley's Empire (1963) and Poulter's Passage (1967). A number of these entries were distributed solely in the United Kingdom.

Under the cover identity of Duncan MacNeil, McCutchan penned the James Ogilvie series, a historical saga about Victorian-era soldiers in India. He also wrote as T. I. G. Wigg and Robert Connington Galway (see separate reference).

McCutchan, like many spy novelists, conceived suspense novels with strong contemporary overtones, chiefly The Oil Bastards (1972).

Three years after the Shaw series ended, McCutchan recruited one Simon Shard for the Security Service in Call for Simon Shard (1974), A Very Big Bang (1975), and Blood Run East (1976). Unlike Commander Shaw's exploits, Shard's activities were not disclosed in U.S. territory.

McCutchan once functioned as chairman for the British Crime Writers Association.

CWF AGENT: Shaw, Esmonde (Commander).

CWF HISTORY: British subject. At the outset of World War II, Shaw was designated as a midshipman for the British fleet on a weathered destroyer. Assigned to the North Atlantic, the destroyer initially served as a convoy escort, under the most perilous weather conditions.

Shaw developed an ulcer early in his service term and he was temporarily consigned to shore duty. However, the ulcer symptoms persisted, and Shaw's orders took him abroad to Spain, Egypt, and elsewhere in Northeast Africa. Shaw spent the remainder of the war journeying to similarly volatile locales and, despite his disability, established an enviable record as intelligence officer for the Admiralty.

After the war Shaw reluctantly remained in intelligence, employed by a clandestine unit known as the Special Services of the Naval Intelligence Division (N. I. D.), often described as the department within a department.

Shaw's superior was identified as a man named Latymer, "cover identity" of Vice Admiral Sir Henry Charteris, K. C. B. , D. S. O. , two bars, D. S. C. , and several foreign decorations. Full details to follow.

During the war Sir Henry Charteris had been in grave peril as Special Services chief. Seriously injured by a bomb assault on his Eaton Square flat, he was declared dead by the Admiralty.

By means of plastic surgery, Charteris was "transformed" into Mr. G. E. D. Latymer, newly appointed head of the Special Services. Although officially the department ceased to exist after the war, Latymer was recognized ostensibly as the Under Secretary for a section affiliated with the Royal Navy, and under this cover the Special Services silently prospered through the Cold War era. The Special Services group was situated in Room 12 in the Old Admiralty Building, Whitehall.

In 1968 Commander Shaw joined a secret intelligence organization, identified only as 6D2, controlled by a man known only as Max. This action resulted from a 1966 mission in which Shaw infiltrated Soviet territory without the official authorization of the Special Services, let alone Whitehall. Full details under OPERA-TIVE DATA.

Commander Shaw was recommended by Latymer for a field position with 6D2.

No further record of Commander Shaw after 1971.

OPERATIVE DATA: McCutchan's Shaw series was conceived along the general lines of Ian Fleming's James Bond (see separate reference), especially in terms of concern with technical expertise and menacing plots.

Beginning with the first Shaw assignment, Gibraltar Road (1960), McCutchan's format, however, differed from Fleming's in two major respects:

1) McCutchan sharpened his plots with a sense of logical suspense.

2) The archetypal McCutchan nemesis was credibly delineated and blended in naturally with the plot.

In Gibraltar Road McCutchan probed the relatively virgin area of nuclear proliferation, a theme intensified in many of the later Shaw missions. During a briefing with Latymer, Shaw learned of "Project Sinker," a highly secret Naval operation outlining the development of Gibraltar as the initial link for an arsenal of atomic-powered submarines.

The crucial figure of "Project Sinker" was revealed as Ackroyd, a British physicist responsible for the production unit that generated ALG-SIX, the required fuel for the submarine battery. When Ackroyd suddenly disappeared, Latymer placed Commander Shaw on his trail.

Karina, a tempestuous Soviet agent who had allied with Shaw during the war, was also searching for Ackroyd, on behalf of the Kremlin.

Gibraltar Road defined McCutchan's series concept. With the author's meticulous description of the technology associated with "Project Sinker" and ALG-SIX, Shaw's initial assignment translated into an authentic yet destructive blueprint.

McCutchan superbly balanced the mesmerizing locales with the cataclysmic threat posed by Ackroyd's absence, while McCutchan's double-agent figure, Andrés, transpired as a model for future adversaries. Pursuant to this level of characterization, McCutchan sketched Karina as a daringly devious challenge for his protagonist. It was in this entry, too, that Shaw encountered the provocative Debonnair Delacroix, with whom he was casually involved in later initiatives.

Although the Shaw books were not distributed in the U.S. until the mid-sixties, they were immediately accepted in the British sector. Patrick Gaffney noted in his review in The Scotsman: "The plot ... is worked out in credibly fearsome detail ... McCutchan has an eye for the macabre situation and the skill and restraint to put it across."

McCutchan advanced the basic premise of Gibraltar Road in the subsequent Shaw missions of the early sixties. In the next three entries, the names of principal nuclear weapons served as the titles.

In Redcap (1961) Shaw was ordered to find Lubin, a Soviet electronics expert, who was the significant link to R.E.D.C.A.P., a.k.a. Radio Regulator Equipment for Defense Coordination Atom Powers. M.A.P.I.A.C.C.I.N.D. (Major Atom Powers International Authority for Centralized Control and Inspection of Nuclear Devices), a global nuclear reduction organization based in Geneva, constituted the core of R.E.D.C.A.P.

It was well known that Red China, unlike the Soviet Union, was not a member of M.A.P.I.A.C.C.I.N.D. The Special Services logically considered the Chi-Coms as the most likely source of sabotage while R.E.D.C.A.P. was being shipped to its base in the Central Australian Desert.

In Bluebolt One (1962), Latymer sanctioned Shaw to unearth Edo, the enigmatic master of a voodoo cult in the African jungle. It was believed that Edo's vengeful rites jeopardized the security of an Anglo-American radio center in Nogolia, West Africa, the control site of "Bluebolt One," the nuclear satellite system capable of launching missiles to any global target. This weapons-guidance unit is presently outmoded.

Latymer's directive was motivated by the liquidation of one Hanley Mason, a former representative of the Foreign Office, who was spotted in Nogolia, West Africa, before his death--for reasons unknown.

In terms of locales, McCutchan's graphic African settings in Bluebolt One surpassed the settings of Gibraltar Road and Redcap.

The Birmingham Post, undeniably impressed with this entry, declared that "His third Commander Shaw story puts Mr. McCutchan indisputably among our best writers of thrillers."

Having established Shaw's character in his first three missions, McCutchan prepared his operative for the expansion of the Cold War in Warmaster (1963) and Moscow Coach (1964).

A dock manufactured in Hamburg and subsequently transported to Luanda, Angola, provided the most promising lead to a nebulous consortium, one which the Special Services suspected had discerned the devastating secret of "Warmaster," the nuclear missile designed as the ultimate deterrent to Armageddon during the Cold War era.

Informed of the termination of a U.S. Naval Intelligence agent known by the cover name of Dolly Gray, Latymer dispatched Shaw to New York to penetrate the inimical network surrounding the explosive potential of "Warmaster."

Specifically, Shaw's assignment dealt with a communications complex concealed beneath an elite manufacturing concern, the Frazer Harfield Packaging Corporation, located in Brooklyn.

The following identifications proved useful to Commander Shaw in the completion of his mission:

1) Gottlieb-Hauser, the German firm responsible for the construction of the dock.

2) Otto Keller, the treacherous German physicist credited with the design of "Warmaster." This second fragment materialized as the more crucial of the two, in view of Keller's purported defection to Soviet Russia.

Ultimately, Shaw's task was to connect these segments with the activities of the Frazer Harfield Packaging Corporation in New York.

McCutchan fused these elements to realize a satisfying conclusion while adhering to his typical predilection for technical detail, as manifested by the expertise relating to "Warmaster" as well as the war ships Dakota and the Moehne, both of which were involved in the book's gripping climax.

The threats delivered by McCutchan's chief conspirators, Fleck and Schillenhorst, shaped up as the formidable challenges of the series, and McCutchan displayed a strong global quality in Warmaster, with the well-conveyed locales of New York, Argentina, and the desolate beauty of Cape Horn.

Of Commander Shaw's fifth mission, the London Evening Standard lauded, "... a fine, full-blooded, extrovert, exciting affair."

Shaw's assignment in Moscow Coach (1964) was the assassination of one Ivan Conroy, a fanatical British Communist. To successfully accomplish this directive Shaw was required to shadow Conroy on the West Berlin bus journey to Moscow.

Skyprobe (1966) emerged as a transition for Commander

Shaw as McCutchan presented his agent with his most challenging mission. Allying with intelligence agencies in the U.S., Shaw attempted to isolate the threat to Skyprobe IV, a U.S. spacecraft involved in the evaluation of future exploration beyond the moon. Orbiting near the earth, Skyprobe IV was endangered by the possibility of belligerent interference that could result in all-out atomic war.

McCutchan developed the plot of Skyprobe on a far more intricate level than in previous entries, for he skillfully captured the awesome sensation of Skyprobe IV in flight while maintaining the tension of the mounting menace to the spacecraft.

Further, McCutchan dexterously fused the absorbing characters of a former Polish Army officer, Colonel Stefan Spalinski, now working for the N.I.S., a British anti-Communist network, and a renowned English scientist traveling on Skyprobe IV, identified from Special Services files as Dr. Neil Danvers-Marshall.

In the midst of the Skyprobe IV crisis, Spalinski was found tragically murdered.

Skyprobe differed from the Bondian-oriented espionage novel in that McCutchan also approached the opposing realistic sector.

Pursuing through the darkest streets of Hong Kong a Swiss assassin identified as Rudolf Rencke, purportedly responsible for Colonel Spalinski's death, Shaw eventually penetrated the Sea of Okhotsk in the Soviet Union where he believed Skyprobe IV would descend.

In a balance of the contrasting elements of Skyprobe, McCutchan employed Shaw's arrogant field action to inject a personal dilemma into the mission, thus enhancing the spectacle of suspense created by the Skyprobe IV crisis.

It was this incident which led to Commander Shaw's transfer to 6D2 in 1968 and categorized Skyprobe as an action-genre thriller embodied with both the richly conceived fantasy typical of Ian Fleming (see separate reference) and the grimly conveyed inevitability depicted by John le Carré (see separate reference).

Skyprobe emerged as a prophetic statement of the generic Cold War secret agent's purpose, conflict, and future; and without doubt was the best entry in the Shaw dossier.

Following the trail paved by John Creasey's The Terror (1966) (see separate reference), Skyprobe advanced the marriage of espionage and outer space, which was exploited by such diverse practitioners as Edward S. Aarons, James Dark, and Van Wyck Mason (see separate references).

The Hartford Courant said of the spy-space epic, "McCutchan holds his reader through the skillful use of mystery and suspense.... Skyprobe is richly embellished with violence, sadism, and sex."

In The Screaming Dead Balloons (1968), Shaw's first assignment for 6D2, properly defined as a global fact-finding agency, he was sanctioned to eliminate a megalomaniacal Maltese scientist, one John Zan, who had fostered a parasitic fungus capable of reproducing itself.

Exploring in this satisfying entry a new scientific-espionage realm, McCutchan countered Ian Fleming's (see separate reference) S. P. E. C. T. R. E. with the technological machinations of G.R.A.S.P.

SUMMARY: Philip McCutchan's Commander Shaw counterspy series honored the style of Ian Fleming's James Bond (see separate reference), except in the plot and characterization arenas where the author infused his specialized brand of credible suspense. Indeed, McCutchan's Skyprobe (1966) was a provocative mixture reminiscent of both Fleming (see separate reference) and le Carré (see separate reference). Further, McCutchan's penchant for absorbingly intricate technical explanations heightened the credibility of the series.

Berkley-Medallion Books commenced its U.S. distribution of the Shaw dossier in 1965, and the following promotional review from Books and Bookmen revealed the paperback publisher's competitive bid for the domain of Agent 007: "Throws a strong challenge to James Bond. At the moment, Bond is leading by a short head, but Shaw is hot on his trail."

John Day originally published six of the Shaw books in hardback.

STATUS: As with the works of Desmond Cory (see separate reference), the style and complexion of the Shaw dossier is sufficient recommendation for reissue in the current market. SOP.

FIELD BIBLIOGRAPHY

McCutchan, Philip. The All-Purpose Bodies. London: Harrap, 1969. HB-HB. See also The All-Purpose Bodies in Appendix I.

_____. Bluebolt One. London: Harrap, 1962; New York: Berkley-Medallion paperback, 1965. HB-R.

_____. The Bright Red Business Men. New York: John Day, 1969. HB.

_____. The Dead Line. London: Harrap, 1966; New York: Berkley-Medallion paperback, 1966. HB-R.

_____. Gibraltar Road. London: Harrap, 1960; New York: Berkley-Medallion paperback, 1965. HB-R.

_____. The Man from Moscow. London: Harrap, 1963; New York: John Day, 1965; New York: Berkley-Medallion paperback, 1966. HB-HB-R.

_____. Moscow Coach. London: Harrap, 1964; New York: John Day, 1966; New York: Berkley-Medallion paperback, 1967. HB-HB-R.

_____. Redcap. London: Harrap, 1961; New York: Berkley-Medallion paperback, 1965. HB-R.

_____. The Screaming Dead Balloons. New York: John Day, 1968; New York: Berkley-Medallion paperback, 1969. HB-R.

_____. Skyprobe. London: Harrap, 1966; New York: John Day, 1967; New York: Berkley-Medallion paperback, 1968. HB-HB-R.

_____. Warmaster. London: Harrap, 1963; New York: John Day, 1964; New York: Berkley-Medallion paperback, 1965. HB-HB-R.

CONSULT APPENDIX I FOR SERIES CONTINUATION

END OF CWF 44

† CWF 45. McDANIEL, DAVID †

BACKGROUND: American science-fiction-oriented author dominantly associated with the "The Man from U.N.C.L.E." home series. Also wrote a space epic, The Arsenal out of Time (1967), and The Prisoner--#2 (1969), adapted from the popular science-fiction visual project. Born in 1939.

Of all the U.N.C.L.E. authors drafted by the Ace Intelligence Group (see separate reference), McDaniel quickly achieved top status. Between 1965 and 1969 McDaniel shadowed six U.N.C.L.E. missions, evaluated by many operatives as the best of the series.

A major representative of the Ace Intelligence Group (see separate reference) during the mid- and late sixties, McDaniel literally symbolized the objectives of the U.N.C.L.E. novelization project. It therefore seems appropriate to dedicate this file to David McDaniel who left an indelible mark on the espionage novelization genre before his untimely death in 1977.

In 1970 McDaniel penned his seventh U. N. C. L. E. thriller, The Final Affair, which is yet to be distributed in the general intrigue market.

CWF AGENTS: Solo, Napoleon, and Illya Kuryakin.

CWF HISTORIES: See also Avallone, Michael--CWF 6.

OPERATIVE DATA: In his six U. N. C. L. E. assignments, McDaniel consistently animated the principal values of the series, capturing its visual mystique on the printed page.

Prompted by a series of mysterious incidents, including the movement of $3,000,000 in gold out of Los Angeles, Mr. Waverly ordered Solo and Kuryakin to collaborate with the Los Angeles-based U. N. C. L. E. command center in The Dagger Affair (1965).

McDaniel intensified this entry with a graphically blistering pace which shaped the progression of his future U. N. C. L. E. missions.

Abducted by elusive T. H. R. U. S. H. agents in Los Angeles, Solo and Kuryakin uncovered the existence of another inimical organization, DAGGER, and its suspected head, identified as one Kim Keldur. Solo and Kuryakin then embarked on a hazardous foray from Los Angeles to San Francisco, subsequently discovering a plan to eradicate the human race.

McDaniel interjected into The Dagger Affair several original elements which greatly enhanced the series:

1) A major plot reverting back to the concept of Hitler's "Final Solution."

2) Mr. Waverly, relieved of his desk-bound duties at U.N.C.L.E. headquarters in New York, conferred with San Francisco bureau chief Jerry Davis on the DAGGER crisis.

3) Equally threatened by DAGGER, T. H. R. U. S. H. was forced to cooperate with U. N. C. L. E.

4) McDaniel integrated the dynamic settings of Los Angeles and San Francisco into the plot.

Regarding this entry's action values, McDaniel accelerated to a pulsating pitch Solo and Kuryakin's battle with hostile operatives in a San Francisco warehouse.

Further, McDaniel invested The Dagger Affair with a strong measure of credibility, including the detailed background on Kim

Keldur and his previous affiliation with T. H. R. U. S. H., the palpable
notions of the "Energy Damper" and the GX-40-B9 tubes in relation
to the plot. McDaniel also offered a brief yet intriguing history of
T. H. R. U. S. H.

David McDaniel's The Dagger Affair represented spy novelization at its finest. In his later U. N. C. L. E. efforts McDaniel refined
his style while retaining his sharply defined sense of novelty and authenticity.

In The Vampire Affair (1966) Mr. Waverly assigned Solo and
Kuryakin to investigate the savage death of U. N. C. L. E. operative
Carl Endros--purportedly attacked by a bat in the Transylvanian
Alps.

Mass obliteration from outer space figured in The Monster
Wheel Affair (1967) in which Mr. Waverly summoned Solo and Kuryakin to trace the origin of a contentious space station orbiting the
globe. McDaniel's fictitious Egyptian locales, where Solo and Kuryakin attempted to unmask the mystery of the space station, ranked
as one of the series' most inventive developments.

In The Rainbow Affair (1967) Mr. Waverly was concerned
over the possible alliance between T. H. R. U. S. H. and an infamous
master criminal known only as Johnny Rainbow, whom the author
portrayed as the definitive elitist mastermind.

Allied with the C. I. D. in London, Solo and Kuryakin sought
to discern the mutual interests of T. H. R. U. S. H. and Rainbow.
T. H. R. U. S. H. 's Ultimate Computer was effectively presented as the
apparat's nerve center, and McDaniel's utilization of London and
other British settings made this U. N. C. L. E. entry unusually entertaining.

In a more critical mood, The Utopia Affair (1968) featured
Napoleon Solo at the helm of U. N. C. L. E. Learning that Mr. Waverly was vacationing for six weeks at the exclusive Utopia resort in
Southern Australia, T. H. R. U. S. H. conspired a devious ploy to liquidate the U. N. C. L. E. chief.

Confronted with this imminent crisis at U. N. C. L. E. headquarters in New York, Solo desperately maneuvered Kuryakin into
the Utopia perimeter to reach Mr. Waverly before T. H. R. U. S. H.
could eliminate him.

For reference purposes, it should be noted that Mr. Waverly
designated Kuryakin as Chief Enforcement Officer, which permitted
Solo to assume command of U. N. C. L. E. in Mr. Waverly's absence.

McDaniel eschewed the typical global-menace plot in The
Utopia Affair, shifting into the dramatic sphere with unblemished
delineations of Solo, Kuryakin, and Mr. Waverly in the thick of a
dilemma.

With this new direction of plotting and characterization, The Utopia Affair qualified as one of McDaniel's best U.N.C.L.E. missions.

With an illustration of Solo as the authoritative U. N. C. L. E. chief, gravely poised in front of a global intelligence map, the Ace paperback cover of The Utopia Affair reflected the serious tone of the novel.

With The Hollow Crown Affair (1969), McDaniel returned to more traditional U. N. C. L. E. themes. Joseph King, U. N. C. L. E.'s former Lab Chief, was supposedly killed in 1965 during a test for the new experimental rifle, the P. A. R. (Particle Accelerator Rifle). Four years later, U. N. C. L. E. central turned up information that King had survived the incident and defected to T. H. R. U. S. H., taking with him the blueprint for the lethal P. A. R.

Ward Baldwin, the head of T. H. R. U. S. H.'s satrap in San Francisco, disclosed King's relationship to U. N. C. L. E. and requested their assistance, fearing that King was preparing to use the P. A. R. in an attempt to gain control of T. H. R. U. S. H.

McDaniel punctuated The Hollow Crown Affair with a convincing treachery plot that unwound as Solo and Kuryakin uncovered the truth about King.

SUMMARY: In his six U. N. C. L. E. assignments David McDaniel covered an admirable range of plot variations, ranging from the archetypal global domination theme to the unexpected depiction of U. N. C. L. E. in a state of chaos.

In each entry McDaniel manifested a unique mixture of originality and credibility that led many U. N. C. L. E. students to favor McDaniel's field interpretations over those of other Ace Intelligence Group (see separate reference) analysts.

Assisted by the efforts of U. N. C. L. E. contributors Michael Avallone, Peter Leslie, and J. Hunter Holly (see separate references), as well as prolific author Jack Pearl (see separate reference), David McDaniel helped fashion the spy novelization into a respectable paperback original genre.

STATUS: As of this report (7-27-82), McDaniel's The Final Affair remains unpublished, due to legal disputes.

See also Avallone, Michael--CWF 6.

FIELD BIBLIOGRAPHY

McDaniel, David. The Dagger Affair. New York: Ace Books, 1965. PBO. TN.

_____. The Hollow Crown Affair. New York: Ace Books, 1969.
PBO. TN.

_____. The Monster Wheel Affair. New York: Ace Books,
1967. PBO. TN.

_____. The Rainbow Affair. New York: Ace Books, 1967.
PBO. TN.

_____. The Utopia Affair. New York: Ace Books, 1968. PBO.
TN.

_____. The Vampire Affair. New York: Ace Books, 1966.
PBO. TN.

CONSULT ACE INTELLIGENCE GROUP FOR ADDITIONAL AUTHOR
REFERENCES

END OF CWF 45

† CWF 46. MAIR, GEORGE B. †

BACKGROUND: Born in 1914 in the city of Troon, Scotland.

Mair studied medicine at the universities of Glasgow and
Edinburgh before serving as a surgeon from 1946 to 1953. Until
1968, Dr. Mair functioned as medical director of a clinic in Central Scotland.

While in his early twenties, Mair went to Spain where he
fought against the Nazis and the Fascists in the Spanish Civil War.
This experience fostered a passionate desire for world travel.

With increased affluence, Mair ventured to Asia, Japan,
South America, the Caribbean, Canada, the United States, and
Europe. Pursuant to this last sector, Dr. Mair and his Dutch-
born wife, Trudie, visited nearly all the Iron Curtain nations.

Dr. Mair also lectured on the Pacific and Orient Lines summer cruises from 1953 to 1972, and often helmed the Royal Scottish
Geographical Society Expeditions to Greece, Turkey, and Anatolia.

With some relevance to the subject of this file, N. A. T. O.
"representative" Dr. David Grant, the Mairs were the first tourists
to photograph Kremlin interiors, and on a daring trip to Poland,
Dr. Mair was arrested on espionage charges.

Although Mair's early thriller, The Day Khrushchev Panicked (1962), contained ominous political implications, most of his subsequent Cold War-era books, namely the missions of Dr. David Grant, were unmistakably Bondian in nature.

Despite the fact that the Grant dossier was initiated in 1963 with Death's Foot Forward, it was 1968 before the series was reprinted in the U.S. paperback market, despite the consistently excellent reviews garnered by the early books.

Curiously, 1968 signaled the end of Grant's hardback field service in the domestic sector, as typified by Black Champagne (1968). Beginning with Goddesses Never Die (1969), the later Grant entries were confined to British distribution.

Before recruiting Dr. Grant, Mair penned several fiction and non-fiction volumes pertaining to medicine, notably Surgeon's Saga (1950) and three works containing the designation of "Doctor": Doctor Goes East (1952), Doctor Goes North (1958), and Doctor Goes West (1958). Dr. Mair entered the suspense genre with Destination Moscow (1960) and Doctor in Turkey (1961).

In 1974 Dr. Mair invaded the competitive action-avenger field with The Jade Cat, and while he performed admirably in this flourishing market, a new series failed to materialize. That same year Mair returned to writing about medicine in the highly acclaimed Confessions of a Surgeon (1974).

Arranging and Enjoying Your Package Holiday (1975) reflected Mair's unfailing interest in global tourism.

Dr. Mair is a former member of the Mystery Writers of America and the British Crime Writers Association.

CWF AGENT: Grant, Dr. David.

CWF HISTORY: Reminiscent of the resemblance between Ian Fleming (see separate reference) and James Bond, is that between George Brown Mair and Dr. David Grant. Both Mair and Grant are of Scottish origin; both became recognized as physicians of the highest caliber during the early fifties; and both share a penchant for exotic wayfaring.

The similarities end with these three points, however, for Dr. Grant's foreign travels were often besieged with the peril indicative of the Cold War--although in fairness to Dr. Mair, his itinerary matched that of Dr. Grant. But despite the resourcefulness displayed by Dr. Mair during his journeys behind the Iron Curtain, unlike Dr. Grant, he was not affiliated with any global intelligence organization.

After 1963 Dr. Grant served as a field operative for A. D. S. A. D., the Administrative Department of N. A. T. O. responsible for controlling Security measures relating to Attack and Defense. Established in 1958, this apparat, situated in an obscure 18th-century house in Paris known as Maison Candide, became one of N. A. T. O.'s most potent instruments during the Cold War.

A. D. S. A. D. was commanded by Admiral John Silas Cooper who drafted Dr. Grant for a special mission to Moscow in 1963. Initially, Dr. Grant was attached to S. H. A. P. E. as Deputy Adviser Medical Aspects of Physical Survival (D. A. M. P. S.).

Grant's 1963 assignment for A. D. S. A. D. revealed, however, that his early medical years with the U. N. had fashioned D.A.M.P.S. into an intricately designed cover for him as a key intelligence agent for S. H. A. P. E. (Supreme Headquarters Allied Powers Europe), nerve center of N. A. T. O.

Although Grant's immediate superior at S. H. A. P. E. was one Colonel Fengsted, he received his A. D. S. A. D. orders from Admiral Cooper. (Tragically, Colonel Fengsted was killed under hazardous circumstances in 1964).

Grant's alluring secretary at S. H. A. P. E., Jacqueline de Massacré, purportedly from one of France's most distinguished families, was involved in a 1967 Chi-Com conspiracy directed against Britain and France.

During the Cold War period Grant's missions embroiled him in the intrigues of the Soviet Union and Red China. However, Dr. Grant's A. D. S. A. D. directives repeatedly confronted a malevolent organization known appropriately as S. A. T. A. N., Society for the Activation of Terror, Anarchy, and Nihilism. S. A. T. A. N. penetrated global governments on five continents and, in the thick of the Cold War, infiltrated the U. N.

As of 1965 S. A. T. A. N. was believed to have existed for approximately 80 years, mastered during that time by S. A. T. A. N. 's Chairman of the Board, known as Zero. Zero was specifically mentioned by Disraeli in his notorious revelation of the "unseen powers" which influence world politics.

S. A. T. A. N. 's objective: the global accumulation of money and power. After 1945, however, S. A. T. A. N. concentrated its virulent energy on the second of these tenets.

By 1966 S. A. T. A. N. employed over 50, 000 men and women, most of whom were ignorant of its venomous scope throughout the world--especially in those sectors susceptible to armed and/or nuclear conflict.

Although the headquarters for S. A. T. A. N. changed with

shifting geopolitics, its permanent conference center was identified as a decaying house situated between Les Diablerets and Gstaad, Switzerland, northeast of Gsteig. According to a confidential A.D.S.A.D. report, dated 1966, this base has been occupied by S.A.T.A.N. for over 50 years. The directors of S.A.T.A.N. ranged in age from 25 to 80.

Pertaining to Dr. Grant's field abilities, he achieved proficiency in standard armed and unarmed combat techniques. Employed a Smith & Wesson .357 in the field.

Dr. Grant, also known as Treble-A, often utilized his medical acumen when engaged on an assignment for A.D.S.A.D.

Given the termination of Dr. Grant's U.S. profile after 1968, the present status of both A.D.S.A.D. and S.A.T.A.N. is unknown.

OPERATIVE DATA: To understand Mair's intention with Dr. Grant, it is necessary to recognize that he endowed each entry with a tantalizing tongue-in-cheek quality, especially in his outlandish depiction of S.A.T.A.N.

Generally, Mair's character delineation was influenced by the immense magnitude of his plotting. Mair's overall objective with the series was reflected in the satirical chapter headings that punctuated each Grant initiative.

Simply, Mair was inspired by Ian Fleming (see separate reference) in his realization of the Dr. Grant dossier. To Dr. Mair's credit, he made no attempt to blemish Fleming's standing in the espionage genre.

Assigned to the Spanish Sahara in Miss Turquoise (1964), Grant was ordered to preserve a vital mineral, known as Riodorium, crucial to the Western powers in their plans for moon exploration.

Ultimately, Grant's mission required him to establish transportation facilities for securing the Riodorium. This involved gaining the cooperation of the Caid Bobaida Farrachi, ruling sheik of the desert region which contained the coveted mineral.

In this entry Mair initiated S.A.T.A.N. into the drama, adroitly interplaying Grant's calculated manipulation of Turquoise, the sheik's alluring niece, with the organization's insidious maneuvers. Mair balanced his introduction of S.A.T.A.N. with an equally measured sketch of Zero, placing him above the power and defenses of N.A.T.O.

Mair generated a strong line of tension within the plot of Miss Turquoise, based on a Chi-Com scheme to liquidate Dr. Grant. Engineered by Ling Tao, the plan employed the prized talents of Jacqueline de Massacré. A belligerent group identified as Force-X was responsible for this conspiracy, and its role in Miss Turquoise strengthened the malevolent designs of S. A. T. A. N., making the challenge to Dr. Grant all the more menacing.

The intrigue maze also focused on R-AM-EN, a Russian, American, and English alliance dedicated to space discoveries, and Maya Koren, a sensuous Soviet ballerina with whom Dr. Grant "operated" in later A. D. S. A. D. projects, was introduced in Miss Turquoise.

Miss Turquoise mirrored Dr. Mair's erudite knowledge of the Spanish Sahara, as typified by Rio de Oro, and other locales, notably Madrid.

In Live, Love, and Cry (1965), Mair approached a threatening scientific premise from a purely escapist viewpoint.

FOR YOUR EYES ONLY: Penter-15, characterized as "worse than the bomb," was disclosed by Professor Juin, A. D. S. A. D.'s director of science.

Associated with the advancement of birth control, Penter-15 was labeled as an excessively lethal chemical, tasteless and odorless, that in its simplest form caused permanent sterility.

On a larger scale, Penter-15 was capable of eroding a nation's population in the face of any given enemy siege.

The disappearance of Dr. Alex Carpenter, the creator of Penter-15, prompted Admiral Cooper to dispatch Grant and Professor Juin to Perth, Australia, to terminate the Scottish scientist before S. A. T. A. N. appropriated the formula.

With Deidre, Carpenter's ravishing daughter, Grant anatomized S. A. T. A. N.'s motives in procuring the Penter-15 blueprint. The somewhat bizarre sexual implications of the plot in this Grant effort enabled Dr. Mair to manifest his medical acumen.

With Live, Love, and Cry, Mair completed the definition of the S. A. T. A. N. -Zero union so that they materialized in the reader's mind as a genuinely destructive force.

Because of the apocalyptic challenge presented to the U. S. in Kisses from Satan (1966), this entry not only symbolized Mair's series but scored as Dr. Grant's most impressive field performance for A. D. S. A. D. This S. A. T. A. N. initiative is outlined below.

The Director General of N. A. T. O. briefed Admiral Cooper on a suspected conspiracy to foster massive civil conflict in the U. S., with the end objective of fomenting global racism.

From a top-secret N. A. T. O. memorandum, Cooper learned of the activities of one Charles W. E. Miller, an ambitious oil magnate who invested nearly all of his financial reserves to promote his own policy of U. S. isolationism in world affairs.

Therefore, a sanction was duly authorized to assassinate Miller during a visit to Professor Hancke's Health Clinique in Geneva. Selected for this assignment were three highly competent female agents of varied Negroid origins, identified by the names Winona, Sultry M. Mbawa, and Maria Suza. Each of these operatives had at one time been victimized by racial prejudice.

Stefanie Carmichael was designated as the principal contact for the three A. D. S. A. D. agents-in-place, although they received their orders from Dr. Grant, who had been assigned by Cooper to head this liquidation project, which A. D. S. A. D. termed "Operation Noah."

As the operation progressed in Geneva, it became apparent that S. A. T. A. N. was manipulating this situation for its own purposes.

The appearance at the Health Clinique of Señor Tomás Martinez, Spanish subject, heightened Grant's suspicions of S. A. T. A. N. provocation, and the savage deaths of Miller and Maria Suza unmasked a more explosive element in the racial intrigues.

A threat to Maya Koren and a seemingly unrelated meeting of the major financiers in Switzerland provided circumstantial links in Kisses from Satan.

Unlike his previous Grant thrillers, Kisses from Satan contained a Mair plot that was both indigenous and sensitive to the sixties, and as a result, it portrayed Grant in a more sympathetic light than did Miss Turquoise and Live, Love, and Cry.

Mair's realistic civil conflict was regarded as an unconventional theme for a Cold War-era series entry. From this point, considering S. A. T. A. N. 's volatile scheme to exploit this divisive weakness, Kisses from Satan not only evolved as Mair's premier Grant novel but also qualified as one of the most inventively crafted espionage thrillers of the decade.

In addition, Mair's travelogue-style description of the mesmerizing Swiss settings, and the businesslike S. A. T. A. N. conference (presided over by Fernando Coia, identified as the Chairman-elect) evoked an authentic background absent from the preceding yarns.

Purportedly, S. A. T. A. N. was dismantled after "Operation Noah," resulting in conviction of the organization's executives by the Swiss authorities.

Both The Girl from Peking (1967) and Black Champagne
(1968) were intricately plotted but lacked the magnetism of Dr.
Grant's earlier A. D. S. A. D. intrigues.

The Girl from Peking revealed Jacqueline de Massacré as a
key Chi-Com agent in a convoluted scheme to place Red China in
the U. N. Set against the chaotic repercussions of U. S. involvement
in Vietnam, The Girl from Peking focused on a high-level diplomatic
gathering at the fashionable Elysée Palace in Paris where a major
Anglo-French treaty was commemorated.

Jacqueline was transformed, by means of plastic surgery,
into "Tania Monham," whose cover established her as born in
Macao, wealthy, educated in Saigon, and married to a Peking refugee who was killed in an air raid in Da Nang while working for the
U. S.

Tania's assignment was to compromise both the British
Prime Minister and the French President as a crucial step in
achieving the installation of Red China in the U. N.

The main deficiency in this entry was the paranoid dimensions of the plot generated by the presence of a U. S. spy satellite,
Samos, which intercepted intelligence data from two crucial points
in Peking:

1) An important Chi-Com training center which existed under
the cover of the House of 100 Eternal Lives.

2) The office of a top-ranking counterintelligence chief, Maksud.

Mair apparently infused this element to intensify the Chi-Com
conspiracy against Britain and France by eliciting the power-ploys
of the U. S. into the Paris strategy. This complicated the progression of Jacqueline/Tania's mission, and diverted an otherwise logically conceived premise. Apart from their inclusion in the U. N.
body, there was no justifiable reason for U. S. intervention in The
Girl from Peking.

The enigmatic Krystelle, whom Grant accosted in a French
brothel at a later stage of his assignment, developed as his most
resourceful ally against the venomous Jacqueline/Tania. It should
be emphasized that Krystelle was a former S. A. T. A. N. confederate.
Mair also summoned the provocative beauty in Black Champagne,
Dr. Grant's next mission for A. D. S. A. D.

Dr. Mair's electrifying French and Asian settings, especially Peking and Thailand, seriously rivaled those of Dr. Grant's previous escapist journeys. However, the lack of continuity manifested
throughout The Girl from Peking sacrificed the plausibility of the
Chi-Com diplomatic threat.

An imprisoned S. A. T. A. N. executive, identified only as

Ferguson, was sentenced to death at the Santé prison in Paris at the outset of Black Champagne (1968). Unfortunately, Ferguson escaped only seconds before his appointed execution, resulting in grave injury to Dr. Grant who had been ordered to interview the S.A.T.A.N. leader.

A. D. S. A. D. used the explosive Santé incident to publicly declare Dr. Grant dead. Secretly, however, Grant assumed the cover of Largo Juan Fabregas. His mission: infiltrate a remote sector of St. Thomas in the Virgin Islands where Ferguson reportedly was expanding, on S. A. T. A. N.'s behalf, the region's civil strife into U. S. territory.

Deriving this information from Ferguson's prior testimony while under the influence of a drug called Epontol, Admiral Cooper and Professor Juin realized that Grant's directive could be imperiled on the basis of such unreliable data.

Joining forces with Krystelle, Grant unveiled a destructive scheme aimed at the influential decision-making quarters of global power within the U. N., deploying the darkest applications of drugs and black magic.

Black Champagne emerged as a complex series entry, far removed from the entertaining designs of Miss Turquoise, Live, Love, and Cry, and Kisses from Satan.

Dr. Mair smoothly enacted his plot in Black Champagne, depicting Grant and Krystelle as natural colleagues as they confronted S. A. T. A. N.'s revival project after it was purportedly dissolved in Kisses from Satan.

Since her initial appearance in The Girl from Peking, Krystelle triumphed as an adventurous, independent woman-of-action, despite her past allegiance to S. A. T. A. N.

Accepting S. A. T. A. N.'s manipulation of Maya Koren in Kisses from Satan, Mair achieved an identity-crisis analogy for Dr. Grant through his relationship with Krystelle in Black Champagne, employing these diverse women as the source of the A. D. S. A. D. agent's intensely personal conflict.

Besieged by the effect of the Cold War on the espionage fiction of the late sixties, Black Champagne nonetheless succeeded as a strong challenge to the gradual decline of the genre, which began manifesting itself in 1968.

Sadly, Dr. Grant had matured to such an extent in Black Champagne that he was barely recognizable as against his more spirited performances in Miss Turquoise, Live, Love, and Cry, and Kisses from Satan.

Similarly, the new S. A. T. A. N. represented in Black Champagne failed to radiate the vengeful enthusiasm of the earlier entries.

Occasionally, S. A. T. A. N.'s reliance on voodoo in Black Champagne vaguely recalled Ian Fleming's Live and Let Die (1954) (see separate reference) and, more definitely, Mair's medical expertise with lethal drugs was an improvement on the previous Dr. Grant excursions.

SUMMARY: Influenced by Ian Fleming (see separate reference), George B. Mair conceived a generally satisfying spy series, characterized by an engaging tongue-in-cheek approach that often produced compelling plots and escapist-oriented characters.

Mair's self-parodying chapter headings refined his unique concept and prevented it from becoming ludicrous.

However, the constant modifications in the espionage series format, not to mention the Cold War itself, served to familiarize the novelty of the Dr. Grant counterspy dossier by the late sixties.

Although Dr. Mair was exposed to the critical battle for Ian Fleming's (see separate reference) position, the attitude expressed in some of the Grant reviews was noticeably less contentious than in the evaluations of James Leasor and Philip McCutchan (see separate references), among others: For instance, the Berkley Gazette: "Much better and fully as fantastic as James Bond"; the Buffalo Evening News: "In the best 007 tradition, Grant gets gold stars for wooing, indestructibility, and exotic gadgetry."

STATUS: Three years after launching Philip McCutchan's (see separate reference) Commander Shaw series, Berkley-Medallion Books initiated a sensational campaign for five of the Dr. Grant thrillers.

Outdoing the illustrated Shaw paperback promotion with sexually suggestive color covers depicting Dr. Grant and the "femme fatale" of the reprinted entry, Mair's series failed to achieve a measurable sales volume in the United States. This perhaps can be explained by the year of the series' appearance in paperback, 1968, which signaled the decline of the secret agent genre.

Given the above, it does not seem feasible to consider the Dr. Grant dossier for reactivation in the present market. SOP.

FIELD BIBLIOGRAPHY

Mair, George B. Black Champagne. London: Jarrolds, 1968; New York: Berkley-Medallion paperback, 1969. HB-R.

_____. Death's Foot Forward. London: Jarrolds, 1963; New York: Random House, 1964. HB-HB.

_____. The Girl from Peking. London: Jarrolds, 1967; New York: Berkley-Medallion paperback, 1968. HB-R.

_____. _Goddesses Never Die._ London: Jarrolds, 1969. HB.

_____. _Kisses from Satan._ London: Jarrolds, 1966; New York: Berkley-Medallion paperback, 1968. HB-R.

_____. _Live, Love, and Cry._ London: Jarrolds, 1965; New York: Berkley-Medallion paperback, 1968. HB-R.

_____. _Miss Turquoise._ London: Jarrolds, 1964; New York: Random House, 1965; New York: Berkley-Medallion paperback, 1968. HB-HB-R.

CONSULT APPENDIX I FOR SERIES CONTINUATION

END OF CWF 46

† CWF 47. MARK, TED †

BACKGROUND: Cover identity of Theodore Mark Gottfried, prolific American author of paperback originals. Born in Bronx, New York, in 1928.

Although Gottfried has alternated between straight fiction and the spy format, most of his books have been "marked" by lines of self-parodying sex.

Gottfried's satirical secret agent, Steve Victor--"The Man from O. R. G. Y. "--is the subject of this file.

After attending the University of Miami, the New York School of Journalism, and the New School for Social Research in the late forties, Gottfried held various jobs, including publicist for Warner Brothers, reporter and film reviewer for _Boxoffice_ magazine, cab driver, and numerous editing and advertising positions with such New York-based publishing firms as Penthouse, Stearn, and Westpark Publications.

Became a free-lance writer in 1963, and more recently served as an editor for _High Society_ magazine in 1976. The following year, secured the post of publisher with Drake, a hardback house situated in New York until a bankruptcy suit put it out of business in 1979.

In addition to the Ted Mark cover, Gottfried has employed several pseudonyms, notably Leslie Behan, Harry Gregory, Lou Marco, and Katherine Tobias; has also written books for Playboy Press under various identities, although none of these were in the espionage field.

As Mark, Gottfried wrote two sequel series to the Victor dossier: "The Girl from Pussycat," commencing with a 1965 entry of that title, and "The Man from Charisma," which he initiated in the early seventies.

Further, Mark/Gottfried penned the screenplay for The Man from O. R. G. Y. and the Real Gone Girls, a 1970 visual project distributed by the Cinemation Corporation.

Although an author of sex-laden novels, Gottfried is noted as a supporter of the Equal Rights Amendment. He also has been active in civil rights and peace movements and has participated in numerous protests, among them the 1968 demonstrations at the Democratic Convention in Chicago.

CWF AGENT: Victor, Steve.

CWF HISTORY: Born on July 4, 1933, in Columbus, Ohio. Son of a toolmaker and a public school teacher.

Attended grammar and high school in Columbus. Entered the University of Ohio in the late forties.

In 1950 Victor enlisted in the U.S. Army to serve in the Korean War, subsequently earning the Silver Star for heroism and three separate citations of commendation from his C.O.

After the war Victor resumed his schooling at the University of Indiana where he engaged in postgraduate studies with the famed Kinsey organization: Steve Victor garnered a Ph.D. in the subject of sex.

Having established a solid reputation as an expert in this field, Victor operated on a free-lance basis through a number of acquired foundation grants, including one in 1965 which allowed Victor to visit Damascus to study Arabic and Oriental copulation customs.

During the Damascus assignment Victor was escorted to the city's U.S. Embassy where he was interviewed by a Mr. Putnam who was fully aware of Victor's past, including his unique qualifications in the area of sexual relationships.

Mr. Putnam's objective was to verify Victor's patriotism before according him a hazardous mission in the Middle East.

As the consummate master of sex, Steve Victor alone symbolizes O. R. G. Y. --the Organization for the Rational Guidance of Youth--which he continues to represent today in the capacities of researcher and secret agent.

OPERATIVE DATA: "The Man from O. R. G. Y. " was the first sex-oriented spy series to materialize during the espionage genre of the sixties, preceding by two years both "The Lady from L. U. S. T. " and "The Man from T. O. M. C. A. T. "

Where the later efforts focused, in varying degrees, on the sexual acumen of their athletic "provocateurs," Mark used Victor's sex researcher status to seek a broader satirical scope than was manifested in the L. U. S. T. series by Rod Gray (see separate reference) or the T. O. M. C. A. T. series by Mallory T. Knight (see separate reference).

In the O. R. G. Y. entry as in the other sex-and-spy species, the initial entry typified the shape of the series.

Posing as a defector in The Man from O. R. G. Y. (1965), Victor allied with the Soviets and the Egyptians in Syria to avert a Chi-Com nuclear weaponry build-up in the Middle East.

Victor's involvement with the "harem" of Sheik Taj-ed el Atassi, particularly Teska, a fiery Syrian beauty from the exotic Druze cult, allowed him the luxury of testing his sexual expertise in alien lands.

The later Victor books closely followed The Man from O. R. G. Y., but two are worthy of mention because of their self-parodying overtones.

In Dr. Nyet (1966) Putnam assigned Victor to prevent a sultry Soviet chemist from defecting to a mysterious cartel, identified only as S. M. U. T., which harbored a network that extended from New York to Delhi.

Victor's sexual prowess was suitably challenged by Dr. Nyet and by the voluptuous Prudence Highman, amidst a formidable Chi-Com threat.

In Room at the Topless (1967) Victor infiltrated the liberated Hollywood scene, a preliminary to eliminating a ruthless enemy operative known to O. R. G. Y. as Ex-Lax.

SUMMARY: Ted Mark's "The Man from O. R. G. Y. " series developed as the best of the sex-oriented spy series because of its brazen mockery of the super-agent archetype.

In The Man from O. R. G. Y., Victor's first recorded mission, Mark integrated authentic Arabic backgrounds and customs, which served to elevate the style of the series.

As noted earlier, Mark adapted The Man from O. R. G. Y. and the Real Gone Girls from the respectively titled Victor books. The 1970 visual project featured Robert Walker as Steve Victor.

The O. R. G. Y. series has accumulated paperback sales totaling in the millions, with distribution extending throughout the United Kingdom and Scandinavia, in addition to the U. S. market.

STATUS: Steve Victor remains on active duty, although the paperback source has changed since 1965. SSP, subject to periodic rotation.

FIELD BIBLIOGRAPHY

Mark, Ted. Back Home at O. R. G. Y. New York: Berkley-Medallion, 1968. PBO.

_____. Come Be My O. R. G. Y. New York: Berkley-Medallion, 1968. PBO.

_____. Dr. Nyet. New York: Lancer Books, 1966. PBO.

_____. Hard Day's Knight. New York: Lancer Books, 1966. PBO.

_____. The Man from O. R. G. Y. New York: Lancer Books, 1965. PBO.

_____. My Son, the Double Agent. New York: Lancer Books, 1966. PBO.

_____. The Nine-Month Caper. New York: Lancer Books, 1965. PBO.

_____. The Real Gone Girls. New York: Lancer Books, 1966. PBO.

_____. Room at the Topless. New York: Lancer Books, 1967. PBO.

_____. The Square Root of Sex. New York: Berkley-Medallion, 1967. PBO.

_____. The Ted Mark Reader. New York: Lancer Books, 1966. PBO. Short-story collection.

_____. The Unhatched Egghead. New York: Lancer Books, 1966. PBO.

_____. Where's Your O. R. G. Y. ? New York: Berkley-Medallion, 1969. PBO.

CONSULT APPENDIX I FOR SERIES CONTINUATION

CONSULT APPENDIX II FOR SERIES TRANSITION

END OF CWF 47

† CWF 48. MARLOWE, DAN J. †

BACKGROUND: Born in 1914 in Lowell, Massachusetts; long regarded as an outstanding author of paperback original mysteries.

After completing his studies at the Bentley School of Accounting and Finance in Boston, Marlowe began a rewarding business career.

However, in 1957, after his wife died, Marlowe vacated the
business sector to enter the free-lance writing market.

In 1960 Marlowe moved to Harbor Beach, Michigan, where
he wrote a weekly column, featured in numerous newspapers throughout the state. In addition Marlowe has contributed book reviews to
the Detroit Free Press.

Marlowe's first mystery series concerned Johnny Killain, a
tough New York private detective: Doorway to Death (1959), Killer
with a Key (1959), Doom Service (1960), The Fatal Frails (1960),
and Shake a Crooked Town (1961).

Marlowe also wrote several gripping non-series suspense
novels, principally Strongarm (1963), Never Live Twice (1964),
The Vengeance Man (1966), and Route of the Red Gold (1967).

However, The Name of the Game Is Death (1962) certified
Marlowe as a top mystery author, for it was in this novel that
Earl Drake, the subject of this file, was initially conceived (as
Chet Arnold).

Marlowe attracted national attention with his disturbing character analysis of a ruthless and hunted man.

In the New York Times Book Review Anthony Boucher observed: "This is the story of a completely callous and amoral
criminal, told in his own self-justified and casual terms, tensely
plotted, forcefully written, and extraordinarily effective in its presentation of a viewpoint quite outside humanity's expected patterns."

As a result of the novel's popularity, Marlowe came into
contact with Albert Nussbaum, a bank robber whose communication
with the author supposedly led the F. B. I. to the apprehension of
Nussbaum's partner, Bobby Wilcoxson. Since that time, Marlowe

has guided Nussbaum through his prison term and its aftermath, and his subsequent writing career.

Although Drake emerged as a crime figure, some of his later entries contained elements of the espionage genre. One of them, Flashpoint (1970), earned Marlowe the first Mystery Writers of America best paperback mystery award.

The book was later reissued as Operation Flashpoint; all the Drake books of the seventies bear the code identification "Operation."

Marlowe served as a leading constituent of the Fawcett Intelligence Group (see separate reference), and has remained in the upper ranks of the Mystery Writers of America.

Mr. Marlowe presently resides in Tarzana, California.

CWF AGENT: Drake, Earl.

CWF HISTORY: Real name: Chet Arnold, a convicted murderer and bank robber who in 1962 led Sheriff Blaze Franklin on a perilous chase across Florida.

Arnold's accomplice was identified as a man named Bunny. Arnold, aware of a Lucille Grimes who was involved with Sheriff Franklin (whose treachery was unknown to the citizens in his domain) forced her to reveal Bunny's whereabouts.

Discovering Bunny's mutilated body in an isolated cabin outside Hudson, Arnold shot Ms. Grimes three times in the throat with a Smith & Wesson .38 Special.

Arnold was romantically associated with a woman identified as Hazel Andrews, owner of the Dixie Pig, a bar situated outside Hudson. Ms. Andrews, described as a fiery, six-foot redhead, was abandoned by Arnold prior to his confrontation with the Florida police.

Arnold penetrated a roadblock on U.S. 19, sparing the lives of Deputy Jed Raymond, his only ally in the Sheriff's department, and Kaiser, Raymond's police dog. However, the bullet of a rifle, reported as a .30-06, punctured Arnold's car, triggering an explosive battle with Sheriff Franklin and his deputies. Arnold was engulfed in flames when the .30-06 ignited the gas tank of his car.

Retained in the state hospital, Arnold was totally disfigured from the accident. Refusing to talk to anyone, Arnold silently planned both the perfect escape and his private vengeance against Blaze Franklin.

Arnold endured plastic surgery under the supervision of one

Dr. Afzul, a surgeon attached to the hospital. Then, executing a faultless escape, Chet Arnold, upon removal of the surgical bandages, ceased to exist.

In his place Earl Drake materialized as "the man with nobody's face."

OPERATIVE DATA: This CWF evaluation differs from most of the other file entries by virtue of its recognition of Drake's barbarous character in the context of his field duty as an intelligence agent during the seventies.

Usually employed on a free-lance basis, Drake accepted assignments from Commander Karl Erikson, whom he had rescued from a Bahamian prison in 1971. All missions were prefixed by the designation, "Operation," although this recognition code was officially initiated in 1969 with Operation Fireball. Consult APPEN-DIX I for specific title sanctions.

During this period Drake reunited with Hazel Andrews, who aided him admirably in the field.

Drake's savage nature endowed him with a fearsome reputation as a counterespionage agent during the seventies.

In the first two Arnold-to-Drake crime entries, The Name of the Game Is Death (1962) and One Endless Hour (1969), Marlowe utilized the first person in the narrative manner of Fawcett allies Donald Hamilton and Stephen Marlowe (see separate references) to convey the total desolation of his creation.

Through the seventies Drake's progression as a ruthless operative reflected and often surpassed that of the action-avenger figure, as typified by Don Pendleton's Mack Bolan and his imitators.

SUMMARY: Beginning with Chet Arnold's detailed history as an amoral criminal in The Name of the Game Is Death, and encompassing his transformation into Earl Drake in One Endless Hour and Operation Fireball, Dan J. Marlowe laid the foundation for a series about one of the most lethal secret agents of the seventies.

STATUS: For some inexplicable reason, the Arnold-Drake dossier was removed from active service in the late seventies.

With the continued success of both the avenger and the current man-of-action genres, the Drake entries would command a solid following in the present adventure market. SOP.

FIELD BIBLIOGRAPHY

Marlowe, Dan J. The Name of the Game Is Death. New York: Fawcett-Gold Medal, 1962. PBO.

_____. One Endless Hour. New York: Fawcett-Gold Medal, 1969. PBO.

_____. Operation Fireball. New York: Fawcett-Gold Medal, 1969. PBO.

CONSULT APPENDIX I FOR SERIES CONTINUATION

END OF CWF 48

† CWF 49. MARLOWE, STEPHEN †

BACKGROUND: Cover identity of Milton Lesser, author of mystery and science fiction. Born in New York in 1928; graduated from William and Mary College in 1949; served in the U.S. Army from 1952 to 1954.

Also wrote suspense novels under the names of Andrew Frazer, Jason Ridgway, and C. H. Thames, but Stephen Marlowe is probably the most recognizable of Lesser's assumed author identities. Has been employed frequently in the suspense field, notably in the Chester Drum series, the subject of this file. Drum was recruited in The Second Longest Night (1955).

Pursuant to the Drum dossier, Lesser collaborated with Richard S. Prather, creator of Los Angeles-based private-eye Shell Scott, on Double in Trouble (1959) in which the two detectives pooled their violent resources on a difficult case.

In the broader non-series mystery category, Lesser, writing as Marlowe, has written a plethora of books, as either paperback originals or hardback editions. These include Catch the Brass Ring (1954), Blonde Bait (1959), The Search for Bruno Heidler (1966), The Summit (1970), The Man with No Shadow (1974), and The Cawthorn Journals (1975).

More recently Lesser has retained the Marlowe cover for such contemporary efforts as The Valkyrie Encounter (1978) and Nineteen-Fifty-Six (1981).

Whatever his in-print identity, Lesser's books have been distributed by such prestigious paperback houses as Ace, Avon,

Fawcett, and Pocket Books while Bernard Geis, Macmillan, and Prentice-Hall have published his hardbound contributions.

Stephen Marlowe has left an indelible mark on the suspense world, as has his author-wife, Ann. Both are members of the Mystery Writers of America. For that distinguished organization, Lesser served as regional vice-president for the New York chapter from 1961 to 1963 and later as a member of the board of directors.

Lesser was also a principal constituent of the Fawcett Intelligence Group (see separate reference).

For the purpose of this evaluation, the cover identity of "Marlowe" is used.

CWF AGENT: Drum, Chester (Chet).

CWF HISTORY: American. Washington, D. C.-based private detective whose cases often transcended international borders. This distinction was due to the location of Drum's office in Washington, D. C., specifically on the seventh floor of the Farrell Building on F Street.

Initiating his practice in 1955, Drum quickly educated himself in the subtle diplomatic and sexual interplay of Washington.

Although Drum possessed no direct affiliations with the intelligence community, his activities often resembled those of a counterespionage agent. This was particularly evident in assignments dated from 1964 to 1968, which were prefixed by the designation "Drum Beat" on his dossier with the Fawcett Intelligence Group (see separate reference).

Given the unconventional nature of his work, Drum cultivated a broader scope of abilities than might be expected of his freelance brethren in New York and Los Angeles, including the aforementioned Shell Scott.

Highly proficient in unarmed combat techniques indigenous to both the East and the West. Also adept at such skills as negotiating a motorcycle over hazardous terrain. Effectively employed, in numerous global sectors, both the .357 and .44 Magnum calibers.

In 1960 Drum renewed his acquaintance with Wally and Marianne Baker, a husband-and-wife writing team with View magazine in Washington, a publication similar in concept to Life and Time. In fact, Drum first encountered Wally and Marianne at the Afro-Asian conference in Benares, India, in the late fifties when the couple had been attached to the old Time-Life staff.

During a 1960 murder investigation, Drum's car was wired

with explosives, and it was Wally Baker's fate to start the vehicle, resulting in his death in a residential area of Georgetown.

In spite of a brief affair that began a few months after Wally's death, Drum and Marianne remained good friends throughout the sixties. According to a Drum file dated 1964, Marianne was still a View writer.

Perhaps Drum's most striking talent was his attraction to treacherous women, especially an elusive French woman named Dominique Guilbert, whom he met during a 1965 assignment in Paris. See OPERATIVE DATA for details.

No information has been reported on Drum since 1968 when he was involved in a perilous case with Marianne.

OPERATIVE DATA: Aside from Drum's infiltration of the espionage genre, Marlowe's development of the series focused on two basic points.

First, beginning with the third Drum entry (Trouble Is My Name (1957)), the ten subsequent books evidenced similar signals (ending with Jeopardy Is My Job (1962)), as contrasted to the first two Drum mysteries: The Second Longest Night (1955) and Mecca for Murder (1956), both of which were of the hard-boiled school.

Marlowe, in these thirteen Drum cases, crafted a taut narrative style that equaled the suspenseful manner of Fawcett confederate Edward S. Aarons (see separate reference).

The 007 phenomenon inevitably influenced the direction of the later Drum missions. Bearing the code "Drum Beat," the last five entries progressed more in the Bondian mold than was apparent in the earlier books, but it should be emphasized here that Marlowe perfected his unique narrative format during the mid- and late sixties and did not attempt, as others have contended, to imitate Ian Fleming (see separate reference).

Francesca, Drum's recorded 1963 case, might be considered, at least in titular terms, as his passage into the peak of the Cold War.

Second, Marlowe's use of the first person signified a new dimension for the espionage genre, although it was not innovative for the private-eye school. In any event, Marlowe initiated a pathfinding framework that would later be refined by such practitioners as Len Deighton and Donald Hamilton (see separate references).

Marlowe's evolution of the Drum series was a careful one, and by the time the "Drum Beat" efforts began appearing in 1964, he had achieved a smooth mixture of escapism and suspense. Even Danger Is My Line (1960) reflected Marlowe's seasoned ability to fuse the series' elements of detection and intrigue into a cohesive whole.

Drum shadowed the threatened liquidation of a free-lance assassin, identified as George Brandvik, and found himself involved in the manipulative schemes of a mysterious Swedish stewardess, Maja Kolding. Utilizing the resources of View magazine, Drum unmasked a murder plot aimed at the very nerve center of the U.N., and a rebellious diplomat, Jorgen Kolding--Maja's father.

Going to Stockholm, Drum penetrated the mystery of Maja's movements, eventually encompassing the machinations of Baroness Margaretha, a 20-year-old secret, torture through the use of LSD, and a ruthless "provocateur" named Einar Laxness. Further, it was in this entry that Drum rekindled his friendship with Wally and Marianne Baker--only to be shattered by Wally's tragic death.

Danger Is My Line represented Marlowe's skillful use of his first-person technique integrated into an espionage plot spiced by a haunting twist.

While the majestic Scandinavian backdrop of Danger Is My Line undeniably enhanced the entry, Manhunt Is My Mission (1961) intensified the travelogue aspect of Marlowe's concept.

Amidst an incendiary civil war in an Arab nation known as Motamar, Drum was asked to find an American surgeon, Dr. Turner Capehart, who had vanished in the thick of the divisive conflict.

With Manhunt Is My Mission, Marlowe concerned himself with the chaotic Arab power politics of the early sixties as he defined the ideologies of the mythical Motamar against the violent and authentic regions of the Middle East. Specifically, Marlowe delineated the core of his plot through the democratic objectives of Motamar.

Conceding that Manhunt Is My Mission denoted Marlowe's transition into new mystery territory, he utilized the fictional Arabic locales to flesh out a complex plot that satisifed the implied realities of Capehart's dilemma as well as Motamar's struggle for independence.

Manifesting a judicious attitude toward the opposing political factions in Manhunt Is My Mission, especially in his depictions of El Thamad, tyrannical head of Motamar's secret police, and the ambitious Princess Farat, Marlowe conveyed a credible and gripping portrayal of an Arab country ravaged by the calculated designs of the major global powers.

This entry, which also involved the Middle Eastern opium market and the assassination of a passionately pro-Western monarch, King Khalil, surpassed Drum's earlier cases in all areas except that of the detective's fatal fascination with dangerous women.

Drum's relationship with the placid Samia Falcon, whom he encountered at the outset of the assignment, lacked the electrifying
quality of his earlier conquests.

With the "Drum Beat" imprint, the sexual passivity of Manhunt Is My Mission was altered.   The precise authenticity of that
1961 Drum entry afforded the author no alternative, although it was
followed by Jeopardy Is My Job (1962) and Francesca (1963) before
the first "Drum Beat" mission appeared.

The abduction of Heinrich Graeber, a German human-rights
activist, and Quentin K. Hammond, View's Berlin correspondent,
established the conflict of Drum Beat--Berlin (1964).

Set in divided Berlin during one of the more volatile Cold
War periods in Europe, this entry radiated Marlowe's knowledge of
East-West geopolitics.

Traveling to Berlin with Marianne under the allied cover of
View representatives, Drum became involved with Lorelei, Graeber's
tempestuous daughter, and her boyfriend, one Helmut Steinbrenner,
who was fingered in certain intelligence quarters as a double agent.

With the existence of the Berlin Wall a factor in Drum Beat--
Berlin, Marlowe balanced the Graeber-Hammond incident with the
revelation of a secret tunnel designed to aid 300 refugees imprisoned
in the Soviet sector of Berlin.

Marlowe elicited a decidedly serious tone in this entry,
strengthened by Marianne's engagement to Hammond and Drum's
sincere affection for Lorelei Graeber.   Until he met Dominique
Guilbert the following year, Drum's experience with Lorelei Graeber ranked as his most intense sexual exercise.

The Cold War intrigues of Drum Beat--Berlin unmasked the
machinations of one Otto Fuchs, an ex-Nazi who figured in the
Graeber-Hammond crisis.

With Drum Beat--Berlin Marlowe conceived a sharp line between the realism of John le Carré (see separate reference) and the
feverish narrative pace of Ian Fleming (see separate reference).

Further, Marlowe displayed an admirable grasp of detail,
from the enigmatic Berlin locales to the workings of U.S. and Soviet intelligence organs in Europe's most ravaged city of the Cold
War.

Drum Beat--Dominique (1965) focused on the scandalous accusation of Jack Morley, a key State Department official in Paris,
as the architect of an insidious international extortion scheme, with
U.S. Senator Clay Bundy its suspected victim.

Drum, accepting the assignment of defending Morley's reputation, eventually accosted Dominique Guilbert, a smooth and calculating Parisian beauty who triggered a treacherous path of deception and murder during Drum's Paris mission.

With Drum Beat--Dominique Marlowe's compelling depiction of the antagonism which undermined the diplomatic surface of U.S.-European relations during the Cold War surpassed the more confined menace of Drum Beat--Berlin.

Further, Marlowe's characterization of the extortion blueprint, which extended from Washington into the highest realms of the French government and N.A.T.O., created one of the most chillingly memorable tales to originate in the espionage fiction of the Cold War.

Within the sphere of the extortion element, an unscrupulous plastic surgeon and the mystery surrounding a U.S. soldier figured in the shadowy Washington-Paris ploys in Drum Beat--Dominique.

If these qualities weren't enough to certify Drum Beat--Dominique as Marlowe's best Drum book, then the manipulative role of sex in the yarn's U.S.-French interplay, masterfully demonstrated through Dominique's knife-edged talents, invested this entry with a near-classic dimension. Unquestionably, Dominique scored as a satanic sexual challenge to Chester Drum, excelling even the formidable lure of Lorelei Graeber in Drum Beat--Berlin.

SUMMARY: Stephen Marlowe's Chet Drum series materialized as a major development of the spy fiction of the sixties for two reasons:

1) The author's innovative fusion of a cynical detective figure with provocative espionage plots.

2) Marlowe's use of the first person defined his alliance of the two formats identified in 1).

STATUS: Given the consistent success of Fawcett confederates Edward S. Aarons and Donald Hamilton (see separate references) from the spy wave of the sixties to the present day, the Drum dossier should be actively solicited as a positive reissue candidate. SOP.

FIELD BIBLIOGRAPHY

Marlowe, Stephen. Danger Is My Line. New York: Fawcett-Gold Medal, 1960. PBO.

_____. Death Is My Comrade. New York: Fawcett-Gold Medal, 1960. PBO.

_____. Drum Beat--Berlin. New York: Fawcett-Gold Medal, 1964. PBO.

_____. Drum Beat--Dominique. New York: Fawcett-Gold Medal, 1965. PBO.

_____. Drum Beat--Erica. New York: Fawcett-Gold Medal, 1967. PBO.

_____. Drum Beat--Madrid. New York: Fawcett-Gold Medal, 1966. PBO.

_____. Drum Beat--Marianne. New York: Fawcett-Gold Medal, 1968. PBO.

_____. Francesca. New York: Fawcett-Gold Medal, 1963. PBO.

_____. Homicide Is My Game. New York: Fawcett-Gold Medal, 1959. PBO.

_____. Jeopardy Is My Job. New York: Fawcett-Gold Medal, 1962. PBO.

_____. Killers Are My Meat. New York: Fawcett-Gold Medal, 1957. PBO.

_____. Manhunt Is My Mission. New York: Fawcett-Gold Medal, 1961. PBO.

_____. Mecca for Murder. New York: Fawcett-Gold Medal, 1956. PBO.

_____. Murder Is My Dish. New York: Fawcett-Gold Medal, 1957. PBO.

_____. Peril Is My Pay. New York: Fawcett-Gold Medal, 1960. PBO.

_____. The Second Longest Night. New York: Fawcett-Gold Medal, 1955. PBO.

_____. Terror Is My Trade. New York: Fawcett-Gold Medal, 1958. PBO.

_____. Trouble Is My Name. New York: Fawcett-Gold Medal, 1957. PBO.

_____. Violence Is My Business. New York: Fawcett-Gold Medal, 1958. PBO.

END OF CWF 49

† CWF 50.   MASON, F. VAN WYCK †

BACKGROUND: Born in 1901 in Boston. Attended the Berkshire School for two years; graduated from Harvard in 1924. Full name: Francis Van Wyck Mason.

Beginning with his U.S. Army service in France during World War I, Mason registered twenty-six years of active and reserve duty, including an appointment to the Supreme Headquarters of the Allied Expeditionary Forces from 1943 to 1945 and the honor of the French "Croix de Guerre." He attained the rank of colonel by the end of World War II.

Although initially planning a diplomatic career, Mason established his own importing firm after his father's sudden death. Traveling extensively throughout Europe and North Africa, Mason purchased embroideries, rugs, and rare books for his private concern.

Mason's first wife, the former Dorothy Louise Macready, whom he married in 1927, died in March, 1958; seven months later, Mason married Jean-Louise Hand. Mr. Mason died in 1978.

Becoming a full-time writer in 1928, Mason instantly sold articles and short stories to the finest popular magazines. Two years later Mason published his first novel, Seeds of Murder (1930), which introduced the subject of this file, Hugh North--the man from G-2.

Many of Mason's books have been serialized in such publications as Argosy and Saturday Evening Post, and he developed an immense following as an author of historical fiction, producing such classics as Captain Nemesis (1931), Stars on the Sea (1940), Proud New Flags (1951), and The Young Titans (1959). Several of Mason's books in this competitive genre achieved bestseller status, and of them, Three Harbours (1938) remained on the top sales lists for nearly a year.

Mason has also written a number of juvenile novels with historical themes, such as Battles for Quebec (1965), and other works under the cover identities of Frank W. Mason and Ward Weaver.

Mason, as Geoffrey Coffin, authored two memorable mysteries in collaboration with H. Brawner, both of which featured Inspector Scott Stuart: Murder in the Senate (1935) and The Forgotten Fleet Mystery (1936).

However, it was the intrigues of Hugh North that secured Mason's reputation as a gifted writer and his mass acceptance with the mystery audience. The North series, lasting for nearly forty years, transcended the changing politics of the postwar period and continued to captivate new and seasoned readers alike during the secret-agent phenomenon of the sixties.

CWF AGENT: North, Hugh (Captain/Major/Colonel).

CWF HISTORY: Born in 1883 in Portsmouth, New Hampshire. North's father served as Attorney General of the U.S., often engaged in global inquiries for the Consular Service.   Consequently Hugh North received his early education in France and Germany. However, he subsequently returned to the U.S. to gain admittance into West Point.

Graduating with top honors from the American military academy, North later became assistant military attaché in Vienna.   During this posting North cultivated an interest in criminology, often working with noted experts who were bringing distinction to Vienna in police circles.

Prior to World War I, North attracted the attention of Washington when he successfully recovered a cache of confidential documents which had been stolen from the U.S. Embassy in Vienna.

During the early years of the war North acted as a secret agent on several hazardous missions in Europe.   With the formal declaration, he was designated as the head of U.S. Army counterespionage operations in France.   He was responsible for averting the assassination of certain diplomats at the Versailles Peace Conference in 1919 and by this time, had attained the rank of captain.

By the end of the war North was permanently attached to the Military Intelligence division of the U.S. Army, otherwise known as G-2, which he continued to serve with distinction through the Cold War era.

Achieving the position of colonel by the conclusion of World War II, North fashioned an enviable reputation for resourcefulness and sophistication that preceded him wherever he was summoned for G-2.   He also manifested a seasoned knowledge of the continental arts, for his global assignments often tested his acumen in the areas of culinary and casino expertise.

As demanded of all G-2 agents, North was highly proficient in the recognized techniques of armed and unarmed defense.   Standard field weapon listed as .38 caliber, generally carried in a shoulder holster.

During the Cold War Colonel North occasionally received his orders from one General R. D. (Request Denied) Armiston.

No further record of Colonel North since a 1968 mission for G-2 in Tangier.

OPERATIVE DATA: Before initiating the CWF evaluation of Colonel North, it must be stressed that Van Wyck Mason probably didn't envision a four-decade series when he recruited North in 1930.   For this reason, it might be helpful to regard Colonel Hugh North as "the Hercule Poirot of espionage," given the similar chronological circumstances that characterized the evolution of Agatha Christie's famed Belgian detective.

The passage of the North dossier into the complex fiction of the Cold War may have resulted from Mason's consistent emphasis on three integral elements:

1)   Logical narrative progression.

2)   Sharply defined character delineation.

3)   Hypnotic locales for G-2's top operative.

Concerning himself less with the geopolitical attitudes of the era, Mason simply identified these ideologies to place the archetypal North plot in the context of the East-West struggle.

Mason gradually guided North's movement into the Cold War battleground, anticipating the sensationalism that would dominate the spy fiction of the mid-sixties, as typified by Ian Fleming (see separate references) and his imitators.

Secret Mission to Bangkok (1960) developed as a potential murder mystery within the framework of the espionage blueprint.

Assigned to protect an important Western missile expert, identified as Dr. Hans Bracht, on a plane destined for Bangkok, Colonel North encountered several passengers who signified a possible threat to his mission, chiefly:

1)   Mary Hollberg: Elusive German tourist; profession given as concert pianist.

2)   Chu Huong: Chinese multimillionaire; creator of Dragon's Tooth Elixir.   Mr. Huong's industrial status in the Orient refuted any alleged Chi-Com affiliations.

3)   Boris Salenkov: Soviet passenger who closely resembled Joseph Stalin, physically and politically.

4)   M. Georges Marchet: French planter based in Cholon, South Vietnam.

5)   Henry Barrows: Cover identity of Dr. Hans Bracht; established as a respectable citizen of Washington, D. C.

6)   Lita Naline: Tempestuous American film actress who revealed a sudden attraction to Colonel North.

7)   Anton Carss: Belligerent Hollywood director.

8) Lex Ross: Celebrated American actor with former Communist associations.

9) John Wallen: Calculating film star with international box-office following.

10) Aloysius Robinson: Free-lance agitator; based in Macao.

Utilizing the cover of Charles Boyden, an importing agent from New York, North discerned a surprising number of motives from a selection of these passengers who purportedly never had seen Dr. Bracht prior to the Bangkok flight. Bracht was journeying around the world to locate his missing Siamese wife, Tao Muong, described as adventurous and alluring.

Mason used this single fragment to fuse all of the characterization and plotting segments of Secret Mission to Bangkok, including Colonel North's intrusion into Bracht's personal plans.

The opening chapters, taking place on the plane, suggest the notion of the traditional locked-room mystery, as evidenced by the diverse backgrounds and secrets of the travelers. However, the vital concern of G-2 was a top-priority missile initiative, "Project Galaxy," of which Dr. Bracht was the appointed head.

Viewing Bracht's search for his wife as a lethal danger to the project, G-2 instructed North to insure the rocket scientist's safe passage to Bangkok where, in their estimation, he would be less vulnerable to liquidation by Redland or Peking. One major factor in G-2's decision was the location of the headquarters for S. E. A. T. O. (the Southeast Asian Treaty Organization) in the ancient city.

A brutal murder resulting from an automobile ambush brought North into contact with the Bangkok Imperial Troop's Captain Pilanung Pokh, a tenacious Thai officer with whom the G-2 agent allied in Trouble in Burma (1962).

An array of malicious intentions, a global opium network based in Indochina, and a convincing Bracht double frustrated North and Pokh in their attempt to isolate the threat to the missile genius's life.

Van Wyck Mason has been consistently praised for his smoothly satisfying style as an espionage novelist, and nowhere was this style more apparent than in Secret Mission to Bangkok.

2) The entry constituted a dexterous integration of the mystery and spy formats.

2) It emerged as a classic novel of transition, rich in plot and characterization, and moved Colonel North from the dated

relics of postwar politics into the ambiguous challenges of
the Cold War.

From this point, Mason intensified the activities of G-2 into
the volatile deceptions of the era.

Trouble in Burma (1962) concerned a missing rocket capsule,
Voyageur I, which vanished in the seething Burmese Jungle.

In Rangoon, working once again with Captain Pokh, North uncovered a host of avaricious designs while journeying into the jungles of Burma on a riverboat, accompanied by, among others, a
megalomaniacal Chi-Com general and three devastatingly beautiful
women: Marianne, Madame Bo Lintin, and Tola Duvaine.

Although Mason conveyed the darkly sensuous Southeast Asian
settings of Trouble in Burma in much the same graphic fashion as
in Secret Mission to Bangkok, the former surpassed the narrative
aspect of North's 1960 G-2 mission with its disturbingly authentic
menace of Chi-Com power in Indochina during the early sixties.

In Zanzibar Intrigue (1963), the C.I.A. approached G-2 to
rescue an operative who had disappeared near the East African
Coast. During a briefing with G-2's General Armiston, North
learned that this "agent" was one Willis Bonhart, a seemingly devoted black master sergeant (C.M.P.) who had suddenly defected to
East Berlin while assigned to the American sector as part of U.S.
Army duty.

According to G-2 files, North initially accosted Bonhart in
1939 during an investigation of a black market ring specializing in
U.S. Army goods. Bonhart, a P.F.C. at the time, was suspected
by G-2 of involvement in this operation.

Proving Bonhart's innocence to the satisfaction of the Pro-
vost Marshall's office, North took an active interest in Bonhart's
subsequent military career. Consequently Zanzibar Intrigue transpired as one of Colonel North's most difficult missions for G-2 because of his personal relationship with Bonhart. It should be emphasized, however, that the East Berlin fiasco changed North's attitude toward Bonhart.

Armiston revealed to North that Bonhart's "defection" was
arranged by the C.I.A., to infiltrate the Soviet sector. Objective:
to obtain crucial intelligence data on the U.S.S.R.'s machinations
in the new African states.

Given this explosive situation, North was immediately dispatched to Nairobi with the name of an eventual contact in Zanzibar,
being advised also on Britain's hostility toward external influence in
the region.

Posing as Reid Douglas, a spice buyer from the Baltimore-based MacKettrick importing firm, North was initially confronted with the death of a hotel proprietor in Zanzibar, identified as Jaol Silvera--North's designated G-2 contact in the area.

Allying with G-2's Captain Kenneth Trotter, North contended with a number of puzzling characters whom he viewed as possible enemies in the Bonhart crisis:

1) Rodney Phillpotts: M. I. 5. agent whom North had encountered on a previous assignment in Malaya.

2) James Mnoyah: A gregarious Kenyan whom North recognized as a former Mau-Mau master terrorist.

3) Ionel Zelrenu: Described as an elusive Rumanian; a favored target of M. I. 5.

4) Sahami Buma: The mysterious widow of a prestigious Briton, tagged by M. I. 5. as a key Mau-Mau agent.

5) Tommy Henderson: British subject, obsessed with a mission of vengeance.

6) Meklov and Nulgin: Known as two of the K. G. B.'s top assassins, the Kremlin reserved their special talents for East Africa.

Zanzibar Intrigue came from the same mold as Secret Mission to Bangkok, given the attention devoted to the secret malefactions of the principal characters (excluding Colonel North and Captain Trotter) and the peril surrounding Willis Bonhart. Accenting the zealous political motives of KADOK, the East African Liberation Party, Mason advanced the character interaction and the Bonhart dilemma to a staggering climax.

Expressing the realistic threat of Soviet domination in Africa and graced with the electrifying mystery element of Secret Mission to Bangkok, Zanzibar Intrigue developed as Van Wyck Mason's finest Colonel North entry of the sixties--with the improbability of the C. I. A. seeking the help of G-2 imparting an ironical twist.

Maracaibo Mission (1965) and The Deadly Orbit Mission (1968) displayed Mason's acute awareness of the technological terror of the Cold War.

In Maracaibo Mission General Armiston sent North to Venezuela to seek out and destroy "Kugelblitz," an apocalyptic weapon created by the Soviets. Concealed in the upper regions of the Andes Mountains, "Kugelblitz" was capable of unleashing cataclysmic fireballs on the oil-rich fields of Maracaibo, the seaport and capital of Zulia State, Venezuela.

Resembling, in some respects, John Creasey's The Terror

(1966) (see separate reference), The Deadly Orbit Mission (1968)
(Colonel North's last recorded mission for G-2 to date) involved a
Soviet warhead encircling the earth, whose path the Russians as-
serted they were unable to control.   According to G-2 intelligence
reports, the missile was launched from a clandestine Soviet base
in the Ural Mountains.

Assigned to Tangier as assistant to Charles Gregory, technical director of the Voice of America, North played a major role
in the desperate attempt to defuse the hovering Soviet weapon.

While The Deadly Orbit Mission clearly represented Mason's
acknowledgment of the proliferation of nuclear-space flight themes
which dominated the espionage sector in the late sixties, this entry
was invested with an atmosphere of impending and inevitable doom
that excelled the narrative scope of previous G-2 missions of the
decade.

In accelerating this facet of the spy blueprint, however,
Mason sorely neglected the mystery element of The Deadly Orbit
Mission.   For this reason it did not quite measure up to the suspense level of Secret Mission to Bangkok and Zanzibar Intrigue,
although Mason retained North's dedicated and sophisticated manner.
Saturday Review was undeniably impressed with this G-2 initiative,
observing that it was "A novel of intrigue and Cold War terror to
match Fail-Safe. "

SUMMARY: The durability of the Hugh North series can be linked
to Van Wyck Mason's logical sense of plotting and characterization
while recognizing, to a lesser extent, the influences of the Cold
War upon the espionage fiction of the era.

Despite Mason's success, North was curiously ignored by
the visual sector during his four-decade term of service with G-2.
However, ABC (radio) launched "The Man from G-2, " a popular
audio project starring Staats Cotsworth as Major Hugh North.   The
program debuted in 1945, garnering an international audience.

STATUS: Like Agatha Christie and Erle Stanley Gardner, Van
Wyck Mason became one of Pocket Books' most distinguished mystery authors in the U.S. paperback market.

Although the North series generated excellent sales for
Pocket Books through the mid-sixties, in 1968 several G-2 files
were acquired by Popular Library for future distribution.

Unfortunately, the latter publisher did not enjoy the same
impressive commercial response as Pocket Books, and by 1975 the
Colonel Hugh North/G-2 dossier was no longer a feature of the
U.S. mystery paperback landscape.

North performed equally well in the hardback arena, and (unlike the series' paperback status) occasional hardbound editions of the classic G-2 missions have turned up in the field, such as The Rio Casino Intrigue (1941), which Doubleday reprinted in 1975. Otherwise, SOP.

As a prospective reissue project, the North series, especially its Cold War entries, speaks for itself.

FIELD BIBLIOGRAPHY

Note: Although Pocket Books reprinted a considerable number of the Hugh North adventures, the passage of time has virtually eradicated the recorded information on many of the Mason paperback titles. For this reason, only the most fully documented paperbound releases have been listed below.

Mason, F. Van Wyck. The Branded Spy Murders. Garden City, N. Y.: Doubleday, 1932; London: Eldon, 1936. HB-HB.

_____. The Bucharest Ballerina Murders. New York: Stokes, 1940; London: Jarrolds, 1941. HB-HB.

_____. The Budapest Parade Murders. Garden City, N. Y.: Doubleday, 1935. HB.

_____. The Cairo Garter Murders. Garden City, N. Y.: Doubleday, 1938. HB.

_____. Captain North's Three Biggest Cases. New York: Grosset & Dunlap, 1934. HB. Omnibus Edition: The Branded Spy Murders, The Vesper Service Murders, and The Yellow Arrow Murders.

_____. The Castle Island Case. New York: Reynal, 1937; London: Jarrolds, 1938. HB-HB. See also The Multi-Million-Dollar Murders.

_____. The China Sea Murders. New York: Pocket Books paperback, 1959. R. Revised edition of The Shanghai Bund Murders.

_____. The Dardanelles Derelict. Garden City, N. Y.: Doubleday, 1949; London: Barker, 1950; New York: Pocket Books paperback, 1958. HB-HB-R-R. See also The Dardanelles Derelict in Appendix II.

_____. The Deadly Orbit Mission. Garden City, N. Y.: Doubleday, 1968; New York: Popular Library paperback, 1969. HB-R.

_____. The Fort Terror Murders. Garden City, N. Y.: Doubleday, 1931; London: Eldon, 1936. HB-HB.

_____. The Gracious Lily Affair. Garden City, N. Y.: Double-day, 1957; London: Hale, 1958; New York: Pocket Books paper-back, 1960. HB-HB-R-R. See also The Gracious Lily Affair in Appendix II.

_____. Himalayan Assignment. Garden City, N. Y.: Doubleday, 1952; London: Hale, 1953; New York: Pocket Books paperback, 1959; New York: Popular Library paperback, 1969. HB-HB-R-R.

_____. The Hong Kong Airbase Murders. Garden City, N. Y.: Doubleday, 1937; London: Jarrolds, 1940. HB-HB.

_____. Maracaibo Mission. Garden City, N. Y.: Doubleday, 1965; New York: Pocket Books paperback, 1967. HB-R.

_____. The Multi-Million-Dollar Murders. New York: Pocket Books paperback, 1960; London: Hale, 1961. R-HB. Revised edition of The Castle Island Case, with the addition of the Hugh North character.

_____. The Rio Casino Intrigue. New York: Reynal, 1941; London: Jarrolds, 1942. HB-HB.

_____. Saigon Singer. Garden City, N. Y.: Doubleday, 1946; London: Barker, 1948. HB-HB.

_____. Secret Mission to Bangkok. Garden City, N. Y.: Double-day, 1960; New York: Pocket Books paperback, 1961; New York: Popular Library paperback, 1969. HB-R-R.

_____. Seeds of Murder. Garden City, N. Y.: Doubleday, 1930; London: Eldon, 1937. HB-HB.

_____. The Seven Seas Murders. Garden City, N. Y.: Double-day, 1936; London: Eldon, 1937. HB-HB. Collection of four Hugh North novelettes.

_____. The Shanghai Bund Murders. Garden City, N. Y.: Doubleday, 1933; London: Eldon, 1934. HB-HB. See also The China Sea Murders.

_____. The Singapore Exile Murders. Garden City, N. Y.: Doubleday, 1939. HB.

_____. The Sulu Sea Murders. Garden City, N. Y.: Doubleday, 1933; London: Eldon, 1936; New York: Pocket Books paperback, 1958 (revised edition). HB-HB-R.

_____. Trouble in Burma. Garden City, N. Y.: Doubleday, 1962; London: Hale, 1963; New York: Pocket Books paperback, 1963; New York: Popular Library paperback, 1969. HB-HB-R-R.

_____. Two Tickets to Tangier. Garden City, N. Y.: Doubleday, 1955; London: Hale, 1956; New York: Pocket Books paper-back, 1958. HB-HB-R-R. See also Two Tickets to Tangier in Appendix II.

_____. The Vesper Service Murders. Garden City, N. Y.: Doubleday, 1931; London: Eldon, 1935. HB-HB.

_____. The Washington Legation Murders. Garden City, N. Y.: Doubleday, 1935; London: Eldon, 1937. HB-HB.

_____. The Yellow Arrow Murders. Garden City, N. Y.: Doubleday, 1932; London: Eldon, 1937. HB-HB.

_____. Zanzibar Intrigue. Garden City, N. Y.: Doubleday, 1963; London: Hale, 1964; New York: Pocket Books paperback, 1965. HB-HB-R.

CONSULT APPENDIX II FOR SERIES TRANSITION

END OF CWF 50

† CWF 51. MAYO, JAMES †

BACKGROUND: Cover identity of Stephen Coulter, British journal-ist, intelligence officer, and author of suspense and spy fiction. Born in 1914.

Coulter started as a newspaperman in select English counties, eventually becoming a Parliamentary staff correspondent for Reuters New Agency.

Appointed as one of General Eisenhower's staff officers with S. H. A. P. E. during World War II, Coulter evaluated intelligence op-erations in France and Scandinavia.

After the war Coulter was employed for two decades as a staff correspondent with the Kemsley Newspaper Syndicate, notably with the Sunday Times in Paris. It was during this period that Coulter became acquainted with Ian Fleming (see separate refer-ence), who was foreign manager with Kemsley.

Coulter, widely known as a devotee of casinos, supposedly provided Fleming with the research to write Casino Royale (1953). Bond's potential impact became apparent to Coulter, and, as James Mayo, he infiltrated the field with The Quickness of the Hand (1952) while The Loved Enemy appeared the same year under his own name.

In 1964, the year of Fleming's untimely death, Coulter, under the Mayo cover, recruited Charles Hood, the subject of this file. Preceding the spy wave by over a year, the Hood series was one of the first to excel in both the critical and commercial arenas in both the U.S. and Britain.

As Mayo, Coulter has written such non-series thrillers as Rebound (1961) and Asking for It (1971). Retaining his own name during the sixties, Coulter contributed several well-received books to the mystery genre, namely Threshold (1964), Offshore (1965), and A Stranger Called the Blues (1968). The last title was published the same year in the U.S. as Players in a Dark Game.

In the non-fiction sector, Coulter wrote Damned Shall Be Desire (1958), an excellent study of Guy de Maupassant.

As noted in the CWF segment on James Dark (see separate reference), Mayo's operative was not affiliated in any way with Intertrust agent Mark Hood, whom Dark drafted for field duty in 1965.

CWF AGENT: Hood, Charles.

CWF HISTORY: British subject. Although described in Who's Who as a sportsman and art connoisseur, his recorded history reveals a background totally isolated from these cosmopolitan pursuits.

During World War II Hood distinguished himself as one of Sir William Stephenson's best Secret Service agents in the United States. He eventually came into contact with Sir George Tread, head of M.I.5. While Hood was not a registered member of this Military Intelligence branch, he accepted and successfully completed a confidential postwar mission.

Hood gradually fashioned an admirable reputation within the highest spheres of Whitehall, leading to assignments with the Foreign Office and Special Intelligence Security.

By the early sixties, Hood was a principal operative for a consortium of Britain's major economic powers. Hood's initial project for the group focused upon a series of delicate financial entanglements in an obscure foreign territory.

Known only to a select group of men who controlled the financial destiny of the City, this small yet formidable network became known as the Circle, an organization so exclusive that even global magnates and multinational corporations (non-British) were not considered for admission. In view of its clandestine origins, the Circle was privately funded.

When engaged on "business" for the Circle, Hood commanded the services of its charter constituents. These included 1) International Chemical Corporation (I. C. C.), 2) Lavery Brothers, the industrial products trust, 3) Rothsteil & Company, bankers, 4) Kristoby's, auctioneers and art dealers, 5) Combined Steel, 6) Jordan Matthews & Son, shipping and finance, 7) Lords of London, the renowned underwriting concern, 8) Royal Banner Oil, 9) the Diamond Trust, and 10) International Tobacco.

Hood also remained on active duty with both the Foreign Office and Special Intelligence Security, and the interests of the Circle frequently coincided with these two entities.

Regarding Special Intelligence Security (S. I. S.), Hood received his orders from one George Conder and from an intelligence chief known only as "the Head Man." The presidents of the various Circle organizations generally served as Hood's superiors whenever he was summoned by that body.

Apart from Hood's activities with the Foreign Office, the S. I. S. , and the Circle, his dossier includes the following information:

1) HEIGHT: $6'\frac{1}{2}''$

2) WEIGHT: 177 Lbs.

3) APPEARANCE: Eyes dark gray and humorous; clean-cut English looks.

4) CLOTHES: Shirtmakers in London, New York, Paris, and Hong Kong; bootmaker in St. James; sports trousers from Rio; suits from Blades of Dover Street.

5) WEAPONRY: Israeli Yassidi, fired with a .38 Special.

6) FOOD: Lunch-lark paté, truite bleu, wild strawberries, a Chateau Olivier, and Armagnac.

7) GIRLS: Kit, a cabaret ecdysiast--among others.

8) RESIDENCE: Curzon Street, London. However, at the insistence of the Circle, in 1966 Hood moved to a flat in Fiveman's Court.

9) LIQUIDATION RATING: Perfect.

OPERATIVE DATA: Beginning with the first series entry, Hammerhead (1964), Mayo accomplished the difficult feat of balancing Hood's elitist tastes with absorbing plots.

At the outset of Hammerhead, Hood was on an assignment for the S. I. S. when he learned of the secret activities of a respected art dealer, identified as Espiritu Lobar. In a briefing by

George Conder, Lobar's past was disclosed as a treacherous history of international sea piracy in which he utilized at least six identities. Although Lobar's real name was purportedly Urip, he was known to his enemies as "Hammerhead."

Providing Hood with a collection of prized paintings, Conder ordered him to penetrate Lobar's yacht, the Triton, which was reportedly shadowing two crucial areas: the Eastern Mediterranean and Fernando Po, a Spanish island off the West coast of Africa. The S.I.S. suspected that Lobar was using his yacht as a spy ship in a sector viewed as strategically critical to both the U.S. and the Soviet Union--the Eastern Mediterranean.

Mayo conceived Lobar as a malicious sensualist devoted to the consumption of all that attracted his twisted preferences. Thus, Mayo achieved a malevolent counterpart to Charles Hood, carefully delineating this conflict with the appearance of two alluring passengers on the Triton, namely Ivory, an enticing Indonesian beauty, and Sue Trenton, a tempestuous Englishwoman.

Depicting Ivory and Sue as tragically vulnerable women, Mayo defined Lobar as an amoral manipulator, within the context of his machinations as Hammerhead. This aspect of the series' development typified Mayo's basic premise, which he integrated into the plot involving the feared sabotage of a vital Western nuclear defense program.

Certain allegations surrounding the British Ambassador to N.A.T.O., Sir Richard Calvert, entered into the intrigues of this entry in a way that effectively accelerated its suspenseful progression.

Mayo capably invaded Ian Fleming's (see separate reference) domain in the areas of gambling and sea lore, the former during a game of baccarat in which Hood challenged Lobar at the elegant Chapelle St. Michel Casino. Mr. Mayo's operative displayed a complete mastery of this passionate contest, and the author's graphic sketch of the casino's hypnotic interiors reflected the knowledge which Coulter may have passed on to Ian Fleming for Casino Royale (1953) (see separate reference).

In a serious fashion, Mayo surpassed Ian Fleming (see separate reference) with Hood's expertise in the fine arts, for in Hammerhead it was the British agent's knowledge of art that afforded him access to Lobar's exclusive yacht.

Mayo's detailed description of the Triton, encompassing both the craft's resplendent and technical features, boldly rivaled that of Fleming's Disco Volante in Thunderball (1961) (see separate reference). In Hammerhead Mayo created a deadly navigational device for the Triton, which blended perfectly with the devious central plot.

The striking locales present in this entry--Cap Ferrat,

Beaulieu, Monaco, Chapelle St. Michel, and elsewhere--endowed this Hood mission with a worldly touch.

While the segments concerning the environs of N. A. T. O., including its headquarters on the Bois de Boulogne in Paris, were less extensive than the principal settings, Mayo authentically initiated the reader into the complex motives of the global alliance.

Mayo's characterization of Andreas, Lobar's calculating valet, created one of the most electrifying figures to emerge from the genre, especially considering his surprising involvement in the shaded interplay of Hammerhead. (Mayo's Hammerhead is not, of course, related in any way to Desmond Cory's (see separate reference) 1963 novel of the same name, which was published in the U. S. the following year as Shockwave.)

After Hammerhead, Mayo deviated little from his carefully molded concept.

In Let Sleeping Girls Lie (1965) Hood was associated more closely with the Circle as the I. C. C. summoned the agent to protect the fiery Evenly girls, Tiara and Tickle, both of whom literally controlled the corporation's security file. The chairman of I. C. C., Lord Claymore, persuaded Hood to employ his special talents when one of the girls inexplicably began vanishing at intervals.

A major scientific endeavor, identified from Circle files as the Newton Project, fitted into the avaricious maze of Let Sleeping Girls Lie.

A ruinous financial crisis punctuated Shamelady (1966), although the specifics of this Circle effort were not immediately revealed to Hood. Initially dispatched to New York on a clandestine mission for Rothsteil's, Hood attended a Christmas Eve party at the glittering Sessel mansion where he encountered Bonbon, a mysterious and sensual auburn-haired woman who played a dangerous role in the Rothsteil affair.

Hood's assigned task in New York was to contact one Alexis Falkenberg and form a solid relationship with her. Nothing more.

Mayo penned Shamelady more in the manner of a traditional mystery, as he fused the introductory elements into revelation of an ingenious accounting scheme whereby large funds appeared to originate from Soviet Russia.

The resources of one Narcisso Rosario, an immensely wealthy international playboy, were invested in the global aircraft industry and a computer that operated on the microgroove principle in this tautly written espionage novel. The scope of Mayo's plot in which Hood discovered that the activities of the Circle had become known to his antagonists, extended from New York to Rosario's private Moroccan paradise, identified as El Tabela. Of all the Hood assignments, Shamelady shaped up as the most exotic.

SUMMARY: James Mayo's Charles Hood series emerged as one of
the pioneering species of the Bondian mold. His lean style and
erudition in certain areas, notably casinos, elevated the Hood dossier above many of its competitors.

In 1965 Dell Books launched an impressive paperback reprint
campaign for the first three Hood missions, with a strong sales re-
sponse in the highly competitive U.S. market. However Sergeant
Death (1968), the fourth Hood entry, failed to materialize in the
U.S. paperback arena, and the last of the series, The Man Above
Suspicion (1969), was confined to distribution in the British sector.

Matt Helm conspirator Irving Allen recruited Vince Edwards
as Charles Hood in Hammerhead (Columbia, 1968), a visual project
featuring Judy Geeson as Sue Trenton, Patrick Cargill as Conder,
Beverly Adams as Ivory, and veteran British actor Peter Vaughan
in the title role.

STATUS: The continuation of the current James Bond revival could
assist the successful reactivation of James Mayo's intrepid operative, a recommendation that would also apply to reissue of Desmond
Cory, John Gardner, Philip McCutchan, and possibly James Leasor
(see separate references). SOP.

FIELD BIBLIOGRAPHY

Mayo, James. Hammerhead. New York: William Morrow, 1964;
New York: Dell paperback, 1965. HB-R.

_____. Let Sleeping Girls Lie. London: Heinemann, 1965;
New York: William Morrow, 1966; New York: Dell paperback,
1967. HB-HB-R.

_____. The Man Above Suspicion. London: Heinemann, 1969.
HB.

_____. Once in a Lifetime. London: Heinemann, 1968. HB.
See also Sergeant Death.

_____. Sergeant Death. New York: William Morrow, 1968.
HB. U.S. title for Once in a Lifetime.

_____. Shamelady. New York: William Morrow, 1966; New
York: Dell paperback, 1967. HB-R.

END OF CWF 51

† CWF 52. MILTON, JOSEPH †

BACKGROUND: Cover identity of the late Joseph Hilton Smith, American author of paperback originals.

Most of Smith's contributions featured secret agent Bart Gould, subject of this file, but his epic novel, Ship of the Damned (1972), appeared under his own name.

The Bart Gould books were published by Lancer Books, no longer in existence.

President's Agent (1963), the first Milton/Gould book, was reissued under the cover of Joseph Hilton, and Magnum Books, a New York-based paperback firm, reprinted two installments. Like Lancer, Magnum has ceased operations.

No additional information available.

CWF AGENT: Gould, Bart.

CWF HISTORY: Former U.S. Marine Corps commando. During the Korean War, Gould led a raid into the North sector, successfully routing a division of Chi-Com and allied Korean troops.

Earning the Congressional Medal of Honor for his distinguished record in Korea, Gould subsequently achieved the rank of major.

The death of Gould's fiancée in 1953 plunged him into a state of deep depression. However, an incident at the Brazilian Embassy in Washington ten years later triggered a sequence of events that resulted in Gould's honored Cold War status: Secret agent to the President of the United States.

Accepting orders from one Titus Banning, an immensely powerful White House figure during the Cold War era, Gould functioned as an executive operative from 1963 to 1966. No further record of agent Gould since that time.

OPERATIVE DATA: Milton's Bart Gould series followed closely the concept of Michael Avallone's Ed Noon--"spy to the President" dossier (see separate reference).

Generally, the Gould entries lacked the biting cynicism of the Noon efforts, and the main recommendation for the series is Milton's consistency of feverish action throughout its three-year term. Otherwise, the formularized plot and characterization elements in each sequel offered little diversion as the series progressed.

President's Agent (1963) defined Gould's new occupation, and in this first White House mission Gould was ordered to avert a scheme to destroy the Panama Canal.

In Baron Sinister (1965) the mysterious disappearance of several U.S. government representatives in Europe prompted Titus Banning to send Gould on a global probe. Here Milton's nefarious Baron Wiesner, who commanded an army of world-class scientists from his impenetrable Austrian bastion, triumphed as Gould's most menacing nemesis.

In The Big Blue Death (1965) the White House expressed concern when a top Mafia assassin, identified as Nick Blue, revealed his intention of extending the power of the criminal organization far beyond U.S. borders. This Gould mission offered an unusually violent view of Las Vegas where the executive agent began his hunt for Blue.

The post-1965 Gould assignments reflected the rising nuclear pulse of the Cold War.

The Man Who Bombed the World (1966) involved Gould's sanction to penetrate the apocalyptic kingdom of J. Hunter Savage, whose Peking obliteration project virtually insured a global nuclear war.

Operation: World War III (1966) transpired as Milton's most complex series entry: Dispatched to Turkey with the task of accompanying Zoltan Kracodilu, a pro-Western liberator, back to the U.S., Gould unwittingly provoked the belligerent attention of the Soviets when he failed to complete his mission.

The Soviet hostilities erupted into a plan to demolish the White House.

Gould's stunning Turkish confederate, Adriana, was most challenging as the "femme fatale."

Gould's final assginment, The Death Makers (1966), presented an array of mesmerizing Oriental and Southeast Asian locales for the Presidential agent, ranging from Hong Kong to South Vietnam, as well as accurate allusions to Djakarta, Indonesia and Macao.

Focusing on this volatile global sphere, Milton embroiled his protagonist in a satisfying Cold War tale concerning one Major Thatcher Graybar, an O.S.S. officer who supposedly was killed in the Tsinghai province of China in 1944.

In 1966 reports materialized in Washington to the effect that Major Graybar was alive somewhere in Southeast Asia, mapping out a decisive strategy calling for the irrevocable defeat of all U.S. combat forces in the region.

Gould's orders: execute immediate covert action against Major Graybar.

SUMMARY: The Bart Gould series developed as a passable paperback original enterprise, characterized by a strong line of action.

Gould was recruited at an early phase of the spy movement, and his overall performance was surpassed by later contenders.

STATUS: Given the dated themes conveyed in the Milton/Gould dossier, it is not a probable reissue candidate. SOP.

FIELD BIBLIOGRAPHY

Milton, Joseph. Assignment: Assassination. New York: Lancer Books, 1964. PBO. See also The Running Spy.

_____. Baron Sinister. New York: Lancer Books, 1965; New York: Magnum Books, 1969. PBO.

_____. The Big Blue Death. New York: Lancer Books, 1965. PBO.

_____. The Death Makers. New York: Lancer Books, 1966. PBO.

_____. The Man Who Bombed the World. New York: Lancer Books, 1966. PBO.

_____. Operation: World War III. New York: Lancer Books, 1966. PBO.

_____. President's Agent. New York: Lancer Books, 1963; New York: Magnum Books, 1967. PBO. Magnum edition signed as Joseph Hilton.

_____. The Running Spy. New York: Lancer Books, 1967. PBO. Reissue title of Assignment: Assassination.

_____. Worldbreaker. New York: Lancer Books, 1964. PBO.

END OF CWF 52

† CWF 53. MUNRO, JAMES †

BACKGROUND: Cover identity of James Mitchell, British

suspense writer with wide experience ranging from teaching to acting.

Born in 1926 in South Shields, England. Received a B. A. degree from Oxford in 1948, then worked as both an actor and travel agent in the United Kingdom and Paris.

By 1963 Mitchell had taught courses in English and the liberal arts, with credits as a writer for British television (where he eventually authored twelve plays).

Mitchell began selling serious fiction in 1957 with Here's a Villain. Before recruiting series operative John Craig, the subject of this file, Mitchell wrote several straight novels that achieved critical and commercial success in England, chiefly Steady, Boys, Steady (1960) and Among Arabian Sands (1963).

The John Craig series, written under the Munro cover, began in 1964 with The Man Who Sold Death and endowed Mitchell with an enviable literary-public acceptance that placed him on a par with Ian Fleming and John le Carré (see separate references).

After the Craig dossier was terminated in 1969, Mitchell drafted a new "provocateur," David Callan, in A Magnum for Schneider (1969). This highly acclaimed spy thriller was published two years later in the U.S. as A Red File for Callan (1971). The Callan books were enthusiastically received in both the U.S. and Britain, with the most recent entry being Smear Job (1975). The Callan series appeared under his own name but he has authored other suspense works as James Meldrum.

Mitchell has contributed book reviews to such publications as The New Statesman and Books and Art, and he prepared the screenplay from his last Craig novel, The Innocent Bystanders (1969), which surfaced as a 1973 visual project starring the late Sir Stanley Baker as John Craig.

Mr. Mitchell is a member of the Screen Writers Guild and the Society of Film and Television Arts. In 1959 Mitchell was bestowed with the British Crime Writers Association Award for his mystery, A Way Back (1959).

CWF AGENT: Craig, John.

CWF HISTORY: Born in 1924. Joined the Royal Navy in 1941; initially trained at Devonport. Craig demonstrated an excellent aptitude in the deployment of small boats in a crisis situation.

After a single voyage on a destroyer, Craig was assigned to Special Boat Service in the Mediterranean where he remained until 1945.

During the war Craig quickly ascended the naval ranks, from leading seaman to lieutenant. Twice decorated (D.S.O., D.S.C.), Craig participated in seventeen major raids against the Axis powers in Greece, Italy, and North Africa.

Craig's wartime accomplishments were numerous and served to substantiate his reputation as a fearless officer:

1) All boats under Craig's command consistently assaulted the Axis fleet.

2) By the end of the war Craig had acquired fluency in French, Italian, and Greek, complemented by a serviceable command of German and Arabic.

3) Lieutenant Craig maintained an authoritative manner with all those he encountered.

4) Described as dangerously efficient in the use of unarmed combat and firearms. Recipient of the Black Belt in karate.

5) Craig was captured twice by the enemy, escaping both times.

In 1947 Craig secured employment with the prestigious Rose Line, a British-based shipping concern whose operations were focused in the Mediterranean. He worked his way up in the powerful shipping complex, subsequently becoming the line's general manager.

A bizarre incident in 1961 radically altered Craig's postwar occupation. Craig was reportedly killed when his Bristol motor car exploded, the result of a wired detonation device.

The London police assumed that it was John Craig in the car since his wife, Alice, was a passenger. Unfortunately, the driver's body was burned beyond recognition, and the explosion rendered Alice unconscious. However, as the investigation progressed, the identity of the driver was revealed as one Charlie Green, John Craig's brother-in-law.

Craig was involved, at that time, with a smuggling ring which had been supplying arms to the Algerian Arabs in their war against the French. Allied with Craig were three men identified as Baumer, Lange, and Rutter, all targeted for assassination by the Society for the Solution of the Algerian Problem, a violently pro-French political organization.

John Craig was also marked for liquidation by this vengeful organization but Charlie Green died in his place.

In light of the tense Algerian situation, these events came to the attention of Department K, a secret division situated within M.I.6. Concerned with perilous missions that weren't even whispered about in Whitehall, Department K was controlled by a man named Loomis. Philip Grierson, an ex-Marine commando, capably served as Loomis' number two.

Department K, pressured to select an agent for a mission related to the Algerian crisis, chose John Craig for the assignment --hired killer for Department K.

OPERATIVE DATA: In The Man Who Sold Death (1964) Munro devoted considerable attention to the delineation of Craig, describing the shattering episodes leading up to the introduction of Department K. Munro effectively conveyed the contrast between Craig's personal conflict and the callous objectives of Department K.

In his initial mission for Department K, Craig was ordered to terminate Colonel Pierre-Auguste Lucien de St. Briac, fanatical head of the Society for the Solution of the Algerian Problem.

Based in Nice, the group professed the double aim of intentionally deceiving Britain into military action in Algeria and eliminating all alien influences in the Algerian conflict.

The car explosion and the merciless executions of Baumer, Lange, and Rutter removed the dispassionate edge from Craig's character and, because of this, his penetration of St. Briac's network became an act of vengeance in the le Carré (see separate reference) mold.

Within the grim dimensions of Craig's assignment, Munro brought to mind the style of Ian Fleming (see separate reference) in two important areas: The placement of an exclusive casino, the Quai des Etats Unis, in the city of Nice, and Munro's careful elaboration of Craig's weaponry collection: two Colt .38s, a Luger, and a Colt Woodsman. A throwing knife was added in a later entry.

Playboy's perceptive evaluation of The Man Who Sold Death noted that "Munro is writing of the end of innocence, of the new era in which the C.I.A.'s, Special Services, and S.M.E.R.S.H.'s live by their own laws so that others may live or die. But Munro has installed a giant brain in the smooth James Bond machine, and a half-heart and semi-soul to John Le Carré's burned out Leamas."

Venturing into the barbed-wire perimeters of the Cold War, Munro implanted an isolated tone into his subsequent Department K missions. This was especially apparent in Die Rich, Die Happy (1965) in which Loomis sanctioned Craig to protect Aristides Naxos, a Greek millionaire who owned a significant percentage of Britain's Arbit Oil, a national concern with a massive investment in the crucial Middle East market.

Naxos' voting share in the Arbit group was perceived in Whitehall (and elsewhere) as the critical diplomatic factor in determining the future of British influence in the Arab world.

Set in the most violent core of the Middle East, Die Rich, Die Happy reflected Britain's Cold War struggle to assert itself amidst the cut-throat politics of Arab oil.

The author's Arabic locales, especially his fictitious People's Republic of Zaarb, graphically reflected the calculated danger of the times it depicted in Die Rich, Die Happy.

Although Munro's portrayal of the British battle for oil supremacy in the Arab world of the Cold War era was undeniably authentic, he failed to match the haunting quality of James Leasor's Passport to Oblivion (1964) (see separate reference) or William Haggard's The Powder Barrel (1965) (see separate reference) in this geopolitical arena.

The Los Angeles Times lauded John Craig's second Department K endeavor: "No one ... is more qualified to wear the mantle of the late Ian Fleming than Mr. Munro."

The Money That Money Can't Buy (1967) signified the peak of the Craig series in many respects, but especially in Munro's inflexibly brutal characterization of Department K's principal agent.

The appearance of a Soviet trawler north of England and the murder of a Chinese man from Hong Kong, identified as one James Soong, motivated Loomis to devise a field operation that, at the time, was judged as being out of bounds for M. I. 6.

Munro conceived this entry in a wholly different fashion than The Man Who Sold Death and Die Rich, Die Happy. Here, Munro made Department K the target of evil intrigue that revealed itself as the novel progressed, rather than the aggressive protector of Britain's gilded interests.

Loomis ordered Craig to contact a timid K-contact in Marabella, Spain, identified as George Allen, and manipulate him as the link to a top Soviet agent, one Jean-Luc Calvet, a native Ukrainian who had established a solid cover as an erudite French painter living conveniently near Allen. Craig was briefed on Calvet's background as Oleg Dovzhenko, a major K. G. B. operative, and on the spoils of the Allen assignment--a radio transmitter and 25,000 counterfeit British quid notes.

Unlike the earlier Department K missions, the plot of The Money That Money Can't Buy reached into the sensitive nerve center of the K. G. B. A high-ranking Soviet Intelligence officer, known as Chelichev, contemplated the repercussions of the abduction of Calvet/Dovzhenko and a multimillion dollar account in the Credit Labonne Bank of Tangier. K. G. B. inquiries revealed that the fund was secretly registered to an organization identified only as "BC," a wealthy albeit fanatical consortium committed to hostile activities against the U.S.S.R.

From this point, Munro intensified all of the foregoing elements, fusing them with the figures of C. G. Simmons, an avaricious communications magnate; Jane, Simmons' manipulative daughter; and a malicious Chi-Com agent named Chan. Further, the author inserted a startling twist regarding Craig's sexual inclinations that brought a chilling accent to the plot.

Munro sketched the plot of The Money That Money Can't Buy as deceptive interplay in which the machinations of "BC" emerged as a bitter commentary on the Cold War, related from the British viewpoint.

Munro's meticulous development of the plot qualified this entry as the best of the series while it also confirmed the author's position relative to Ian Fleming (see separate reference) and John le Carré (see separate reference). The absorbingly bloodthirsty Moroccan and Spanish locales helped crown The Money That Money Can't Buy as his classic contribution to the espionage fiction of the Cold War.

The New York Times Book Review extolled this masterful Craig foray as "Enough action, color, and tightly-coiled espionage to suffice a lesser artist for three novels."

Many critics commended The Innocent Bystanders (1969), the final entry in the Craig series, although Munro invested his protagonist with such a foreboding sense of disillusionment that Craig's mission of finding defector-scientist Aaron Kaplan seemed fatally rooted in a type of le Carré (see separate reference) format.

SUMMARY: James Munro's John Craig series represented a serious attempt to depict the realistic secret agent with some of the escapist trappings typified by Ian Fleming (see separate reference).

Generally, Munro achieved his objective, although The Innocent Bystanders radiated the futility of an Alec Leamas or a Quiller.

While the critical observations of the Craig dossier clearly reflected the "James Bond heir" syndrome of the sixties, Munro's series was unique in that all of its entries were published in the U.S., including the domestic paperback market where Bantam Books successfully distributed the series from 1966 to 1971.

As stated earlier, James Mitchell abandoned his Munro cover to do the screenplay for The Innocent Bystanders (Paramount, 1973) featuring Sir Stanley Baker as Craig and Donald Pleasence as Loomis.

Originally intended as a visual-project series agent, Craig failed to display James Bond's box office charisma, and after Sir Stanley's tragic death in 1976, all future Munro treatments were shelved.

STATUS: During 1980-81, Charter Books launched a successful campaign to reissue the first three entries in the Craig dossier. This action makes it clear that, given proper promotion and distribution, the generic Cold War espionage series can still exist as a viable force in the current paperback market.

As of this report (9-12-82), The Man Who Sold Death (1964) and The Money That Money Can't Buy (1967) remain in print, with Die Rich, Die Happy (1965) subject to rotation. EsSP.

FIELD BIBLIOGRAPHY

Munro, James. Die Rich, Die Happy. London: Hammond, 1965; New York: Knopf, 1966; New York: Bantam paperback, 1967. HB-HB-R.

_____. The Innocent Bystanders. London: Jenkins, 1969. HB.

_____. The Man Who Sold Death. London: Hammond, 1964; New York: Knopf, 1965; New York: Bantam paperback, 1966. HB-HB-R.

_____. The Money That Money Can't Buy. New York: Knopf, 1967; New York: Bantam paperback, 1969. HB-R.

CONSULT APPENDIX I FOR SERIES CONTINUATION

CONSULT APPENDIX II FOR SERIES TRANSITION

END OF CWF 53

† CWF 54. THE N. A. L. /SIGNET INTELLIGENCE GROUP †

CONTENTS: Officially recognized as the New American Library, a major U.S. publisher with several paperback divisions. One of them, Signet, figured greatly in the spy fiction of the Cold War era. In CWF terms, this group is identified as N. A. L. S. I. G., while the New American Library is referred to as N. A. L.

The activities of N. A. L. S. I. G. during the mid-sixties represented a broader spectrum than the Fawcett Intelligence Group (F. I. G.) (see separate reference). While N. A. L. S. I. G. 's contributions to the espionage genre were certainly impressive, they generally lacked the collective focus of the F. I. G., encompassing the incompatible works of Ian Fleming and John le Carré under the same imprint.

Unlike the F. I. G., the development of N. A. L. S. I. G. can be
linked to the paperback reprint sector. Several major events figure
in the evolution of this N. A. L. S. I. G. facet. In 1958 Ian Fleming's
fifth James Bond thriller, From Russia, With Love (1957), appeared
as a Signet paperback. However, the four previous 007 entries,
Casino Royale (1953), Live and Let Die (1954), Moonraker (1955),
and Diamonds Are Forever (1956), had already been reprinted elsewhere. (Consult Fleming, Ian--CWF 25 for specific sources and
dates.)

From that point, the subsequent Fleming-Bond books, beginning with Doctor No (1958), were distributed as Signet editions a
year after each title's hardcover publication. By late 1961 the first
four Bond missions had appeared with the N. A. L. paperbound imprint.

By the summer of 1967 Signet possessed the complete Ian
Fleming--Agent 007 "oeuvre," and even with the later distribution
initiatives launched by Bantam, Jove, and Berkley, the N. A. L.
branch remains the only U. S. paperback house to hold this distinction.

William Haggard's The Telemann Touch (1958) was reprinted
by N. A. L. in 1963. While this expertly written tale of diplomatic
intrigue was not a series item, Haggard's second assignment for the
urbane Colonel Charles Russell, Venetian Blind (1959), materialized
the same year as a Signet paperback. Five more Haggard-Russell
books would be published under the Signet flag by 1967, although
N. A. L. 's promotional efforts to sell the series in the competitive
mass market eventually failed.

Richard Condon's The Manchurian Candidate (1959) exploded
onto the international espionage scene as an unforgettable novel of
deception and treason, played out in the most critical spheres of
U. S. government. Issued as a Signet paperback in 1960, The Manchurian Candidate penetrated areas previously untouched by Fleming
and Haggard.

John le Carré's first two novels featuring George Smiley,
Call for the Dead (1961) and A Murder of Quality (1962), were recruited into the fledgling N. A. L. S. I. G. in 1964, but le Carré's
later Cold War classics, including The Spy Who Came In from the
Cold (1963), were reprinted by Dell Books during the spy phenomenon.

The later reprints in N. A. L. S. I. G. reflected the impact of
James Bond on the American espionage field, although the effect
was not fully realized until 1965, seven years after From Russia,
With Love (1957) appeared as a Signet paperback.

The advanced phases of N. A. L. S. I. G. 's infiltration of the
paperback reprint arena included Mickey Spillane, who was firmly
established as a mystery writer by the time he invaded the intrigue

market in 1964 with secret agent Tiger Mann. Consisting of Day of
the Guns (1964), Bloody Sunrise (1965), The Death Dealers (1965),
and The By-Pass Control (1966), the Mann series achieved instant
bestseller status and enjoyed great success as Signet paperbacks,
beginning with the distribution of Day of the Guns and Bloody Sunrise in 1965. Unlike most of the other N. A. L. S. I. G. members,
the Mann dossier has retained the N. A. L. stamp into the present
day.

Two of Desmond Cory's Johnny Fedora thrillers, Undertow
(1962) and Shockwave (1963), were presented as Signet editions in
1965, followed in 1966 by a 1959 Cory project, Johnny Goes South.

In 1966 James Leasor's first perilous journey for Dr. Jason
Love, Passport to Oblivion (1964), was published for the first time
in the U. S. paperback alley as Where the Spies Are, a Signet tie-in
for the M. G. M. -David Niven visual project of the same title. Spylight (1966), Leasor's haunting sequel to Passport to Oblivion, was
summoned as a Signet reprint in 1967.

The works of the late Francis Clifford represented a departure for N. A. L. S. I. G. in that the celebrated British novelist was
not involved in the series maze. Beginning with a 1967 reprint of
Clifford's bestselling The Naked Runner (1966), N. A. L. S. I. G. thereafter featured several of Clifford's thrillers. (Surfacing as a successful visual project, The Naked Runner (Warner Brothers, 1967),
offered Frank Sinatra as Clifford's world-weary protagonist, Sam
Laker.)

During this period, N. A. L. published Martin Woodhouse's
initial Giles Yeoman novel, Tree Frog (1966), under the Signet imprint. In the non-series sector, they issued such diverse hardcover
successes as Irwin R. Blacker's The Kilroy Gambit (1960), a story
of diplomatic-military interplay from Washington to Afghanistan,
which Signet represented in 1962; and Richard Mason's masterful
fusion of romance and espionage set in India, The Fever Tree
(1962), which turned up the following year as a Signet paperback.

With one exception, N. A. L. S. I. G. 's Cold-War era achievements in the paperback original field were mostly in the Bondian
category and consisted primarily of series projects (unlike the F. I. G.,
N. A. L. S. I. G. did not actively pursue this format until 1965). A
chronological summary is provided below.

1)   Bill S. Ballinger's dossier concerning one Joaquin Hawks, an
     intrepid C. I. A. agent assigned to Southeast Asia in the thick
     of the Vietnam War, was disclosed in 1965 with three mis-
     sions: The Spy in the Jungle, The Chinese Mask, and The
     Spy in Bangkok. The series was terminated in 1966 with
     The Spy at Angkor Wat and The Spy in the Java Sea.

2)   David St. John's Peter Ward series was distinguished from
     its N. A. L. S. I. G. allies by the author's realistic depiction of

global C. I. A. operations. Beginning with <u>On Hazardous Duty</u> and <u>Return from Vorkuta</u> (both 1965), six entries were sponsored under the auspices of N. A. L. S. I. G. (Once St. John was unmasked as E. Howard Hunt, N. A. L. reissued the Ward series in 1974, in the midst of the Watergate scandal.)

3) Mark Hood emerged as one of the more durable PBO operatives. Commencing in 1965 with <u>Come Die with Me</u> and <u>The Bamboo Bomb</u>, James Dark's file, with twelve representative N. A. L. missions, involved Intertrust, a Geneva-based global intelligence network devoted to the aversion of nuclear proliferation. The series continued until 1971.

4) Richard Hershatter adroitly blended sex and espionage in his three-volume Rand Stannard series. However, only the first entry, <u>The Spy Who Hated Licorice</u> (1966), was featured as a Signet paperback.

5) Although N. A. L. S. I. G. evidenced little interest in the nonseries spy novel within the PBO sector, Michael P. Faur's <u>A Friendly Place to Die</u> (1966) was a worthy exception in a startling Chi-Com plot to assassinate Fidel Castro at the United Nations.

6) 1967 marked the transformation of Michael Avallone's cynical private eye, Ed Noon, into a secret agent in several PBO assignments, notably <u>The February Doll Murders</u> (1967), <u>Assassins Don't Die in Bed</u> (1968), and <u>The Doomsday Bag</u> (1969).

An evaluation of N. A. L. 's hardcover line has been delayed until this point so that all of the publisher's strengths as a primary force in the paperback espionage market could be properly outlined.

N. A. L. established this division in 1963 when they realized that James Bond was developing into a worldwide sensation. As such, the new imprint initially functioned as Ian Fleming's hardbound publisher after Viking Press terminated their involvement with the distribution of the tenth Bond entry, <u>The Spy Who Loved Me</u> (1962).

Beginning with <u>On Her Majesty's Secret Service</u> in 1963, N. A. L. went on to issue in hardback <u>You Only Live Twice</u> (1964), <u>The Man with the Golden Gun</u> (1965), and <u>Octopussy and the Living Daylights</u> (1966). The first three of these invaded global bestseller terrain; of them, <u>The Man with the Golden Gun</u> generated the largest hardcover sales volume of all the Fleming-Bond books. Prior to publication, all four N. A. L. titles were serialized in <u>Playboy</u>.

Concurrent with the publication of <u>The Man with the Golden Gun</u> in 1965, N. A. L. released Kingsley Amis' acclaimed Fleming-007 study, <u>The James Bond Dossier</u>. A year later, Amis' scholarly tome accompanied the posthumous Bond novel to the paperback racks as a Signet reprint.

Ian Fleming's worldly travelogue, <u>Thrilling Cities</u>, was launched in hardback by N. A. L. in 1964, followed by a Signet edition in June 1965. Two months earlier, Signet distributed O. F. Snelling's <u>007 James Bond: A Report</u>, a pre-Amis commentary which first appeared in Britain in 1964.

In 1966 N. A. L. S. I. G. expanded its espionage line with William Garner's first Mike Jagger book, <u>Overkill</u>, succeeded the following year by a Signet paperbound version.

While Fleming's involvement with N. A. L. is long past, the publisher's hardback imprint has gone on to represent such contemporary authors as Erica Jong and the late Henry Fonda (offering his bestselling autobiography). In the future N. A. L. will be distributing the works of other popular novelists in hardback editions.

N. A. L. S. I. G. supported a sizeable number of tie-ins, covering both the theatrical and home visual sectors, listed at the end of this CWF File. This category can be divided into two formats:

1) The previously published spy thriller, promoting an adapted visual project. Perhaps the most striking example of this group was Signet's 1964 tie-in for Ian Fleming's <u>Goldfinger</u>, which reportedly sold over 1,000,000 copies in that edition alone.

2) The novelization. The best illustration of this type was probably Henry Reymond's <u>Deadlier Than the Male</u> (1967), based on the Universal visual project featuring Richard Johnson as Bulldog Drummond. Also, Michael Avallone and Peter Leslie contributed three novelizations from the M. G. M. visual series, "The Girl from U. N. C. L. E. " (A nonfiction entry, John Hill's <u>The Man from U. N. C. L. E. 's ABC of Espionage</u>, surfaced as a Signet paperback in 1966.)

N. A. L. S. I. G. is no longer in existence today, and only the works of Mickey Spillane and Ian Fleming's last four Bond books* have survived as Signet paperbacks. The remaining 007 entries are now available in the U. S. from Berkley, once the outlet for such Bond competitors as Philip McCutchan and George Brown Mair (see separate references).

From 1971 to 1973 Bantam Books reprinted the first seven Bond thrillers, two of which appeared as visual tie-ins, namely <u>Diamonds Are Forever</u> (Bantam, 1971) and <u>Live and Let Die</u> (Bantam, 1973). Eight years later, <u>For Your Eyes Only</u> surfaced from Berkley ally Jove as a tie-in for the 007 theatrical mission.

In October 1982 Signet reissued <u>Octopussy</u>, and will feature

---

*<u>On Her Majesty</u>'s Secret Service (1963), <u>You Only Live Twice</u> (1964), <u>The Man with the Golden Gun</u> (1965), and <u>Octopussy and the Living Daylights</u> (1966).

it as a tie-in when the visual project starring Roger Moore as
James Bond is released in June 1983.

The other N. A. L. S. I. G. allies have generally vanished from
the paperback intrigue field, replaced in N. A. L. 's current "Action-
Adventure" project by such series as Peter Buck's Marc Dean--
"The Mercenary," Robert Emmett's Mike McVeigh--"American
Avenger," Gregory St. Germain's Scott Gideon--"Resistance" (World
War II, Europe), and even one set during the Crusades, Mark Ram-
say's "The Falcon." In recent years, N. A. L. also has successfully probed new ground in the areas of horror, romance, and science
fiction.

It should not be construed that this CWF evaluation has
covered all of the memorable N. A. L. espionage artists of the Cold
War era; for instance, Don Von Elsner (see separate reference).
Rather its objective has been to simply outline N. A. L. S. I. G. 's major developments during the period.

Excluding Irwin R. Blacker, Francis Clifford, Richard Condon, Michael P. Faur, Richard Hershatter, Richard Mason, and
Henry Reymond, N. A. L. S. I. G. 's CWF identities can be found under
the appropriate file sections.

FIELD VISUAL PROJECT BIBLIOGRAPHY

Note: The dates given refer to project release and not necessarily
to original publication.

Avallone, Michael. The Birds of a Feather Affair. New York:
New American Library, 1966. PBO. TN. ("The Girl from
U. N. C. L. E. ")

_____. The Blazing Affair. New York: New American Library,
1966. PBO. TN. ("The Girl from U. N. C. L. E. ")

Clifford, Francis. The Naked Runner. New York: New American
Library paperback, 1967. R. MT.

Condon, Richard. The Manchurian Candidate. New York: New
American Library paperback, 1962. R. MT.

Fleming, Ian. Casino Royale. New York: New American Library
paperback, 1967. R. MT.

_____. Doctor No. New York: New American Library paper-
back, 1963. R. MT.

_____. From Russia, With Love. New York: New American
Library paperback, 1964. R. MT.

_____. Goldfinger. New York: New American Library paper-
back, 1964. R. MT.

_____. On Her Majesty's Secret Service. New York: New
American Library paperback, 1969. R. MT. Tie-in edition
reissued in 1977.

_____. Thunderball. New York: New American Library paper-
back, 1965. R. MT. 1971 reissue featured the artwork of the
1965 tie-in edition.

_____. You Only Live Twice. New York: New American Li-
brary paperback, 1965. R. MT. Consisted of a pressure-
sensitive sticker attached to the 1965 edition, advertising the
1967 Sean Connery visual project. No artwork, credits, or
stills.

Hill, John. The Man from U.N.C.L.E.'s ABC of Espionage. New
York: New American Library, 1966. PBO. TN.

Leasor, James. Where the Spies Are. New York: New American
Library paperback, 1966. R. MT. Visual project title for
Passport to Oblivion.

le Carré, John. The Deadly Affair. New York: New American
Library paperback, 1967. R. MT. Visual project title for
Call for the Dead.

Leslie, Peter. The Cornish Pixie Affair. New York: New American Library, 1967. PBO. TN. ("The Girl from U.N.C.L.E.")

Reymond, Henry. Deadlier Than the Male. New York: New
American Library, 1967. PBO. MN.

CONSULT APPENDIX I FOR SERIES CONTINUATION

END OF CWF 54

† CWF 55. O'DONNELL, PETER †

BACKGROUND: Born in London in 1920. O'Donnell left school at
the age of sixteen, eventually joining the British Army. Served in
the Signal Corps in Iran (known as Persia at the time) and witnessed the exodus of countless war-ravaged refugees, which probably played a significant role in his conception of Modesty Blaise,
subject of this file.

First appearing as a syndicated comic feature, in 1963, Modesty Blaise rapidly attracted an enthusiastic following throughout Europe and elsewhere, but not, ironically, in the United States. Yet when Doubleday published Modesty Blaise, O'Donnell's initial tongue-in-cheek exercise for his enigmatic "femme fatale," the yarn became an alternate selection of the Doubleday One-Dollar Book Club.

Modesty Blaise was reprinted three times in as many months after its issuance in June 1965, and it inspired a slightly distorted visual project starring Monica Vitti as Modesty, which surfaced the following year in the midst of the super-spy explosion.

The Blaise series has continued into the eighties with nine entries, including a short-story collection, Pieces of Modesty (1972).

Mr. O'Donnell functioned as a principal member of the Fawcett Intelligence Group (see separate reference) during the mid- and late sixties.

CWF AGENT: Blaise, Modesty.

CWF HISTORY: Despite Ms. Blaise's known reputation in the field, her exact origins continue to be shadowed in an atmosphere of mystery and speculation. Therefore, the operative is advised to bear this in mind in reviewing her file.

Classified as a refugee in the postwar Middle East, Modesty Blaise survived a savage back-alley existence in Turkey and Iran (she purportedly attended kindergarten in a Greek prison camp). During this time, Modesty saved the life of an elderly male, identified as a philosophy professor from Budapest. Fluent in five languages, the "professor" cultivated in Modesty the general art of worldliness that would dominate her life.

The "professor" also endowed Modesty with her flamboyant Christian name; Modesty herself borrowed her last name from the tutor of Merlin the magician.

Though the "professor" was a master of scholarly pursuits, he was timid to a fault, and Modesty often used her ferocious instincts to protect him. Modesty and the "professor" shared a richly balanced relationship that might be likened to that of a devoted daughter and father, based on unconditional reciprocation.

It is well documented that Modesty never knew her true parents, and her brief tutelage under the "professor" seemed to compensate at least partially this deficiency in her life.

Wandering aimlessly through the Arabic desert, Modesty was miraculously found by Sheik Abu-Tahir, the ruler of Malaurak, who would figure in her first mission for British Intelligence in 1965. See OPERATIVE DATA for full details.

Several years later Modesty was working in a Tangier casino, which was controlled by an elite criminal group, when its head, Henri Louche, was liquidated by an avaricious competitor.

Acquiring and expanding the organization, Modesty appropriately designated it the Network and proceeded to concentrate its energies on art and jewelry thefts, gold and currency manipulations, smuggling, and espionage. The Network stringently avoided, however, two areas of endeavor in its global operations: drugs and vice.

After the Network was firmly established as a multinational concern, Modesty encountered a man in Saigon who would play a major role in her future involvement with British Intelligence. Willie Garvin, identified as a former member of the Foreign Legion, was transformed by Modesty Blaise from a drifter into a man of culture and sophistication. Garvin's loyalty to Ms. Blaise eventually earned him the position as her A.D.C. in the Network.

Through her illicit projects Modesty attained financial independence, and, while in her mid-twenties, she "retired," luxuriating in an environment of magnificent wealth. She owned several homes, including a small English cottage in Wiltshire, and was dutifully served by her Indochinese valet, Weng. Willie Garvin opened a pub, the Treadmill, on the Thames.

However, the legal ramifications of Modesty's unknown nationality posed a serious threat to her paradisiacal lifestyle and, in 1962, she married and subsequently divorced an unworthy Englishman in Beirut as a means of obtaining British citizenship.

The enigma surrounding the Network had always fascinated Sir Gerald Tarrant, a high-ranking official of British Intelligence. Acknowledging Modesty's affluent status, Sir Gerald also perceived her main weakness and maneuvered her into realizing that she desired above all else the intrigue of her memorable past. Thus, Modesty Blaise was duly recruited by Sir Gerald as a special agent for British Intelligence. Sir Gerald's assistant was identified as one James Fraser.

The official dossier on Ms. Blaise, apart from her command of the Network, dates back to 1965. Since that time she has engraved her legend as a sleek, efficient, and lethal operative, feared and insatiably desired by men throughout the world.

Although not possessed of the Grecian style of beauty, Modesty's dispassionate mystique enslaved any male adversary who crossed her path. Moreover, Modesty's physical abilities rivaled those of one James Bond, and the fusion of her devastating magnetism and unique talents distinguished Modesty Blaise from even the

most professional male "provocateur." Ms. Blaise manifested her
proficiency in a number of critical areas, chiefly:

1) Mastery of unarmed combat methods, including judo and a
technique of her own design, the Nailer. The Nailer consisted of Modesty's stripped-to-the-waist entrance into a
roomful of male antagonists. Fully executed by agent Blaise,
this achieved the effect of "nailing" her intended prey.

2) Firearms. Although Ms. Blaise rarely carried a gun, she
preferred the Brevete, or the .32 Colt for more demanding
work. Also skilled in the use of the Colt Python. She wore
a snap-holster attached to the back of her hip, covered with
a short jacket so that the standard F.B.I. draw could be
satisfied in the field.

3) Archery. Ms. Blaise practiced this art to intensify her vision.

The Treadmill housed a number of interesting weapons utilized by Modesty and Willie, notably bows, ranging from the Mongol recurve to the laminated Japanese wood bow, which measures
eight feet in length, and such firearms as the Ruger 10/22 carbine
rifle, the hammerless Smith & Wesson Centennial, the .38 Special
Colt Cobra, the Astra Firecat, and the MAB Brevete.

Willie Garvin accented Modesty's performance with his knife-
throwing skill. In a stitched sheath inside the left breast of his
windbreaker Garvin nested two knives, one of which was hazardous-
ly unconventional in function and design.

Modesty's espionage abilities were sensuously heightened by
her skin-tight apparel, such as the black polo-neck sweater and
matching denim slacks she displayed when she rescued a confederate from a South American prison in 1965.

According to recent intelligence reports, Modesty Blaise remains on active duty, as reflected in her 1979 entry, Dragon's
Claw.

OPERATIVE DATA: From the earliest days of her affiliation with
British Intelligence, Modesty Blaise has been aptly termed the female James Bond, a comparison that has evolved from the incredible action sequences.

Since agent Blaise began her operative career as a comic-
strip figure, it's hardly surprising that she has been linked to that
format, despite O'Donnell's literary prowess.

The Blaise adventures, when measured against those of James
Eastwood's (see separate reference) Anna Zordan, pale in terms of
characterization and story development. Nonetheless, Modesty has

long since outlasted Anna's brief term of duty, and the myth surrounding the Blaise chronicles transcends any literary criticism.

Modesty Blaise (1965) was underscored by the critical oil
concession negotiations between Britain and the Skeikdom of Malaurak. During a briefing with Tarrant, Modesty learned that a
cache of diamonds, valued at ten million pounds sterling, was part
of an intricate financial arrangement with Malaurak's ruler, Sheik
Abu-Tahir.

According to a plan drafted by British Intelligence, the stones
were scheduled to be transported to Beirut on a passenger ship identified as the Tyboria. However, the intervention of a mysterious
multinational figure known as Gabriel gave Ms. Blaise the opportunity to employ her physical-sexual acumen. Ms. Blaise had, in fact,
encountered Gabriel during her days with the Network when both
were competing for a gold shipment in Calcutta.

O'Donnell graphically conveyed his concept in Modesty Blaise
with the depiction of Modesty and Willie's incomparable talents
throughout the mission, not to mention the stunning Middle Eastern
and Mediterranean locales, such as Cairo and Tel Aviv.

Modesty's expertise at unarmed combat was at its finest in
this entry when she employed the Nailer to liberate Willie Garvin
from an Argentine prison.

In another realm, Gabriel's insidious henchwoman, Mrs.
Fothergill, contributed a certain savagery to Modesty Blaise.

The Chicago Tribune regarded Modesty Blaise with great
fervor: "In bed or hot water, Modesty is Bond's counterpart with
cleavage ... always ready for a little action."

In Sabre-Tooth (1966) and I, Lucifer (1967) O'Donnell maintained with conviction both the Blaise charisma and the action.
Sabre-Tooth concerned Modesty and Willie's penetration of the mystery surrounding one Es-Sabah Solon, an enigmatic Arab-Greek who
mastered a fanatical freedom movement in Kuwait amidst the prosperity created by the current Kuwaitis ruler, Sheik Abdulla, descendant of the First Emir.

Publishers Weekly exulted, "This new adventure tops its
type in toughness ... fabulous, fantastic."

O'Donnell adroitly focused all the integral Blaise elements
in I, Lucifer (1967). In this assignment Modesty and Willie allied
with Deuxième Bureau chief René Vaubois to dismantle a blackmail
ring that was infiltrating the most influential levels of global power.

O'Donnell distinguished this entry from its predecessors by
an overpowering sense of malevolence that reached the reader as
well as his key operatives.

The author consummated this disturbing tone in the characterization of Lucifer, who "calculated" the deaths of the blackmailers' chosen victims. O'Donnell's Lucifer ploy elevated this imaginative thriller to the highest dimensions of the series.

Book Press observed, "Plenty of fast-paced action ... full of sex, sadism, mystery, and violence."

SUMMARY: Peter O'Donnell conceived the ideal fusion of action and fantasy when he advanced Modesty Blaise from a comic-strip adventuress to an engaging Cold War protagonist.

While the series generally lacked the suspenseful movement of James Eastwood's (see separate reference) Anna Zordan dossier, its blistering pace and undeniable charm insured agent Blaise's future beyond the boundaries of Cold War fiction.

As mentioned earlier, Monica Vitti appeared as Modesty Blaise in a 20th Century-Fox visual project of the same title which, however, failed to honor the style and humor of O'Donnell's creation. Released in 1966 Modesty Blaise featured Terence Stamp as Willie Garvin, Dirk Bogarde as Gabriel, and Harry Andrews as Sir Gerald Tarrant.

ABC's pilot of Modesty Blaise (1982) was not derived from a specific O'Donnell book, but this second visual-project adaptation perfectly reflected the author's premise, though the characterization was undeniably Americanized. Ann Turkel vividly portrayed Modesty Blaise, complemented by Keene Curtis as Tarrant, and Lewis Van Bergen as Willie Garvin. It is to be hoped that this electrifying visual project will lead to a future series in the home sector, with Ms. Turkel as Modesty Blaise.

STATUS: Despite the fact that the Blaise books, following The Impossible Virgin (1971), were not generally available in the U.S., publication of the series has continued unabated in Britain. Modesty Blaise (1965), which London's Souvenir Press reprinted in a hardback edition in 1977, has since been distributed in the U.S. through International School Book Service, along with the more recent Dragon's Claw (1979). The Silver Mistress (1973) was reissued in the U.K. in 1981 by Archival Press, but has yet to appear in U.S. territory. Otherwise, SOP.

FIELD BIBLIOGRAPHY

O'Donnell, Peter. I, Lucifer. Garden City, N.Y.: Doubleday, 1967; New York: Fawcett-Crest paperback, 1969. HB-R.

_____. Modesty Blaise. Garden City, N.Y.: Doubleday, 1965; New York: Fawcett-Crest paperback, 1966. HB-R. MT.

_____. Sabre-Tooth. Garden City, N. Y.: Doubleday, 1966; New York: Fawcett-Crest paperback, 1967. HB-R.

_____. A Taste for Death. Garden City, N. Y.: Doubleday, 1969; HB-R. See also A Taste for Death in Appendix I.

CONSULT APPENDIX I FOR SERIES CONTINUATION

CONSULT APPENDIX II FOR SERIES TRANSITION

END OF CWF 55

† CWF 56. ORAM, JOHN †

BACKGROUND: Drafted by the Ace Intelligence Group (see separate reference) as author of two entries for the "Man from U. N. C. L. E." novelization project, namely The Copenhagen Affair (1965) and The Stone-Cold Dead in the Market Affair (1966).

No further information available.

CWF AGENTS: Solo, Napoleon, and Illya Kuryakin.

CWF HISTORIES: See also Avallone, Michael--CWF 6.

All operatives should make special note of the following: The paperback cover of The Copenhagen Affair featured an authentic file photograph depicting agents Solo and Kuryakin at U. N. C. L. E. headquarters in New York, each armed with the U. N. C. L. E. field weapon.

Derived from the P-38 automatic, details of the early anatomy of the U. N. C. L. E. gun include 1) mounted scope, 2) long-bullet magazine extension, 3) silenced-barrel extension, 4) shoulder stock, and 5) muzzle break. The U. N. C. L. E. pistol could be deployed with or without these attachments, and in its advanced version, the barrel of the field weapon was replaced with a cage.

In the aforementioned photo, dated 1965, Solo was attired in a black, casino-style tuxedo while Kuryakin appeared in a dark sports jacket and his legendary turtleneck sweater. Shown in the background of the photograph, Kuryakin manifested the triangular U. N. C. L. E. recognition badge.

OPERATIVE DATA: John Oram displayed an agreeable narrative

manner in his two U. N. C. L. E. assignments. However, since The Stone-Cold Dead in the Market Affair (1966) wasn't distributed in the U.S. until 1970, only the first Oram entry will be evaluated in this file.

In The Copenhagen Affair (1965) Mr. Waverly acquired a series of subminiature film rolls from a British businessman, identified as Mike Stanning. During an S. A. S. Convair Coronado 990 flight to Copenhagen, Stanning had encountered U. N. C. L. E. agent Norah Bland, who was liquidated after passing the film cache to Stanning as a pack of Danish North State cigarettes.

Examining several of the films with Solo and Kuryakin, Mr. Waverly briefed the U. N. C. L. E. operatives on a sequence of disturbing events involving unexplained explosions and apparent U. F. O. aircraft sightings. The recent report of a circular segment of scorched earth on the Danish island of Jutland convinced Mr. Waverly of T. H. R. U. S. H. scientific aggression, suspicions that were heightened by the organization's aeronautical expertise.

Further, the dossier of one Major Garbridge, a renegade Irish Army officer who had acted as a double agent in Denmark for the Nazis and the Resistance during World War II, revealed him as the director of T. H. R. U. S. H. satraps in Denmark and Sweden.

Fearing that T. H. R. U. S. H. could conceivably manipulate the U. F. O. ploy to seriously jeopardize the defense response of the Western powers, Mr. Waverly ordered Solo and Kuryakin to penetrate Jutland and uncover the link between Major Garbridge and T. H. R. U. S. H. 's experimental U. F. O. project.

SUMMARY: John Oram's 1965 U. N. C. L. E. entry, The Copenhagen Affair, reflected a confident, uncomplicated style that satisfied most field operatives, even if it didn't quite measure up to the efforts of series contributors Michael Avallone, J. Hunter Holly, Peter Leslie, and David McDaniel (see separate references).

In addition, Oram's knowledge of Danish locales greatly enhanced the escapist values of this entry.

STATUS: See also Avallone, Michael--CWF 6. SOP.

FIELD BIBLIOGRAPHY

Oram, John. The Copenhagen Affair. New York: Ace Books, 1965. PBO. TN.

_____. The Stone-Cold Dead in the Market Affair. London: Four Square, 1966. PBO. TN.

CONSULT ACE INTELLIGENCE GROUP FOR ADDITIONAL AUTHOR
REFERENCES

CONSULT APPENDIX I FOR SERIES CONTINUATION

END OF CWF 56

† CWF 57.   PEARL, JACK   †

BACKGROUND: Cover identity of Jacques Bain Pearl, prolific
American author of mystery and general fiction, non-fiction, and
visual-project novelizations.

Born in 1923 in Richmond Hill, New York. Served in Africa
and Italy in the U.S. Army during World War II. By 1950 Pearl
had received A.B. and M.A. degrees from Columbia University.

Between 1947 and 1960 Pearl held a variety of positions,
from advertising copywriter to editor, for MacFadden Publications
and Saga magazine. In 1961 he became a free-lance writer.

By the mid-sixties Pearl had established his reputation as a
major author of novelizations, notably Our Man Flint (1965), the
first recorded mission of U.S. secret agent Derek Flint, the subject
of this file.

Pearl also has adapted a wide variety of visual projects as
paperback originals, namely Robin and the Seven Hoods (1964), Ambush Bay (1966), Funny Girl (1968), and Lepke (1975).

In the fiction sector, Pearl wrote several novels which critics praised for their savage realism. These include: Stockade
(1965) and The Crucifixion of Pete McCabe (1966). Along with most
of his paperback novelizations, these Pearl titles were reprinted by
Pocket Books.

Throughout the seventies Pearl focused his talents on the
suspense genre, with amazing diversity in both the paperback original and hardback formats, as represented by The Plot to Kill the
President (1970) and A Jury of His Peers (1975).

Pearl's achievements in the non-fiction area easily rivaled
his fiction credits. His first book, Blood and Guts (1961), was regarded as one of the most incisive biographies of General George S.
Patton ever written.

Shortly thereafter Pearl prepared a visual-project script for

20th Century-Fox, derived from his book. However, it is not known whether Pearl's version was the one used in the same studio's Oscar-winning biography, Patton (1970), starring George C. Scott.

Pearl employed his biographical skill again in General Douglas MacArthur (1962) and Admiral Bull Halsey (1963). During this period, he also diverted his non-fiction objectives into the sphere of general military history, as represented by The Great Air Battles of World War II (1963) and Battleground, World War I (1964).

A member of the Writers Guild of America--East, Mr. Pearl has produced over 200 short stories and articles for numerous popular magazines.

CWF AGENT: Flint, Derek.

CWF HISTORY: American citizen. Derek Flint served with honor during World War II, earning the Medal of Honor and the Croix de Guerre. After the war he fought as a mercenary in a score of foreign wars and civil conflicts--exact dates and places unknown.

At various times, Flint has been a doctor, dentist, lawyer, and honorary Indian chief. The astounding range of Flint's accomplishments reflect the many degrees he has received from seventeen international universities.

During the Cold War era, Flint often utilized his medical expertise in the field. For instance, prior to departing on a mission for the American Intelligence Agency (A. I. A.) in 1965, Flint recognized the characteristics of plastic surgery on a murdered enemy agent at A. I. A. headquarters in Washington, D. C.

Perhaps Flint's most ingenious and impressive physical ploy was his heart-stop technique, which enabled him to arrest his heartbeat to deceive an opponent, and then revive the organ through the use of a special pulse-watch.

Flint's physical prowess has often been compared to that of Superman, and he superbly demonstrated his seemingly boundless energy as a professional boxer, ballet dancer, and acrobat. As a seasoned athlete, he garnered Olympic championships in Grecian wrestling, dueling, fencing, and the military pentathlon.

Flint expertly employed his physical skill as an undercover operative. At the climax of a critical assignment on a remote Caribbean island in 1965, Flint leaped through a huge pipe into an air bubble, accompanied by five tantalizing women as he landed on the blue sea.

Although not summoned into counterespionage service until 1965, Flint's possession of the Black Belt in Judo prepared him for the demanding challenges of this hazardous profession. Also highly skilled as a frogman.

Renowned as an artist, Flint's oil paintings were displayed by the finest galleries. Being appreciative of classical art as well, Flint adorned his exclusive New York penthouse apartment with the works of Monet, Picasso, and Renoir, as well as a world-class collection of nude female portraits.

Gaining recognition as an accomplished musician, Flint once gave an organ recital in Notre Dame Cathedral and he was equally proficient in the intricacies of the piano, horn, fiddle, and drum movements. He designed his own numerical code system, supposedly based on one of Bach's fugues, but its deployment in the field often suggested rather striking female measurements.

Flint was also revered in New York's publishing circles, developing a strong academic following with a scientific tome on isomcrisms and a dictionary of dolphin sounds. During a 1967 mission Flint used his knowledge of hypnotism to obtain crucial information.

Fluent in no fewer than forty-two languages and dialects, Flint was a man of continental tastes. An incident in an exquisite New York restaurant involving a venomous dart and Flint's wartime commander, Bruce Cramden, revealed his rare ability to identify the precise region and proportions of certain culinary preparations--in this instance, bouillabaisse.

Flint's diverse talents eventually made him an extremely wealthy man, so that his magnificent New York penthouse apartment embodied such affluent touches as a library, massive bed, a television monitor installed in the ceiling, barber's station, three protective dogs, and the affectionate attention of four ravishing women. He also owned a private jet.

While Flint's sexual reputation with women was acknowledged, his concern with the females who lived with him was to evoke the individuality of each.

"The Derek Flint Fan Club" was formed to accommodate the legion of his female admirers throughout the world. Flint's handsome, rugged features have been compared to the likes of Cary Grant and Rock Hudson, and he was even honored with a theme song that boasted that he was superior to all mortal men.

If there's an ironical facet to Derek Flint's enigmatic personality, it's the mystery surrounding his origins. The date and place of his birth remain unknown.

Flint's military superior, Bruce Cramden, found him to be arrogant and conceited and, in his postwar role as the head of the A.I.A., Cramden expressed his reluctance to give Flint a special mission though it was suited to his unique talents. As the danger mounted, Cramden and other allied intelligence chiefs unanimously decided to recruit an operative outside the counterespionage sector.

Derek Flint was the agent selected by the computerized World Selective Service Files, and Camden was faced with convincing Flint to accept the assignment. Flint subsequently agreed to execute the A. I. A. project, but on his own terms. His specialized weaponry for instance, a cigarette lighter capable of performing eighty-three functions, served to reinforce Cramden's hostility toward the American legend. The standard arsenal recommended by Cramden consisted of a stylish attaché case, complete with sixty-five weapons and the Walther PPK.

OPERATIVE DATA: A sequence of cataclysmic weather conditions around the globe preceded Derek Flint's "appointment" as the ideal operative for the mission in Our Man Flint (1965).

Flint's elimination of one Hans Gruber, a former Nazi, at the Bistro Restaurant in New Orleans unmasked the activities of a mysterious espionage network, known as Galaxy.

Galaxy agent Gila had been ordered to liquidate the A. I. A. representative, but Flint, penetrating Galaxy's cover in San Francisco (the Exotica Beauty Company), accosted Gila's lethal ally Malcolm Rodney, who was later fingered as Galaxy's U. S. liaison for their weather project.

Discovering Galaxy's island complex in the Caribbean, Flint employed his heart-stop technique to infiltrate Galaxy's command center, where the scientific directors of Galaxy, identified as Doctors Krupov, Schneider, and Wu, generated a series of volcanos to provide the global intelligence sector with proof of their destructive intentions.

Unknown to Gila and Rodney, Flint posed as a Galaxy construction worker and successfully averted Galaxy's attempt to dominate the world through weather control.

In his novelization for Our Man Flint, Jack Pearl masterfully conveyed the visual project's mocking dimensions, which focused on Cold War society in general as well as the menacing concept of global weather manipulation.

Like the visual project, Pearl's novelization spoofed both the general Bondian format and the nebulous complexion of the Cold War. In this respect, the operative should be reminded that Derek Flint was initially recognized as a tongue-in-cheek reaction to Agent 007.

As to the weather plot, Galaxy's island fortress was not defensively equipped, and Pearl depicted hordes of mindless inhabitants, enslaved to conformity through the guise of commercialized pleasure. Here, Pearl cleverly mirrored the visual project's satirical acknowledgment of Communism's "defeat from within" threat, which dated to early days of the Cold War.

Jack Pearl's Our Man Flint, reflecting the best of its genre, was a novelization which provocatively animated its outlandish protagonist and the spectacular elements which surrounded him.

There were, however, some noticeable differences between the visual effort and the novelization. The book's locales of San Francisco and New Orleans were replaced by Rome and Marseilles in the 1966 visual project. The American Intelligence Agency was referred to as Z. O. W. I. E. (Zonal Organization of World Intelligence and Espionage), and Cramden's theatrical Christian name was Lloyd. In the visual climax, Flint jumped over a waterfall instead of through the novelization's large pipe.

SUMMARY: Distributed by Pocket Books in December 1965, Jack Pearl's novelization for Our Man Flint featured eighteen black-and-white stills from the visual project, complete with satirical captions.

Although not realized at that time, this pictorial format would have an indelible effect on Pocket Books' later involvement with science fiction, specifically their series of books inspired by Star Trek. Utilizing detailed photographs of the U. S. S. Enterprise crew, these titles include the "foto-novels" adapted from Star Trek: The Motion Picture (1979), Star Trek II: The Wrath of Khan (1982), The Official Star Trek Trivia Book (1980), and the publisher's Wallaby trade paperback edition of The Star Trek Compendium (1981).

Although Pocket Books wasn't associated with science fiction in 1965, Our Man Flint manifested some interesting overtones, as typified by Pearl's interpretation of Galaxy.

Considering the fact that Our Man Flint was a novelization, and not a previously published spy entry, it fared extremely well in the paperback intrigue market. Pearl's adaptation surfaced at about the same time as the more highly publicized tie-ins for Ian Fleming's Thunderball, James Leasor's Where the Spies Are, and Peter O'Donnell's Modesty Blaise, among others. (See the Fawcett and N. A. L. /Signet Intelligence Groups for specific visual project release dates.)

James Coburn conveyed to perfection Derek Flint's hypnotic charm in Our Man Flint (1966), 20th Century-Fox's visual project featuring the late Lee J. Cobb as Cramden, Gila Golan as Gila, and Edward Mulhare as Malcolm Rodney.

Flint's second recorded mission, In Like Flint (1967), will be evaluated in CWF 67.

STATUS: A new Derek Flint visual project is currently being

developed by James Coburn and producer Saul David. As of this report (9-27-82), no announcement has been made concerning the return of the legendary secret agent.

Nonetheless, it is recommended that Jack Pearl's novelization for Our Man Flint be reissued as an example of imaginative visual-project adaptation and the potential of the genre. EOP.

FIELD BIBLIOGRAPHY

Pearl, Jack. Our Man Flint. New York: Pocket Books, 1965.
    PBO. MN.

CONSULT CWF 67 FOR SERIES CONTINUATION

END OF CWF 57

† CWF 58. PHILLIFENT, JOHN T. †

BACKGROUND: British science-fiction novelist; extensive experience in engineering. Assigned to the "Man from U.N.C.L.E." novelization project in 1965.

Born in 1916. Served in the Royal Navy from 1935 to 1947, and functioned as a planning engineer for the English Electrical Board.

Employing the cover identity of John Rackham, Phillifent contributed to Pearson's Tit-Bits SF Library in the early fifties, and went on to produce such genre novels as Danger from Vega (1966), The Proxima Project (1968), (...).

Phillifent, as Rackham, also created the Chappie Jones short-story collection for Science Fantasy magazine, and under his own name produced several space epics, including Genius Unlimited (1972) and King from Argent (1973). Outside his major sphere as a recognized science-fiction talent, Phillifent published a mystery novel, The Lonely Man, in 1965.

A representative of the Ace Intelligence Group (see separate reference). Mr. Phillifent died in 1976.

CWF AGENTS: Solo, Napoleon, and Illya Kuryakin.

CWF HISTORIES: See also Avallone, Michael--CWF 6.

OPERATIVE DATA: Although John T. Phillifent contributed only three entries to the U. N. C. L. E. novelization series, his science-fiction approach generated some unusually harsh criticism from purists who refused to accept the common ground shared between Phillifent's chosen genre and the espionage format.

While Phillifent was not regarded with the same fervor as Michael Avallone, J. Hunter Holly, Peter Leslie, and David McDaniel (see separate references), he injected some inventive elements into the popular series.

Set against a high-level scientific conference in Shannon, Ireland, The Mad Scientist Affair (1966) initially focused on Sarah O'Rourke, the daughter of one "King Mike" O'Rourke, an eccentric Irish biochemist, and an academic paper scheduled to be delivered by Ms. O'Rourke.

Mr. Waverly dispatched Solo and Kuryakin to Shannon after he learned of T. H. R. U. S. H.'s interest in Dr. O'Rourke's latest enterprise, a brewery situated near Conway, Clare, Eire.

Phillifent balanced these elements of the plot with the liquidation of Dr. Amazov, an inquisitive scientist who dismissed Sarah's study at the convention; the activities of Dr. Vittorio Trilli, renowned Genovese biochemist and suspected T. H. R. U. S. H. agent; a mysterious castle; and the cryptic significance of Sarah O'Rourke's scientific document, which previously had been dismissed as illogical.

In The Power Cube Affair (1968) Solo and Kuryakin were not specifically assigned to any field duty, but after evaluating the scandalous contents of a tape casette, the U. N. C. L. E. agents pursued the scattered clues of a crazed genius and the puzzle surrounding twenty-seven crystals.

Properly assembled into a perfect cube, the crystals held the elusive key to global domination.

Endowing this U. N. C. L. E. mission with colorful British locales, Phillifent utilized the authentic trappings of Admiralty House and offered the English command center for the intelligence network, which was placed on the Thames Embankment near New Scotland Yard.

While many devotees dismissed The Power Cube Affair, this 1968 U. N. C. L. E. initiative effectively displayed Phillifent's science-fiction skill with his detailed anatomy of the cubic particles and their relationship to certain hallucinatory drugs.

The Corfu Affair (1967), which is not covered in this CWF file, was not immediately distributed in the U. S. sector. Details in FIELD BIBLIOGRAPHY.

SUMMARY: In his U. N. C. L. E. assignments, John T. Phillifent neatly blended science fiction with action-espionage. However, many U. N. C. L. E. field observers strongly disapproved of his treatment within the series framework.

STATUS: See also Avallone, Michael--CWF 6.

FIELD BIBLIOGRAPHY

Phillifent, John T. The Corfu Affair. London: Four Square, 1967; New York: Ace Books, 1969. PBO. TN.

_____. The Mad Scientist Affair. New York: Ace Books, 1966. PBO. TN.

_____. The Power Cube Affair. New York: Ace Books, 1968. PBO. TN.

CONSULT ACE INTELLIGENCE GROUP FOR ADDITIONAL AUTHOR REFERENCES

END OF CWF 58

† CWF 59. PICARD, SAM †

BACKGROUND: Paperback-original author of the "Notebooks" espionage series. Member of the Universal-Award Intelligence Group (see separate reference). Since this CWF entity is no longer in existence, no additional information on Mr. Picard is available.

CWF AGENT: Anonymous.

CWF HISTORY: The nebulous profile of this CWF agent resembles that of Picard himself.

In his first series entry, The Notebooks (1969), Picard utilized the first person to depict a protagonist in the fashion of Len Deighton (see separate reference) while revealing the full identities of the supporting characters.

For the purpose of this file, Picard's operative shall be designated Ns-A, meaning Notebooks Agent.

Date and place of birth unknown.   Nationality probably American, as suggested by his occupation as Washington-based foreign correspondent since 1948.

Ns-A executed numerous magazine assignments during the Greek Civil War, the Korean War, the Berlin Wall Crisis, and the Vietnam War, among others.

In 1969 Ns-A was situated in the Press Building on 14th Street in Washington, D. C. as a traveling journalist for <u>Contact</u> magazine.

Reportedly served in Europe during World War II; war record unverified through field inquiries.

OPERATIVE DATA: <u>The Notebooks</u> (1969) signified a new phase in the development of the Universal-Award Intelligence Group (see separate reference).   Following the global missions of Nick Carter (see separate reference) and the more sobering activities of Don Smith's (see separate reference) Phil Sherman, Picard's series centered around the potential of a conspiracy, rather than a field agent.

In <u>The Notebooks</u> Ns-A acquired a photograph which had been linked to the deaths of four men:

1)   Mort Beach: professional photographer with whom Ns-A had often worked, including a 1968 pictorial assignment in the Mekong delta.

2)   Dr. Thomas A. Stamler and Lafcadio Woodbridge: contracted to write two separate books on the same topic; they had both seen the photograph.

3)   Robbin Prentice III: prominent State Department official who was assigned to Hong Kong as First Secretary.

Ns-A's possession of the photo revealed the existence of a cable stretching from Washington to Germany, encircling both sectors of Berlin.   The book derived its title from Ns-A's detailed diary account of the story surrounding the photograph.   <u>The Notebooks</u> began from the viewpoint of Ns-A's recollection of the conspiracy, revealing the avaricious motives of a U.S. Senator and a top East German nuclear physicist, Dr. Hans Tobler, who worked for both the Soviet Union and Red China after World War II.

Picard gradually revealed the significance of Ns-A's seemingly innocent photograph and, fusing it with the complexities of the foregoing elements, he shifted the plot to the suspicion surrounding a possible Chi-Com operative in Washington and the truth behind one of the most shattering events in U. S.-Cold War history.

The C. I. A. and the F. B. I. also figured in the photo scandal, but along with the mystery surrounding the authentic incident alluded to above, their intrigues, as recorded in The Notebooks, must remain classified.

SUMMARY: Sam Picard's The Notebooks represented one of the many transitional points from the secret agent genre of the sixties to the acceptance of the conspiracy theme in the espionage fiction of the seventies.

Narrated in the first person, The Notebooks emerged as a convincing medium for a mystery-suspense format that would dominate the paperback machinations of the détente era.

The Notebooks, with its graphic reference to an authentic incident, perceptively demonstrated the credible mixture of fact and fiction.

STATUS: When The Notebooks was originally published, in 1969, Picard's provocative approach to the spy novel appeared to be before its time, for readers and critics alike. However, Charter Books' reissue of this entry in 1980 has generated a more receptive audience, and it is likely to remain in the field indefinitely.

It should be pointed out that Picard's sequel efforts, The Man Who Never Was and Dead Man Running, both distributed by Universal-Award in 1971, have yet to resurface in the current market. ESP.

FIELD BIBLIOGRAPHY

Picard, Sam. The Notebooks. New York: Universal-Award, 1969. PBO.

CONSULT APPENDIX I FOR SERIES CONTINUATION

CONSULT APPENDIX II FOR SERIES TRANSITION

END OF CWF 59

† CWF 60. PICKERING, R. E. †

BACKGROUND: As with CWF 26 on Robert C. Galway (see separate reference), the purpose here is informative, rather than evaluative.

Specifically, R. E. Pickering's Himself Again (1966) was published the following year in the U.S. as The Uncommitted Man. Until recently these alternate titles have been regarded as two distinct entries. In some cases these books have been listed in various sources as a limited series featuring Dick Philip, protagonist of the original novel.

As far as current field inquiries indicate, Mr. Philip was not summoned for intelligence duty after 1967. For this reason, the operative is advised to make special note of the titular differences.

Robert Easton Pickering was born in Carlisle, England, in 1934, and received a B. A. degree from Queen's College, Oxford, in 1958. He served in the Royal Navy from 1952 to 1954, achieving the rank of sub-lieutenant. During 1959 and 1960, Pickering was employed by the International Atomic Energy Agency in Vienna.

Elected twice as vice-president of the International Association of Conference Translators, Pickering was engaged as a freelance translator from 1960, primarily for the United Nations.

Pickering's In Transit was published in Britain in 1968 but its classification (fiction or non-fiction) is unknown.

Himself Again (1966) concerned British businessman Dick Philip's nostalgic journey to Vienna in search of his missing wife and some treasured postwar memories.

The Christian Science Monitor endorsed with feeling Pickering's initiation into the espionage fiction of the Cold War: "Every spy story worth its salt these days stars a disillusioned hero. R. E. Pickering's Dick Philip is more disillusioned than most. He is also far more compelling, and far more difficult to disbelieve."

Given the atypical nature of CWF 60, the remaining standard evaluative sections have been omitted. EOP.

FIELD BIBLIOGRAPHY

Pickering, R. E. Himself Again. London: Gollancz, 1966. HB. See also The Uncommitted Man.

_____. The Uncommitted Man. New York: Farrar, Straus, and Giroux, 1967; New York: Berkley-Medallion paperback, 1968. HB-R. U.S. title for Himself Again.

END OF CWF 60

† CWF 61.   RABE, PETER †

BACKGROUND: Multi-faceted author of paperback originals; member of the exclusive clique represented by Michael Avallone and Norman Daniels (see separate references).   Unlike the situation regarding these CWF conspirators, virtually no information about Rabe's personal life is available.

Although Rabe's dossier on file subject Manny deWitt earned him a valued position in the Fawcett Intelligence Group (see separate reference), his long-term relationship with the publisher's Gold-Medal division extended beyond the realm of spy fiction.

Rabe attracted a devoted following in the late fifties with his four-volume mystery series featuring cynical ex-hood Daniel Port: It's My Funeral (1957), The Out Is Death (1957), Bring Me Another Corpse (1959), and Time Enough to Die (1959).

Several years earlier, however, Rabe entered the non-series suspense arena with three tautly written books, all of which appeared in 1955: Benny Muscles In, Stop This Man!, and A Shroud for Jesso.

During the brief term of the Port series, Rabe continued to successfully employ this viable format, and by 1960 his became a conspicuous name on paperback mystery stands.

Rabe's later efforts in the non-series sector included Journey in Terror (1957), Mission for Vengeance (1958), My Lovely Executioner (1960), The Box (1962), (...).

The first entry in the Manny deWitt series, Girl in a Big Brass Bed, was published in 1965, and when Rabe's elusive secret agent retired from "the game" two years later, it was generally accepted that Rabe could adapt his productive talents to any category of popular fiction.   This was soundly confirmed when he ventured into the mafia genre of the seventies with two compelling novels, War of the Dons (1972) and Black Mafia (1974).

Not all of Rabe's books were published as Fawcett paperback originals--The Cut of the Whip (1958) surfaced as an Ace paperback original while Anatomy of a Killer (1960) was issued in hardback in both the U.S. and England.

Mr. Rabe has been inactive as a writer in recent years.

CWF AGENT: deWitt, Manny.

CWF HISTORY: American lawyer employed by Lobbe Industriel, a global business enterprise with a variety of interests.

Dating from the mid-sixteen-hundreds, the Lobbe family capitalized on such commodities as spice and rubber. They monopolized the rubber market for about 300 years, but the outbreak of World War II seriously jeopardized the substance's availability in the family's native Holland. After the war, Lobbe channeled its dynamic resources in the area of synthetics.

During the Cold War era, Lobbe Industriel was based in the thirty-story, glass-encased Lobbe Building in New York. Although primarily recognized as a major synthetics producer, the Lobbe consortium extended its influential tentacles throughout the industrial world, as symbolized by the diverse concerns which inhabited the Lobbe Building.

The Lobbe empire was mastered by Mijnheer Hans Lobbe, a family descendant characterized as a deceptively placid man, but who in fact ruled the Lobbe enterprise with ruthless precision.

Manford deWitt, described by certain Lobbe intimates as smooth and calculating, ostensibly acted as legal negotiator for numerous Lobbe interests around the world. However, deWitt's activities on behalf of Lobbe Industriel, especially in Europe and the Orient, entailed a previously unsuspected tangent of the Lobbe dynasty--espionage.

Engaged as a field operative for Lobbe from 1965 to 1967, deWitt was referred to as Manny by close associates.

No record after 1967.

OPERATIVE DATA: Rabe's intrigue series was relatively conventional in its plotting, characterization, and overall presentation.

In his three missions for Lobbe, deWitt expertly demonstrated his skill as a secret agent, going far beyond the boundaries of his legal duties.

Like many Fawcett allies, notably Donald Hamilton and Stephen Marlowe (see separate references), Rabe utilized the first person in the deWitt series.

Girl in a Big Brass Bed (1965) graphically defined Manny deWitt and the enigmatic dimensions of Lobbe Industriel.

In The Spy Who Was Only 3 Feet Tall (1966) deWitt was ordered to protect the interests of a Lobbe subsidiary in Essen, Germany, which was contracted for a road development project in the new African state of Motana.

Confronted with the tempestuous charms of Inge, Lobbe's niece, deWitt was also menaced by a decadent Italian prince and a murderous Pygmy spy, known only as Baby, who attempted to sabotage Lobbe Industriel's investment in Motana.

Code Name: Gadget (1967) concerned deWitt's assignment to find an apocalyptic nuclear weapon--which actually had never been sighted in any of the critical defense sectors.

This entry transpired as the most suspenseful of the series, as Rabe heightened the tension with the slightest possible lead for deWitt: the connection between the death of a mysterious industrialist, Spyros Cervassette, and his London-based factory, Special Developments Ltd.

SUMMARY: Peter Rabe's three-volume Manny deWitt series displayed his talents as a mystery writer but was not particularly distinctive as a constituent of the paperback original espionage genre.

STATUS: The works of such prolific paperback authors as Peter Rabe are rarely reissued, and since his brief dossier on Manny deWitt failed to leave any durable mark on the cloak-and-dagger market during the mid-sixties, it is unlikely to be considered as a reactivation prospect. SOP.

FIELD BIBLIOGRAPHY

Rabe, Peter. Code Name: Gadget. New York: Fawcett-Gold Medal, 1967. PBO.

_____. Girl in a Big Brass Bed. New York: Fawcett-Gold Medal, 1965. PBO.

_____. The Spy Who Was 3 Feet Tall. New York: Fawcett-Gold Medal, 1966. PBO.

END OF CWF 61

† CWF 62. SANGSTER, JIMMY †

BACKGROUND: Suspense novelist and visual-adaptation writer, especially the latter.

Born in North Wales in 1927. Left school at age 15 to pursue a career in the visual arena. However, it wasn't until Sangster had completed three years of military service in the R.A.F. that he gained recognition in the visual industry.

From 1948 to 1955 Sangster worked as a free-lance assistant director and production manager. By 1957 he was operating as a free-lance writer and visual-project producer.

In 1959 Sangster collaborated with Barre Lyndon on The Man Who Could Cheat Death (1959) and three years later he penned a British novelization, Terror of the Tongs (1962).

As a visual project author, Sangster has adapted over forty theatrical works, notably The Criminal (1960), Maniac (1963), and The Anniversary (1968) as well as several Dracula and Frankenstein excursions for Britain's Hammer Films. Sangster also doubled as producer on some of his script assignments, including The Nanny (1965).

Pursuant to this file, Sangster charted the Cold War reactivation of Bulldog Drummond in Deadlier Than the Male (1967). (See also N. A. L. /Signet Intelligence Group--CWF 54.)

Equally active in the home sector, Sangster served as a script consultant for CBS in 1972.

Sangster turned his attention to the spy genre in the late sixties with Private i (1967), which featured investigator-secret agent John Smith. A sequel, Foreign Exchange, appeared in 1968.

In his dual role of producer and writer, Sangster turned both books into visual projects featuring Robert Horton as John Smith. Private i was presented as The Spy Killer in 1969 while the original title was retained for the 1970 release of Foreign Exchange.

Distributed theatrically in British territory by Hammer Films, the Smith missions were issued in the U.S. through the home market (ABC).

Sangster recruited operative Katy Touchfeather in Touchfeather (1968), and since only two female CWF agents, notably Modesty Blaise and Anna Zordan, have been considered as yet in this file book, she has been selected as the subject of this Sangster evaluation.

Since 1963 Sangster has been affiliated with a variety of creative organizations, chiefly the Screen Writers Guild of Great Britain, the Directors Guild of America, and the Writers Guild of America--West.

CWF AGENT: Touchfeather, Katherine.

CWF HISTORY: British subject; born in Streatham.

Ms. Touchfeather was employed as an air hostess by a number of international airlines, notably B. O. A. C., T. W. A., Pan-Am, Air India, and Air Pakistan. Her profession required an extensive knowledge of foreign languages and she duly acquired fluency in Spanish, French, German, and Italian, and at least six additional tongues. During her basic training period Ms. Touchfeather responded poorly in other subject areas, such as domestic science and biology.

On her first assignment, Ms. Touchfeather fell in love with the flight captain and married him two weeks later in Mexico City. Three months after their marriage was consummated, Ms. Touchfeather's husband was killed in a motor-car crash outside Rome.

Ms. Touchfeather's global occupation and her husband's tragic death eventually brought her into contact with one C. W. Blaser (C. B. E.), head of a secret intelligence unit linked to Whitehall.

Ironically, Blaser controlled his counterespionage network from 32 Pandam Street in London, the same deteriorating building that housed an adjunct of the Ministry of Civil Aviation.

Katherine, otherwise known as Katy, Touchfeather became one of Mr. Blaser's most reliable agents. After her second mission, she was indoctrinated in the field techniques of weaponry, assassination, and concealment.

OPERATIVE DATA: Although Sangster's Touchfeather series lasted for only two years, the seasoned writer deftly conceived his sensual creation through use of the first person narrative, exhibiting a worldly knowledge of the aircraft industry and the global locales pertaining to it.

Katy accepted her initial mission in Touchfeather (1968) after learning that her late husband had served as a courier for Blaser.

Blaser's briefing of Ms. Touchfeather concerned the death of a mysterious man in Bombay, the background of the arrogant head of a specialized British research team, and the operations of Gerastan Industries, a joint U. S. -British corporation involved in electronics and aircraft instruments. The head of the research unit was identified as Professor William Partman, and on the body of the dead man in Bombay was found a microfilmed dossier on Professor Partman's working project.

Assigned to contact Partman on an Air India flight to Bombay, Ms. Touchfeather's orders were to discover the significance of the murder in the Indian city. After their first meeting, Ms. Touchfeather and Professor Partman formed a romantic liaison that didn't escape the notice of Blaser's department.

An air piracy incident in Cairo eventually unveiled an insidious scheme within the highest spheres of the British aircraft industry, of intent to disclose the nation's most sensitive defense secrets.

Allying with Bertelli and Martin, Blaser's respective Italian and U.S. confederates, Ms. Touchfeather penetrated an enemy spy network which had been meticulously assembled to execute the systematic leakage of the critical secrets.   The design of the I.C.B.M. prototype also figured into the blueprint.

After suspensefully constructing his menacing plot, Sangster inserted a chilling twist on a climactic flight to Egypt which served to alter both the reader's initial impression of Katy Touchfeather and the texture of the plot itself.

In Touchfeather, Sangster fully characterized his heroine as a tough, alluring, and engaging secret agent who challenged Modesty Blaise in many areas, somewhat similar to James Eastwood's (see separate reference) Anna Zordan.

SUMMARY: Although Katy Touchfeather entered the field after Peter O'Donnell's Modesty Blaise and James Eastwood's Anna Zordan (see separate references), Jimmy Sangster still invested some originality into the female 007 format, despite her appearance in the early declining stages of the spy phenomenon.

Sangster extended Ms. Touchfeather's term of active duty to 1970 with two additional assignments, Touchfeather Too and Touch Gold.

STATUS: As in the case of Modesty Blaise, reissue of the Touchfeather series could be expected to prove successful in the current espionage market.   SOP.

FIELD BIBLIOGRAPHY

Sangster, Jimmy.   Touchfeather.   New York: Norton, 1968.   HB-R.   See also   Touchfeather in Appendix I.

CONSULT APPENDIX I FOR SERIES CONTINUATION

END OF CWF 62

† CWF 63.   SEWARD, JACK †

BACKGROUND: Born in 1924.   Leading American authority on Japan, Jack Seward has integrated this cultural passion with his business and writing pursuits, including the subject of this file, Curt Stone.

Seward's first exposure to the Japanese language came from two co-workers on an Oklahoma ranch, sometime between 1939 and 1942. He subsequently attended the University of Michigan, which housed the Military Intelligence Service Japanese Language School, where he completed his studies in Japanese history, literature, economics, and geography, receiving the B. A. degree. From 1943 to 1947, he was commissioned in U. S. Army Military Intelligence. Ranked second in his class, he continued his Japanese studies at the Horace H. Rackham School of Graduate Studies in Ann Arbor, Michigan, and the University of Hawaii during 1950-51.

Between 1946 and 1949 Seward was attached to the Civil Censorship Detachment in the Japanese cities of Kyushu as a liaison officer, and in Osaka as a telecommunications censor and public opinion analyst. This section was part of General MacArthur's postwar occupation project in Japan.

After a year as vice-president and Tokyo branch manager for the Pan-Pacific Trading Company, Seward worked in Japan as an intelligence analyst for the C. I. A. From 1951 to 1956 he evaluated business and economic trends as well as public and political opinion. By 1966 Seward had worked extensively in the Japanese market, principally as export sales manager for the Yashica Camera Company in Tokyo and Far East representative for the Chicago-based Sunbeam Corporation.

Seward, who has four new works on Japan scheduled for future publication, has authored two dozen books about Japan. The Japanese (1972) sold over 4, 000, 000 copies in a special edition published by the Reader's Digest Condensed Book Club, the most widely read Japanese study to appear in any language. Unlike most American writers, Seward developed a strong following in Japan, a result of his personal involvement with the country.

During the early seventies Seward became the Far East representative for the New York-based Scholastic Books and Magazines, establishing a sales office in Tokyo.

The first in the Curt Stone series, The Cave of the Chinese Skeletons (1964), which Seward derived from his experiences in the Civil Censorship Detachment, was originally issued in Japan before Tower Books distributed it in the U. S. as a paperback mystery in 1968.

Represented by such prestigious Japanese publishers as Tuttle and Lotus Press, Seward wrote, among others, such works as Hara-Kiri (1968) and The Diplomat (1972), a novel of intrigue which might be described as the serious counterpart to Richard Mason's The World of Suzie Wong (1958).

During 1973-74 Seward lectured on Japanese language and culture at the University of Texas and Austin College, and, until 1979, he served as Director of International Operations for Ecology and Environment, Inc. Today he is president of International Consulting Services, a management firm with its main office in Houston, Texas (where he currently resides), and subsidiary branches in Bangkok, Hong Kong, Osaka, Peking, Singapore, and Tokyo.

CWF AGENT: Stone, Curt.

CWF HISTORY: American. Former intelligence officer with the C. I. C. (U. S. Army Counter Intelligence Corps). Stone was recalled by the C. I. C. in the early sixties for a special mission. Although the C. I. C. 's principal headquarters are situated in Washington, D.C., the network's division in Tokyo was involved in this field selection.

After attending the University of Colorado for two years (1939 to 1941), Stone transferred to the Military Intelligence Langauge School at the University of Michigan. Eventually earned an A. B. degree from the university.

During World War II Stone acted as a combat intelligence officer in the Pacific where he was required to interrogate Japanese prisoners behind Japanese front-lines.

Posted to the 24th U. S. Army Division, Stone entered Japan in September 1945. Later assigned to the C. I. C. in Fukoka, Japan, followed by a six-month term as Civil Property Custodian.

Achieving the rank of major in the C. I. C., Stone launched espionage operations in enemy sectors during the Korean War. He resigned his commission in 1953.

Two years later Stone formed Far East Investigations, Inc. in Tokyo. Stone's activities generally focused on supplying commercial and credit evaluations to U. S. companies interested in conducting business in the competitive Japanese market. In this capacity, Stone was assisted by 1) Jeanne Auber, Eurasian secretary; 2) Augustus (Gus) Nakano, Nisei A. D. C.; and 3) four part-time agents.

Address listed as: No. 6, 4-chome, Nishi-Ginza, Chuo-ku, Tokyo.

Characterized as successful in his chosen profession, purportedly with numbered accounts in Hong Kong and Switzerland, Stone's affluence was evidenced by his exclusive Higashi-Toriizaka apartment in Tokyo, a motor cruiser anchored in Manazuru (40 miles from Tokyo), a mountain villa in Hakone, and a late-model Mercedes.

Served as a postwar agent until 1969. During the Cold War era Stone utilized his diverse talents in the field, chiefly:

1) Fluency in written and spoken Japanese, complemented by a proficient knowledge of Chinese.

2) Mountaineering.

3) Scuba diving.

4) Standard and advanced techniques of armed and unarmed combat.

On the personal side Stone was often described as a man of sophistication and superior intellect, although moderate in his culinary consumption. Relevant to his scholarly interests, Stone was acknowledged as a major authority on the Tokugawa era of Japanese history.

Stone was distinguished by a three-inch bayonet scar on the left side of his neck; with bullet wounds on the right rear calf, right side, and left shoulder. Also manifested grenade fragment scars on upper right arm and shoulder.

Suggested for operative duty by one Colonel Riddle, identified as an active C. I. C. officer during the early sixties. Stone was generally assigned to the Far East, notably Japan. However, a 1969 mission summoned him briefly to Hawaii. Details under OPERATIVE DATA.

No further record.

OPERATIVE DATA: Seward invested his extensive knowledge of Japan into the Stone series, resulting in one of the most inventive espionage sagas to come out of the sixties.

Where Gavin Black (see separate reference) concentrated on Malaya and Southeast Asia in his dossier on Paul Harris, Seward mastered the Japanese spy thriller, surpassing such CWF conspirators as Ian Fleming and James Dark (see separate references) whose respective "provocateurs, " James Bond and Mark Hood, were each accorded a Japanese initiative during the Cold War.

Seward lent his Japanese expertise to every aspect of the series, from characterization to locales to smallest details. While this meticulous attention might have completely occupied some espionage novelists, Seward achieved an effective balance through his consistently suspenseful plots and interesting characters.

Curt Stone was formally drafted for Cold War service in The Cave of the Chinese Skeletons (1964). Seward initiated this entry with an intriguing background on "intoku busshi" or concealed goods, which the Japanese desperately secured in August 1945 prior to the arrival of U.S. forces at Atsugi.

During the briefing between one Major Dillon and Colonel Riddle at C. I. C. headquarters in Tokyo, it was revealed that a certain cave had been selected to hide countless Japanese artifacts--

and that the three Japanese Army officers entrusted with knowledge of the cave's location had all died.

C. I. C. believed that the cave was situated in the mountains of the Izu Peninsula, 60 miles south of Tokyo, and that both black market agents and a Chi-Com espionage network based in Tsukiji, Japan, identified as the Overseas Chinese Communist Group (O. C. C. G.), were adequately informed of the World War II cache. Stone was ordered to find the cave before it was infiltrated by these antagonists.

Utilizing the resources of Far East Investigations, Stone turned up one lead: Yasuko Tashiro, the daughter of the third Army officer. According to C. I. C. files, Tashiro's father had been tortured to death by the Chi-Coms.

Seward developed Stone's deductive capabilities in a mesmerizing plot, and beyond this realized objective, The Cave of the Chinese Skeletons evolved into an odyssey of Cold War intrigue as Stone challenged the O. C. C. G. from Tokyo to the mountains of Hakone.

The segment of the book in which Stone and Gus Nakano explored the skeleton-protected Izu cave emerged as a mission in itself, with the discovery of such treasured goods as military weaponry, precision machinery, optical equipment, and an unexpected collection which intensified the mystery element.

Seward's description of the cryptic cave conveyed a sense of geographical wonder while his briefer portraits of Mt. Amagi and Lake Hakone were no less striking.

Stone displayed his mastery of scuba diving as he probed Lake Hakone in a ploy designed to deceive the O. C. C. G. , and his skill as a mountain climber also was suitably demonstrated.

The Cave of the Chinese Skeletons was an expertly conceived novel of Japanese intrigue, rich in taut progression, provocative characterization, and fascinating Japanese lore.

The later Stone efforts appeared in the U. S. as previously unpublished paperback spy thrillers, and Seward was required to heighten both the sexual angle and the Cold War machinations for the mass market.

The Frogman Assassination (1968) concerned the attempted liquidation of the Emperor of Japan, an incident which stressed the precarious relationship between the U. S. and Japan, and the movements of an efficiently lethal killer identified as the Porcupine.

In The Eurasian Virgins (1968) Stone was assigned to find Rose Hasegawa, a captivating Eurasian beauty who had become enslaved by the parasitical "jinshin baibai" (human flesh market) in the Far East.

Assignment: Find Cherry (1969) was accented by a fanatical consortium, recognized as the Pure Nation Society, and a priceless treasure map.

Adding Hawaii to the expected Japanese locales, this entry focused on Stone's mission of locating Charmaine Oka, professionally known as Cherry, a stripper operating in Waikiki who possessed a secret coveted by enemy agents.

Defining the objective of the Pure Nation Society as the fervent revival of traditional Japanese values, Seward devised a startling plot that seriously questioned the U.S. role in Cold War Japan, at the same time offering a brief yet fascinating historical account of a battle between the Tokugawa Shogun and the Imperial Forces that related to the principal story line.

SUMMARY: Emanating a wealth of Japanese culture, Jack Seward's Curt Stone series was distinguished by impressive plots and provocative characters. Seward's meticulous interaction of these elements presented the Oriental spy thriller in its purest form, wisely avoiding the shortcomings suggested by the boundaries of Cold War fiction.

STATUS: Tower Books reissued the Stone dossier in 1973, and given the current world view of Japan in the political and economic sectors, the series should be actively solicited as a reactivation candidate. SOP.

FIELD BIBLIOGRAPHY

Seward, Jack. Assignment: Find Cherry. New York: Tower Books, 1969. PBO.

_____. The Cave of the Chinese Skeletons. Tokyo, Japan: Charles Tuttle, 1964; New York: Tower Books, 1968. HB-R.

_____. The Chinese Pleasure Girl. New York: Tower Books, 1969. PBO.

_____. The Eurasian Virgins. New York: Tower Books, 1968. PBO.

_____. The Frogman Assassination. New York: Tower Books, 1968. PBO.

END OF CWF 63

† CWF 64. SMITH, DON †

BACKGROUND: Canadian author of paperback original suspense and espionage novels; also credited with several hardbound contributions. Born in 1909 in Port Colborne, Ontario, Canada.

Donald Taylor Smith fashioned an illustrious career that began with his assignment as China correspondent for the Toronto Daily Star from 1934 to 1939. After receiving the Distinguished Flying Cross for his wartime service as an R.A.F. fighter pilot, Smith traveled extensively, working as a yachtsman in Tangiers and free-trader in Majorca.

Smith became a full-time writer in 1964, drawing on his military and traveling experiences for many of his books, including the subject of this file, the Phil Sherman-"Secret Mission" series.

Prior to the initiation of the "Secret Mission" dossier for the Universal-Award Intelligence Group (see separate reference) in 1968, Smith was author of several non-series suspense works, including Perilous Holiday (1951) and China Coaster (1953).

In the general fiction arena, Smith displayed a worldly style in several novels that reflected their time: Out of the Sea (1952) and Red Curtain (1966).

A year after he recruited Phil Sherman, Smith began his Tim Parnell series with The Man Who Played Thief (1969), which quickly became one of the more popular mafia-avenger sagas of the seventies.

Still active as an author, Smith currently resides in Paris.

CWF AGENT: Sherman, Phil.

CWF HISTORY: American C.I.A. operative assigned as a resident agent in Paris. Cover established as a free-lance operator of export-import firm, the Transeastern Supply Company. Although Sherman's business activities touched upon many global markets, he specialized in computers.

Born in Boston, Massachusetts; exact date unknown. Recruited for the C.I.A. by a commercial attaché to the U.S. State Department in Paris, identified as one Robert Frobrisher, who acted as his field contact in 1968. Assigned to the agency's anti-nuclear section, Sherman later received his orders from a C.I.A. superior known as Ross McCullough.

In light of the fact that Sherman's active C.I.A. duty began during the height of U.S. antagonism towards Peking, two incidents which affected Sherman's conception of the Chi-Coms should be mentioned.

First, in 1945 Sherman set up the original base for the Transeastern Supply Company in Shanghai, with considerable success until Mao Tse-tung assumed power in 1949. The Chi-Coms tortured Sherman's partner, an elderly Chinese national, in an effort to obtain from him financial information concerning Transeastern, of which he was completely ignorant. Sherman was allowed to depart from China.

Second, Sherman's brother lost both legs in a forced amputation in a Chi-Com P. O. W. camp during the Korean War. After his release he endured two years of considerable pain until his death.

Sherman, fully trained as a C. I. A. agent in all the armed and unarmed techniques of defense, served with the agency until 1979. No further record.

OPERATIVE DATA: The Universal-Award Intelligence Group (see separate reference) initiated their distribution of the Sherman dossier four years after they had accumulated a wide audience with the Nick Carter (see separate reference) Killmaster series. During this interim period, the Cold War had reached an advanced stage verging on the era of détente.

Similar to the general format of the Carter missions, the Sherman books explored this transitional passage strictly in terms of volatile global locales. In this respect, Smith evoked the anti-American ideologies of the late sixties through his relevant settings. Therefore, this file will emphasize this one aspect of the series, acknowledging Smith's constancy of plotting and characterization.

Secret Mission: Peking (1968): Sherman was assigned to sell a sophisticated computer to the Chi-Coms as part of an intricate plan to sabotage their atomic weaponry complex.

This "Secret Mission" was heightened when the Chinese discovered that the computer had been "modified," and the C. I. A. dispatched Sherman to Peking to confiscate the contraband calculator.

Secret Mission: Prague (1968): Sherman intercepted $5, 000, 000 worth of weapons in divisive Prague--destined for a U. S. extremist force committed to fomenting a massive racial war in America.

Ironically, this Sherman entry appeared at the time of two pertinent crises: the Soviet invasion of Czechoslovakia and the profusion of violent racial protests throughout the United States.

Secret Mission: Corsica (1968): Sherman averted a Chi-Com opium network that was revealed as part of an apocalyptic conspiracy directed against the United States. Further, the vast resources of the Corsican drug market also imperiled this Sherman assignment.

Secret Mission: Morocco (1968): Sherman probed a U.S. agent-assassination plague. This initiative also involved a Swiss financier, identified as Berno Wolfgang Steigendorf, and the purported penetration of Fort Knox. (During the Cold War period, Tangiers, Morocco, was acknowledged as a preferred free port for gold smuggling.)

SUMMARY: Don Smith's "Secret Mission" series was related in the first person, in a departure from the pattern established by Nick Carter (see separate reference).

Smith convincingly delineated the crossing point from the Cold War to détente. Despite the fact that Smith was one of the first espionage novelists to perceive this change in world attitudes, the "Secret Mission" stamp on each successive Sherman entry signaled the deficiency of formularization. However, the basic concept of Smith's chaotic-locale series effectively complemented Sherman's image as an urbane, globe-trotting secret agent.

The operative might wish to compare the development of the "Secret Mission" docket to that of the Sam Durell-"Assignment" series by the late Edward S. Aarons (see separate reference).

STATUS: The Sherman books scored impressively in 1968, and it was casually assumed that Smith's protagonist would gradually replace Nick Carter (see separate reference) as the archetypal paperback spy. However, Universal-Award's departure from commercial publishing in 1977 drastically reversed the viability of the "Secret Mission" project. Charter Books had distributed only two new Sherman yarns by 1979. Despite the fact that the series had generated a sales volume of 2,000,000 copies by 1972, Charter elected not to reissue any of the Cold War-dated entries.

However, Sherman's durable escapist values would lend themselves to an aggressive reactivation campaign in the current action-oriented market. SOP.

FIELD BIBLIOGRAPHY

Smith, Don. Secret Mission: Corsica. New York: Universal-Award, 1968. PBO.

_____. Secret Mission: Istanbul. New York: Universal-Award, 1969. PBO.

_____. Secret Mission: Morocco. New York: Universal-Award, 1968. PBO.

_____. Secret Mission: Peking. New York: Universal-Award,
1968. PBO.

_____. Secret Mission: Prague. New York: Universal-Award,
1968. PBO.

_____. Secret Mission: Tibet. New York: Universal-Award,
1969. PBO.

CONSULT APPENDIX I FOR SERIES CONTINUATION

END OF CWF 64

† CWF 65. SPILLANE, MICKEY †

BACKGROUND: Cover identity of Frank Morrison Spillane, American mystery writer.

Born in 1918 in Brooklyn, New York, Spillane began selling
fiction to popular magazines while still in his teens; later entered
the pulp field where he contributed to the conception of such super-
heroes as Captain Marvel and Captain America. Of these, Mike
Danger eventually provided the inspiration for his tough private eye,
Mike Hammer.

After serving with the U.S. Air Force during World War II
as a trainer and combat flyer, Spillane continued to produce comic
features and short stories at an astounding rate.

Mike Hammer's first published case, I, the Jury (1947),
generated an unprecedented commercial response for a first mystery of the postwar period. However, a number of critics strongly objected to the book's scathing violence.

The ten subsequent Hammer entries, concluding with Survival ... Zero (1970), though honoring the format established in
I, the Jury, met with a more agreeable response from the
critical sector.

It is now common knowledge that Spillane's first seven books
are ranked among the ten bestselling novels of the twentieth century.
Global sales of the Spillane thrillers have reportedly exceeded
55,000,000.

Spillane's visibility as an author has undeniably enhanced his
popularity; over the years, Spillane has made numerous appearances

in the home visual arena and he even portrayed Hammer in the 1963 visual project, The Girl Hunters.

More recently, New American Library has reissued all of Spillane's books, complete with new, darkly graphic covers depicting the suspense master embroiled in a shadowy, Hammeresque background, armed only with his typewriter and a generous supply of beer.

Just as Mike Hammer has been characterized as a man of irrevocable justice, so have Spillane's later protagonists, including the subject of this file, Tiger Mann, as well as Morgan the Raider, Ryan, Deep, and others.

Spillane has also authored several non-series efforts, notably The Delta Factor (1967), The Erection Set (1972), and The Last Cop Out (1973). An earlier entry in this category, The Long Wait (1951), a tautly written novel about an ex-G.I. who suddenly loses his memory, has sold over 4,000,000 copies alone. The Delta Factor materialized in 1971 as a visual project starring Christopher George, as Morgan the Raider, and Yvette Mimieux; Spillane's wife, Sheri, was featured in a supporting role.

The Spillane "oeuvre" has been supplemented by novelette collections, namely Me, Hood! (1963), Killer Mine (1965), and The Tough Guys, a 1969 Signet paperback edition featuring "The Seven Year Kill," which was originally published in The Flier (1964). The volume contained two additional stories: "The Bastard Bannerman" and "Kick It or Kill!"

A number of Spillane's mysteries, especially his Mike Hammer books, have been adapted as visual projects. I, the Jury, released in 1953, offered Biff Elliott as the first visual Hammer. Twenty-nine years later, French actor Armand Assante turned up as a more modern Mike Hammer in a remake of the 1947 suspense classic. Other theatrical visual projects include The Long Wait (1954), Kiss Me Deadly (1955), and My Gun Is Quick (1957).

Hammer has also been portrayed in the audio and home sectors, with the latter represented by Darren McGavin in a 1958 home visual series, "Mike Hammer, Detective," and Kevin Dobson in a 1981 home visual project.

Spillane's career has been marked by periods of inactivity. Eight years passed before The Deep (1961) reaffirmed his narrative power, and the surprising revelation of his skill with the juvenile genre, as typified by The Day the Sea Rolled Back (1979), ended a second similar term.

With two previously written Hammer mysteries remaining unpublished, Spillane is reportedly preparing to launch his grim detective into the eighties. Unlike other vintage authors of the hardboiled, private-eye school, all of Spillane's works continue to sell in huge numbers today.

With the issuance of the first Tiger Mann entry, Day of the Guns (1964), Spillane entered the N. A. L. /Signet Intelligence Group (see separate reference).

CWF AGENT: Mann, Tiger.

CWF HISTORY: American. Regarded as a dedicated and vicious soldier, Mann served in the O.S.S. in Europe during World War II. Mann's C.O. was identified as Colonel Charles Corbinet, who later figured in his counterespionage duties during the Cold War.

During a 1964 luncheon date at the Cavalier Restaurant in New York, Mann noticed a tall, auburn-haired woman. Mann's companion, local journalist Wally Gibbons, identified the woman as Edith Caine, a translator for the United Nations. Gibbons also described Ms. Caine as a member of a prominent London family.

Mann, however, recognized her as Rondine Lund, an Austrian national who had defected to the Nazis in 1941.

As an O.S.S. agent, Mann had been assigned to terminate Rondine in occupied France. Despite their conflicting loyalties the two formed a romantic liaison, but the decisive turn of the tide against the Axis forces in Europe drastically altered Tiger Mann's relationship with Ms. Lund.

In 1945 Rondine shot Mann twice, believing that she had thus liquidated the O.S.S. operative. Mann, however, survived the incident, thereafter fostering a desire for retribution against Rondine Lund.

Now twenty years later, it was revealed that Rondine had long since been eliminated as a Nazi agent in Europe. The woman in the restaurant was actually Rondine's younger sister, Edith, whose position as a U. N. translator was subsequently confirmed. It was similarly disclosed that Caine was Rondine's true surname, her family ancestry going back to the English nobles who contested King John over the Magna Carta.

After the war Mann had been recruited by an elusive man named Martin Grady for a highly secret civilian intelligence unit that penetrated the highest spheres of U.S. military and political power.

By the end of a 1964 initiative for the Grady network, Mann had come to regard Edith as Rondine, exactly as he remembered her. One year later they were committed to a future wedding. The union was never consummated, and Rondine-Edith utilized her role as U. N. translator as an effective cover to work for her own embassy.

The activities of the Grady organization were a matter of public record to the major Washington agencies, including the powerful I. A. T. S.

Former O. S. S. officer Colonel Charles Corbinet, who had also acted for I. A. T. S. during the war, was drafted back into that intelligence body.

As an agent for the Grady interests, Mann often worked closely with Corbinet, although considerable friction existed between the two counterespionage entities, as demonstrated during a 1965 mission involving a suspected plot to assassinate an Arab king. Full details under OPERATIVE DATA.

The New York division of I. A. T. S. was situated on the upper floor of the Carboy Building on Church Street, and was controlled by Hal Randolph. Despite the cooperative relationship between Mann and Colonel Corbinet, Randolph made no secret of his contempt for Martin Grady.

A resident of New York, Tiger Mann possessed an intricate knowledge of the U. N. and also a lethal expertise with firearms. These talents superbly aided Mr. Grady in the pursuit of his intelligence objectives from 1964 to 1966.

Among other Grady principals was Ernie Bentley, the network's special equipment consultant.

No further record of either Tiger Mann or the Martin Grady organization after 1966.

OPERATIVE DATA: Mike Hammer has been compared to James Bond, specifically in the dimensions of each character's murderous amorality. However, in the strict context of Cold-War espionage fiction, a closer affinity existed between Bond and Tiger Mann.

Despite the bestseller status of the first Mann book, Day of the Guns (1964), the era in which it appeared prompted some critics to define Tiger Mann as either an extension of Mike Hammer or a leaner, grimmer version of James Bond. Mike Hammer has thus overshadowed Spillane's other characters to such an extent that their individual personalities never have been fully realized.

Although Mann reflected Hammer's unbiased code of vengeance, they have little else in common. The world in which Mann lived was considerably more subtle in its political trappings and, because of the placement of the U. N. throughout the series, more disturbing in the violence which threatened it. Beyond this level, the diplomatic figures who inhabited the New York of the Mann thrillers signified a different place and time than the dark Manhattan landscape of Mike Hammer's existence.

Within the four-book span of the series, Spillane established his own concept of realistic expionage fiction, which differed noticeably from le Carré and Deighton (see separate references). As for Mann's likeness to Bond, only the last book in the Mann dossier, The By-Pass Control (1966), approached the style of the Cold War spy thriller as fashioned by Ian Fleming (see separate reference).

The New York Times adequately summed up the secret of Spillane's mastery in its review of the third Tiger Mann entry, The Death Dealers (1965): "It's unfair to apply rules to Spillane, who observes only one: that the story must keep you reading."

From this viewpoint, it should be recognized that Spillane's readership has evolved not only on the basis of his provocative plots but also from the feverish narrative pace evidenced in all his books, including the Mann novels.

In its purest form, the Mann series represents Spillane's progression beyond the private-eye genre, as well as his sharpened perception of contemporary justice through the complexities of the Cold War.

Tiger Mann reflected his time in much the same manner as Mike Hammer did the postwar world. But Hammer and Mann were equally vehement in their contempt toward Communists.

Beginning with the first Mann thriller, Day of the Guns (1964), Spillane seemed to have shaped a commentary on both the Cold War and the popular fiction which encompassed it, emphasizing Mann's reaction to the era's ideologies rather than the avaricious designs of the Kremlin.

In Day of the Guns Spillane defined, with a measured balance, Mann's hostility toward Rondine and also the functional core of the U.N., ultimately generating a Communist conspiracy that served to unite them into a formidable alliance.

The New York Times vigorously endorsed Spillane's initial foray into Cold War espionage: "It possesses the authentic narrative drive and almost hypnotic conviction that set Spillane apart from all his imitators ... Spillane is a master in compelling you always to read the next page."

In Bloody Sunrise (1965) Spillane offered a more decisive portrait of the Grady organization than was immediately apparent in Day of the Guns. Mann was given an apocalyptic assignment, identified only by the operative code, "Plato."

The mystery surrounding one Gabin Martrel, a highly publicized Soviet defector, and the revelation of a dreadful U.S.S.R. initiative, Project Valchek, provided Mann with an intense and menacing conflict.

Bloody Sunrise emerged as the most challenging of the series, as Spillane tested Mann's talents through his ambiguous relationship with Rondine and his perilous interplay with a lethal female operative known as Sonia Dutko.

The climax violently fused all these diverse elements with a shattering effect that typified Spillane's taut narrative style and Mann's amoral nature.

In its evaluation of Bloody Sunrise, the Charlotte Observer commented, "A gala one for mystery fans ... Tiger slugs, shoots, and loves through international intrigue at a fast pace."

Spillane explored the devious designs of power politics in The Death Dealers (1965): the contentious motives of the Grady "apparat" and I. A. T. S. were infused into the diplomatically explosive threat to the life of an influential Arab king, Teish El Abin.

The conflict in this Mann entry resulted from the belligerent suspicion between Martin Grady and Hal Randolph; a development project involving Abin's country; and the enigma of the multinational AmPet Corporation.

The Death Dealers portended the mutual interests that the U. S. and the Arab world would inevitably share during the seventies, and, within this framework, Spillane conceived a mesmerizing tale of betrayal and deception that eclipsed any political considerations, qualifying The Death Dealers as the best of the series.

In The By-Pass Control (1966) Spillane accelerated the ultimate fear of the Cold War. Mann was ordered to find Louis Agrounsky, a missing atomic scientist who had perfected the destruct device on America's I. C. B. M. system that could lead to the total annihilation of the United States.

Incorporating the intricately technological complexion of this entry, Spillane equalized the precision of the potential threat with his typically blistering movement.

The climax ranks with that of Bloody Sunrise, as Mann confronts Niger Hoppes on a desolate North Carolina beach. The final battle and the barbarous figure of Hoppes develop, respectively, as the most significant event and villain in the series.

With The By-Pass Control, Mann's relationship with Rondine-Edith has become sexually cooperative, totally separated from the malice that marked their postwar encounter in Day of the Guns.

Spillane advanced the operative resources of the Grady network in this Mann mission. As Newsday was quick to point out, "Killer Tiger, who seems to enjoy his work, has come up with a new killing device in this book [a deadly modification of the Bezex sinus inhaler] and one that the late Ian Fleming might have appreciated."

SUMMARY: Like Mickey Spillane's later mystery protagonists, Tiger Mann was inevitably compared to Mike Hammer. In fact, Spillane's four-title series penetrated the dimensions of the Cold War with the conviction and magnetism that characterized the Hammer books (along with the likes of Morgan the Raider, Ryan, and Deep).

Punctuated by an incisive view of the New York background around the U.N. during the Cold War years, the Mann dossier probed both the Bondian and realistic arenas while it also demonstrated Spillane's narrative skill.

Despite the considerable number of visual projects that have been derived from various other Spillane works, the Tiger Mann thrillers were curiously ignored for this purpose.

STATUS: Unlike most of the espionage novelists represented by the N.A.L./Signet Intelligence Group (see separate reference) during the mid-sixties, Mickey Spillane's have continued to register excellent sales as Signet paperbacks. This applies also to his other contributions to the suspense genre. SSP.

FIELD BIBLIOGRAPHY

Spillane, Mickey. Bloody Sunrise. New York: E. P. Dutton, 1965; New York: New American Library paperback, 1965. HB-R.

_____. The By-Pass Control. New York: E. P. Dutton, 1966; New York: New American Library paperback, 1967. HB-R.

_____. Day of the Guns. New York: E. P. Dutton, 1964; New York: New American Library paperback, 1965. HB-R.

_____. The Death Dealers. New York: E. P. Dutton, 1965; New York: New American Library paperback, 1966. HB-R.

END OF CWF 65

† CWF 66. STRATTON, THOMAS †

BACKGROUND: Allied cover identity of Thomas Eugene DeWeese and Robert Stratton Coulson.

DeWeese, born in 1934, has a solid reputation in both the mystery and science-fiction fields. In the former genre, DeWeese has operated alone, altering his Christian name to "Jean" for three suspense works, all published in 1975: The Carnelian Cat, The Moonstone Spirit, and The Reimann Curse.

In collaboration with Coulson, DeWeese wrote two parodies involving science-fiction convention reporter Joe Karnes, chiefly: Now You See It--Him--Them (1975) and Charles Fort Never Mentioned Wombats (1977). In the non-series arena, they produced Gates of the Universe (1975).

A decade earlier, DeWeese and Coulson, as Thomas Stratton, had conspired two entries for the "Man from U. N. C. L. E." novelization project, The Invisibility Affair and The Mind-Twisters Affair (both 1967). These two missions are the subject of this file.

An active member of the Mystery Writers of America, DeWeese has written numerous short stories for suspense publications, among them Mike Shayne Mystery Magazine.

Coulson, more closely associated with science fiction, was born in 1924. He and his wife, science-fiction novelist Juanita Coulson, jointly received in 1965 the Hugo award for best amateur publication for their popular fan magazine, Yandro, for which Mr. Coulson served as editor.

Retaining his solo identity, Coulson penned To Renew the Ages (1976). During this period, he revised Pier Anthony's But What of Earth? Issued as a collaborative effort in 1976, Anthony disputed the volume on the grounds that it was an unauthorized version of his novel.

Both DeWeese and Coulson represented the Ace Intelligence Group (see separate reference).

CWF AGENTS: Solo, Napoleon, and Illya Kuryakin.

CWF HISTORIES: See also Avallone, Michael--CWF 6.

OPERATIVE DATA: As were the U. N. C. L. E. novelizations prepared by John T. Phillifent (see separate reference), Stratton's contributions to the series were more inclined toward science fiction than those of the other U. N. C. L. E. authors. However, Stratton's assignments were more favorably received than Phillifent's.

The mysterious disappearance of a top U. N. C. L. E. scientist in Wisconsin, identified as Dr. Morthley, and a T. H. R. U. S. H. - financed revolution in Cerro Bueno, San Sebastian, characterized The Invisibility Affair (1967).

Combining U. N. C. L. E. resources in the U. S. and South America, Mr. Waverly ordered Solo and Kuryakin to seek and destroy T. H. R. U. S. H. 's newest weapon--a device capable of rendering any person or object invisible, without sound or trace. Thus Stratton conceived one of T. H. R. U. S. H. 's most deadly aeronautical defenses: an invisible dirigible.

In The Mind-Twisters Affair (1967) a bizarre incident in Del Floria's and the return of Dr. Morthley signaled the antagonistic behavior of Dr. Richard Armden, a scientific advisor for U. N. C. L. E. According to official field reports, Armden exhibited belligerence toward U. N. C. L. E. and its global objectives.

Utilizing the facilities of the U. N. C. L. E. branches in Chicago and in Fort Wayne, Indiana, Solo and Kuryakin were to probe the landscape of the Midford University campus, where Dr. Armden resided, to find the cause of the scientific advisor's misanthropic posture.

Stratton's expertise in the science-fiction genre was especially evident in The Mind-Twisters Affair, for he skillfully and credibly blended an abstruse theme--mind control--into the durable U.N.C.L.E. format.

SUMMARY: Thomas Stratton invested a sense of continuity into the two U. N. C. L. E. initiatives, as typified by the consistent function of scientists and by Dr. Morthley's sequel appearance in The Mind-Twisters Affair.

While Stratton's offensives were not regarded in the same vein as the efforts of Michael Avallone, Peter Leslie, and David McDaniel (see separate references), most U. N. C. L. E. observers approved of his smooth, science-fiction-oriented approach to the series.

STATUS: See also Avallone, Michael--CWF 6.

FIELD BIBLIOGRAPHY

Stratton, Thomas. The Invisibility Affair. New York: Ace Books, 1967. PBO. TN.

_____. The Mind-Twisters Affair. New York: Ace Books, 1967. PBO. TN.

CONSULT ACE INTELLIGENCE GROUP FOR ADDITIONAL AUTHOR REFERENCES

END OF CWF 66

† CWF 67. STREET, BRADFORD †

BACKGROUND: Author of visual-project novelizations. In addition to adapting <u>In Like Flint</u> (1967), the subject of this file, Street has penned several visual titles in both the theatrical and home quadrants, namely <u>The Glass Bottom Boat</u> (1966), <u>Primus</u> (1971), and <u>For Pete's Sake</u> (1974).

No other details available.

CWF AGENT: Flint, Derek.

CWF HISTORY: <u>See also</u> Pearl, Jack--CWF 57.

OPERATIVE DATA: The launching of a manned space platform into a perfect orbit, three missing minutes from a golf game between the President of the United States and Z. O. W. I. E. chief Cramden, and a scandalous incident in a New York hotel room involving Cramden and one Norma Benson, a schoolteacher from Roanoke, Virginia, set the tone for <u>In Like Flint</u> (1967).

Disturbed by both the golf fiasco and his encounter with Ms. Benson, Cramden requested Flint's assistance. Penetrating the Z. O. W. I. E. security complex, Flint discovered that the U. S. intelligence organization had been infiltrated by traitors headed by Colonel David Carter, Z. O. W. I. E. 's Control Administrator. Ironically, Carter was eventually promoted to the rank of general.

A feverish confrontation with Carter's security agents permitted Flint to simulate his own death. Then, employing the guises of a ballet dancer and Cuban guerilla, Flint invaded an exclusive health resort in the Virgin Islands, identified as Fabulous Face. Here, a secret society of women, under mastery of the sensually enigmatic Lisa Norton, was involved in a plot that concerned two female Soviet cosmonauts based in a distant galaxy, an apocalyptic defense initiative known as "Project Damocles," and an exact double of the President of the United States.

Ms. Norton was assisted by three prominent women, who literally controlled the kingdoms of publishing, high fashion, cosmetics, and communications: Elizabeth, Helena, and Simone.

The machinations of General Carter caused Lisa's network to convert into Flint's allies, and, journeying into space, Z.O.W.I.E.'s matchless operative decisively averted Carter's cataclysmic scheme.

Flint's cooperative movements with the two female cosmonauts, as they soared in a space capsule destined for Central Park in New York, boded well for the possibilities of global peace.

When the visual sequel to Our Man Flint (1966) appeared in 1967, it was unduly criticized for lacking the satirical energy of its predecessor.

In his novelization for In Like Flint, Bradford Street accented the project's mocking attitude toward the women's liberation phenomenon and the U.S. military-political power structure with such conviction that it proved prophetic.

SUMMARY: Despite the fact that In Like Flint was one of Street's first novelization missions, he displayed an admirable narrative talent that unfortunately has been neglected in recent years.

While Street lacked the tested style of Jack Pearl (see separate reference), his paperback interpretation of In Like Flint unquestionably excels anything currently being issued in this highly competitive genre.

In contrast to Pearl's Our Man Flint (1965) (see separate reference), Street integrated the stock elements of 20th Century-Fox's 1967 visual project (featuring James Coburn as Derek Flint, Lee J. Cobb as Cramden, Jean Hale as Lisa, Andrew Duggan as the President, and the late Steve Inhat as Colonel/General Carter), as in the retention in the novelization of Z.O.W.I.E. and of Cramden's Christian name of Lloyd. Another difference in the second Flint adaptation was the inclusion of only three voluptuous women in the lavish New York penthouse apartment.

In 1976 Ray Danton accepted a Flint mission for Our Man Flint: Dead on Target, a CBS home visual project. However, no further reports have been issued on the progress of James Coburn's planned return to the intelligence field as Derek Flint.

STATUS: Bradford Street's In Like Flint, as well as Jack Pearl's Our Man Flint (see separate reference), should be reactivated, which would also help illustrate the deficiencies of present novelization formats. EOP.

FIELD BIBLIOGRAPHY

Street, Bradford. In Like Flint. New York: Dell Books, 1967. PBO. MN.

CONSULT PEARL, JACK--CWF 57 FOR ADDITIONAL AUTHOR REFERENCES

END OF CWF 67

† CWF 68. THOMAS, ROSS †

BACKGROUND: Born in Oklahoma City in 1926. A fledgling reporter for the Daily Oklahoman during his freshmen year at the University of Oklahoma, Thomas was summoned to U.S. Army duty in the
later stages of World War II, serving as a combat soldier in the
Philippines. After the war Thomas returned to graduate in 1949.

Thomas based several of his novels on his experiences as a
publicist. The Seersucker Whipsaw (1967) and The Brass Go-
Between (1969) reflected his term as publicity director for Chief
Obafemi Awolowo of Nigeria.

The second title was written under the cover identity of Oli-
ver Bleeck as the first entry in his dossier concerning one Philip
St. Ives, a free-lance interagent.

A later series title, The Procane Chronicle (1972), was
adapted as St. Ives (1976), a theatrical visual project starring
Charles Bronson as Bleeck's slick intermediary, with John House-
man, Maximilian Schell, and Jacqueline Bisset.

Other Thomas novels have focused on the theme of corrup-
tion in the highest spheres of power, chiefly The Fools in Town
Are on Our Side (1971), The Porkchoppers (1972), and If You Can't
Be Good (1973).

A member of the Mystery Writers of America, Thomas received that organization's Edgar, in the category of best first mystery novel of the year, for his first novel, The Cold War Swap
(1966), in which he introduced the crack counterintelligence team of
McCorkle and Padillo, allied subject of this file.

Thomas is one of the few mystery writers whose works have
been reprinted in paperback at regular intervals. During the seventies Pocket Books reissued The Cold War Swap (1966) and The Backup Men (1971), as well as some of Thomas' non-series contributions
and all of the Bleeck-St. Ives books. And Thomas's first paperback
publisher, Avon, distributed new editions of his suspense classics,
notably Cast a Yellow Shadow (1967), McCorkle and Padillo's second
mission, and The Singapore Wink (1969).

Retaining what the New Yorker called "A seasoned hand at
catching the reader's interest and keeping it," Thomas' recent
thrillers include Chinaman's Chance (1979), The Eighth Dwarf (1980),
and The Mordida Man (1981).

Mr. Thomas lives in Malibu.

CWF AGENTS: McCorkle, Mac, and Mike Padillo.

CWF HISTORIES: McCorkle was born in San Francisco.

He fought behind enemy lines during World War II, as a U.S. Army combat soldier in Burma. After being discharged, he surfaced in Germany, and in 1953 he opened a bar in Bad Godesberg, called Mac's Place.

Summoned for 20 months reserve duty at the U.S. Embassy on the Rhine. Adept in armed strategy, using the .38 caliber.

McCorkle's entire span as a Cold War operative was in association with Mike Padillo, whose dossier is outlined below. Padillo was of mixed Estonian-Spanish origin. His father, a Spanish lawyer, was killed in 1937 during the Spanish Civil War.

Over the next four years, Mike and his Estonian mother migrated from Portugal to Mexico, supported by means of her pedantic talents with piano and language lessons. As a result of this experience, Padillo became well-versed in several tongues, including German and Russian.

After his mother died of tuberculosis in 1941, young Michael ventured across the Mexican border into El Paso, Texas, where he worked briefly as bellhop, tour guide, and smuggler.

After a long trek stretching from the Big Bend country of Texas into Albuquerque, New Mexico, onto the famed Route 66 into Los Angeles, Padillo found himself sought by the F.B.I. for draft evasion.

Padillo joined the U.S. Army in the summer of 1942 and operated the officers' club at a training replacement center in north Texas near Dallas and Fort Worth.

Padillo's language skill was eventually discovered, and upon completing a battery of indoctrination courses in Maryland and Washington, he was assigned as a U.S. liaison with the Maquis in Paris, where he remained until 1945.

After the war Padillo returned to the U.S., eventually finding employment as a bartender in Santa Monica, California. Shortly thereafter he was visited by two nondescript men who promised him lucrative compensation if he accepted as "assignment" that required travel--to Warsaw, Poland.

Having completed at least two dozen similar tasks, during which time he had resided in Denver, Chicago, Pittsburgh, and New York, Padillo met McCorkle in the early fifties, and taught him the rudiments of the bar trade. Together, Padillo and McCorkle successfully established Mac's Place, which catered to the Cold War diplomatic traffic that frequently passed through Bonn and Berlin.

Responsible for the financial aspects of the business, McCorkle periodically went to London and the U.S. in search of new furniture sources and bar-merchandising concepts.

In the mid-sixties Padillo revealed his clandestine activities to McCorkle, resulting in their combined counterintelligence field term, evaluated below.

OPERATIVE DATA: The appearance of one Herr Maas, unofficially identified as an attaché to the Jordanian Embassy in Bonn, and the brutal murder of a mysterious man in Mac's Place underscored the topical tension in The Cold War Swap (1966).

In considering Thomas's espionage initiative, it should be acknowledged that he punctuated his mission with the ravaged-Berlin settings indigenous to certain works of John le Carré, Len Deighton, and Adam Hall (see separate references). Once this point is in proper perspective, the scope of Thomas's plotting as a contemporary spy novelist can be isolated.

The Cold War Swap possessed realistic tones similar to le Carré's The Spy Who Came In from the Cold (1963) (see separate reference), Deighton's Funeral in Berlin (1964) (see separate reference), and Hall's The Quiller Memorandum (1965) (see separate reference). However, that which set Thomas apart from his predecessors was the interaction between McCorkle and Padillo-- although enacted within the expected perimeters of the Cold War, including divided Berlin.

Although Thomas has not been discussed within the context of the aforementioned CWF authors, his irrefutable achievement with The Cold War Swap seems to have complemented the evolution of the realistic spy novel, as typified by le Carré, Deighton, and Hall (see separate references).

Going beyond the elements of Maas and the murder victim in The Cold War Swap, Thomas included in the plot Padillo's disappearance during an assignment in East Berlin.

Having established the direction of his espionage theme, Thomas utilized Maas for the narrative thrust of this entry in which he informed McCorkle of two mathematicians with the N.S.A. (National Security Agency) who had defected to the U.S.S.R. Maas identified the defectors as Gerald R. Symmes and Russell C. Burchwood, both of whom were alleged homosexuals.

Padillo's initiative in the Eastern sector was fully detailed as being the transfer of Symmes and Burchwood to Bonn on a U.S.A.F. aircraft, to which the Soviets agreed on the condition that a U.S. agent be exchanged for Symmes and Burchwood.

Fearing that Moscow would create a scandal focusing on

Symmes and Burchwood as homosexual traitors, Washington con-
sented to the "swap."

The U.S. operative selected for exchange: Mike Padillo.

From this point, Thomas heightened The Cold War Swap into
a tautly written thriller that included McCorkle's alliance with several resourceful patriots, chiefly Cook Baker, identified as the Bonn
correspondent for an international radio service known as Global
Reports, Inc., in order to penetrate the Soviet sector in a desperate attempt to liberate Padillo.

The Cold War Swap materialized as a chilling foray into the
diplomatic world of Bonn as well as the sex-perverted domain of
the alleys of Berlin. Its integration with the principal plot imparted
a haunting quality that, in some respects, equaled the effects of
le Carré and Deighton (see separate references).

Thomas also fused the intrigues of a Chi-Com agent into his
Berlin-Bonn conspiracy. Identified as Ku, he summoned the services of Peking's European ally, Albania, for his counterintelligence
maneuver in East Berlin. (Subsequently it was revealed that Ku and
Padillo had served together during World War II.)

Further, Thomas's narrative power was at its most compelling when he depicted the devious rivalries between the Soviet K.G.B.
and the German Gehlen network.

At the conclusion of this entry, McCorkle proposed marriage
to Dr. Fredl Arndt, a political correspondent for a newspaper in
Frankfurt.

The critical praise bestowed upon The Cold War Swap instantly elevated Ross Thomas into the top rung of contemporary espionage
novelists. The New York Times Book Review observed: "A good,
nasty Le Carresque plot of opportunism and betrayal within the intelligence service, a well-observed background of Berlin and Bonn,
some violent surprises and a fine individual tone of wry, tough humor in its telling," while the New Yorker proclaimed: "An admirable story of American agents and counteragents, and counter-
counteragents, and their English and German and Russian counter-
and counter-counterparts, playing a desperate game of wits and guns
on both sides of the Berlin Wall."

In 1967 The Cold War Swap was published as The Spy in the
Vodka in British territory.

In Cast a Yellow Shadow (1967), Thomas dexterously blended
the abduction of Fredl McCorkle with Padillo's most perilous
counterintelligence project--the termination of the white prime minister of an emerging African nation, Hennings Van Zandt.

In the context of the Cold War, Van Zandt's small African

kingdom controlled the global supply of chromium and was committed to following Rhodesia's liberation from British influence.

No longer residing in Bad Godesberg, McCorkle transported Mac's Place, along with his alluring wife, to Washington, D.C.

Cast a Yellow Shadow compared favorably with The Cold War Swap, and Thomas's use of the first person throughout the series intensified the overall sense of the unknown in the dark pathways of the Cold War.

As the Chicago Tribune commented in its evaluation of this entry, "You cannot tell anything for certain until the last chapter. Don't miss any of it!"

SUMMARY: With the publication of Ross Thomas's Edgar-winning The Cold War Swap, the realistic spy thriller manifested dimensions beyond the disturbing complexities of le Carré, Deighton, and Hall (see separate references).

Despite the critical acclaim that followed the McCorkle-Padillo series, Thomas has never been widely regarded on a par with his predecessors.

Regarding his suspense works as a whole, mystery critic Dorothy B. Hughes praised Ross Thomas as, "... without peer in American suspense."

STATUS: Cast a Yellow Shadow (1967) is currently in reissue as an Avon paperback, and, although the recent Pocket Books editions of The Cold War Swap (1966) and The Backup Men (1971) have since expired, their future return to the intrigue market is highly probable. SSP, subject to title rotation and possible transfer of paperback sources.

FIELD BIBLIOGRAPHY

Thomas, Ross. Cast a Yellow Shadow. New York: William Morrow, 1967; New York: Avon paperback, 1968. HB-R.

_____. The Cold War Swap. New York: William Morrow, 1966; New York: Avon paperback, 1967. HB-R. See also The Spy in the Vodka.

_____. The Spy in the Vodka. London: Hodder, 1967. HB. British title for The Cold War Swap.

CONSULT APPENDIX I FOR SERIES CONTINUATION

CONSULT APPENDIX II FOR SERIES TRANSITION

END OF CWF 68

† CWF 69. TIGER, JOHN †

BACKGROUND: Cover identity of Walter Wager, American author, editor, and producer. Born in 1924 in New York.

Received degrees from Columbia College, Harvard, and Northwestern universities. During 1949-50 Wager attended the Institut des Hautes Etudes Internationales, and the University of Paris as a Fulbright Fellow.

Working extensively as an editor after 1947, Wager secured valued positions in the field with such varying entities as Aeroroutes, Inc., the U. N., and Playbill magazine. Also gained experience as a writer for CBS in 1956, and the following year, he ventured into the visual project arena as a producer for NBC.

Relevant to this last pursuit, Wager fashioned a considerable reputation as a producer of documentaries on such provocative subjects as disarmament, atomic weapons in World War II, and organized crime in the United States.

Wager's suspense fiction has touched other forms of the genre. Two of his books appeared as visual projects in 1977. Viper Three (1971) was adapted as Twilight's Last Gleaming, a cataclysmic nuclear thriller with overtones of Fail-Safe (1962). The Allied Artists release featured Burt Lancaster and Charles Durning. And Charles Bronson starred as a top K. G. B. agent in Telefon (1975) in which he was assigned to disband a dormant yet potentially destructive Soviet spy network in the U. S.

Sledgehammer (1970) and Swap (1972) contrasted with Wager's crisis-oriented works and established him as a major mystery talent.

In the non-fiction sector Wager is represented by such works as The O.S.S. --A Short History and How Broadway Works (both 1966). He also edited The Playwright Speaks (1967).

The John Tiger cover, employed for nine novelization titles derived from the home visual series "I Spy" and "Mission: Impossible," was first reported in 1954 when Wager conceived Death Hits the Jackpot. Wager's infiltration of the novelized espionage territory is the subject of this file.

In 1956 as Walter Herman, Wager wrote Operation Intrigue. More recently he recruited sensual private detective Alison Gordon in two mysteries: Blue Leader (1979) and Blue Moon (1980).

Mr. Wager is a prominent member of the Mystery Writers of America and the Writers Guild of America--East.

CWF AGENTS: 1) Robinson, Kelly, and Alexander Scott.
2) The I. M. F. (Impossible Missions Force) unit.

CWF HISTORIES: 1) Kelly Robinson and Alexander Scott: Americans.

Born in Los Angeles, Kelly Robinson earned a reputation as world-class tennis player, and in 1959 was a major contender at Wimbledon. Described as a complex man with the seemingly incompatible qualities of a romantic and adventurer, Robinson was equally proficient in the arts of seduction and assassination.

Alexander Scott overcame racial barriers and an impoverished childhood to gain success as an All-Eastern college football celebrity in the late fifties. He later became a championship tennis star and advanced his athletic prowess as Robinson's tennis trainer in the early sixties. Scott also was a Rhodes Scholar and among his many intellectual talents was fluency in eleven languages.

Publicly, Robinson was regarded as a socialite tennis jock and Scott as his glib mentor. In fact, Robinson and Scott formed a relationship that both complemented and camouflaged their true profession: agents for the C. I. A.

Designated by the Pentagon as "Domino," the operative code for the global spy squad represented solely by these two men, Robinson and Scott were summoned to a garage beneath the Hotel Pershing at 11th and Penn in Washington, D. C., into a secret command center activated by dialing an "inside" number in a basement phone booth. The "Domino" base contained extensive counterintelligence files and a global television monitor, as well as the expected furnishings.

Robinson and Scott's chief was identified as one Donald Mars, although he was known in other agency spheres as Harry Borton and Colonel Kent.

As C. I. A. agents, Robinson and Scott effectively utilized their allied cover of tennis player and trainer engaged on the tournament circuit (the Director of the C. I. A. once referred to them as "The Varsity").

In terms of their "company" service, it should be properly

noted that Robinson was adept in the use of the .357 Magnum and the throwing-knife (sleeve-sling type), and that Scott was similarly lethal with firearms. Scott also specialized in cryptography, tapping techniques, and deception.

Robinson and Scott acted as global C. I. A. agents from 1961 to 1968, although their assignments were not properly documented until 1965. No further record.

2) The I. M. F. unit: The Impossible Missions Force, a clandestine intelligence group initially controlled by one Dan Briggs. During the Cold War era, the I. M. F. was composed of the following affiliates:

1) Barney Collier: electronics and engineering expert.

2) Cinnamon Carter: infiltration specialist.

3) Rollin Hand: deception strategist; ex-actor and magician.

4) Willy Armitage: master safecracker; former Olympic weight-lifing champion.

By 1967 the I. M. F. had successfully executed a number of perilous objectives, including the acquisition of a cache of nuclear warheads from the guarded vault of a Latin American dictator, the removal of the barbarous warden of a penal colony in French Guinea, and the multimillion dollar circumvention of an avaricious prince who planned to supply arms for an explosive conflict in the Near East.

The crucial element of the I. M. F. was the meticulous planning invested into each initiative, with each member receiving a task suited to his or her special talents.

Jim Phelps assumed Briggs's position as I. M. F. head in September 1967, and, until its termination in 1973, new agents replaced departing constituents of the original unit.

Throughout the term of the I. M. F. Briggs and Phelps were appropriately briefed on their missions by means of a concealed tape recorder, carefully implanted in locations specially selected for isolation from external forces.

OPERATIVE DATA: As John Tiger, Wager approached both novelization series in a similar fashion, accenting the escapist values of each home visual design with pace and style.

1) I Spy (1965) concerned penetration by "Domino" of an insidious spy network known only as "Force 1," which sought to influence mentally the top military architects in the Pentagon. Employing their usual tennis tournament ploy, Robinson and Scott probed the flamboyant environs of Kingston, Jamaica, and the most exclusive pleasures of Paris, France.

In Superkill (1967) the precarious global balance of N. A. T. O.
in Cold War-ravaged Berlin and a torturous Japanese asylum affected Robinson and Scott's assignment.

Death-Twist (1968) focused on their suicidal attempt to undermine the cruel right-wing regime of General Giron in Costa Verde,
in an entry that reflected the sobering realities of the Cold War in
the U. S. sector during the late sixties.

Into the principal plot, Tiger integrated the mysterious
deaths of two U. S. A. F. sentries, the theft of critical combat and
nuclear weaponry from the Homestead Air Force Base, south of
Miami, and the intrigues of a small but ruthless band of Communist guerillas opposed to Giron.

2) In Mission: Impossible (1967), the first in the novelization
series, Tiger graphically defined the core and function of Dan
Briggs's Impossible Missions Force.

The I. M. F. combined their various skills to halt the production of DEXON-9, a psychologically paralyzing gas, linked to the activities of two Nazi war criminals: Dr. Kurt Dersh, Director of
the Third Reich's Chemical Warfare Research, and Colonel Fritz
Messelman, Deputy Chief of Security for Himmler's S. S.

Infiltrating the malignant jungles of Santilla, a South American nation inhabited by renegade Nazis (including Dersh and Messel-
men) and the oppressive military junta of General Rafael Belissario
Lorca, the I. M. F. 's DEXON-9 crisis was heightened by the top-
priority need to return Dersh and Messelman to West Germany before expiration of the statute of limitations on war crimes.

Utilizing the cover of Max Walker, Michael Avallone (see
separate reference) recorded the second and third I. M. F. dockets
in 1968, namely Code Name: Judas and Code Name: Rapier.

Tiger's Code Name: Little Ivan (1969), the fourth series assignment, involved new I. M. F. chief Jim Phelps's objective of fil-
tering his crack intelligence group into East Germany to seek out
and destroy a formidable tank capable of provoking a devastating
East-West confrontation in Europe.

SUMMARY: In his novelization contributions for "I Spy" and "Mission: Impossible, " John Tiger effectively conveyed the special qualities of both home visual projects.

In the context of his Tiger identity, Wager separated his distinctive narrative style from the format he used in his novelization
efforts.

From 1965 to 1968, Robert Culp and Bill Cosby served in
the field as Kelly Robinson and Alexander Scott in "I Spy, " produced by NBC and Three-F Productions.

With Steven Hill as Dan Briggs during 1966-67, succeeded by Peter Graves as Jim Phelps, "Mission: Impossible" operated world-wide for CBS, Desilu Productions, and Paramount Pictures from 1966 to 1973.

Initially, the following I. M. F. operatives were summoned: Greg Morris as Barney Collier, Barbara Bain as Cinnamon Carter, Martin Landau as Rollin Hand, and Peter Lupus as Willy Armitage. As the I. M. F. dossier advanced beyond the Cold War, Leonard Nimoy was recruited as Paris and Leslie Ann Warren as Dana Lambert, replacing Rollin Hand and Cinnamon Carter, respectively.

Lynda Day George, as I. M. F. strategist Casey, eventually superseded Ms. Warren, while Nimoy's term was not extended after his departure. Sam Elliott, Barbara Anderson, Jessica Walters, Lee Meriwether, and Elizabeth Ashley all served briefly as I. M. F. agents.

STATUS: "I Spy" and "Mission: Impossible" are not scheduled for reactivation (a projected return of the I. M. F. was subsequently shelved), and therefore it would not be feasible to authorize the corresponding novelization files for future distribution. SOP.

FIELD BIBLIOGRAPHY

Tiger, John. Code Name: Little Ivan. New York: Popular Library, 1969. PBO. TN. ("Mission: Impossible")

_____. Countertrap. New York: Popular Library, 1967. PBO. TN. ("I Spy")

_____. Death-Twist. New York: Popular Library, 1968. PBO. TN. ("I Spy")

_____. Doomdate. New York: Popular Library, 1967. PBO. TN. ("I Spy")

_____. I Spy. New York: Popular Library, 1965. PBO. TN.

_____. Masterstroke. New York: Popular Library, 1966. PBO. TN. ("I Spy")

_____. Mission: Impossible. New York: Popular Library, 1967. PBO. TN.

_____. Superkill. New York: Popular Library, 1967. PBO. TN. ("I Spy")

_____. Wipeout. New York: Popular Library, 1967. PBO. TN. ("I Spy")

† CWF 70. THE UNIVERSAL-AWARD INTELLIGENCE GROUP †

CONTENTS: Known variably as Universal-Award House, Award Books, and Universal Publishing and Distributing, this New York-based paperback firm concentrated heavily on espionage series fiction during the Cold War era. Universal-Award ceased operations in 1977.

Generally, the efforts of the U. A. I. G. were influenced by the Nick Carter-Killmaster series, which was initiated in 1964 with Run-Spy-Run.

Prior to their departure from the U. S. paperback market, the U. A. I. G. issued, on a regular basis, over 100 Carter missions.

Although the Carter docket garnered global sales exceeding 8, 000, 000 by 1968, Universal-Award advanced slowly into the intrigue field, relying more on the PBO format for their genre constituents. However, the intelligence group was involved in the reprint sector. The post-Carter PBO development of the U. A. I. G. is outlined below:

1) Don Von Elsner's spy series involving bridge-playing connoisseur Jake Winkman was actually initiated by N. A. L. in 1963 with How to Succeed at Murder Without Really Trying. However, after Universal-Award published the second Winkman entry, The Ace of Spies (1966), Von Elsner's first series thriller was reissued by the U. A. I. G. in 1967 as The Jake of Diamonds. The Winkman competition played into 1968 with The Jack of Hearts.

2) "Peter Winston" was devised by the U. A. I. G. as both the house cover and principal agent for their dossier on "The Adjusters." Acknowledging the general Carter-Killmaster design, the series consisted of: Assignment to Bahrein (1967), The ABC Affair (1967), Doomsday Vendetta (1968), The Glass Cipher (1968), and The Temple at Ilumquh (1969).

3) Recognized as a radical departure from the other U. A. I. G. members, Mallory T. Knight's Tim O'Shane-"The Man from T. O. M. C. A. T." series belonged to the sex-oriented class of Ted Mark's "The Man from O. R. G. Y." (see separate reference). The first O'Shane book, The Dozen Deadly Dragons of Joy, was published in 1967, and the T. O. M. C. A. T. file extended until 1971 with ten titles.

4) Don Smith's Phil Sherman-"Secret Mission" series was one of the first to reflect the changing climate of the Cold War. Beginning in 1968 with Secret Mission: Peking, Secret Mission: Prague, Secret Mission: Corsica, and Secret Mission: Morocco, Smith carried his action dossier into the mid-seventies with nearly twenty representative assignments.

5) In 1969 Albert Barker's Reefe King series and Sam Picard's

file on "The Notebooks" illustrated the U. A. I. G. 's diversity during the period.

Characterized by imitative plotting and characterization, Barker's two-volume King sequence included: Gift from Berlin (1969) and The Apollo Legacy (1970).

By contrast, Sam Picard's dossier focusing on The Notebooks (1969) probed the complexities of the politically motivated conspiracy, which in itself portended a trend of the seventies. Defined by an anonymous agent and skillful use of the first person, Picard supplemented his notebooks with Dead Man Running and The Man Who Never Was (both 1971).

Most of the PBO fare distributed by Universal-Award continued into the seventies, and a few new ones were introduced, notably Paul Richards' "Hot Line-Espionage" series.

To cultivate an active interest in the espionage genre, the U. A. I. G. published two entries aimed at the seasoned devotee, chiefly The Award Espionage Reader (1965), edited by Hans Stefan Santesson, and Arthur Kaplan's collection of classic tales of intrigue, The Fine Art of Espionage (1967), which offered the works of such undisputed masters as W. Somerset Maugham, Graham Greene, and J. P. Marquand, among others.

The U. A. I. G. 's efforts in the reprint sector were less extensive than the contributions of the Fawcett and N. A. L. /Signet Intelligence Groups (see separate references). This aspect of the U. A. I. G. 's activities during the sixties embodied two phases.

1) Three of Desmond Cory's Johnny Fedora books had already appeared as Signet paperbacks by the time Universal-Award took up the series.

In 1968 the U. A. I. G. issued Feramontov (1966) and Timelock (1967) as paperback spy entries while several of the earlier Fedora missions were published under new titles. Intrigue (1954) surfaced as Trieste in 1968; The Hitler Diamonds was the title given to the 1969 Universal-Award edition of Dead Man Falling. By 1971 eleven Cory titles had been reissued under the auspices of the U. A. I. G.

John Boland's dossier on "The Gentlemen" originally materialized in Britain in the late fifties and early sixties, with only scattered distribution in the United States. Two books in the series, The Gentlemen Reform (1961) and The Gentlemen at Large (1962), were distributed as Universal-Award paperbacks in 1968.

2) In the broader espionage range, the U. A. I. G. regularly featured the works of Victor Canning and John Creasey.

In 1970 Stephen Frances's John Gail series, which reportedly registered sales surpassing 10, 000, 000 in Europe, was less successfully promoted by the U. A. I. G. in the U. S. paperback market.

groups, the U. A. I. G. did
il the seventies, as typified
Alfred Hitchcock's Family
roject title for Victor Can-

Jniversal-Award properties
rena in 1977. Consequent-
he Tiger (1965) and The
e Charter imprint while new
gularly.

er, Sam Picard, Don Von
issued as Charter paper-
rrently known as Ace-
on Smith's "Secret Mis-
sal-Award contributions to
on the Charter list).

Frances, the aforemen-
nder the appropriate CWF

n London, Universal-Tandem
les in British territory, in-
cluding the Nick Carter series.   Like their American counterpart,
Universal-Tandem was terminated in 1977.

END OF CWF 70

† CWF 71.   VON ELSNER, DON †

BACKGROUND: Born in 1909 in Oak Park, Illinois. Don Byron
Von Elsner--singer, sales executive, industrial banker, and vice-
president of a construction firm--became a free-lance writer in the
early sixties. He entered the suspense field in 1961 with Those
Who Prey Together Slay Together, the first in his paperback series
about corporation sleuth David Danning.

While most of the Danning entries were classified as pure
mysteries, Countdown for a Spy (1966) blended the global secret
agent theme with the Danning formula. Most of these novels were
published by N. A. L.

Since the distribution of the detective-oriented Danning books
preceded the espionage wave of the mid-sixties, Von Elsner wasn't
placed within The N. A. L. /Signet Intelligence Group (see separate
reference). However, his involvement with N. A. L. played a major

role in the recruitment of the subject of this file, master bridge player-spy Jake Winkman.

In 1963 N. A. L. issued How to Succeed at Murder Without Really Trying as the first in a projected Winkman series. When Universal-Award published the second Winkman thriller, The Ace of Spies (1966), the latter house acquired the N. A. L. property and re-issued it in 1967 as The Jake of Diamonds. A third Winkman effort, The Jack of Hearts, followed in 1968.

Winkman's bridge acumen was derived from the author's status as a Life Master of the American Contract Bridge League and his term as a member of the Bridge World panel of consultants. Von Elsner was also knowledgeable in photography, golf, music, and the martial arts.

Unlike many CWF conspirators, Von Elsner maintained a professional life outside the publishing sector, chiefly as a successful real estate broker and appraiser in Hilo, Hawaii, the state which served as the common locale for Countdown for a Spy and The Jake of Diamonds.

A former constituent of the Mystery Writers of America, Von Elsner was a principal representative of the Universal-Award Intelligence Group (see separate reference).

CWF AGENT: Winkman, Jake.

CWF HISTORY: American; born in 1925. Jake Winkman, at times characterized as a "bridge bum," earned a sterling reputation as a championship bridge player; by the early sixties, he was known to have participated in at least twenty-six major annual tournaments.

These events were generally sponsored by the conferences of the American Contract Bridge League (A. C. B. L.), which gained Winkman access to some of the most exclusive hotels in the U. S. , from Florida to Hawaii.

Having achieved the honor of Life Master, signifying a player who had accumulated 300 master points from regional and national contests, Winkman developed a clientele of candidates wishing to meet the challenges of the A. C. B. L.

Winkman, known to all as Wink, prepared his students for the weekend competitions, which literally punctuated the average year in the bridge world.

Specifically, Winkman taught his clients to compete aggressively in the tournaments for fractional master points; the winner of a given weekend playoff was awarded 26 fractional master points, and once the participant has accrued 100 of these, he or she is bestowed with a single master point. The various levels of bridge mastery, on the basis of ascending master points, are as follows: 1) Junior Master = 1 master point, 2) Full Master = 20 master points, 3) National Master = 50 master points, 4) Senior Master = 100 master points, 5) Advanced Senior Master = 200 master points, and 6) Life Master = 300 master points.

Many of Winkman's protegés attained the class of Life Master and went on to pursue the frenzied existence of the publicity-ridden bridge star.

Winkman's matchless proficiency in the art of contract bridge and the hypnotic locales to which he was beckoned, often exposed him to murder, deception, theft, and espionage. Full details under OPERATIVE DATA.

Winkman has remained on the tournament circuit, as chronicled in Von Elsner's Everything's Jake with Me (1980) and The Best of Jake Winkman (1981).

OPERATIVE DATA: Because Winkman was more dominantly associated with the Universal-Award Intelligence Group than the N. A. L. / Signet, Von Elsner's first entry is designated The Jake of Diamonds, followed by the original release date.

The Winkman series was one of the most inventive spy concepts to come out of the sixties, due partly to Von Elsner's impressive knowledge of bridge. A gifted mystery writer, Von Elsner deftly integrated his bridge acumen into a credibly effective suspense framework so that he immediately captured the reader's interest.

However, Von Elsner's unique narrative approach to the series elevated Winkman, with a world-class adroitness in a high-risk quest, above the level of the archetypal secret agent.

In The Jake of Diamonds (1963), Von Elsner identified himself with Winkman in the first chapter and initiated the reader by revealing his objective of writing a tongue-in-cheek guide to tournament bridge. Having established this glib tone, Von Elsner achieved a startling contrast through the subsequent development of a compelling plot, set in the competitive world of contract bridge.

Essentially Von Elsner reached a wide audience by providing simple escapism through his self-parodying introduction, while satisfying the most seasoned suspense observer with precise descriptions of a perplexing game and a logically conceived story.

Delineating Jake Winkman's daring character and the intricate mechanics of championship bridge and the A. C. B. L., The Jake of Diamonds involved the Mid-Pacific Regional Tournament at the resplendent Princess Kaiulani Hotel in Honolulu, where Winkman was registered as a key contestant.

Penetrating the challenges of the regional game, Winkman encountered a savage murder, a valuable cache of missing diamonds, four venomously calculating women, and a relentless Chinese detective. He also included bridge expert Charlie Goren in the intrigues of this entry.

Von Elsner accelerated the pace in The Ace of Spies (1966). Winkman was engaged at the Summer Nationals Tournament, at the Sheraton Park Hotel in Washington, D. C., where one opponent was General Hunter Hayes, a former intelligence commander who served with distinction in Europe during World War II.

Authentically depicting Washington in a state of transition in the context of the Cold War, Von Elsner also conveyed an unusually tense bridge competition, accented by the explosive potential of the city.

The discovery of a mysterious murder victim in Winkman's New York hotel room, preceding the actual tournament, triggered the puzzling intervention of the F. B. I. and C. I. A. and was a link to the insidious motives concealed behind the glamor of the Mid-Pacific event in Washington.

Von Elsner heightened this entry with some richly deceptive character portraits, crucial to a meticulously planned scheme concerning the hijacking of commercial U. S. aircraft into Cuban territory.

The Ace of Spies was a remarkable accomplishment for Von Elsner as he chillingly fused the passion of contract bridge, strongly conceived characters, and a pulsating plot.

SUMMARY: In The Jake of Diamonds (1963) and The Ace of Spies (1966), Don Von Elsner captured the detailed trappings of professional bridge with a taut style that was both satisfying and informative, devising themes indigenous to the intensely pressured environment of championship bridge, and adapted to the polished finesse of Jake Winkman.

Winkman transcended the image of the jet-trekking secret agent marked by an insatiable taste for womanizing. All of Winkman's energy was focused on his bridge expertise, making him a distinctive figure of Cold War espionage.

Throughout the series Von Elsner strengthened his concept with the use of graphic table sketches, depicting the various tournaments during their most dramatic moments. However, it should be pointed out that this device was used earlier by Ian Fleming (see separate reference) in Moonraker (1955) to illustrate the bridge game between James Bond and Sir Hugo Drax.

STATUS: In 1980 Charter Books reissued The Ace of Spies (1966) to a fairly responsive audience. Two years later The Ace of Spies and The Jack of Hearts (1968) appeared under the M. Hardy imprint. Two newer entries, Everything's Jake with Me (1980) and The Best of Jake Winkman (1981), are also available from M. Hardy. SSP.

FIELD BIBLIOGRAPHY

Von Elsner, Don. The Ace of Spies. New York: Universal-Award, 1966. PBO.

_____. How to Succeed at Murder Without Really Trying. New York: New American Library, 1963. PBO. See also The Jake of Diamonds.

_____. The Jack of Hearts. New York: Universal-Award, 1968. PBO.

_____. The Jake of Diamonds. New York: Universal-Award, 1967. PBO. Reprint title for How to Succeed at Murder Without Really Trying.

CONSULT APPENDIX I FOR SERIES CONTINUATION

CONSULT APPENDIX II FOR SERIES TRANSITION

END OF CWF 71

† CWF 72. WADDELL, MARTIN †

BACKGROUND: Recent CWF inquiries have revealed that Mr. Waddell's agent is no longer engaged in the U.S. publishing sector.   In addition, Waddell's respective U.S. hardback and paperback publishers during the sixties, Stein & Day and Pocket Books, have no information on the mystery author in their current files.

The reviews of Mr. Waddell's four-volume dossier on Gerald Arthur Otley, the subject of this file, suggest that he is British. However, the certainty of this as Mr. Waddell's background remains unconfirmed.

Provided there is no cover identity involved, the author has been inactive in the field since the Otley series terminated in 1969. Waddell was credited that year with a non-mystery novel, Come Back When I'm Sober (1969).

CWF AGENT: Otley, Gerald Arthur.

CWF HISTORY: British subject. Exact date and place of birth un-known.

Described as parasitic and manipulative, Otley operated as a thief specializing in the lucrative antique market. Otley, establishing a number of contacts knowledgeable in outlets for rare collectibles, utilized his uniquely calculating talents to "satisfy" the needs of the "clients" who approached him.

Otley distinguished himself in the sexual arena, sharing notoriously passionate relationships with several females, including two alluring Englishwomen, known under the names of Grace and Jean.

Although achieving success in his clandestine pursuits, Otley was officially recorded as an unemployed actor.

No further information after 1969.

OPERATIVE DATA: To understand the basic concept of Waddell's spy concept, it is essential for the reader-agent to consider these two points:

1) Otley was conceived as a British anti-hero.

2) Otley reflected the growing contempt toward traditional English values, as expressed by an increasing number of young adults in the mid- and late sixties.

As did the protagonists of le Carré and Deighton (see separate references), Otley embodied the time in which he initially appeared.

Waddell adroitly integrated his working elements throughout the series, with a menacing note of unpredictability in each entry.

The author's accomplished use of the first person heightened the overall effect of suspense, and, unlike other serious espionage novelists of the period, Waddell preferred narrative energy to depiction of the alarming dangers of the Cold War.

In Otley (1966) Waddell's recalcitrant manipulator, after stealing the figurine of a hunchback, accepted an invitation to lodge at the London flat of a local antique collector, identified as Lambert.

The subsequent discovery of Lambert's body on Clapham Common implicated Otley in his murder, and he eventually found himself embroiled in the malefactions of a mysterious network, the I.C.S.

Anthony Boucher's evaluation of Otley in the New York Times Book Review emphasized the complexities of Waddell's cynical approach to the spy thriller:

> "A different (and in its way equally delightful) kind of wild spy story is Martin Waddell's Otley, a brightly-written, near-parody thriller with a fine anti-hero of the malcontent British generation. As I've often objected, most of today's spy fiction (and films and television) is too clear-cut.... Waddell has rediscovered the great principle of uncertainty, of early Ambler and early Hitchcock.... The result is fresh, funny, tricky, and often breathtaking."

Waddell skillfully maintained the biting satirical edge of Otley in Otley Pursued (1967). Acting more ready in the capacity of a secret agent, Otley penetrated a Neo-Nazi organization whose objectives were focused against Britain and France.

Once again Anthony Boucher praised the audacity of Waddell's glib hero: "Gerald Arthur Otley, second-rate actor, third-rate secret agent, and first-rate opportunist, is Martin Waddell's anti-heroic and entertaining contribution to the gallery of espionage...."

SUMMARY: Waddell's unconventional perception of the Cold War spy rates him a special place among his realistic allies for preserving a delicate balance of style and originality throughout his four Otley books.

The path laid by Waddell aided the modern espionage novel to evidence more radical tones, as represented by Adam Diment's Philip McAlpine (see separate reference).

In 1968 Pocket Books launched an imaginative campaign for Otley and Otley Pursued, which consisted of unusually vivid paperback covers depicting Otley in outrageously sexy situations of peril and intrigue.

British actor Tom Courtenay superbly portrayed Waddell's reluctant "provocateur" in a tightly adapted version of Otley, which Columbia distributed as a theatrical visual project in 1968. The late Romy Schneider and Alan Badel were also featured in the large European cast.

STATUS: Although the U.S. commercial response to Gerald Otley didn't quite measure up to Waddell's critical acceptance, it might be interesting to observe his performance in the present market, given Waddell's lack of concern with the specifics of the Cold War, and the continued success of le Carré and Deighton (see separate references). SOP.

FIELD BIBLIOGRAPHY

Waddell, Martin. Otley. New York: Stein & Day, 1966; New
   York: Pocket Books paperback, 1968. HB-R-MT.

————. Otley Forever. New York: Stein & Day, 1968. HB.

————. Otley Pursued. New York: Stein & Day, 1967; New
   York: Pocket Books paperback, 1968. HB-R.

————. Otley Victorious. New York: Stein & Day, 1969. HB.

END OF CWF 72

† CWF 73. WAYLAND, PATRICK †

BACKGROUND: Cover identity of Richard O'Connor, prolific American author of mysteries, biographies, and historical studies. Born in 1915 in LaPorte, Indiana.

O'Connor also worked briefly as an actor, appearing in two Broadway plays. Between 1936 and 1957 O'Connor was employed as a newspaperman in a number of large U.S. cities, among them Los Angeles and Washington.

O'Connor's first book, Thomas: Rock of Chickamunga, was published in 1948, but he continued his journalism career until 1957 when he became a full-time writer. Prior to his death in 1975, O'Connor produced over 60 books in both the fiction and non-fiction sectors.

Regarded as a leading biographer, O'Connor completed such penetrating studies as Wild Bill Hickok (1959), Black Jack Pershing (1961), and A Biography of John Reed (1967). O'Connor's 1957 portrait of Bat Masterson served as the basis for the popular home visual series with Gene Barry, and he also wrote several juvenile biographies, including Sitting Bull: War Chief of the Sioux (1968).

Equally acclaimed as a historian, O'Connor probed diverse subjects with Hell's Kitchen: The Roaring Days of New York's Wild Side (1958), An Informal History of the U.S. in the Far East, 1776-1968 (1969), The Oil Barons: Men of Greed and Grandeur (1971), (...).

O'Connor entered the suspense field in 1964, operating simultaneously under the identities of Frank Archer and Patrick Wayland.

As Archer, O'Connor conspired two mysteries involving private detective Joe Delaney, The Malabang Pearl (1964) and The Turquoise Spike (1967); and three non-series entries: Out of the Blue (1964), The Widow Watchers (1965), and The Naked Crusaders (1972). (Under the cover of John Burke, O'Connor expanded his biographical collection with Winged Legend: The Story of Amelia Earhart (1970).)

O'Connor's activities as Patrick Wayland concerned secret agent Lloyd Nicolson, the subject of this file, in Counterstroke (1964), Double Defector (1964), and The Waiting Game (1965).

Although O'Connor's works were distributed by various major publishers, his suspense efforts were associated primarily with Doubleday, and several of them appeared as Doubleday Crime Club editions. However, The Turquoise Spike was issued as a Fawcett-Gold Medal paperback.

CWF AGENT: Nicolson, Lloyd.

CWF HISTORY: American. Graduated with honors from West Point in 1951. By 1953 Nicolson was attached to the Eighth U.S. Army Division in Korea as a language expert.

During his posting in the Orient, Nicolson employed his acumen with the spoken word as a junior officer for G-2, revealing himself capable of mastering any language or dialect--a talent which served him well in the Cold War alleys of the Far East.

After completing his assignment in Korea, Nicolson, now a captain, was dispatched to the Pentagon for an indefinite period. For no apparent reason, Captain Nicolson's superior summoned him to his office in early 1960 and "suggested" that Nicolson embark on an "extended leave." The "suggestion" was actually an order and the "leave" was a conditional release: Captain Nicolson was transferred to an organization in New York, on record as the International Trade Research Bureau (I.T.R.B.). Nicolson was designated as "trade researcher."

In 1964 Nicolson lost his right leg when a car he was driving exploded in Mexico City, the result of a bomb planted in the motor. The I.T.R.B. lavished a generous amount of medical and prosthetic attention on Nicolson and he emerged with a remarkable aluminum leg that compensated for his physical deficiency.

Situated on Stone Street, in a building dominated by import and export firms, with Old Slip and the weathered East River docks a few blocks away, the New York-based I.T.R.B. was the field cover for a clandestine U.S. counterespionage network known as "Counterstroke." Objective: immediate counteraction against any threat to U.S. interests. Since the I.T.R.B. was privately financed, it possessed no association or allegiance to any of the official Western intelligence networks.

Nicolson was informed of new missions by a phone call from an "unregistered number" in New York--Whitehall 7-8242. Nicolson was fully briefed on his impending assignment and provision made for needed documents and funds. Nicolson's only connection with the I.T.R.B. was his "in-house" contact, a Mr. Cramer, and the regular deposit of cashier's checks to his account in a New York bank.

As key agent for "Counterstroke," Nicolson was authorized to travel to any global sector, including territories influenced by the U.S.S.R. and the Chi-Coms.

Nicolson was highly skilled in the use of firearms, especially the .38 caliber revolver, and proficient in unarmed combat techniques.

Despite his physical handicap, Nicolson served as a "Counterstroke" field operative for five years, although only three missions were recorded from 1964 to 1965.

No further record of either Nicolson of the I.T.R.B. - "Counterstroke" after 1965.

OPERATIVE DATA: When Richard O'Connor devised his Patrick Wayland cover for the "Counterstroke" project, he was still relatively new to the suspense field, despite his reputation as a historian-biographer.   The three-volume Nicolson series secured an enthusiastic audience.

Wayland's formula in the Nicolson books was a simple one: blistering action blended with gripping yet uncomplicated plots.   As Wayland, O'Connor displayed an admirable narrative precision in his ability to satisfy the demanding tastes of the espionage advocate.

Supplied with only two names, one being that of an immensely powerful U.S. lawyer, Nicolson's mission in Counterstroke (1964) was to avert a Chi-Com scheme to smuggle a multimillion dollar cache of heroin into the U.S.

Double Defector (1964) concerned Nicolson's assignment of finding two treacherous agents: Miller Hagen, a U.S. Army lieutenant who had disappeared with critical microfilms, and Don Sinclair, the devious "Counterstroke" operative who had been ordered to unmask Hagen as a traitor.   Wayland developed an unusually sharp line of tension as Nicolson pursued his quarry, testing "Counterstroke" resources from Washington to a Soviet spy cell in Montreal.

In The Waiting Game (1965) Nicolson was faced with the task of locating a beautiful Russian ballerina who had vanished from Kennedy Airport.

SUMMARY: Patrick Wayland's Lloyd Nicolson-"Counterstroke" dossier was marked by feverish action and compelling plots, with Wayland's sense of narrative balance placing it above the typical secret agent series.

Although Nicolson preceded the 007 mania by one year, it was 1968 before Counterstroke appeared in paperback. Consequently, the mass saturation evidenced in the paperback intrigue market by that time seriously hindered its competitive potential as a Paperback Library title.

Although Paperback Library promoted Counterstroke as the first in a reprinted Nicolson spy series, the response to the initial Wayland entry failed to warrant the future distribution of "Counterstroke" missions in the U.S. paperback sector.

STATUS: Considering the mass-production quality of current paperback espionage series fare, the literate tone of Patrick Wayland's "Counterstroke" file makes it an excellent candidate for reissue. Its satisfying readability conceivably would transcend the question of viability. SOP.

FIELD BIBLIOGRAPHY

Wayland, Patrick. Counterstroke. Garden City, N.Y.: Doubleday, 1964; New York: Paperback Library, 1968. HB-R.

_____. Double Defector. Garden City, N.Y.: Doubleday, 1964. HB.

_____. The Waiting Game. Garden City, N.Y.: Doubleday, 1965. HB.

END OF CWF 73

† CWF 74. WHITTINGTON, HARRY †

BACKGROUND: Born in 1915 in Ocala, Florida. Held a variety of jobs during the thirties, from postal clerk to advertising copywriter. Later worked as an editor for Labor Advocate and other publications. Served two years in the U.S. Navy.

Whittington became a successful author of paperback originals, notably in the mystery, western, and novelization categories.

In the suspense arena, Whittington's efforts have leaned toward the cynical, hard-boiled school, as typified by The Naked Jungle (1955), One Deadly Dawn (1957), Journey into Violence (1961), Hot As Fire, Cold As Ice (1962), (...).

Under the cover identity of Whit Harrison, Whittington has written such taut mysteries as Rapture Alley (1952) and Strip the Town Naked (1960). He has also written numerous books under the following names: Kel Holland, Harriet Kathryn Myers, Clay Stuart, Harry White, and Hallam Whitney.

While Whittington's works were published by several paperback houses, it was probably his association with Ace Books, dating back to the early fifties, that earned him the "Man from U.N.C.L.E." novelization assignment, The Doomsday Affair (1965). This espionage entry is the subject of this file.

Under the Ace imprint, Whittington has penned a plethora of mysteries and westerns, the latter genre represented by such novels as Searching Rider (1962), Drygulch Town (1963), Prairie Raiders (1963), and Valley of the Savage Men (1965). Some of his westerns have been featured in Ace's classic Double Western series.

Whittington established himself as a visual project writer with credits for Black Gold (1963); and two of his books, Desire in the Dust (1956) and A Ticket to Hell (1959), were made into theatrical visual projects.

Besides his U.N.C.L.E. novelization initiative, Whittington has adapted several visual efforts, namely Man in the Shadow (1957) and Charro! (1969), the latter starring Elvis Presley. Whittington has also scripted episodes for a host of home visual series, including "Lawman" and "The Alaskans."

Under his own name and the identities of Steve Phillips and Hondo Wells, Whittington has produced over 100 short stories and novelettes, which have appeared in such magazines as Male, Stag, Manhunt, Mammoth Western, and Detective Tales, among others.

A member of the Mystery Writers of America, Whittington once functioned as a board member, and has been affiliated with the Authors' Guild and the Western Writers of America. Representative of the Ace Intelligence Group (see separate reference).

CWF AGENTS: Solo, Napoleon, and Illya Kuryakin.

CWF HISTORIES: See also Avallone, Michael--CWF 6.

OPERATIVE DATA: Unlike the science-fiction-oriented contributions of John T. Phillifent and Thomas Stratton (see separate references), Harry Whittington's execution of The Doomsday Affair (1965) reflected a thoroughly developed mystery plot, blended with the U. N. C. L. E. format.

In this entry, Whittington meticulously conceived a sequence of seemingly isolated incidents, enacted in different geographical sectors, each of which played a crucial role in one of Solo and Kuryakin's most perplexing missions. These events are described below.

1) HONOLULU INTERNATIONAL AIRPORT: Solo was assigned to assist in the defection of a top T. H. R. U. S. H. agent, identified as Ursula Baynes-Neefirth. However, Ms. Baynes-Neefirth was killed when a lei of ginger flowers draped around her neck exploded.

2) ACAPULCO, MEXICO: Kuryakin shadowed one Sam Su Yan, a Chinese-American who reportedly had died in a 1963 plane crash. In 1965 U. N. C. L. E. targeted Su Yan as one of T. H. R. U. S. H. 's most lethal operatives.

3) THE HUNGRY PUSSYCAT--SAN FRANCISCO: Solo pursued a tempestuous cabaret performer known as Barbry Coast.

Whittington adroitly webbed these occurrences with several suspenseful elements: a clandestine laboratory concealed in the mountains of California, the activities of a treacherous enemy agent--Tixe Ylno, a cataclysmic atomic weapon, and a T.H.R.U.S.H. blueprint for destruction.

SUMMARY: Measured against the diversity of structure in other U. N. C. L. E. assignments herein, Harry Whittington's novelization, The Doomsday Affair, represents a balance between the unremitting pace of Avallone and McDaniel (see separate references) and the fantastic dimensions of Phillifent and Stratton (see separate references).

In addition to the typically graphic cover photographs, this entry contained detailed sketches of Solo and Kuryakin.

STATUS: See also Avallone, Michael--CWF 6.

FIELD BIBLIOGRAPHY

Whittington, Harry. The Doomsday Affair. New York: Ace Books, 1965. PBO. TN.

CONSULT ACE INTELLIGENCE GROUP FOR ADDITIONAL AUTHOR REFERENCES

END OF CWF 74

† CWF 75. WINSTON, PETER †

BACKGROUND: House cover. Similar in concept to the "creation" of Nick Carter (see separate reference), "Peter Winston" was devised as a cover identity by Universal-Award in 1967 for the development of "The Adjusters," a privately financed intelligence network in which Winston was engaged as an agent.

Represented within the Universal-Award Intelligence Group (see separate reference), this espionage series has been listed in certain sectors as novelization entries. However, no such acknowledgment existed on the original Universal-Award paperback editions, and recent field inquiries have failed to verify any home visual project under the title of "The Adjusters" in either the U.S. or British territories during the late sixties.

CWF AGENT: Winston, Peter.

CWF HISTORY: Principal member of a crack counterespionage unit, known as "The Adjusters."

Officially, Winston was employed by White Whittle Ltd., a global enterprise involved in construction, shipping, and other interests. The corporate head of this multinational combine, Edgar White Whittle, reportedly one of the richest men in the world, utilized contacts in the C.I.A. and the U.S. State Department in his private role as a guardian of world peace.

Secretly, Winston worked for a Whittle subsidiary, the International Adjustments Department--"The Adjusters."

Winston was known in the field as A-2. Whittle held the designation of A-1, unknown to his associations in the international business sector.

The appointed chief of "The Adjusters" was one Leslie Vandervelde and his key operatives included Mike Sawtelle, Fred Cotts, and a provocative French woman, Jeanne-Marie Martin.

"The Adjusters" were based in an impenetrable Georgetown residence, containing an extensive library suited to the demands of global intelligence. The headquarters for "The Adjusters" reflected the highest levels of exclusivity and security.

Winston was keenly proficient in armed combat, especially in the deployment of the .357 Magnum. Also skilled in the martial arts.

No further record after 1969.

OPERATIVE DATA: "The Adjusters" series was firmly structured in the mold of Nick Carter (see separate reference), with the emphasis on fast-paced action. The books reflected the crisp style fashioned by the Universal-Award Intelligence Group (see separate reference).

In Assignment to Bahrein (1967), "The Adjusters" were assigned to avert an assassination and potentially explosive situation in the war-ravaged Middle East.

The ABC Affair (1967) concerned Winston's confrontation with Christopher Donne, an immensely wealthy European conspirator, in his resplendent suite at Chicago's exclusive Conover House, and a diplomatic party in South America identified as the ABC group.

An insidious espionage network was at work in Doomsday Vendetta (1968). A-2, ordered to investigate a brutal murder in Tangier, eventually discovered an apocalyptic blueprint to destroy critical U.S. missile bases.

SUMMARY: Peter Winston's "The Adjusters" series faithfully followed the format of Nick Carter (see separate reference) and the category of paperback espionage fiction distributed by the Universal-Award Intelligence Group (see separate reference).

STATUS: In 1980 Charter Books reissued Assignment to Bahrein and The ABC Affair (both 1967), generating a receptive response in the competitive paperback intrigue market. Currently SOP, but subject to reactivation.

FIELD BIBLIOGRAPHY

Winston, Peter. The ABC Affair. New York: Universal-Award, 1967. PBO.

_____. Assignment to Bahrein. New York: Universal-Award, 1967. PBO.

_____. Doomsday Vendetta. New York: Universal-Award, 1968. PBO.

_____. The Glass Cipher. New York: Universal-Award, 1968. PBO.

_____. The Temple at Ilumquh. New York: Universal-Award, 1969. PBO.

CONSULT APPENDIX II FOR SERIES TRANSITION

END OF CWF 75

† CWF 76.   WOODHOUSE, MARTIN †

BACKGROUND: British espionage novelist who served as the first
lead writer for the home visual project, "The Avengers." (See also
Daniels, Norman--CWF 18, and Garforth, John--CWF 28.)

Born in 1932 in Romford, Essex, England, Woodhouse received degrees from Cambridge University and St. Mary's Hospital
Medical School, London.   (During his term at Cambridge, Woodhouse
sold science-fiction stories to various American pulp magazines.)

After completing his military obligation with the R. A. F.,
Woodhouse worked for one year as a research scholar with the
Medical Research Council Applied Psychology Unit at Cambridge.

Before scripting "The Avengers" in the early sixties, Woodhouse had adapted episodes for a children's home visual series and,
later, a theatrical comedy feature.

Woodhouse eventually left "The Avengers" in pursuit of a
career as an author of spy novels.   His first book, Tree Frog
(1966), enthusiastically received in both the U. S. and Britain, introduced Dr. Giles Yeoman, the subject of this file.

A distinguished member of the Institute of Electrical Engineers (Medical Division), Woodhouse built one of the world's first
pure logic computers and also designed a dashboard instrument that
has been accepted as standard aeronautical equipment.

Representative of the N. A. L. /Signet Intelligence Group (see
separate reference).

CWF AGENT: Yeoman, Dr. Giles.

CWF HISTORY: British subject.   Former R. A. F. pilot.   Entered
the field of aircraft research because of his interest in aeronautical
science.

Yeoman was often employed on a free-lance basis by "Seeker," otherwise known as the Scientific Section of the Department of
Special Intelligence.

Established in the immediate postwar period, "Seeker" functioned as a clearinghouse for atomic information.   By the time of
the Cold War, this duty had been passed on to another scientific
branch of the Ministry, "ELECTRON."

Yeoman was concerned with the detailed analysis of damaged
military aircraft, in recognition of his skill in the conception of
control system components.

Advancing into the dark corridors of ministry research, Yeoman was eventually accorded the status of scientist, and title of doctor.

By the mid-sixties Dr. Yeoman had achieved the rank of senior scientific officer with a research unit loosely attached to the Air Ministry, referred to as the Institute.

Headed by one Dr. Michaelson, the Institute was constantly arguing with the Admiralty over the utilization of a computer in their work. Ironically, the Admiralty refused to recognize that Dr. Yeoman and his research associate, Dr. McTeague, had computed the critical statistics for a series of defense projects bearing the code designation, "Flittermouse."

It was Dr. Yeoman's experience with ministry research that led to his subsequent involvement in the Tree Frog initiative, evaluated below.

OPERATIVE DATA: Leaning somewhat toward the cynical style of Len Deighton (see separate reference), Martin Woodhouse's Giles Yeoman series probed the impenetrable scientific façade of Cold War Britain in the face of the nation's declining global status.

The outlandish style of Woodhouse's approach to "The Avengers" was apparent in the Yeoman books, for he often infringed on the delicate boundaries of parody. Woodhouse's placement of Yeoman as a scientist accounted for a certain degree of this dominant tone, coupled with his glorified personification of English society (another facet frequently reflected in Woodhouse's treatment of "The Avengers").

Beginning with Tree Frog (1966) Woodhouse devoted meticulous attention to the inscrutable levels of the British scientific community and its contemptuous attitude toward the military establishment. But even with all these abstruse elements, he maintained a taut narrative manner throughout the series.

After receiving accurate information on Britain's pilotless, high-altitude reconnaissance aircraft Tree Frog, Dr. Yeoman was sent into the Austrian Alps to filter incorrect intelligence on the spy plane into an inimical sector.

Allied with a select group of Institute personnel, including statistician Binnie Abrams posing as his secretary, Dr. Yeoman infiltrated Al Qarif in the torturous Libyan Sahara where Tree Frog was manipulated in a devastating desert test.

The Los Angeles Herald Examiner endorsed Woodhouse's excursion into espionage: "Swift-paced and ultra-smooth suspense story ... Woodhouse is a master story craftsman and an outstanding writer."

Woodhouse preserved his unconventional motif beyond Tree Frog, especially so in Bush Baby (1968), the last series entry of the sixties.

Assigned to recover a top-secret seismology device, Dr. Yeoman encountered a lethal laser crystal, which was being pursued passionately by Chi-Com-financed agents.

SUMMARY: The cynical fashion Martin Woodhouse exhibited in his Giles Yeoman series reflected the influence of Len Deighton (see separate reference) on his basic format.

Woodhouse presented a somewhat idealistic view of England in the midst of the Cold War, intensified by the characterization of Yeoman as a dispassionate scientist and by the intricate structure of the British scientific world.

Despite the critical praise that greeted Yeoman when Tree Frog was published, the series ultimately failed to generate a strong sales response in the United States. By contrast, Woodhouse's offbeat brand of intrigue was widely embraced in his native Britain.

STATUS: The abstract complexion of the Dr. Yeoman docket does not suggest it as a likely reissue possibility. SOP.

FIELD BIBLIOGRAPHY

Woodhouse, Martin. Bush Baby. New York: Coward-McCann, 1968. HB-R. See also Bush Baby in Appendix I. See also Rock Baby below.

_____. Rock Baby. London: Heinemann, 1968. HB. British title for Bush Baby.

_____. Tree Frog. New York: Coward-McCann, 1966; New York: New American Library paperback, 1967. HB-R.

CONSULT APPENDIX I FOR SERIES CONTINUATION

END OF CWF 76

† CWF 77. YORK, ANDREW †

BACKGROUND: Cover identity of Christopher Robin Nicole, author of spy and historical fiction. Born in 1930 in Georgetown, Guyana.

Lured early by the attractions of global travel, Nicole left school at the age of sixteen and traveled extensively throughout the Caribbean, Europe, and the U.S., providing the exotic locales for secret agent Jonas Wilde, the subject of this file.

In 1969, three years after the Wilde series was initiated, Nicole recruited a second Cold War operative, Jonathan Anders, whose assignments were prefixed with the designation "Operation": Operation Destruct (1969), Operation Manhunt (1970), (...). He wrote the Anders books under his own name, as he had his historical novels. Then, as Robin Cade, Nicole penned the suspense effort, The Fear Dealers (1974).

However, it was the activities of Jonas Wilde that engraved Nicole's cover as Andrew York in the espionage field. Unlike other Cold War-era spies, Wilde remained "in place" until 1975.

Dark Passage (1976) suggested that Nicole was progressing away from the general intrigue genre, for his protagonist, Big Tommy Angel, developed as a fatalistic character.

In recent years Mr. Nicole has resided with his wife on Guernsey in the Channel Islands where he pursues his passion for bridge and chess, although not to the exclusion of his old love of travel, source of backgrounds for new fictional projects.

CWF AGENT: Wilde, Jonas.

CWF HISTORY: Born in Santiago, Chile, Jonas Wilde was the son of an Englishman, Harry Wilde, and his American wife, Cynthia. Tragically, Wilde's parents were killed in an airplane crash in 1953.

Wilde served in the British Army during both World War II and the Korean War, earning a reputation as a savage commando.

Shortly after the Korean conflict, Wilde was involved in a mysterious incident that resulted in his premature release from military duty. However, his particular talents were recalled in the mid-sixties by an independent, clandestine intelligence unit known as the Elimination Section, who tagged him for a hazardous mission concerning a Soviet spy master identified as Kieserit.

The Kieserit initiative also embodied the participation of a U.S. counterespionage organization, the Special Section, controlled by one Coolidge Lucinda.

Wilde's code name: "The Eliminator."

The Kieserit affair developed into one of the most explosive scandals of the Cold War, and, in the face of increasing centralization within the British Intelligence network, the Elimination Section was incorporated into the new operative system.

Shortly after this transition was fully executed in 1967, Wilde resumed his status as "The Eliminator" under Commander Mocka, Controller of the Elimination Section.

Wilde remained in the field as an assassin until 1975.

OPERATIVE DATA: Although in many respects York fashioned Jonas Wilde after James Bond, he intensified his agent's role as a liquidator until it dominated every facet of his personality.

The Guardian's evaluation of Wilde after publication of The Eliminator (1966), the first series entry, acknowledged this line: "Wilde has everything that James Bond had and perhaps more."

In The Eliminator, York defined the ambiguities of the Elimination Section and Wilde's function as "The Eliminator," intensifying Wilde's talent as the series' constant, and adapting the plots to reflect the Cold War and beyond.

Wilde allied with the Special Section in the Channel Islands to pursue K. G. B. strategist Kieserit.

Appointed as the Director of Soviet Counterintelligence (N. A. T. O. section), Kieserit returned in The Co-ordinator (1967), in which Wilde was under the orders of Commander Mocka.

In this entry Wilde was sanctioned to terminate a Scandinavian fashion magnate, identified as Gunnar Moel, known in intelligence sectors as an elusive master spy, the Swedish Falcon.

The Deviator (1969) focused on the assassination of Sir Everett Langtree, a prominent British metallurgical scientist whose knowledge was coveted by Kieserit and the K. G. B.

SUMMARY: Andrew York offered a taut portrait of the secret service "terminator" in his Jonas Wilde series.

Shortly after completing his visual-project assignment as Bulldog Drummond in Deadlier Than the Male (1967), Richard Johnson assumed the more dangerous role of Jonas Wilde-"The Eliminator" in Danger Route (United Artists), a 1968 adaptation of The Eliminator.

STATUS: Given the endurance of the Wilde series, and its similarity to the Bond books, York's dossier would perform well in the current espionage market. SOP.

FIELD BIBLIOGRAPHY

York, Andrew. The Co-ordinator. New York: J. B. Lippincott,

1967; New York: Lancer paperback, 1968.
HB-R.

_____. Danger Route. New York: Lancer paperback, 1968.
R.   MT.   Visual project title for The Eliminator.

_____. The Deviator. New York: J. B. Lippincott, 1969.
HB-R. See also The Deviator in Appendix I.

_____. The Dominator. London: Hutchinson, 1969. HB.

_____. The Eliminator. New York: J. B. Lippincott, 1966;
New York: Lancer paperback, 1967. HB-R. See also Danger
Route.

_____. The Predator. New York: J. B. Lippincott, 1968.
HB-R. See also The Predator in Appendix I.

CONSULT APPENDIX I FOR SERIES CONTINUATION

END OF CWF 77

†† THE COLD WAR FILE IS OFFICIALLY CLOSED ††

This appendix enumerates CWF series that continued
after 1969, incorporating both new releases and reprints of earlier works. Absence of a Cold War File
reference indicates that the series did not extend beyond 1969.

† CWF 1. AARONS, EDWARD S. †

Aarons, Edward S. Assignment: Afghan Dragon. New York:
Fawcett-Gold Medal, 1976. PBO.

_____. Assignment: Amazon Queen. New York: Fawcett-Gold
Medal, 1974. PBO.

_____. Assignment: Bangkok. New York: Fawcett-Gold Medal,
1972. PBO.

_____. Assignment: Black Gold. New York: Fawcett-Gold
Medal, 1975. PBO.

_____. Assignment: Ceylon. New York: Fawcett-Gold Medal,
1973. PBO.

_____. Assignment: Golden Girl. New York: Fawcett-Gold
Medal, 1972. PBO.

_____. Assignment: Maltese Maiden. New York: Fawcett-
Gold Medal, 1972. PBO.

_____. Assignment: Quayle Question. New York: Fawcett-
Gold Medal, 1975. PBO.

_____. Assignment: Silver Scorpion. New York: Fawcett-
Gold Medal, 1973. PBO.

_____. Assignment: Star Stealers. New York: Fawcett-Gold
Medal, 1970. PBO.

_____. Assignment: Sumatra. New York: Fawcett-Gold Medal,
1974. PBO.

_____. Assignment: Tokyo. New York: Fawcett-Gold Medal,
1971. PBO.

_____. Assignment: Unicorn. New York: Fawcett-Gold Medal,
1976. PBO.

_____. Assignment: White Rajah. New York: Fawcett-Gold
Medal, 1970. PBO.

Aarons, Will B. Assignment: Mermaid. New York: Fawcett-
Gold Medal, 1979. PBO.

_____. Assignment: Sheba. New York: Fawcett-Gold Medal,
1976. PBO.

_____. Assignment: 13th Princess. New York: Fawcett-Gold
Medal, 1977. PBO.

_____. Assignment: Tiger Devil. New York: Fawcett-Gold
Medal, 1977. PBO.

_____. Assignment: Tyrant's Bride. New York: Fawcett-
Gold Medal, 1980. PBO.

† CWF 5.   ATLEE, PHILIP   †

Atlee, Philip. The Black Venus Contract. New York: Fawcett-
Gold Medal, 1975. PBO.

_____. The Canadian Bomber Contract. New York: Fawcett-
Gold Medal, 1971. PBO.

_____. The Fer-de-Lance Contract. New York: Fawcett-Gold
Medal, 1970. PBO.

_____. The Judah Lion Contract. New York: Fawcett-Gold
Medal, 1972. PBO.

_____. The Kiwi Contract. New York: Fawcett-Gold Medal,
1972. PBO.

_____. The Kowloon Contract. New York: Fawcett-Gold
Medal, 1974. PBO.

_____. The Last Domino Contract. New York: Fawcett-Gold
Medal, 1976. PBO.

_____. The Makassar Straits Contract. New York: Fawcett-
Gold Medal, 1976. PBO.

_____. The Shankill Road Contract. New York: Fawcett-Gold
Medal, 1973. PBO.

_____. The Spice Route Contract. New York: Fawcett-Gold
Medal, 1973. PBO.

_____. The Underground Cities Contract. New York: Fawcett-
Gold Medal, 1974. PBO.

_____. The White Wolverine Contract. New York: Fawcett-
Gold Medal, 1971. PBO.

† CWF 6. AVALLONE, MICHAEL †

Avallone, Michael. Death Dives Deep. New York: New American
Library, 1971. PBO. (Ed Noon)

_____. Little Miss Murder. New York: New American Library,
1971. PBO. (Ed Noon)

† CWF 8. BARKER, ALBERT †

Barker, Albert. The Apollo Legacy. New York: Universal-Award,
1970. PBO.

† CWF 9. BLACK, GAVIN †

Black, Gavin. A Big Wind for Summer. London: Collins, 1975;
New York: Harper and Row, 1976. HB-HB.

_____. The Bitter Tea. New York: Harper and Row, 1972;
London: Collins, 1973. HB-HB.

_____. The Cold Jungle. New York: Popular Library paper-
back, 1970. R.

_____. The Eyes Around Me. New York: Popular Library pa-
perback, 1970. R.

_____. The Golden Cockatrice. London: Collins, 1974; New
York: Harper and Row, 1975. HB-HB.

_____.   A Time for Pirates.   New York: Harper and Row, 1971.
HB.

_____.   A Wind of Death.   New York: Popular Library paper-
back, 1970.   R.

_____.   You Want to Die, Johnny?   New York: Popular Library
paperback, 1970.   R.

† CWF 11.   BREWER, GIL †

Brewer, Gil.   Appointment in Cairo.   New York: Ace Books, 1970.
      PBO.   TN.   ("It Takes a Thief")

† CWF 13.   CAILLOU, ALAN †

Caillou, Allan.   Assault on Agathon.   New York: Avon Books, 1972.
      PBO.

_____.   Assault on Aimata.   New York: Avon Books, 1975.
PBO.

_____.   Assault on Fellawi.   New York: Avon Books, 1972.
PBO.

† CWF 14.   CARTER, NICK †

Carter, Nick.   Agent Counter Agent.   New York: Universal-Award,
      1973.   PBO.

_____.   And Next the King.   New York: Charter Books, 1980.
PBO.

_____.   Appointment in Haiphong.   New York: Charter Books,
1982.   PBO.

_____.   The Arab Plague.   New York: Universal-Award, 1970.
PBO.   See also The Slavemaster.

_____.   The Asian Mantrap.   New York: Charter Books, 1979.
PBO.

_____. The Gallagher Plot. New York: Universal-Award, 1976.
PBO.

_____. The Golden Bull. New York: Charter Books, 1981.
PBO.

_____. The Greek Summit. New York: Charter Books, 1983.
PBO.

_____. The Green Wolf Connection. New York: Universal-
Award, 1976. PBO.

_____. Hawaii. New York: Charter Books, 1979. PBO.

_____. A High Yield in Death. New York: Universal-Award,
1976. PBO.

_____. Hour of the Wolf. New York: Universal-Award, 1973.
PBO.

_____. The Hunter. New York: Charter Books, 1982. PBO.

_____. Ice Bomb Zero. New York: Universal-Award, 1971.
PBO.

_____. Ice Trap Terror. New York: Universal-Award, 1974.
PBO.

_____. Inca Death Squad. New York: Universal-Award, 1972.
PBO.

_____. The Israeli Connection. New York: Charter Books,
1982. PBO.

_____. The Jamaican Exchange. New York: Charter Books,
1979. PBO.

_____. The Jerusalem File. New York: Universal-Award,
1975. PBO.

_____. Jewel of Doom. New York: Universal-Award, 1970.
PBO.

_____. Katmandu Contract. New York: Universal-Award, 1975.
PBO.

_____. The Kremlin File. New York: Universal-Award, 1973.
PBO.

_____. The Last Samurai. New York: Charter Books, 1982.
PBO.

_____. The Liquidator. New York: Universal-Award, 1973.
PBO.

_____. The List. New York: Universal-Award, 1976. PBO.

_____. The Man Who Sold Death. New York: Universal-Award,
1974. PBO.

_____. The Mark of Cosa Nostra. New York: Universal-
Award, 1971. PBO.

_____. Massacre in Milan. New York: Universal-Award, 1974.
PBO.

_____. The Mendoza Manuscript. New York: Charter Books,
1982. PBO.

_____. The Mind Killers. New York: Universal-Award, 1970.
PBO.

_____. Moscow. New York: Universal-Award, 1970. PBO.

_____. The N-3 Conspiracy. New York: Universal-Award,
1974. PBO.

_____. The Nichovev Plot. New York: Universal-Award, 1976.
PBO.

_____. Nick Carter-100. New York: Universal-Award, 1975.
PBO. Special Collector's Edition: Dr. Death, the 100th Killmaster novel; Run-Spy-Run, the first Nick Carter espionage
thriller; and the Nick Carter detective story, "The Preposterous
Theft."

_____. Night of the Avenger. New York: Universal-Award,
1973. PBO.

_____. Norwegian Typhoon. New York: Charter Books, 1982.
PBO.

_____. The Nowhere Weapon. New York: Charter Books,
1979. PBO.

_____. The Omega Terror. New York: Universal-Award,
1972. PBO.

_____. Operation: McMurdo Sound. New York: Charter Books,
1982. PBO.

_____. Our Agent in Rome is Missing. New York: Universal-
Award, 1973. PBO.

_____. The Ouster Conspiracy. New York: Charter Books,
1981. PBO.

_____. The Pamplona Affair. New York: Charter Books, 1978.
PBO.

_____. The Parisian Affair. New York: Charter Books, 1981.
PBO.

_____. The Peking Dossier. New York: Universal-Award,
1973. PBO.

_____. The Pemex Chart. New York: Charter Books, 1979.
PBO.

_____. Pleasure Island. New York: Charter Books, 1981.
PBO.

_____. The Puppet Master. New York: Charter Books, 1982.
PBO.

_____. The Q-Man. New York: Charter Books, 1981. PBO.

_____. Race of Death. New York: Charter Books, 1978.
PBO.

_____. Red Rebellion. New York: Universal-Award, 1970.
PBO.

_____. The Redolmo Affair. New York: Charter Books, 1979.
PBO.

_____. Reich Four. New York: Charter Books, 1979. PBO.

_____. Retreat for Death. New York: Charter Books, 1982.
PBO.

_____. Revenge of the Generals. New York: Charter Books,
1978. PBO.

_____. The Satan Trap. New York: Charter Books, 1979.
PBO.

_____. Sign of the Cobra. New York: Universal-Award, 1974.
PBO.

_____. Sign of the Prayer Shawl. New York: Universal-
Award, 1976. PBO.

_____. Six Bloody Summer Days. New York: Universal-
Award, 1975. PBO.

_____. The Slavemaster. London: Universal-Tandem, 1970.
PBO. British title for The Arab Plague.

_____. The Snake Flag Conspiracy. New York: Universal-
Award, 1976. PBO.

_____. Society of Nine. New York: Charter Books, 1981.
PBO.

_____. Solar Menace. New York: Charter Books, 1981. PBO.

_____. The Spanish Connection. New York: Universal-Award,
1973. PBO.

_____. Strike Force Terror. New York: Universal-Award,
1973. PBO.

_____. Strike of the Hawk. New York: Charter Books, 1980.
PBO. Contains two Nick Carter books: Strike of the Hawk
(1980) and reissue of Double Identity (Universal-Award, 1967).
See also Double Identity in Appendix II.

_____. The Strontium Code. New York: Charter Books, 1981.
PBO.

_____. Suicide Seat. New York: Charter Books, 1980. PBO.

_____. Tarantula Strike. New York: Charter Books, 1980.
PBO.

_____. Target: Doomsday Island. New York: Universal-
Award, 1973. PBO.

_____. Ten Times Dynamite. New York: Charter Books, 1980.
PBO.

_____. Thunderstrike in Syria. New York: Charter Books,
1979. PBO.

_____. Time Clock of Death. New York: Universal-Award,
1970. PBO.

_____. The Treason Game. New York: Charter Books, 1982.
PBO.

_____. Triple Cross. New York: Universal-Award, 1976.
PBO.

_____. Trouble in Paradise. New York: Charter Books, 1978.
PBO.

_____. Turkish Bloodbath. New York: Charter Books, 1981.
PBO.

_____. The Turncoat. New York: Universal-Award, 1976.
PBO.

_____. Typhoon Ray. New York: Charter Books, 1980. PBO.

_____. The Ultimate Code. New York: Universal-Award, 1975.
PBO.

_____. Under the Wall. New York: Charter Books, 1978.
PBO.

_____. Vatican Vendetta. New York: Universal-Award, 1974.
PBO.

_____. The Vulcan Disaster. New York: Universal-Award,
1976. PBO.

_____. War from the Clouds. New York: Charter Books,
1980. PBO.

_____. The Z-Document. New York: Universal-Award, 1975.
PBO.

† CWF 16. CORY, DESMOND †

Cory, Desmond. The Gestapo File. New York: Universal-Award
paperback, 1971. R. U.S. paperback title for This Traitor,
Death.

_____. The Nazi Assassins. New York: Universal-Award
paperback, 1970. R. U.S. paperback title for Secret Ministry.

_____. Secret Ministry. See also CWF 16 and The Nazi
Assassins.

_____. Sunburst. New York: Walker, 1971. HB.

_____. This Traitor, Death. See also CWF 16 and The Ges-
tapo File.

† CWF 17. CREASEY, JOHN †

Creasey, John. The Blight. New York: Lancer paperback, 1970.
R.

_____. The Children of Despair. See also CWF 17 and The
Killers of Innocence.

_____. The Children of Hate. See also CWF 17 and The Kill-
ers of Innocence.

_____. Dark Harvest. New York: Walker, 1977. HB.

_____. Death in the Rising Sun. New York: Walker, 1976.
HB.

_____. The Depths. New York: Berkley-Medallion paperback,
1970. R.

_____. The Famine. New York: Lancer paperback, 1970. R.

_____. The Flood. New York: Lancer paperback, 1970. R.

_____. The House of the Bears. New York: Walker, 1975.
HB.

_____. The Inferno. New York: Berkley-Medallion paperback,
1970. R.

_____. The Insulators. London: Hodder, 1972; New York:
Walker, 1973. HB-HB.

_____. The Killers of Innocence. New York: Walker, 1971;
New York: Universal-Award paperback, 1973. HB-R. U.S.
title for The Children of Despair and The Children of Hate.

_____. The Mists of Fear. New York: Walker, 1977. HB.

_____. The Oasis. New York: Walker, 1970. HB.

_____. The Perilous Country. New York: Walker, 1973. HB.
U.S. title for The Valley of Fear.

_____. The Plague of Silence. New York: Lancer paperback,
1970. R.

_____. The Sleep. New York: Lancer paperback, 1971. R.

_____. The Smog. London: Hodder, 1970; New York: Walker,
1971; New York: Universal-Award paperback, 1973. HB-HB-R.

_____. The Touch of Death. New York: Lancer paperback,
1971. R.

_____. Traitor's Doom. New York: Walker, 1970; New York:
Universal-Award paperback, 1972. HB-R.

_____. The Unbegotten. London: Hodder, 1971; New York:
Walker, 1972. HB-HB.

_____. The Valley of Fear. See also CWF 17 and The Perilous
Country.

_____. The Voiceless Ones. London: Hodder, 1973; New York:
Walker, 1974. HB-HB.

_____. The Wings of Peace. New York: Walker, 1978. HB.

† CWF 18.   DANIELS, NORMAN †

Daniels, Norman. Operation S-L. New York: Pyramid Publica-
    tions, 1971. PBO. (Keith)

† CWF 19.   DARK, JAMES †

Dark, James. Sea Scrape. Sydney, Australia: Horwitz Publica-
    tions, 1970; New York: New American Library, 1971. PBO-
    PBO.

† CWF 21.   DEIGHTON, LEN †

Deighton, Len. Spy Story. New York: Harcourt Brace Jovanovich,
    1974; New York: Pocket Books paperback, 1975. HB-R.

† CWF 22.   DIMENT, ADAM †

Diment, Adam. Think Inc. London: Joseph, 1971.

† CWF 23.   EASTWOOD, JAMES †

Eastwood, James. Come Die with Me. London: Macmillan, 1970.
    HB. British title for Diamonds Are Deadly.

_____. Diamonds Are Deadly. New York: Pocket Books paper-
    back, 1971. R.

† CWF 25.   FLEMING, IAN †

Gardner, John. For Special Services. New York: Coward,
    McCann, and Geoghegan, 1982; New York: Berkley paperback,
    1983. HB-R.

_____. License Renewed. New York: Richard Marek, 1981;
New York: Berkley paperback, 1982. HB-R. A third Gardner-
Bond entry is scheduled for 1983.

Wood, Christopher. James Bond and Moonraker. New York: Jove
Books, 1979. PBO. MN.

_____. The Spy Who Loved Me. New York: Warner Books,
1977. PBO. MN.

† CWF 26. GALWAY, ROBERT C. †

Galway, Robert C. Assignment: Death Squad. London: Hale,
1970. HB.

_____. Assignment: Sydney. London: Hale, 1970. HB.

† CWF 27. GARDNER, JOHN †

Gardner, John. Air Apparent. New York: Putnam, 1971. HB.
U.S. title for The Airline Pirates.

_____. The Airline Pirates. London: Hodder, 1970. HB.
See also Air Apparent.

_____. A Killer for a Song. London: Hodder, 1975. HB.

_____. Traitor's Exit. London: Muller, 1970. HB.

† CWF 28. GARFORTH, JOHN †

Cave, Peter. The House of Cards. New York: Berkley, 1979.
PBO. TN. ("The New Avengers")

† CWF 29. GARNER, WILLIAM †

Garner, William. The Us or Them War. New York: Berkley-
Medallion paperback, 1970. R.

† CWF 30. GILMAN, DOROTHY †

Gillman, Dorothy. The Amazing Mrs. Pollifax. Garden City, N.Y.:
Doubleday, 1970; London: Hale, 1971; New York: Fawcett-Crest
paperback, 1972. HB-HB-R.

_____. The Elusive Mrs. Pollifax. Garden City, N. Y.: Double-
day, 1971; London: Hale, 1973; New York: Fawcett-Crest paperback, 1972. HB-HB-R.

_____. Mrs. Pollifax on Safari. Garden City, N. Y.: Double-
day, 1977; New York: Fawcett-Crest paperback, 1978. HB-R.

_____. Mrs. Pollifax, Spy. New York: Fawcett-Crest paper-
back, 1971. R. MT. Visual project title for The Unexpected
Mrs. Pollifax. See also CWF 30.

_____. A Palm for Mrs. Pollifax. Garden City, N. Y.: Double-
day, 1973; London: Hale, 1974; New York: Fawcett-Crest paperback, 1974. HB-HB-R.

_____. The Unexpected Mrs. Pollifax. See also CWF 30 and
Mrs. Pollifax, Spy.

† CWF 31. GRAY, ROD †

Gray, Rod. The Big Snatch. New York: Tower Books, 1970.
PBO. See also Sock It to Me.

_____. Blow My Mind. New York: Tower Books, 1971. PBO.

_____. The Copulation Explosion. New York: Tower Books,
1970. PBO.

_____. Go for Broke. New York: Tower Books, 1975. PBO.

_____. Kill Her with Love. New York: Tower Books, 1975.
PBO.

_____. Lady in Heat. New York: Tower Books, 1970. PBO.

_____. The Lady Takes It All Off. New York: Tower Books,
1971. PBO.

_____. Laid in the Future. New York: Tower Books, 1970.
PBO.

_____. Skin Deep Game. New York: Tower Books, 1972.
PBO.

_____. Sock It to Me. New York: Tower Books, 1974. R.
Reprint title for The Big Snatch.

_____. Turned On to L. U. S. T. New York: Tower Books,
1971. PBO.

† CWF 32. HAGGARD, WILLIAM †

Haggard, William. The Bitter Harvest. London: Cassell, 1971.
    HB. See also Too Many Enemies.

_____. The Hardliners. London: Cassell, 1970; New York:
Walker, 1971. HB-HB.

_____. The Median Line. New York: Walker, 1981. HB.

_____. The Mischief Makers. New York: Walker, 1982. HB.

_____. The Money Men. New York: Walker, 1981. HB.

_____. The Notch on the Knife. New York: Walker, 1973.
    HB. U. S. title for The Old Masters.

_____. The Old Masters. London: Cassell, 1973. HB. See
also The Notch on the Knife.

_____. The Poison People. New York: Walker, 1978. HB.

_____. The Scorpion's Tale. New York: Walker, 1975. HB.

_____. Too Many Enemies. New York: Walker, 1971. HB.
U. S. title for The Bitter Harvest.

_____. Visa to Limbo. New York: Walker, 1979. HB.

_____. Yesterday's Enemy. New York: Walker, 1976. HB.

† CWF 33. HALL, ADAM †

Hall, Adam. The Kobra Manifesto. Garden City, N. Y.: Doubleday, 1976; New York: Dell paperback, 1978. HB-R.

_____. The Mandarin Cypher. Garden City. N. Y.: Doubleday,
1975; New York: Dell paperback, 1977. HB-R.

_____. The Peking Target. New York: Playboy Press, 1982;
New York: Playboy paperback, 1983. HB-R.

_____. The Scorpion Signal. Garden City, N.Y.: Doubleday,
1980; New York: Playboy paperback, 1981. HB-R.

_____. The Sinkiang Executive. Garden City, N.Y.: Double-
day, 1978. HB.

_____. The Striker Portfolio. New York: Pyramid paperback,
1970. R.

_____. The Tango Briefing. Garden City, N.Y.: Doubleday,
1973; New York: Dell paperback, 1974. HB-R.

_____. The Warsaw Document. Garden City, N.Y.: Double-
day, 1970; London: Heinemann, 1971; New York: Pyramid
paperback, 1972. HB-HB-R.

† CWF 34. HAMILTON, DONALD †

Hamilton, Donald. The Intimidators New York: Fawcett-Gold
Medal, 1974. PBO.

_____. The Intriguers. New York: Fawcett-Gold Medal, 1973.
PBO.

_____. The Poisoners. New York: Fawcett-Gold Medal, 1971.
PBO.

_____. The Retaliators. New York: Fawcett-Gold Medal,
1976. PBO.

_____. The Revengers. New York: Fawcett-Gold Medal, 1982.
PBO.

_____. The Terminators. New York: Fawcett-Gold Medal,
1975. PBO.

_____. The Terrorizers. New York: Fawcett-Gold Medal,
1977. PBO.

† CWF 35. HARVESTER, SIMON †

Harvester, Simon. Forgotten Road. New York: Walker, 1974. HB.

_____. Moscow Road. London: Jarrolds, 1970; New York:
Walker, 1971; New York: Manor paperback, 1974. HB-HB-R.

_____. Nameless Road. New York: Walker, 1970. HB.

_____. Sahara Road. New York: Walker, 1972; New York:
Manor paperback, 1974. HB-R.

_____. Siberian Road. New York: Walker, 1976. HB. Pub-
lished posthumously.

_____. Zion Road. New York: MacFadden-Bartell paperback,
1970. R.

† CWF 37. HUNT, E. HOWARD †

Hunt, E. Howard. The Coven. New York: Weybright, 1971. HB.
(As David St. John)

_____. Diabolus. New York: Weybright, 1971; New York:
Fawcett-Crest paperback, 1972. HB-R. (As St. John)

_____. The Sorcerers. New York: Fawcett-Crest paperback,
1970. R. (As St. John)

† CWF 39. KNIGHT, MALLORY T. †

Knight, Mallory T. The Bra-Burners' Brigade. New York:
Universal-Award, 1971. PBO.

_____. The Doom Dollies. New York: Universal-Award, 1970.
PBO.

† CWF 40. LEASOR, JAMES †

Leasor, James. A Host of Extras. London: Heinemann, 1973.
HB.

_____. Love-All. London: Heinemann, 1971. HB.

† CWF 41.   Le CARRE, JOHN †

le Carré, John.   The Honourable Schoolboy.   New York: Knopf,
1977; New York: Bantam paperback, 1978.   HB-R.

_____.   The Quest for Karla.   New York: Knopf, 1982.   HB.
Omnibus Edition: The Honourable Schoolboy, Smiley's People,
and Tinker, Tailor, Soldier, Spy.

_____.   Smiley's People.   New York: Knopf, 1980; New York:
Bantam paperback, 1980.   HB-R.

_____.   Tinker, Tailor, Soldier, Spy.   New York: Knopf, 1974;
New York: Bantam paperback, 1975.   HB-R.

† CWF 43.   LLEWELLYN, RICHARD †

Llewellyn, Richard.   But We Didn't Get the Fox.   London: Joseph,
1970, New York: Popular Library paperback, 1970.   HB-R.

_____.   The Night Is a Child.   Garden City, N. Y.:   Doubleday,
1972; London: Joseph, 1974; New York: Pyramid paperback,
1974.   HB-HB-R.

_____.   White Horse to Banbury Cross.   Garden City, N. Y.:
Doubleday, 1970; London: Joseph, 1972; New York: Pyramid
paperback, 1973.   HB-HB-R.

† CWF 44.   McCUTCHAN, PHILIP †

McCutchan, Philip.   The All-Purpose Bodies.   New York: John
Day, 1970.   HB.

_____.   Hartinger's Mouse.   London: Harrap, 1970.   HB.

_____.   This Drakotny ...   London: Harrap, 1971.   HB.

† CWF 46.   MAIR, GEORGE B. †

Mair, George B.   Crimson Jade.   London: Jarrolds, 1971.   HB.

_____. Paradise Spells Danger. London: Jarrolds, 1973. HB.

_____. A Wreath of Camellias. London: Jarrolds, 1970. HB.

† CWF 47. MARK, TED †

Mark, Ted. Around the World Is Not a Trip. New York: Dell
Books, 1973. PBO.

_____. The Beauty and the Bug. New York: Dell Books, 1973.
        PBO.

_____. Dial O for O. R. G. Y. New York: Dell Books, 1973.
        PBO.

_____. The Girls from O. R. G. Y. New York: Manor Books,
1975. PBO.

_____. Here's Your O. R. G. Y. New York: Berkley-Medallion,
1970. PBO.

_____. Honeymoon in Honolulu. New York: Dell Books, 1974.
        PBO.

_____. Regina Blue. New York: Dell Books, 1972. PBO.

† CWF 48. MARLOWE, DAN J. †

Marlowe, Dan J. Flashpoint. New York: Fawcett-Gold Medal,
    1970. PBO. See also Operation Flashpoint.

_____. Operation Breakthrough. New York: Fawcett-Gold
Medal, 1971. PBO.

_____. Operation Checkmate. New York: Fawcett-Gold Medal,
1972. PBO.

_____. Operation Counterpunch. New York: Fawcett-Gold
Medal, 1976. PBO.

_____. Operation Deathmaker. New York: Fawcett-Gold
Medal, 1975. PBO.

_____. Operation Drumfire. New York: Fawcett-Gold Medal,
1972. PBO.

_____. Operation Flashpoint. New York: Fawcett-Gold Medal, 1970. PBO. Reissue title for Flashpoint. Cover of the second edition emphasized Marlowe's Mystery Writers of America Paperback Award.

_____. Operation Hammerlock. New York: Fawcett-Gold Medal, 1974. PBO.

_____. Operation Stranglehold. New York: Fawcett-Gold Medal, 1973. PBO.

_____. Operation Whiplash. New York: Fawcett-Gold Medal, 1973. PBO.

† CWF 53. MUNRO, JAMES †

Munro, James. The Innocent Bystanders. New York: Knopf, 1970; New York: Bantam paperback, 1971. HB-R.

† CWF 54. THE N. A. L. /SIGNET INTELLICENCE GROUP †

Fleming, Ian. The Man with the Golden Gun. New York: New American Library paperback, 1974. R. MT.

_____. Octopussy. New York: New American Library paperback, 1983. R. MT.

Spillane, Mickey. The Delta Factor. New York: New American Library paperback, 1971. R. MT.

† CWF 55. O'DONNELL, PETER †

O'Donnell, Peter. Dragon's Claw. London: Souvenir Press, 1979. HB.

_____. The Impossible Virgin. Garden City, N. Y.: Doubleday, 1971. HB.

_____. Last Day in Limbo. London: Souvenir Press, 1976. HB.

_____. _Pieces of Modesty_. London: Pan Books, 1972. PBO.
Short-story collection.

_____. _The Silver Mistress_. London: Souvenir Press, 1973;
London: Archival Press, 1981. HB-R.

_____. _A Taste for Death_. New York: Fawcett-Crest paper-
back, 1971. R.

† CWF 56. ORAM, JOHN †

Oram, John. _The Stone-Cold Dead in the Market Affair_. New
York: Ace Books, 1970. PBO. TN. ("The Man from
U. N. C. L. E. ")

† CWF 59. PICARD, SAM †

Picard, Sam. _Dead Man Running_. New York: Universal-Award,
1971. PBO.

_____. _The Man Who Never Was_. New York: Universal-
Award, 1971. PBO.

† CWF 62. SANGSTER, JIMMY †

Sangster, Jimmy. _Touch Gold_. New York: Norton, 1970. HB.

_____. _Touchfeather_. New York: Berkley-Medallion paperback,
1970. R.

_____. _Touchfeather Too_. New York: Norton, 1970; New York:
Berkley-Medallion paperback, 1971. HB-R.

† CWF 64. SMITH, DON †

Smith, Don. _The Bavarian Connection_. New York: Charter Books,
1978. PBO.

_____. The Dalmatian Tapes. New York: Universal-Award,
1976. PBO.

_____. Death Stalk in Spain. New York: Universal-Award,
1972. PBO.

_____. Haitian Vendetta. New York: Universal-Award, 1973.
PBO.

_____. The Libyan Contract. New York: Universal-Award,
1974. PBO.

_____. The Marseilles Enforcer. New York: Universal-Award,
1972. PBO.

_____. Night of the Assassin. New York: Universal-Award,
1972. PBO.

_____. The Peking Connection. New York: Universal-Award,
1975. PBO.

_____. Secret Mission: Angola. New York: Universal-Award,
1970. PBO.

_____. Secret Mission: Athens. New York: Universal-Award,
1971. PBO.

_____. Secret Mission: Cairo. New York: Universal-Award,
1970. PBO.

_____. Secret Mission: The Kremlin Plot. New York:
Universal-Award, 1971. PBO.

_____. Secret Mission: Munich. New York: Universal-Award,
1970. PBO.

_____. Secret Mission: North Korea. New York: Universal-
Award, 1970. PBO.

_____. The Strausser Transfer. New York: Charter Books,
1978. PBO.

† CWF 68. THOMAS, ROSS †

Thomas, Ross. The Backup Men. New York: William Morrow,
1971; New York: Pocket Books paperback, 1976. HB-R.

† CWF 71.   VON ELSNER, DON †

Von Elsner, Don. The Best of Jake Winkman. New York: M.
Hardy, 1981. PBO.

_____. Everything's Jake with Me. New York: M. Hardy,
1980. PBO.

† CWF 76.   WOODHOUSE, MARTIN †

Woodhouse, Martin. Blue Bone. New York: Coward-McCann,
1973; New York: Berkley-Medallion paperback, 1974. HB-R.

_____. Bush Baby. New York: Berkley-Medallion paperback,
1974. R.

_____. Mama Doll. New York: Coward-McCann, 1972. HB.

† CWF 77.   YORK, ANDREW †

York, Andrew. The Captivator. London: Hutchinson, 1973; Garden City, N. Y.: Doubleday, 1974. HB-HB.

_____. The Deviator. New York: Berkley-Medallion paper-
back, 1970. R.

_____. The Expurgator. London: Hutchinson, 1972; Garden
City, N. Y.: Doubleday, 1973; New York: Berkley-Medallion
paperback, 1974. HB-HB-R.

_____. The Fascinator. Garden City, N. Y.: Doubleday, 1975.
HB.

_____. The Infiltrator. Garden City, N. Y.: Doubleday, 1971.
HB.

_____. The Predator. New York: Berkley-Medallion paper-
back, 1970. R.

APPENDIX II

This appendix focuses upon those espionage series which changed paperback outlets after 1969. Since the original Cold War File can be easily referenced, and to avoid repetition, only the reissue date is listed in each entry.

† CWF 8. BARKER, ALBERT †

Barker, Albert. <u>Gift from Berlin</u>. New York: Charter Books, 1980. PBO.

† CWF 9. BLACK, GAVIN †

Black, Gavin. <u>A Dragon for Christmas</u>. New York: Harper-Perennial paperback, 1979. R.

_____. <u>The Eyes Around Me</u>. New York: Harper-Perennial paperback, 1980. R.

_____. <u>You Want to Die, Johnny</u>? New York: Harper-Perennial paperback, 1979. R.

† CWF 14. CARTER, NICK †

(Note: All titles listed below were issued originally as Universal-Award paperbacks.)

Carter, Nick. <u>Beirut Incident</u>. New York: Charter Books, 1978. PBO.

_____. <u>Carnival for Killing</u>. New York: Charter Books, 1981. PBO.

_____. The Casbah Killers. New York: Charter Books, 1980.
PBO.

_____. Checkmate in Rio. New York: Charter Books, 1979.
PBO.

_____. Code Name--Werewolf. New York: Charter Books,
1982. PBO.

_____. The Devil's Dozen. New York: Charter Books, 1982.
PBO.

_____. Double Identity. Included in Strike of the Hawk. New
York: Charter Books, 1980. PBO. See also Strike of the
Hawk in Appendix I.

_____. The Eyes of the Tiger. New York: Charter Books,
1981. PBO.

_____. The Filthy Five. New York: Charter Books, 1978.
PBO.

_____. The Gallagher Plot. New York: Charter Books, 1979.
PBO.

_____. The Green Wolf Connection. New York: Charter Books,
1978. PBO.

_____. The Human Time Bomb. New York: Charter Books,
1981. PBO.

_____. Inca Death Squad. New York: Charter Books, 1982.
PBO.

_____. Istanbul. New York: Charter Books, 1981. PBO.

_____. The Jerusalem File. New York: Chater Books, 1978.
PBO.

_____. The Judas Spy. New York: Charter Books, 1978. PBO.

_____. The Katmandu Contract. New York: Charter Books,
1978. PBO.

_____. The Liquidator. New York: Charter Books, 1978.
PBO.

_____. The List. New York: Charter Books, 1979. PBO.

_____. The Living Death. New York: Charter Books, 1982.
PBO.

_____. Macao. New York: Charter Books, 1981. PBO.

_____. The Man Who Sold Death. New York: Charter Books, 1978. PBO.

_____. The Mind Killers. New York: Charter Books, 1981. PBO.

_____. The Nichovev Plot. New York: Charter Books, 1978. PBO.

_____. The Night of the Avenger. New York: Charter Books, 1978. PBO.

_____. The Omega Terror. New York: Charter Books, 1981. PBO.

_____. The Red Rays. New York: Charter Books, 1981. PBO.

_____. Safari for Spies. New York: Charter Books, 1979. PBO.

_____. Sign of the Cobra. New York: Charter Books, 1978. PBO.

_____. Sign of the Prayer Shawl. New York: Charter Books, 1978. PBO.

_____. Six Bloody Summer Days. New York: Charter Books, 1978. PBO.

_____. Strike of the Hawk. See also Double Identity.

_____. Temple of Fear. New York: Charter Books, 1978. PBO.

_____. Time Clock of Death. New York: Charter Books, 1978. PBO.

_____. Triple Cross. New York: Charter Books, 1980. PBO.

_____. The Turncoat. New York: Charter Books, 1982. PBO.

_____. The Ultimate Code. New York: Charter Books, 1978. PBO.

_____. Under the Wall. New York: Charter Books, 1978. PBO.

_____. The Weapon of Night. New York: Charter Books, 1982. PBO.

_____. The Z-Document. New York: Charter Books, 1978. PBO.

† CWF 17.   CREASEY, JOHN †

Creasey, John. The Killers of Innocence. New York: Ace paper-
    back, 1979. R.

_____. Traitor's Doom. New York: Charter paperback, 1979.
    R.

† CWF 21.   DEIGHTON, LEN †

Deighton, Len. The Billion Dollar Brain. New York: Berkley-
    Medallion paperback, 1977. R.

_____. An Expensive Place to Die. New York: Berkley-
    Medallion paperback, 1977. R.

_____. Funeral in Berlin. New York: Berkley-Medallion
    paperback, 1976. R.

_____. Horse Under Water. New York: Berkley-Medallion
    paperback, 1977. R.

_____. The Ipcress File. New York: Ballantine paperback,
    1974. R.

Note: The "Medallion" imprint no longer exists; more recent editions are featured simply as Berkley reprints.

† CWF 25.   FLEMING, IAN †

Fleming, Ian. Casino Royale. New York: Bantam paperback,
    1971; New York: Jove paperback, 1980; New York: Berkley
    paperback, 1982. R-R-R.

_____. Diamonds Are Forever. New York: Bantam paperback,
    1971; New York: Jove paperback, 1980; New York: Berkley
    paperback, 1982. R. MT. -R-R.

_____. Doctor No. New York: Bantam paperback, 1971; New
    York: Jove paperback, 1980; New York: Berkley paperback,
    1982. R-R-R.

_____. For Your Eyes Only. New York: Jove paperback,
    1981; New York: Berkley paperback, 1982. R. MT. -R.

_____. From Russia, With Love. New York: Bantam paper-
back, 1971; New York: Jove paperback, 1980; New York:
Berkley paperback, 1982. R-R-R.

_____. Goldfinger. New York: Bantam paperback, 1972; New
York: Jove paperback, 1980; New York: Berkley paperback,
1982. R-R-R.

_____. Live and Let Die. New York: Bantam paperback, 1973;
New York: Jove paperback, 1980; New York: Berkley paperback,
1982. R. MT. -R-R.

_____. Moonraker. New York: Bantam paperback, 1973; New
York: Jove paperback, 1981; New York: Berkley paperback,
1983. R-R-R.

_____. The Spy Who Loved Me. New York: Berkley paperback,
1982. R.

_____. Thunderball. New York: Berkley paperback, 1982. R.

† CWF 33. HALL, ADAM †

Hall, Adam. The Quiller Memorandum. New York: Jove paperback, 1979. R.

Note: When Pyramid Publications ceased operations in the late
seventies, several of their properties were transferred to Jove.
See also CWF 33, FIELD BIBLIOGRAPHY.

† CWF 41. Le CARRE, JOHN †

le Carré, John. Call for the Dead. New York: Pocket Books
paperback, 1970; New York: Popular Library paperback, 1975;
New York: Bantam paperback, 1979. R-R-R.

_____. The Looking Glass War. New York: Bantam paperback,
1975. R.

_____. A Murder of Quality. New York: Pocket Books paper-
back, 1970; New York: Popular Library paperback, 1975; New
York: Bantam paperback, 1980. R-R-R.

_____. The Spy Who Came In from the Cold. New York:
Bantam paperback, 1975. R.

† CWF 47. MARK, TED †

Mark, Ted. <u>Dr. Nyet</u>. New York: Dell Books, 1973. PBO.

_____. <u>Hard Day's Knight</u>. New York: Dell Books, 1973. PBO.

_____. <u>The Man from O. R. G. Y.</u> New York: Dell Books, 1973;
New York: Zebra Books, 1981. PBO-PBO.

_____. <u>My Son, the Double Agent</u>. New York: Dell Books,
1973. PBO.

_____. <u>The Nine-Month Caper</u>. New York: Dell Books, 1973.
PBO.

_____. <u>The Real Gone Girls</u>. New York: Dell Books, 1973.
PBO.

_____. <u>Room at the Topless</u>. New York: Dell Books, 1973.
PBO.

_____. <u>The Square Root of Sex</u>. New York: Dell Books, 1973.
PBO.

_____. <u>The Unhatched Egghead</u>. New York: Manor Books,
1976. PBO.

† CWF 50. MASON, F. VAN WYCK †

Mason, Van Wyck. <u>The Dardanelles Derelict</u>. New York: Popular
Library paperback, 1970. R.

_____. <u>The Gracious Lily Affair</u>. New York: Popular Library
paperback, 1970. R.

_____. <u>Two Tickets to Tangier</u>. New York: Popular Library
paperback, 1970. R.

† CWF 53. MUNRO, JAMES †

Munro, James. <u>Die Rich, Die Happy</u>. New York: Charter paperback, 1980. R.

_____. <u>The Man Who Sold Death</u>. New York: Charter paper-
back, 1980. R.

_____. The Money That Money Can't Buy. New York: Charter paperback, 1981. R.

† CWF 55. O'DONNELL, PETER †

O'Donnell, Peter. Modesty Blaise. London: Souvenir Press, 1977. R. Distributed in the U.S. market through International School Book Service.

† CWF 59. PICARD, SAM †

Picard, Sam. The Notebooks. New York: Charter Books, 1980. PBO.

† CWF 68. THOMAS, ROSS †

Thomas, Ross. The Cold War Swap. New York: Pocket Books paperback, 1976. R.

† CWF 71. VON ELSNER, DON †

Von Elsner, Don. The Ace of Spies. New York: Charter Books, 1980; New York: M. Hardy, 1982. PBO-PBO.

_____. The Jack of Hearts. New York: M. Hardy, 1982. PBO.

† CWF 75. WINSTON, PETER †

Winston, Peter. The ABC Affair. New York: Charter Books, 1980. PBO.

_____. Assignment to Bahrein. New York: Charter Books, 1981. PBO.

REFERENCE SOURCES

Amis, Kingsley. The James Bond Dossier. New York: New American Library, 1965.

Breen, Jon L. What About Murder? Metuchen, N.J.: Scarecrow Press, 1981.

Herman, Linda, and Beth Stiel. The Corpus Delicti of Mystery Fiction: A Guide to the Body of the Case. Metuchen, N.J.: Scarecrow Press, 1974.

Hubin, Allen J. The Bibliography of Crime Fiction, 1749-1975. Del Mar: University Extension, University of California, San Diego, in cooperation with Publishers Inc., 1979.

Keating, H. R. F., ed. Whodunit?: A Guide to Crime, Suspense, and Spy Fiction. New York: Van Nostrand Reinhold Co., 1982.

Lane, Sheldon, ed. For Bond Lovers Only. New York: Dell Books, 1965.

McCormick, Donald. Who's Who in Spy Fiction. New York: Taplinger, 1977.

Meyers, Richard. TV Detectives. San Diego: A. S. Barnes, 1981.

Nicholls, Peter, ed. The Science Fiction Encyclopedia. Garden City, N.Y.: Doubleday, 1979.

Parish, James Robert, and Michael R. Pitts. The Great Spy Pictures. Metuchen, N.J.: Scarecrow Press, 1974.

Pearson, John. James Bond: The Authorized Biography of 007. New York: William Morrow, 1973.*

_____. The Life of Ian Fleming. New York: McGraw-Hill, 1966.

Penzler, Otto, ed. The Great Detectives. Boston: Little, Brown, 1978.

---

*This volume was used in the composition of the background on James Bond: see Fleming, Ian, CWF 25.

_____. The Private Lives of Private Eyes, Spies, Crime Fighters, and Other Good Guys. New York: Grosset and Dunlap, 1977.

Rubin, Steven Jay. The James Bond Films. Westport, Conn.: Arlington House, 1981.

Smith, Myron J., Jr. Cloak-and-Dagger Bibliography: An Annotated Guide to Spy Fiction, 1937-1975. Metuchen, N.J.: Scarecrow Press, 1976.

Steinbrunner, Chris and Otto Penzler. Encyclopedia of Mystery and Detection. Marvin Lachman and Charles Shibuk, Senior Editors. New York: McGraw-Hill, 1976.

Wynn, Dilys, perpetrator. Murder Ink: The Mystery Reader's Companion. New York: Workman Press, 1977.

Zieger, Henry A. Ian Fleming: The Spy Who Came In with the Gold. New York: Duell, Sloan, and Pearce, 1965.

SECRET AGENT INDEX

This index has been provided for reference to the
Cold War agents evaluated in this book. Numbers
refer to file entries, not pages.

Intelligence Group Index